THEOLOGY AND FAMILIES

D1368911

Challenges in Contemporary Theology

Series Editors: Gareth Jones and Lewis Ayres
Canterbury Christ Church University College, UK, and Emory University, US

Challenges in Contemporary Theology is a series aimed at producing clear orientations in, and research on, areas of "challenge" in contemporary theology. These carefully co-ordinated books engage traditional theological concerns with mainstreams in modern thought and culture that challenge those concerns. The "challenges" implied are to be understood in two senses: those presented by society to contemporary theology, and those posed by theology to society.

THEOLOGY AND FAMILIES

Adrian Thatcher

Blackwell
Publishing

BLACKWELL PUBLISHING
350 Main Street, Malden, MA 02148–5020, USA
9600 Garsington Road, Oxford OX4 2DQ, UK
550 Swanston Street, Carlton, Victoria 3053, Australia

First published 2007 by Blackwell Publishing Ltd

1 2007

Library of Congress Cataloging-in-Publication Data

Thatcher, Adrian.
    Theology and families / Adrian Thatcher.
        p.   cm.—(Challenges in contemporary theology)
    Includes bibliographical references and index.
    ISBN-13: 978-1405-1-5274-7 (hardcover: alk. paper)
    ISBN-10: 1-4051-5274-5 (hardcover: alk. paper)
    ISBN-13: 978-1-4051-5275-4 (pbk.: alk. paper)
    ISBN-10: 1-4051-5275-3 (pbk.: alk. paper) 1. Family—Religious aspects—
Christianity. I. title. II Series.

    BT707.7.T43 2007
    261.8'3585—dc22

                                        2006012583

A catalog record for this title is available from the British Library.

Set in 10.5/12.5 pt Bembo
by The Running Head Limited, Cambridge, www.therunninghead.com
Printed and bound in Singapore
by COS Printers Pte Ltd

The publisher's policy is to use permanent paper from mills that operate a sustainable
forestry policy, and which has been manufactured from pulp processed using acid-free
and elementary chlorine-free practices. Furthermore, the publisher ensures that the
text paper and cover board used have met acceptable environmental accreditation
standards.

For further information on
Blackwell Publishing, visit our website:
www.blackwellpublishing.com

For James Robert Thatcher
and Loren Rose Thatcher

Contents

viii CONTENTS

Preface

In several previous books I have tried to think theologically about sexuality, marriage and divorce, and the growing practice of cohabitation. A book which tries to think theologically about families and children broadens the range of recent writing and extends the line still further. Previous writing has required me to become familiar with a particular theological literature, and I am still shocked at the lack of attention this literature gives to children. With notable exceptions, theology of all types, schools and branches, past and present, theoretical and practical, stands accused. Given the teaching of Jesus about children, this hiatus is extraordinary. Elsewhere child neglect is a crime. In this volume children are center-stage. The desire to put children (and parenting) first, and to tap into the neglected theological riches that remain available for the purpose, is the reason why I have postponed other projects and written a further volume in an area similar to my other recent writing.

Extraordinary changes are happening to families at the present time. They raise new questions for everyone interested in them, theologians included, and the impetus of the questions prompts fresh theological insights which make the theological enterprise excitingly worthwhile. I have faced conflicting demands. On the one hand, all academics in British universities face peer review of their "research output" in the national Research Assessment Exercise. This book too must be subjected to that fateful scrutiny. On the other hand, researchers are expected to be accountable to their "publics." This is called "dissemination" (an unmistakeably phallic term). The theological "public" is considerably broader than the academic élite who write for one another and read papers to one another at prestigious conferences. A theological book about families has also to be intelligible at least to people in the churches who minister to, and belong within, families, and to the broader academic and professional communities. I have tried to respond to both sets of demands. There is no virtue in obscurity. Originality (whatever that is) and accessibility need not be incompatible. It is equally possible to fail in both these undertakings. Readers (and peer reviewers) will judge the outcome for themselves.

During the writing of this book I came to be blessed with not one, but two, beautiful grandchildren, James and Loren. This book is dedicated to them. They will soon know what granddad does (writes boring books with no pictures in them!). They have taught me afresh what it is to see the face of Christ in the face of a child. Their wise parents, Valerie and John, are superb in the art of parenting. The long sections on parents, and on genuine reciprocity between parents and children, were written with them as my role models.

Also during the writing of this book I left the College of St Mark and St John, Plymouth, after working there for 27 years. I rejoice in my new theological colleagues at the University of Exeter and thank them for their welcome, friendship, geniality, commitment, and remarkable erudition. I also thank Caroline Major for her assiduous proof-reading of the text and compilation of the indexes. This is the fifth book on which we have worked together. She has also provided me with a regular flow of press-cuttings about families and children which have been invaluable.

Adrian Thatcher
Department of Theology
School of Humanities and Social Sciences
The University of Exeter, Devon, UK

Part I

Sources

Chapter One

Beginning with Real Families and Children

1.1 Family Forms

"I kneel in prayer to the Father," exclaimed the writer of the Letter to the Ephesians, "from whom every family in heaven and on earth takes its name" (Eph. 3:14). This tantalizing aside assumes that families are a universal, human institution: indeed families are not even bounded by terrestriality. More than this, we are invited to visualize the identity of every family, past, present, and future, as constituted in some way by their relation to God. The Christian faith names this family-constituting God, "Father." While family forms are relative to time and space, and so to religions and cultures, we are encouraged to envisage human parenting as rooted in the being and will of the divine Parent of all.

This book is a contribution to a Trinitarian theology of families and children, offered both to the Christian community as the fruit of what we *already* tacitly believe about God, and about families as constituted by God; and to the wider community as an honest contribution to multidisciplinary reflection on what families are, what they do, and how best they flourish. It arises out of the conviction that the Christian Gospel speaks transformatively to families and children, and to the societies to which they belong, and that it will continue to do so in ways that have not yet been fully articulated. It addresses the root question "How may the resources of Christian faith and practice contribute to the thriving of families, and in particular, of children?" Indeed, one of the most disturbing features of contemporary theology is the neglect of families and children. Marcia Bunge writes "Until very recently, issues related to children have tended to be marginal in almost every area of contemporary theology."[1]

---

[1] Marcia J. Bunge, "Introduction," in Marcia J. Bunge (ed.), *The Child in Christian Thought* (Grand Rapids, MI/Cambridge, UK: Eerdmans, 2001) [1–28], p. 3.

The book addresses children's marginality in theology and brings them center-stage. Part I of the book marshals together the sources for a theology of families and children. Part II examines relationships within families and between families and the wider community in the light that the theological sources shed upon them. The book reclaims "family values" from the surface rhetoric of certain Christian pressure groups. In order to articulate a Christian theological vision for families and children it is necessary first to understand actual families and the changes that are presently happening to them. The present chapter engages in this preliminary work. It describes some of the changes that are happening to, and within, families, moves to a description of the main currents of theological thought that engage with these changes, and then summarizes the argument of the book as a whole (pages 21–4).

The definition of family remains an intractable problem. The English noun "family" derives from the Latin *familia* which is best translated "household." This included the servants or *famuli* and other possible recipients of patronage, as well as the householder's kin. One recent textbook, *Understanding the Family*, qualifies its title by confessing its "intentionally ironic" intent:[2] to understand "the family" aright is already, apparently, to recognize both the diversity of family forms that exist in most societies, and the "ideological power" that is expressed by speaking of that singular substantive, "the family." An Oxford English Dictionary entry illustrates the difficulties. It provides four non-metaphorical meanings (applicable to human beings): "(1) a group consisting of two parents and their children living together as a unit, (2) a group of people related by blood or marriage, (3) the children of a person or couple, (4) all the descendants of a common ancestor."[3] The first definition appears not to require that the two parents be married, or of opposite sexes, or the biological parents of their children. It does require, however, that they live together. Do children cease to belong to their family when they leave home? The second definition allows that a group of siblings, or an unmarried couple with children, or several generations of people living together are a family. Is a couple without children, a family, or perhaps a household? Is a couple a family? How do stepchildren and adopted children fit in? The third definition seems merely colloquial, as when a parent or couple might say of their children, "This is my family." But that usage excludes parents, and the relationships between parents and children. The fourth definition seems plain archaic, akin more to a tribe than to a household.

---

[2] John Muncie, Margaret Wetherell, Rudi Dallos, Allan Cochrane (eds.), *Understanding the Family* (London: Sage, 1995), p. 1.
[3] *Compact Oxford English Dictionary*. www.askoxford.com./ Accessed 02.09.2006.

Faced with these difficulties sociologists often eschew definitions altogether, preferring to identify families by particular characteristics. One writer speaks of four basic *features* of families (common residence, economic co-operation, reproduction, and sexuality).[4] Other writers speak of *family structures*. According to John and Olive Drane there are "at least seven distinct types of family structure and domestic arrangements in western culture today."[5] (These are "two married parents living together, along with those children who are biologically related to them," "one-parent families," "blended families," "cohabiting couples," "couples without children," "other homes," and "families in transition.") Another writer works with the concept of *family practices*. Raising, but declining to answer, the question "Who and what are 'families'?"[6] she prefers to concentrate instead on the "notion of *family practices*: what we do rather than what we are." These practices are "everyday interactions with close and loved ones." This notion "moves away from the fixed boundaries of co-residence, marriage, ethnicity, and obligation that once defined the white, heterosexual, male breadwinner, nuclear family. It registers the ways in which our networks of affection are not simply given by virtue of blood or marriage but are negotiated and shaped by us, over time and place."[7] But who then are the "we" who engage in these practices? The move from being to doing, from essence to construction, from theory to *praxis* is familiar to students of twentieth-century theology. And so is the list of begged questions that this move raises.

An overtly theological/religious definition can present begged questions of a different kind. An example is the definition in the Roman Catholic Catechism: "A man and a woman united in marriage, together with their children, form a family." The family is a "conjugal community."[8] While few Christians may disagree with this definition, does not the concern for doctrinal orthodoxy, expressed as a necessary connection between "the family" and marriage, have the effect of excluding from the definition those families which, for example, are headed by a single parent, or which are united in marriage no longer, or those members of families who are not the children of the married couple unit? If they are not families, what are they?

Leaving families undefined, however, can imply a fluidity that makes

---

[4] Diana Gittins, *The Family in Question* (2nd edition) (London: Macmillan, 1993), pp. 60–72.

[5] John Drane and Olive M. Fleming Drane, *Family Fortunes: Faith-full Caring for Today's Families* (London: Darton, Longman, and Todd, 2004), pp. 22–41.

[6] Fiona Williams, ESRC CAVA Research Group, *Rethinking Families* (London: Calouste Gulbenkian Foundation, 2004), p. 16.

[7] Williams, *Rethinking Families*, p. 17.

[8] *Catechism of the Catholic Church* (London: Geoffrey Chapman, 1994), paras. 2202, 2201, p. 475.

discussion difficult to pin down. Fluidity of definition may well be the key to understanding the growing fluidity of family form, but our interactions "with close and loved ones" have to be structured somehow, especially if they are young children. The relegation in importance of historical family norms and forms in recent decades is sometimes thought to comprise an organized attack on "the family" or to belong to the malaise of post-modernity. I shall therefore employ a definition, and begin with Lisa Sowle Cahill's: a family is "an organized network of socio-economic and repro-ductive interdependence and support grounded in biological kinship and marriage."[9]

This definition draws on historical family forms while also accommodat-ing some of the contemporary changes to families. "Organized" implies social custom and domestic authority, neither of which is fixed. "Network" implies a common residence. "Socio-economic" implies the wider resources of work, social interaction and exchange, necessary for families to survive. "Reproductive" includes children as a *raison d'être* of families: "interdepen-dence and support" implies both mutuality between members and the dependence of some on others. "Grounded" allows for the extension of families beyond their reproductive base to include adopted and fostered children, elderly relatives, and even residing companions and friends. "Mar-riage" accommodates within the definition the expectation that the core of the family unit still remains the married couple.

With this definition we are prepared for those diverse households that put pressure upon it. As Cahill says, it "is not the only or exclusively legitimate form" of family.[10] But we still need further caveats. A purely structural approach to "the family" is liable to ignore important internal questions of power and gender,[11] and these in turn will enhance or impair relationships within the family. My approach to families will be through relationships, and in particular their qualitative dimension. But "relationships" will need to be grounded in theological sources: of the Persons of God with one another; of Christ with the church; of the new covenantal relationship of God with the world, and so on. If the approach is similar to the family prac-tices approach, it will not ignore deeper questions of the being of family relationships, and therefore of the structures required to sustain them.

[9] Lisa Sowle Cahill, *Family: A Christian Social Perspective* (Minneapolis, MN: Augsburg Fortress, 2000), pp. x–xi.
[10] Cahill, *Family*, p. xi.
[11] Drane and Drane, *Family Fortunes*, p. 6.

1.2 Global Upheavals

Changes to families and households in England and Wales since 1971 provide a convenient snapshot of wider changes in the "Western" world. All the trends referred to in this section will be utilized later in the book. First there are more older people and fewer children. The percentage of people aged 75 and over rose from 4 percent in 1971 to 7 percent in the mid-1990s, while the percentage of children under the age of 16 fell from 25 percent in 1971 to 20 percent, since 1998.[12] In 1971 a married or cohabiting couple headed 92 percent of families. In 2002 that percentage had decreased to 73 percent. At the time of the 2001 Census, nearly one in four children (22.9 percent) lived in lone-parent families (91.2 percent of which were headed by the mother). The percentage of families headed by mothers who have never married rose from 1 percent in 1971 to 12 percent in 2002. But 65 percent of children still live with both natural parents, while more than one in ten dependent children live in a step-family. Approximately 149,000 children under 18 provide unpaid care within their family. Over 45,000 children under 16 still live in communal establishments. Over two million children (or 17.6 percent) live in households where there are no adults in work. In Muslim households this is even higher with more than one-third of children living in households where no adult has work.[13]

In 1961, there were 27,200 divorces in Great Britain, which by 1969 had doubled to 55,600. The number of divorces then doubled again by 1972, to 124,900. This latter increase was partly a "one-off" effect of the Divorce Reform Act 1969 in England and Wales, which came into effect in 1971.[14] In 2003, the number of divorces granted in the United Kingdom increased by 3.7 percent to 166,700, from 160,700 in 2002. This is the highest number of divorces since 1997, and the third successive annual increase. But it is still 7.4 percent less than the peak of 180,000 in 1993.

Fiona Williams provides a very recent summary of some of the changes, all of them detailed by the Office for National Statistics. Divorce rates have doubled in the last 30 years. Cohabitation has trebled in the same period. The proportion of children living with a lone parent or with cohabiting parents has doubled. Single-person households have doubled. The average

---

[12] National Statistics. "Living in Britain." www.statistics.gov.uk/lib2002/default.asp. Accessed 02.09.2006.

[13] All data from National Statistics. Census 2001. Online at www.statistics.gov.uk/cci/. Accessed 02.09.2006.

[14] All data from National Statistics. www.statistics.gov.uk/census/default.asp. Accessed 02.09.2006.

family size has decreased from 2.9 children to 1.6 children. Five times as many babies are born outside of marriage. The average age when women have their first child has increased by five years.[15] Her picture of "parenting and partnering" in the 2000s includes the details that around 40 percent of children experience parental divorce by their sixteenth birthday; that around 40 percent of births occur outside of marriage; and that 70 percent of marriages are preceded by a period of cohabitation.

There are similar trends in the wider European Union. There are fewer marriages, and more marital breakdowns.[16] In 2002, there were only five marriages per 1,000 inhabitants in the EU compared with almost eight in 1970. The average age at which people in Europe first get married has increased: for men, from 26 years in 1980 to over 30 today, and for women from 23 to 28 years. The proportion of divorces is estimated at 15 percent for marriages entered into in 1960, and at around 30 percent for those entered into in 1985. The population of Europe cannot sustain itself at current levels. For this 2.1 children per woman would be required. The total fertility rate decreased from 2.7 in 1965 to below 1.5 in 1995 where it has remained since. The proportion of births outside marriage continues to increase, basically reflecting the growing popularity of cohabitation: from 6 percent of all births in 1970 to over 30 percent in 2002. In Sweden, more than half (56 percent) of the children born in 2002 had unmarried parents.

In Australia, the picture is again similar. 72 percent of couples live with their partner before marriage.[17] The fertility rate in Australia is also similar to that of Europe, at 1.7.[18] Changes to Australian families are reflected in the official government descriptions of them which, bound to a secular ideology, *expunge marriage from the official list of family types.* Instead there are "couple families," "lone parent families" and "other family types." Couple families are defined as families "based on two persons who are in a registered or de facto marriage and who are usually resident in the same household." Couples are families, officially, in Australia. A family consists of "two or more persons, one of whom is aged 15 years and over, who are related by blood, marriage (registered or de facto), adoption, step or foster-

---

[15] Williams, *Rethinking Families*, p. 15.
[16] All European data from *Eurostat Yearbook 2004*, pp. 45–50. Online at epp.eurostat.cec.eu.int/ (pp. 13–19). Accessed 11.17.2004.
[17] David de Vaus, *Diversity and Change in Australian Families: Statistical Profiles* (Australian Institute of Family Studies, 2004). Summarized online at www.aifs.gov.au/inst/pubs/diversity/main.html. Accessed 11.23.2004.
[18] de Vaus, *Diversity and Change.*

ing; and who are usually resident in the same household."[19] Official figures speak no longer of marriage and divorce, but of "partnering and separation." The government estimates that between 32 percent and 46 percent of Australian marriages will end in divorce.

The Australian statistics invite analysis regarding the manner of their compilation. The very framework within which they are presented removes most of the traditional markers of families. The crisis facing marriage is met by demoting "registered marriage" to a sub-set of the larger, generic, "couple-family," while cohabiting couples are promoted to the status of "marriage, de facto." The framework is at least as value-laden as the one it replaces. Another name for cohabitation in these statistics is "de facto relationship." A cohabiting couple is included in the restricted category of marriage (they are "de facto marriages" in the category of couple families), while it is also included in the gratuitously broad category of "relationship." The Australians are reinstating "informal marriage" (*matrimonium presumptum* it used to be called) but many cohabitors do not presume that their relationships are marriages at all.

The literature regarding the crises confronting families in the United States is daunting (below, 5.1–5.2) and well summarized by Michael G. Lawler.[20] The extensive research findings indicate "the greatly elevated divorce rate with negative impact on the former spouses and their children, the increasingly common social phenomena of single motherhood and father absence, and the result feminization and childrenization of poverty." Half of all children in the United States "will spend at least part of their childhood in a single-parent family," where they are "more than six times as likely to be poor." Poverty is implicated in further long-term problems. Summarizing the research Lawler describes how

> Children in single-parent households are more prone to develop serious social and behavioral problems than are children who grow up with both parents. Their socio-emotive skills and their academic achievement are lower, their behavioral problems and delinquency rates higher. Males who experience family disruption in childhood are more likely to drop out of school, leave home, start work, enter relationships, and become fathers earlier. Females who experience family disruption in childhood are more likely to have sexual relations, to have a child at an early age outside of marriage. A

---

[19] Australian Government, Australian Institute of Family Studies. www.aifs.gov.au/institute/ info/charts/glossary.html#couple. Accessed 02.09.2006. These definitions are fixed by the Australian Bureau of Statistics.
[20] Michael G. Lawler, "Towards a Theology of Christian Family," *INTAMS Review*, 8.1 (Spring 2002), [55–71], pp. 55–8.

particularly troubling datum is that the effects of single motherhood and fatherlessness are neither short-lived nor easily remedied. Though the multiple economic, psychological, and social effects on children of family disruption, single parenthood, and father absence may remain submerged until years later, they can extend into continuing problems across time and generations.[21]

The countries where most of the research on the effects of family breakdown has been done are inevitably the world's richest countries. When a *global* perspective on children is adopted, the impact of poverty on children is vastly more striking. While 30 to 35 percent of children in parts of Europe are classified as "overweight or obese,"[22] a recent UNICEF report, *Building a World Fit for Children*, claims that about 150 million children in developing countries still suffer from malnutrition. Nearly 11 million children under five years of age still die each year – most of them from readily preventable causes. About 120 million children of primary school age, a sizeable majority of whom are girls, have no schools to attend. Some 246 million children work, often in abusive conditions. The sexual abuse, prostitution, sale, and trafficking of children continue on a massive global scale. Recruitment of child soldiers and the wartime targeting of children and other civilians have worsened. The report claims that "at the root of this inadequate record for children are long-standing barriers such as poverty, debt burdens, poor use of resources, armed conflict and excessive military spending, as well as more recent challenges such as HIV/AIDS, which infects four young people every minute and has orphaned millions of children."[23] In response UNICEF "calls upon all of society to join in a global movement for children."

Faced with problems of such daunting magnitude, it would be hard to find a reason for *not* lending support for such a movement. It has already been necessary to speak of children at the micro- and macro-levels of societies. Pope John Paul II encompasses a similar range when he says "each

---

[21] Lawler, "Towards a Theology of Christian Family," p. 56, where an extensive United States bibliography is cited.

[22] Report of International Obesity Task Force, *Obesity in Children and Young People: A Crisis in Public Health* (London: 2004). The report claims that there is a "global obesity epidemic;" that one in ten of the world's children (155 million) is overweight; and that "30–45 million within that figure are classified as obese – accounting for 2 to 3 percent of the world's children aged 5–17." Summary at www.news-medical.net/?id=1508. Accessed 02.09.2006.

[23] UNICEF, *Building a World Fit for Children* (New York: United Nations Children's Fund, 2003), p. 10. The report was based on a special session of the United Nations General Assembly, on Children, May 2002. www.unicef.org/publications/. Accessed 02.09.2006.

family" is "as a living 'cell' of the universal 'family' of mankind."[24] That is why Pamela Couture has defined a "social ecology" for children which is useful as a grid for locating, and so for addressing, the range of ethical issues surrounding children.[25] The grid consists of four overlapping systems. There are *microsystems*, which belong at the level of "families, friends, care-takers, and institutions that have direct contact with children." Second, there are *mesosystems*, or "interactions between the systems around the child that influence each other directly and the child indirectly." These might include nurseries, playgroups, schools, doctors' surgeries, public facilities for recreation and sport, a safe space with clean air, an attractive physical environment, etc. At the third level, there are *exosystems*, or "larger institutions, such as governments and businesses, that do not have direct contact with children but affect, or are affected by, children and families." Finally there are *macrosystems*, "that organize and communicate broader sociocultural beliefs and values."

Religions contribute significantly to macrosystems. In a work of amazing breadth Göran Therborn has analyzed changes to families *throughout the world* in the twentieth century. He believes that patriarchy "was the loser of the twentieth century. Probably no other social institution has been forced to retreat as much."[26] Its demise is convincingly documented, but any readerly relief is tempered both by the horrors of what remains and by the religious sanction these horrors receive. An analysis of the "Matrimonials" section of the *Hindustan Times* (in 1999 on one day) found 1,600 advertisements, mostly placed by parents, in 43 categories, including 25 by "Religion/community/Caste."[27] "In India the marriage market is no metaphor," Therborn observes, and concludes "Indian marriage is a professional sport."[28] "*Purdah*, female seclusion, is an upper-caste practice common to Hindus and Muslims, still frequent in conservative rural milieux."[29] Among some Tamils a husband is a god, whose name, for that reason, cannot be uttered.[30] In Egypt, there is "an old patriarchy vigorously alive under new conditions," where nine out of ten adolescents held (in 1997) that "a wife needs to ask

---

[24] Pope John Paul II, *Letter to Families* (1994), section 4. www.vatican.va/holy_father/john_paul_ii/letters/documents/. See also section 13, and *Catechism*, para. 2207, p. 476.
[25] Pamela D. Couture, *Seeing Children, Seeing God: A Practical Theology of Children and Poverty* (Nashville, TN: Abingdon Press, 2000), pp. 23, 42.
[26] Göran Therborn, *Between Sex and Power: Family in the World, 1900–2000* (London and New York: Routledge, 2004), p. 73.
[27] Therborn, *Between Sex and Power*, p. 108.
[28] Therborn, *Between Sex and Power*, p. 109.
[29] Therborn, *Between Sex and Power*, p. 110.
[30] Therborn, *Between Sex and Power*, p. 111.

her husband's permission for everything." Unspeakably worse, "Female genital mutilation was almost universal among Egyptian women in the 1995 Demographic and Health Survey."[31] "Wife-beating is . . . frequent in Southern and Eastern Africa" where it has an "amazing legitimacy."[32] In China (but also in India and elsewhere) "selective abortion, and to a minor extent, the old practice of female infanticide, have created very skewed sex ratios."[33]

First world readers of Therborn's work are likely to put down this remarkable book thankful for their Christian heritage, and happy to affirm his global judgment that "The Western European family was by far the least patriarchal in a very patriarchal world," and that the Catholic emphasis on "marriage by consent only," was a powerful influence on the decline of patriarchal marriage.[34] It is clear that the flourishing of children in individual families, and participation in a global movement for children involve action in all four systems. The systems themselves cannot be exempt from critical analysis, and Christian theology must be alert to them all. Its prescriptions will vary in character, widening in generality according to whether the level of analysis is familial or global. The upheaval in family forms, and the impact of these on children confront the churches and their theologians with a wide range of problems at one level. Equally, a world in which so many children are victims of cruelty and poverty, presents another range of problems at a different level. In many parts of the world an upheaval in family forms, or at least in the power relations within them, is urgently needed and overdue.

A major emphasis of this study, inspired by the doctrine of the Triune God, is a re-thinking of human relations as part embodiments, part iconic reflections of the relations that are God's very self (below, 4.1–4.2). An immediate corollary follows: children's relationships with their parents are therefore a primary subject for theological reflection. Children are a class (of young person), but there are no children in the abstract, only children-in-relationship. Children belong to families and, unless they are homeless, to a household, which resides in a neighborhood, which is topographically and socially specific, and influenced by wider economic and cultural influences.

[31] Therborn, *Between Sex and Power*, p. 113.
[32] Therborn, *Between Sex and Power*, p. 118.
[33] Therborn, *Between Sex and Power*, p. 120.
[34] Therborn, *Between Sex and Power*, p. 297.

1.3 Theological Responses

How does Christian thought cope with the changes to families in which they are caught up? How has the good news of the Gospel impacted on Christian families? In this section I shall briefly outline the controversy generated by family change in secular thought, before examining perspectives from conservative evangelical Christians; from official Roman Catholic thought; and from "revisionist" Roman Catholic and Protestant sources. In the final section I will outline the argument of the book as a whole, in the context of the divergent Christian approaches to families and children.

Optimists and pessimists

Fiona Williams posits a polarity between "the pessimists' demoralization thesis" and the "optimists' democratization thesis."[35] According to pessimists the family crisis is a moral crisis, fed by selfish individualism and lack of commitment, which has "de-moralised" an entire generation. Pessimists *interpret* family breakdown as a major *causal*, but preventable, contribution to human misery, and in particular to the diminution of the happiness and life-chances of children. There are said to be several versions of the thesis: conservative, where traditional values have been corrupted by liberalism and permissive hedonism; socialist, where market values have corrupted the human spirit; and communitarian, where "the movement of both parents into work, the values of careerism and consumption have weakened commitment to care for children." The alternative thesis welcomes "the move away from traditional gender divisions, assumptions of lifelong marriage, duty, and dependence as heralding relationships that are more equal and mutually satisfying, because they are no longer held in place by obligation and convention, but are negotiated." On this view, democratic choice replaces outmoded social expectations and prejudices. Optimists think the consequences of family breakdown are over-dramatized. One version of the democratization thesis holds that people remain just as moral and committed in their relationships as people ever have been. Change is registered rather in the ways by which commitment is expressed. This view "finds people to be energetic moral actors, embedded in webs of valued personal relationships, working to sustain the commitments that matter to them."[36]

---

[35] Williams, *Rethinking Families*, pp. 19–23.
[36] Williams, *Rethinking Families*, p. 41.

Most, but not all, religious thought has sided with, and contributed to, the former thesis. Indeed the term "harmism" now appears, as a name for the expectation, fueled largely by religious groups, that family breakdown will almost invariably cause harm, whatever the circumstances. However, hypotheses have to be established by evidence, and there will be detailed criticism both of the framing of the polarity between optimism and pessimism, and of the further thesis, claimed to be established empirically, that moral commitment is undiminished but different (below, 5.1–5.2). The preliminary point to establish is that while there is agreement that families are changing, there is little agreement in secular thought about either the causes or the consequences. We will not therefore be surprised to discover a similar polarity in religious thought.

Theologies and families

The flagship book in a major project in the United States on "The Family, Religion and Culture" in 1997 posited "three styles of religious response"[37] to the "family crisis" over divorce. Both the crisis and the styles of response can be found far beyond the United States. These are liberal or "mainline" Protestant, conservative Protestant, and Roman Catholic.[38] Each of these styles includes within it much internal diversity. The liberal style is most in tune with culture but most likely to accommodate itself to it. A well-known example is the 1991 Presbyterian Church Report, *Keeping Body and Soul Together*.[39] A mere three and a half pages (out of nearly 200) was devoted to marriage, and that term did not appear in its index. Rosemary Radford Ruether has advocated "a postmodern view of family – that is, one that recognizes a diversity of forms of partnering."[40] This counts as a "liberal" view (and one which does not discriminate between the "forms of partnering" and the different benefits that the different forms may bring).[41] "Conserva-

---

[37] Don S. Browning, Bonnie J. Miller-McLemore, Pamela D. Couture, K. Brynolf Lyon, and Robert M. Franklin, *From Culture Wars to Common Ground: Religion and the American Family Debate* (Louisville, KY: Westminster John Knox Press, 1997), p. 43. Among the many achievements of the project were 19 scholarly books in the area of family and marriage.

[38] A similar schema is used by Fred Guyette in his "Families, Pastoral Counseling, Scripture: Searching for the Connections," *Journal of Pastoral Counseling*, 38 (2003), [5–33], p. 6.

[39] General Assembly Special Committee on Human Sexuality, Presbyterian Church (USA), *Keeping Body and Soul Together: Sexuality, Spirituality and Social Justice*, 1991.

[40] Rosemary Radford Ruether, *Christianity and the Making of the Modern Family* (Boston, MA: Beacon Press, 2000), p. 211.

[41] Adrian Thatcher, "Forming a Family," *Christian Century*, November 1, 2000 [1122–6].

tive-Protestant" is diffuse, encompassing fundamentalists, a range of conservative and liberal evangelicals, and in the United States, the "Religious Right." Roman Catholic thought divides between official and unofficial thought, and the latter divides into progressive and more reactionary types.

The Southern Baptist Convention of the United States, a Protestant denomination of 16 million members, must stand as a reliable representative of a range of conservative Protestant views. Section 18 of "The Baptist Faith and Message," entitled "Family," says "God has ordained the family as the foundational institution of human society. It is composed of persons related to one another by marriage, blood, or adoption."[42] (There is a swathe of supporting biblical references, yet the severe strictures of Jesus himself about biological kin (below, 3.1) are unsurprisingly omitted.) Although the section is entitled "Family," the narrative moves immediately to marriage, which is "the uniting of one man and one woman in covenant commitment for a lifetime." The longest paragraph in the section is about the subordinate role of wives within marriages. While the husband and wife are of equal worth before God, "A husband is to love his wife as Christ loved the church. He has the God-given responsibility to provide for, to protect, and to lead his family. A wife is to submit herself graciously to the servant leadership of her husband even as the church willingly submits to the headship of Christ." The remaining paragraph, on children, describes them, "from the moment of conception," as "a blessing and heritage from the Lord." Parents are "to demonstrate to their children God's pattern for marriage," "to teach their children spiritual and moral values and to lead them, through consistent lifestyle example and loving discipline, to make choices based on biblical truth." Children, in turn, are to "honor and obey their parents."

There are very many more Protestant Christians throughout the world who endorse this approach to families and children. The statement is a direct outcome of what the Bible is believed to be. In this denomination's statement of faith the Bible appears before even the doctrine of God. It "was written by men divinely inspired and is God's revelation of Himself to man. It is a perfect treasure of divine instruction. It has God for its author, salvation for its end, and truth, without any mixture of error, for its matter." The statement is perilously close to idolatry, for it elevates the Bible to a similar status given in Christian faith to that of our Lord himself. What room for Jesus Christ is there if the Bible is "God's revelation of Himself to man"?

The "Family" section is based on a pre-critical reading of the Household

---

[42] Southern Baptist Convention, "The Baptist Faith and Message," section 18. www.sbc.net/bfm/bfm2000.asp#xviii. Accessed 02.09.2006.

Code in Ephesians 5:21–6:9. The husband loves; the wife submits and respects. The asymmetrical relationship between God and God's people, and between Christ and the church, is applied uncritically to the married relationship (so that the husband stands for God and for Christ). Leaving aside the non-existent record of husbands as household managers (and the obsequious oxymoron "servant leadership" that should fool no-one), perhaps the saddest feature of the statement is its lack of awareness of the link between the theology of male power it authorizes and the perpetuation and legitimation of domestic violence that too often results from it.

Neither is there much good news for children in the statement. While an absolute position is taken on the status of the human embryo, one suspects that "loving discipline" is the disingenuous sanctioning of corporal punishment. Children are to be taught, led, and obedient. There is little of the joy of Jesus in the presence of children here: nothing of parents honoring their children; nothing even, of their loving them unconditionally (as Christ loves them?). There is still much in this statement that remains commendable, but the dominance of a particular way of reading the Bible inhibits the need to develop what the Bible gives. It encourages theological complacency by its assumption that with regard to family, sex, and gender, all has already been revealed so there is nothing else to learn, and little to be written either. The male power within the denomination continues to derive its authority from a divinely revealed source that cannot be wrong. What is needed, rather, is a hermeneutic that allows the Christ of the scriptures, of the creeds, and of the church, to be God without remainder or biblical rival, and God the Spirit to be allowed to lead the communities of scripture readers into rather more imaginative and inclusive visions of God's will for families and children. As we shall see, such a shift is crucial to a fresh vision of families and children within the Reign of God.

A different kind of conservatism is expressed in the official writings of the Roman Catholic Church, whose recent leader, Pope John Pope II, regularly and directly intervened in his support for families and children. The best known of these writings, *Familiaris consortio*, or *On the Family* (1981) opens with a statement of regret that "The family in the modern world, as much as and perhaps more than any other institution, has been beset by the many profound and rapid changes that have affected society and culture. Many families are living this situation in fidelity to those values that constitute the foundation of the institution of the family." The Holy Father wished to respond pastorally and sensitively to the crisis:

> Knowing that marriage and the family constitute one of the most precious of human values, the Church wishes to speak and offer her help to those who

are already aware of the value of marriage and the family and seek to live it faithfully, to those who are uncertain and anxious and searching for the truth, and to those who are unjustly impeded from living freely their family lives. Supporting the first, illuminating the second and assisting the others, the Church offers her services to every person who wonders about the destiny of marriage and the family.[43]

Familiaris consortio is discussed in later pages. We are concerned here with the genre of official Catholic thought about families and this quotation provides several pointers to it. In the spirit of Vatican II, the Pope begins with the problems facing families. That is, as a matter of method, he starts with the situation that he wishes to address. Next he has in his sights his audiences. They are faithful Christians; people who no longer find Catholic teaching about the family convincing; people who because of social injustice cannot operate as the families they are; and finally everyone regardless of creed, marital status or sex who ponders over marriage and family as universal institutions. Twenty-five years later this is still an appropriate method for Christian ethics to adopt, and an appropriate set of questions with which to engage. His opening words also suggest an intriguing question. We will not be surprised to hear the Pope say that "marriage and the family constitute one of the most precious of human values." But what is to be made of the implication behind the reference to those "values that constitute the foundation" of both? Are there more fundamental values, values that are not identical with marriage and family but which, just because they are more fundamental, constitute the foundation of both? We will return to this suggestion later (below, 4.2).

In the last 25 years or so, the institution of marriage has become weaker. It is now well separated from parenthood and no longer the assured basis, as we have seen, of families. Talk of the substantive "the family" sounds increasingly archaic, and the conjunction of "marriage and the family" bristles with presumptions. Recent changes to families need not, of course, require a change to Christian teaching: indeed part of the appeal of conservative theology of all kinds is that it defines itself as resistant to change, and thereby strengthens its identity over against sinful "others" (cohabitors, divorced persons, single parents, same-sex couples). But conservative Christians too are deeply affected by these changes, and cannot escape them. The more counter-cultural the Christian message sounds, the harder it is to enter into communication with the very audiences the Pope identifies. Ending a

[43] Pope John Paul II, *Familiaris consortio* (1981), para. 1. www.vatican.va/holy_father/john_paul_ii/apost_exhortations/. Accessed 02.09.2006.

generous review of a century of Roman Catholic teaching about the family Cahill concludes

> Despite significant and admirable advances, the official Roman Catholic approach to family matters is still overly concerned with reproductive issues, not sufficiently attuned to gender and race as intersecting causes of economic inequities that affect families, and too quick to assume that an audience of ecclesial and political rank-holders will endorse and effect wide-ranging changes.[44]

To these concerns we might also add another. Official literature still assumes as normative the indissolubility of marriage, and the further set of assumptions, steadily undermined in practice, that couples and families can be located on the officially approved journey from virginity to lifelong sacramental marriage within which no contraception is practiced and all children thus conceived are wanted. In 1994 it was possible for Pope John Paul II to claim that "these families make up 'the norm,' even admitting the existence of more than a few 'irregular situations.'"[45] Faithful couples are commended for "their service to life," and there are "new reasons for forcefully reaffirming" the "constant teaching" of the church forbidding contraception.[46] The gap between families as they are, and families as they appear through the filter of theological categories, seems to increase annually. Nonetheless some of the insights of official writings, not least the daring and original connections between the being of the Triune God as a communion of divine Persons, or *communio personarum*, and the being of human families as communions of persons,[47] will become a major theme in the re-presentation of families in this volume.

Catholic thought about families also has its revisionists. We have already noted Cahill's critique of certain papal contributions to the debate.[48] Her work combines gentle disapprobations and dissenting analyzes within the broad framework of critical appreciation of the Roman Catholic tradition. The works of Michael Lawler,[49] Florence Caffrey Bourg,[50] the distinguished

---

[44] Cahill, *Families*, p. 95.

[45] Pope John Paul II, *Letter to Families*, section 5.

[46] *Letter to Families*, section 12. *Catechism*, para. 204, p. 476.

[47] Pope John Paul II, *Letter to Families*, sections 6–7.

[48] Cahill, *Family*. And see her *Sex, Gender and Christian Ethics* (Cambridge, UK: Cambridge University Press, 1996).

[49] Michael G. Lawler, *Family: American and Christian* (Chicago, IL: Loyola Press, 1998).

[50] Florence Caffrey Bourg, *Where Two or Three Are Gathered: Christian Families as Domestic Churches* (Notre Dame, IN: University of Notre Dame Press, 2004).

contributors to *Marriage in the Catholic Tradition*,[51] and in the United Kingdom Jack Dominian,[52] among several others, are associated with a full profession of the Catholic faith, an impatience with official natalism and gender intransigence, a sense of the developing social tradition of Catholic thought, and a determination to treat the sexual experience of contemporary people, whether Roman Catholic or not, as spiritually significant. Bourg's rebuke of the Pope for rebuking non-traditional families is a good indicator of the precarious balance in this revisionary style of writing, between a robust affirmation of the Catholic faith, criticism of certain elements of official teaching, and the development of it in ways the Magisterium has not yet approved and may never do so. One of her criticisms of *Familiaris consortio* is that

> much effort is spent in a sort of theoretical pep talk, which aims to inspire families to muster their strengths, conquer temptations and enemies, and go out to save their local communities and the world from error. Where family difficulties are discussed, they are generally described as conquerable, so long as families recognize true priorities and stick to them, praying for God's grace to guide and strengthen them. "Ideals" function as "norms," and on the basis of these norms many types of families are labeled as being in "difficult or irregular situations."[53]

Whatever the difficulties in the papal approach, there is much rich material in Roman Catholic thought, both official and revisionary, that compares favorably with the paucity of official Anglican writing. The Church of England House of Bishops has produced two reports on sexuality since 1991,[54] but these are preoccupied with homosexuality and mention families only rarely and incidentally. The same may be said of a "teaching document" from the bishops on marriage.[55] Anglicans tend to issue discussion documents, not make pronouncements. It may fairly be said that official Anglican teaching about families derives from a prior concern to "defend"

---

[51] Todd A. Salzman, Thomas M. Kelly, and John J. O'Keefe (eds.), *Marriage in the Catholic Tradition – Scripture, Tradition and Experience* (New York: Crossroad, 2004).

[52] His latest work is *Living Love* (London: Darton, Longman, and Todd, 2004).

[53] Bourg, *Where Two or Three Are Gathered*, p. 54.

[54] House of Bishops, *Issues in Human Sexuality* (London: Church House Publishing, 1991). A group of bishops, known as the House of Bishops' Group on Issues on Human Sexuality, produced the sequel, *Some Issues in Human Sexuality: A Guide to the Debate* (London: Church House Publishing, 2003).

[55] *Marriage: A Teaching Document from the House of Bishops of the Church of England* (London: Church House Publishing, 1999).

marriage, and, as part of that defensive strategy, to insist that "Sexual inter-course, as an expression of faithful intimacy, properly belongs within marriage exclusively."[56] An appreciation of families themselves and the rela-tions within them might be fruitful. A more positive approach to families was adopted by the innovative working party of the Board for Social Responsibility of the Church of England, as its title, *Something to Celebrate: Valuing Families in Church and Society*,[57] indicated. But that report was poorly received, and its lack of theological analysis, both historical and contem-porary, made it an easy target from all sides. However, the trends it described are now more advanced than they were in 1995, and the need for a theology of families, which it did not provide, is now greater than ever.

The single, most prolific source of theological writing on families in the last few years is the Family, Religion, and Culture project, directed by Don Browning from Chicago. The flagship volume of the project, *From Culture Wars to Common Ground*, advocated (in 1997) a *"new family ideal, what we call 'the committed, intact, equal-regard, public-private family.'"*[58] The name of the new ideal is "critical familism," and its characteristics include "a full equality between husband and wife," an analysis "of the *power relations* between husband, wife, children, and surrounding economic and governmental insti-tutions," and the deep, co-operative involvement of civil society in promot-ing the "common good." The project promoted "equal-regard marriages and families" and by means of its many books it described "the religio-cultural vision and social supports needed to inspire and maintain them."[59] Later books in the project extended the "religiocultural vision" beyond the United States, and even beyond Christianity.[60]

Critical familism "advances a centrist position" between the liberals and conservatives.[61] It is not denominationally based. Deeply rooted in practical theology it draws freely on psychology, sociology, socio-biology, philosophy, history, psychotherapy, and economics. It wrestles with the key question "Is it the *quality* of family experience, rather than the *form*, that Christianity cele-brates? Or is it both quality and form that it values?"[62] There is a "prima facie presumption toward intactness" in families which is not allowed to "trump all other values under all conditions." Children are less likely to flourish if they

---

[56] *Marriage*, p. 8.
[57] (London: Church House Publishing, 1995).
[58] Browning et al., *Culture Wars*, p. 2 (authors' emphasis).
[59] Browning et al., *Culture Wars*, p. 3.
[60] Don S. Browning, *Marriage and Modernization: How Globalization Threatens Marriage and What to Do about It* (Grand Rapids, MI/Cambridge, UK: Eerdmans, 2003).
[61] Browning et al., *Culture Wars*, p. viii.
[62] Browning et al., *Culture Wars*, p. 5 (author's emphases).

are affected by divorce and raised by a single parent, but intactness can also be an oppressive value. Protestant denominations in the United States are criticized for their liberal family policies from the 1970s on. One of the criticisms is that "A new democracy of loving and just intimate relationships replaced older boundary-creating understandings of marriage as publicly witnessed covenant, sacrament, and contract." Marriages and families became "deinstitutionalized just and loving relationships."[63] Liberal and feminist theologians receive positive but critical treatment. "Beyond proposals to eliminate the family entirely or simply tolerate instability and diversity, with what do feminists propose to replace the failing nuclear family?"[64]

No theologian writing about families and children at the present time can fail to be indebted to the Family, Religion, and Culture project. However at several points in the book I shall diverge, if not from the project's conclusions, then from various arguments leading to them. In particular its hermeneutic procedure is investigated in chapter 2. But Browning's achievement is immense and lasting: any criticism of the project is made with admiration and respect.

1.4 Theology and Families: Arguments and Themes

I have outlined some of the changes that have happened to families in the last 50 years, and some of the lines of theological response to them. It is now possible to present the themes of the book in relation both to the social changes that are occurring, and to the attempts already made to grapple with them theologically. The present work is close to critical familism (though conceived independently of it), but differs from it in several ways. One difference is the hermeneutic procedure. Chapter 2 engages with two of the problems encountered by readers of the Bible seeking guidance about families. These are discontinuity in time and plurality of sources (2.1). The suspicion that critical familism does not deal adequately with these difficulties is examined and allowed to develop into a major reservation regarding the justification of its conclusions (2.2). Several hermeneutical principles for "family-friendly" readings of scripture are then suggested (2.3) which frame the remainder of the present work.

Chapter 3 re-visits the much-neglected teaching of Jesus about families. This will be allowed to impact upon the argument of the book in its sheer

---

[63] Browning et al., *Culture Wars*, p. 45.
[64] Browning et al., *Culture* Wars, p. 161. The question is borrowed from the sociologist Judith Stacey.

power to confront modern assumptions about families and their forms (3.1). The teaching of Jesus about children, better known, but encased in sentiment, is recovered (3.2). Given Jesus' relativization of kin ties and his teaching about the blessedness of *all* children, the question regarding the priorities parents owe to their own children is allowed to be raised in an acute form (3.3). The provisional answer, supported by the doctrinal conclusions of later chapters, is that our children are nearer to us than our neighbors and therefore have a prior entitlement to our love (3.4).

The final chapter in Part I, "Sources," draws its inspiration from the fullness of the divine being in all its relational richness. God's being is presented as the intersection of giving, being, loving, and enabling. The doctrine of the Trinity, applied only rarely in an ethical or familial context, is the ground of all human relations, and in particular, parent–child relations, from which of course the names of two of the divine Persons are taken (4.1). The utilization of Trinitarian doctrine by Karl Barth and Pope John Paul II is examined, and the latter's is preferred (4.2). The realization of, and the participation in, the love of God, is the basis of the flourishing of all human families. The transition from thinking of ourselves as separate selves to thinking of ourselves as relations enables that doctrine to leap into a new relevance inside a Christian family ethic. The notion of the "gifting God,"[65] together with the orthodox belief that God is a Child, becomes the basis of a child theology (4.3). The situatedness of families in the social Trinity, and the reconstruction of the doctrine of the *imago dei* as a relational-social doctrine, enables fresh thinking about families to happen (4.4). These emphases indicate a greater sympathy with metaphysical, and even contemplative and mystical, traditions of theology, that may yield similar results to those of critical familism while arriving at those results via different routes. The four systems within which families operate (above, 1.2) are seen to be disrupted by structural sin, and the overcoming of pervasive global and personal sin is what Christ the Redeemer has already done (4.5).

Part II, "Relations," wraps the theological sources of Part I around families and children. The impasse between optimists and pessimists, both inside and outside the churches, can now be revisited. The form most likely to embody and strengthen the commitment necessary for the flourishing of families and children, namely marriage, is advocated (5.1). The flourishing of children is made the basis for a "theology of liberation for children," and for a critique of the pessimists' case (5.2). It will be suggested, controversially, that there are marital, or conjugal, values in many relationships other than

---

[65] See Stephen H. Webb, *The Gifting God: A Trinitarian Ethics of Excess* (New York and Oxford, UK: Oxford University Press, 1996).

marriage, and an absence of these values in some sacramental marriages. An inclusive understanding of these values will also help to resolve the problem of family form and extend the goods of marriage (5.3).

Chapter 6 addresses the marginalization of children in historical theology. It favorably compares the teaching of Clement of Alexandria about children with that of Augustine and Aquinas and suggests that positive writing about children in the tradition has been impeded by Augustine's influence (6.1). The use of the language of children's rights in relation to the responsibilities of parents and children is endorsed. Children's rights are seen to extend the concern of Jesus for children to a universal and secular context (6.2). These rights are re-sourced in the teaching of Jesus about children, and in his being as the universal Logos of God who becomes the Christ Child (6.3).

Chapter 7 sets human relations between parents and children within the divine relations between the Persons of the Holy Trinity. The symbol "Father" is positively used in a theology of parenthood. The common (and crude) assumption that the divine "Father" is masculine, is subjected to searching criticism (7.1). Several revisionary accounts of divine Fatherhood are noted appreciatively, but the use of the symbol "the Mother of God" in order to restore the gender imbalance of traditional theology, is resisted (7.2). Drawing on earlier arguments in the book, human parent–child relations are situated in the Triune Relations that constitute the Communion of Persons who are God. Two analogies, those of sacrifice and mutuality, are deployed in order to indicate how human parenting can participate in the Fatherly and Motherly action of God (7.3). Several theologians who are also mothers contribute to an original understanding of mutuality between mothers and children. These accounts extend further the Trinitarian theology of parenthood, and help to articulate and sustain essential elements of the parental task, for example, generativity, loving relationality, equality, and appropriate sacrifice. These theological arguments in favor of mutuality are preferred to attempts to find mutuality between mothers and fathers, and parents and children, directly in scripture (7.4).

Chapter 8 considers whether the theological account of families in the book accords with the disruptive teaching of Jesus that the Reign of God, not ties of kin, constitutes the only, or the principal, viable family form for his disciples (8.1–8.3). It then develops a gentle critique of the growing tendency, even among Christians, toward voluntary childlessness (8.4–8.5). "Extended" families are welcomed (8.1). The distinction between "open" and "closed families" is noted, but criticisms of some open families (that they are closed) and the theological personalism that allegedly encourages their closure, are themselves criticized (8.2). The growing practice of voluntary childlessness is examined from a range of viewpoints (8.4), and the conclusion reached that the refusal of the gift of children, at least in many cases, may be influenced by cultural factors of a lamentable kind (8.5).

Chapter 9 examines the idea of "domestic church" and welcomes it as an affirmation of families which is complementary to, and overlaps with, the theology developed in this book (9.1). It next examines the extent to which it is helpful for the local church to consider itself a family, and how families might operate if the Christians who comprise them are churches (9.2). Finally some policy implications for national and global churches are suggested (9.3).

Chapter Two

The Bible in the Service of Families

2.1 Families Then and Now

The spinning of theories about how to read the Bible has become a major theological industry.[1] Much of this endeavour operates at a level of high abstraction. In this chapter I attempt to cut through much of the theoretical discussion by addressing the simple question how best to read the Bible in the service of families and children.

Discontinuity and plurality

There are at least two major sets of problems which today's Bible readers encounter: the series of diachronic discontinuities between biblical times and our own; and the plurality of voices within the biblical witness. Carolyn Osiek and David Balch (in one of the books of The Family, Religion, and Culture project) have provided a detailed and authoritative analysis of the cultural anthropology of Mediterranean families in New Testament times, and they advise us, disarmingly, "not to assume that ancient Mediterranean people meant the same thing we do by such terms as woman, man, child, marriage, divorce, and household."[2] This is a remarkable *caveat*. Since most of the world-wide community of Bible-readers probably still *does* generally

---

[1] See, for example, in this series, Stephen E. Fowl, *Engaging Scripture* (Malden, MA, and Oxford, UK: Blackwell, 1998), and the bibliography there (pp. 207–15).

[2] Carolyn Osiek and David L. Balch, *Families in the New Testament World: Households and House Churches* (Louisville, KY: Westminster John Knox Press, 1997), p. 47. "Friends" might also be added to the list, for the "softer language of friendship" was often a foil for "the hard language of patronage" (p. 50). See also, Bruce J. Malina, *The New Testament World: Insights from Cultural Anthropology* (Louisville, KY: Westminster John Knox Press, 1997). And see Halvor Moxnes (ed.), *Constructing Early Christian Families: Family as Social Reality and Metaphor* (New York: Routledge, 1997).

assume that these very basic terms *do* mean "the same thing" across time, it is necessary to inquire further into this disturbing conclusion. Relations between men and women, Osiek and Balch explain, were governed by codes of honor and shame. Male honor, they say, "consists in maintaining the status, power, and reputation of the male members of a kinship group over against the threats that may be thrown against them by outsiders."[3] Because women "have the power that provides legitimate offspring, they must be protected from outsider males and therefore controlled." Women are "the weak members of the family for whom sexuality is irresistible and sex drive indiscriminate." It is

> women's very weakness that gives them the fearful power of being able to shame their family through its male members by sexual activity with any male other than a legal husband. Virginity before marriage is a girl's highest duty and greatest value. The surest way for a male to dishonor an individual male or family is to seduce or rape its women, for this demonstrates that the males lack the power to protect their vulnerable members.[4]

These highly gendered codes are an important cause of some of the discontinuities between men and women then and now. The equality of the sexes could scarcely be conceived in the ancient world. "No ancient Mediterranean man would have thought that a woman could be his equal; only a man of similar education and social status could be." Marriage, Osiek and Balch remind us, was "a legal and social contract between two *families*," not two individuals, and its purpose was "the promotion and status of each, the production of legitimate offspring, and the appropriate preservation and transferral of property to the next generation."[5] Divorce was "the severance of the relationship between two families at the initiative of one of the marriage partners, with the consequent severance of property agreements."[6]

Many marriages were arranged, of course, by the families themselves, not by the spouses. (I have dealt extensively in another volume with the discontinuities of meaning and practice with regard to marriage in ancient and modern periods.[7]) Children were "the family's most precious possessions." Whether or not they were loved, they were needed: "boys to preserve the family property, protect their women, and beget sons; girls to contract good

---

[3] Osiek and Balch, *Families*, p. 38.
[4] Osiek and Balch, *Families*, p. 39.
[5] Osiek and Balch, *Families*, p. 42 (emphasis added).
[6] Osiek and Balch, *Families*, p. 42.
[7] Adrian Thatcher, *Living Together and Christian Ethics* (Cambridge, UK: Cambridge University Press, 2002).

marriages, assure favorable alliances between families, and produce sons."[8] Households differed considerably from ours. A household would contain kin, "fictive-kin,"[9] a retinue of slaves and possibly patrons. While the married couple would be its nucleus, it would generally contain many more members than the modern nuclear family. As Lawler reminds us, "The 'traditional' American family is a small nuclear unit, comprising some 2.63 people; the biblical family was a large, extended unit, comprising up to 100 people and more."[10]

The Hebrew scriptures confirm these discontinuities. With regard to normative family form (at least in the 1,200 year period of early Judaism), another volume in The Family, Religion, and Culture project confirms that "Family households did not consist of nuclear families in the modern understanding of a married couple and their children but rather were multigenerational (up to four generations) and included the social arrangement of several families, related by blood and marriage, who lived in two or three houses architecturally connected."[11] A household

> was primarily a kinship system that included lineal descent and lateral extension: grandparents, adult male children and their wives and children, unmarried children, and widowed and divorced adult daughters who may have had children. Marginal members of households outside of this immediate kinship structure could include debt servants, slaves, concubines, resident aliens, sojourners, day laborers, orphans, and Levites, together with any family they may have had.[12]

Once these discontinuities are made clear, biblical texts are rendered strange, resistant to our own culture-bound questioning. Men, women, families, and children do *not* mean the same thing. Such discontinuities provide the stuff of much hermeneutical theory. "Discontinuity rather than continuity is the postmodern watchword."[13] But it is important not to overstate discontinuity.

---

[8] Osiek and Balch, *Families*, p. 43.
[9] "Fictive kinship" is the "extension of familiar loyalties . . . to others not related by blood, law, or other traditional ties." See Osiek and Balch, *Families*, p. 54.
[10] Michael G. Lawler, "Towards a Theology of Christian Family," *INTAMS Review*, 8.1 (2002), [55–73], p. 59.
[11] Leo G. Perdue, "The Israelite and Early Jewish Family: Summary and Conclusions," in Leo G. Perdue, Joseph Blenkinsopp, John J. Collins, and Carol Meyers, *Families in Ancient Israel* (Louisville, KY: Westminster John Knox Press, 1997), [163–22], p. 175.
[12] Perdue, "The Israelite and Early Jewish Family," p. 175. See the extensive biblical references there on which these conclusions are soundly based.
[13] Kevin J. Vanhoozer, "Theology and the condition of postmodernity," in Kevin J. Vanhoozer (ed.), *The Cambridge Companion to Postmodern Theology* (Cambridge, UK: Cambridge University Press, 2003), [3–25], p. 11.

There is much in the Hebrew Bible regarding care for strangers, for the "fatherless," the poor, and so on, and the household becomes Yahweh's agent in making provision for them as "marginal members."[14] We would not be able to recognize discontinuities without some deeper appreciation of the historical continuum that allows us to compare one period with another. We also possess a solidarity that unites us with other people through time in the experience of, say, embodiment, mortality, and suffering. If absolutes are banished from postmodern thinking, it would be contradictory to insist on absolute discontinuity. The same may be said of bi-polar or binary oppositions, of which "continuity/discontinuity" is arguably one. Discontinuities upset accustomed readings, but, as we shall see, they occasion exciting new possibilities.

Four awkward questions

Bible readers also have to deal with plurality. Biblical texts are diverse, sometimes to the point of incompatibility. In order to demonstrate the twin problems of discontinuity and plurality, let us ask four awkward questions of the New Testament texts. These are questions that Christians interested in families are bound to ask, even if the New Testament remains partially resistant to them. They are awkward, not at all in the sense of showing our theological sophistication in rendering them inconclusive, but rather in the sense that they defy our lazy requests for simple answers, and so lure us on to more rigorous and more prayerful heuristic and doctrinal work. The difficulty of obtaining answers to the questions will then provide the necessary prompt for handling the biblical witness in a different way. The questions are: does the New Testament teach the priority of men over women, or does it teach the equality of men and women? How does it view children? Does it encourage or discourage marriage? And, does it provide support for nuclear families?

First, does the New Testament teach the priority of men over women, or does it teach equality between them? Clearly it can be found to teach both, but with a heavy masculinist bias over all. St Paul teaches that "There is no such thing as Jew and Greek, slave and freeman, male and female" (Gal. 3:28a). But he also believed "that, while every man has Christ for his head, a woman's head is man, as Christ's head is God" (1 Cor. 11:3). Not for the early Paul is the inclusive understanding of men and woman as jointly made in the image of God, "because man is the image of God, and the mirror of his glory, whereas a woman reflects the glory of man" (1 Cor. 11:7). He based this judgment about women on the temporal priority of the creation of Adam in Genesis 2. The Pauline school responsible for "1 Timothy" puts the idea of Adam's temporal priority over Eve to a severer end: to silence women in the churches. "Their role is to learn, listening quietly and with due submission" (1 Tim. 2:11). Women, not men, brought sin into the world (1 Tim. 2:14).

The ambivalence over the question extends into the Christian household, where the submission of wives (and everyone else) is expected. It is often claimed that the injunction "Be subject to one another out of reverence for Christ" (Eph. 5:21) may be a possible lingering echo of early marital equality. Even so, the hard expectation of the submission of wives to husbands is quickly re-iterated (Eph. 5:22,24b,33c; Col. 3:18; 1 Pet. 3:1–6).[15] There is an uncomfortable implication in these *Haustafeln* or Household Codes that is rarely (if ever?) allowed to surface in contemporary theological discussion. Marital love belongs to the husband only, as a function of his priority, or "headship," in the marriage. The husbands do the loving (Eph. 5:25,28,33b; Col. 3:19), and the wives do the submitting (Eph. 5:22,24b,33c). (Worse, it is even suggested that "whereas Christ *gave* himself, husbands are to *love* themselves," and this is said to be "an alarming shift from altruistic to selfish motivation."[16]) Unpalatable as this one-sided view of marital love may be to the taste of modern readers, including growing numbers of thoughtful evangelical Christians,[17] it is embedded in the ancient world-view of the

[14] Perdue, "The Israelite and Early Jewish Family," pp. 192–203.

[15] Betsy J. Bauman-Martin notes that the wives here were of non-Christian husbands, and the policy of submission was prudential in character, validated by the suffering of Christ. She says "As women negotiating problematic familial and social boundaries, they offer a valuable example of an ancient hermeneutic of *resistance*" (emphasis added). See her "Women on the Edge: New Perspectives on Women in the Petrine *Haustafel*," *Journal of Biblical Literature*, Summer 2004, vol. 123, issue 2 [253–79], p. 254. Despite taking issue with most feminist criticism of the Petrine household code, she leaves us in no doubt about "its vastly destructive influence on the behavior and self-understanding of Christian women" (p. 259).

[16] Osiek and Balch, *Families*, p. 121. And see Elizabeth Johnson, "Ephesians," in Carol A. Newsom and Sharon H. Ringe (eds.), *The Women's Bible Commentary* (Louisville, KY: Westminster John Knox Press, and London: SPCK, 1992), pp. 340–1.

[17] John P. Bartkowski has documented the "internecine" struggle going on among evangelicals about family relations, observing that "more egalitarian evangelical authors tend to embrace an androgynous conceptualization of gender or a 'modified essentialism' that dovetails with their vision of gender-complementary marital teamwork." These commentators rely upon scriptural passages that seem to indicate the reciprocal obligation that all Christians have to submit to one another (interpreted as "mutual submission" for husbands and wives). See his "Debating Patriarchy: Discursive Disputes over Spousal Authority among Evangelical Family Commentators," *Journal for the Scientific Study of Religion*, 36.3, September 1997, [393–410], p. 406. The analysis of discontinuity just undertaken suggests that the common ground between the factions in this "local" culture war, is the fallacy of our immediacy to the text.

relations between the sexes, where the man is the active, and the woman the passive, subject. As Osiek and Balch have shown, "Second-generation, deutero-Pauline Christians acculturating to Roman imperial (tyrannical) society wrote a passive ethic into our canon." They comment on the difficulty this ethic poses for those "many modern Christians," who "are responding to our recent experiences in social and political history by rejecting passive subjection to domestic and political hierarchical institutions."[18] Our question, then, predictably, cannot succeed. Its gets lost in the complexities of discontinuity and plurality.

Second, let us ask: what is the attitude of the New Testament to children? Here surely there is an unambiguous message? Does not the unconditional welcome of children by Jesus, his vivid language about their need for protection, his elevation of them as signs and recipients of the Reign of God, his identification and that of the Father with children, and his blessing of children (Mt. 18:1–5; 19:13–15; 21:14–16; Mk. 9:33–7; 10:13–16) add up to a cumulative manifesto for, and action on behalf of, children?[19] We will certainly make much of these verses (below, 3.2, 6.3). Yet even this amazingly positive picture is qualified by three further factors.

First, the discouragement of marriage and the warning against its attendant cares (including children!) strikes a dissonant chord. If marriage is discouraged, then the approved relationship for having and nurturing children is discouraged also. If celibacy is better than marriage then it is better not to have children than to have them. That remained Augustine's view even after his attempt to justify marriage by means of children as one of its three "goods." Second, the Household Codes introduce a different tone to that of the synoptic Gospels. They affirm a hierarchical order in the household, as in the Empire, and children are required to display unquestioning obedience (Eph. 6:1; Col. 3:20). In the Petrine Code (1 Pet. 2:13–3:7) children make no appearance. Is this because they are valued less than in the other codes? Third, there is evidence already in the New Testament, of the "adultization" of the faith, that is, the vocabulary of "little ones," children and childhood, is metaphorically extended to the adult relation to the divine Father, with the result that the anchoring of child-language in the situation of actual children is easily displaced. This time our question is convincingly answered by the teaching of Jesus himself, but his teaching scarcely receives endorsement elsewhere.

---

[18] Osiek and Balch, *Families*, p. 123.
[19] See Judith M. Gundry-Volf, "The Least and the Greatest: Children in the New Testament," in Marcia J. Bunge (ed.), *The Child in Christian Thought* (Grand Rapids, MI/Cambridge, UK: Eerdmans, 2001) [29–60].

Third, against the grain of almost all Protestant assumption: Does the New Testament encourage or discourage marriage? The answer is that it both encourages and discourages it, and the discouragement of marriage is probably stronger than its encouragement. Luke's Jesus declares that the state of matrimony *imperils one's eternal destiny*: "Jesus said to them, 'The men and women of this world marry; but those who have been judged worthy of a place in the other world, and of the resurrection from the dead, do not marry, for they are no longer subject to death. They are like angels; they are children of God, because they share in the resurrection'" (Lk. 20:34–6).[20] A text that once delighted the Fathers (all of them celibate) is now veiled in embarrassed de-selection from the popular canon. The reservations of Paul regarding marriage are well known. Singleness is better but if the unmarried and widows "do not have self-control, they should marry. It is better to be married than burn with desire"[21] (1 Cor. 7:9; 36b). The path of marriage is one of hardship (1 Cor. 7:28), and of "worldly affairs" (1 Cor. 7:33a, 34d) which is better left untrodden. The imminent return of Christ renders it irrelevant in the last days (1 Cor. 7:29).

What then, is there, in the New Testament, to encourage marriage? It is assumed, rather than commended. The Household Codes assume that Christian households will contain husbands, wives, children, and slaves. A bishop must be a "husband of one wife" (1 Tim. 3:2). A wedding feast at Cana is the place where Jesus performed "the first of his signs which revealed his glory" (Jn. 2:11) but his presence at a wedding reception (and his supernatural generosity) hardly justifies a Christian theology of marriage like the one that has been built upon it.[22] The nucleus of the household is the married couple. When Jesus speaks of marriage it is in the context of then current disputes about divorce. These disputes are more central to the Gospel writers' interests than Jesus' thoughts about marriage. Nevertheless, they indicate the importance of marriage at the time of Jesus, and Jesus heightens it by his opposition to divorce. It can therefore be safely said that the New Testament provides support for marriage. But it discourages it too,

---

[20] See also Lk. 14:20,26; 17:27; and 18:29–30 for Luke's deep suspicions toward marriage.

[21] There are good grounds for thinking that the "unmarried" (*agamoi*) in this verse are in fact the "no longer married," and that Paul was himself once married. See Ken Crispin, *Divorce: The Forgivable Sin?* (London: Hodder and Stoughton, 1988), pp. 44–5. If this interpretation is correct, the permission to marry, given in 1 Cor. 7:8–9, becomes permission to *re*-marry. There are of course many implications for the church's traditional doctrine if this plausible reading is adopted.

[22] See for example, Stavros S. Fotiou, "Water into Wine, and *Eros* into *Agape*: Marriage in the Orthodox Church," in Adrian Thatcher (ed.), *Celebrating Christian Marriage* (Edinburgh and New York: T&T Clark/Continuum, 2001), pp. 89–104.

and that remains a problem. Neither is it solved by the traditional formula whereby all Christians are offered the choice of marriage or of celibacy. There is ambiguity within and between the synoptic Gospels over marriage (and of course over divorce), and between Jesus' advocacy of lifelong marriage, Paul's view of marriage as a concession to desire, and Luke's dislike both of marriage and of divorce. Again our question dissolves in the complexities of discontinuity and plurality.

Finally, does the New Testament provide support for nuclear families? That question predictably dissolves in the same complexities. First, the New Testament does not know of our modern nuclear families. Second, the synoptic Gospels contain several sayings and episodes where Jesus relativizes biological ties in favor of the new family that is established in the Reign of God. "Whoever does the will of God is my brother and sister and mother" (Mk. 3:35). These sayings are examined below (3.1). Third, the relativization of ties of kin is profoundly unsettling to supporters of so-called "family values." Carolyn Osiek muses over how the synoptic tradition, with admonitions such as "Whoever loves father or mother more than me is not worthy of me" (Mt. 10:37) or "Whoever leaves house and family will receive a hundredfold," could have "developed and prospered simultaneously with other writings like the Pastorals" which re-affirm the hierarchical and patriarchal order.[23] Again, plurality threatens to become incommensurability.

These four questions have confirmed and illustrated the particular difficulties of discontinuity and plurality with regard to the interpretation of the New Testament sources about families and children. The project of critical familism offers a "new family ethic," and "a new critical culture of marriage."[24] But that project is itself partly entrapped in these difficulties. While its aims remain laudable, the relation between the aims and the hermeneutic that supports them is more problematic. There may be both a securer foundation in Christian *doctrine* than the critical familists suggest, and a securer hermeneutic that allows the biblical text to respond more fruitfully to our contemporary questions.

[23] Carolyn Osiek, "*Pietas* in and out of the Frying Pan," *Biblical Interpretation*, 11.2 (2003), [166–73], p. 171.

[24] Don S. Browning, Bonnie J. Miller-McLemore, Pamela D. Couture, K. Brynolf Lyon, and Robert M. Franklin, *From Culture Wars to Common Ground: Religion and the American Family Debate* (Louisville, KY: Westminster John Knox Press, 1997), p. 2.

2.2 The Bible and Critical Familism

We have noted (above, 1.3) that critical familism advocates the "egalitarian family"[25] and "equal-regard marriage." How are these *desiderata* themselves derived from scripture and tradition, since scripture teaches them only obliquely, if at all? The flagship volume of the project raises the question directly. "How should Christians and others read the scriptures that pronounce men to be the heads of their families?"[26] The question concedes the difficulty – the egalitarian family is not in the Bible – which is said to be "one of the most perplexing issues facing a family theory informed by a Christian perspective." But the chapter does not engage with our "readerly" difficulties. Instead of reading these passages "flatly" or "dismissively" as conservatives and liberals respectively are said to do, we are offered a "third alternative" which contextualizes the issues. There is a series of strong claims:

> When placed within its full historical context, early Christianity appears as a progressive influence on the family: in contrast to the surrounding Greco-Roman world, it inspired heightened degrees of female equality, a chastened patriarchy, higher levels of male responsibility and servanthood, less of a double standard in sexual ethics, and deeper respect for children. *But all of this was accomplished with ambivalence, hesitation, compromise, and some defensiveness.*[27]

Supporting these claims are others: that there is already "in early Christianity" "an ethic of gender equality," and "a softened patriarchal ethic;" an "unresolved tension" between them; and that "The earliest days of the Jesus movement . . . contained an ethos of genuine egalitarianism between men and women."[28] Elisabeth Schüssler-Fiorenza's depiction of early Christianity as "a discipleship of equals" is invoked,[29] and linked to Warren Carter's novel treatment of Matthew 19 and 20 as a reversal of the Aristotelian Household Codes and the promotion of "a radical equality of discipleship in both household and economic life."[30] The contrasting pairs of believers in the baptismal formula of Gal. 3:28 ("There is no such thing as Jew and Greek,

---

[25] Browning et al., *From Culture Wars*, p. 2.
[26] Browning et al., *From Culture Wars*, p. 129.
[27] Browning et al., *From Culture Wars*, p. 131 (authors' emphasis).
[28] Browning et al., *From Culture Wars*, p. 134.
[29] Browning et al., *From Culture Wars*, p. 135. See Elisabeth Schüssler Fiorenza, *In Memory of Her: A Feminist Theological Reconstruction of Christian Origins* (New York: Crossroad, 1983).
[30] The reference is to Warren Carter, *Households and Discipleship: A Study of Matthew 19–20* (Sheffield, UK: Sheffield Academic Press, 1994).

slave and freeman, male and female; for you are all one person in Christ")
are said to have "enjoyed a heightened equality in the house church because
they were thought to be equal in Christ, thereby having equal status before
God."[31] St Paul affirms that husband and wife have mutual authority over
each other's bodies (1 Cor. 7:8–9). David Balch's judgment that such mutuality is "astounding in Greco-Roman culture," is approvingly noted.[32]

The key to understanding the claimed achievements of the earliest Christianity in relation to issues of family and gender is said to be the
"honor-shame codes" of the ancient world with which the Gospel engaged.
Browning and his team explain "For a man to avoid shame and for a woman
to keep her shame, men had to protect, control, guide, and circumscribe the
lives of their women so that their private space would not be dishonored.
Such an ethic celebrated the virtues of active dominance for males and
passive conformity for females."[33] The Household Codes of the New Testament modify these pagan codes. In particular the extended code of
Ephesians 5:21–6:9 is "a genuine reversal of ancient heroic models of male
authority in families."[34] Much is made of the prefatory injunction of the
code to "Be subject to one another out of reverence for Christ" (Eph. 5:21).
It is only "within the revolutionary framework of mutual subordination that
we should read admonitions for the wife to be subordinate to the husband."
That husbands should love their wives is a "stunning idea," and the appeal to
husbands in Ephesians to "love their wives, as they love their own bodies" is
said to be influenced by the Great Commandment of Jesus to love our
neighbors as ourselves.[35] Finally, the Browning team complain that the "trajectory" of thought and practice, manifest in the text, is incomplete and
even goes into reverse. The Letter "did not tell succeeding generations how
the wife can be an equal, transformative, Christic figure to husband and
children and do so in the *sense of leading as well as following*."[36]

This third alternative is undeniably attractive. It claims to avoid the
excesses of conservatives and liberals. It is a painstaking consensus which has
employed the finest available biblical, historical, and theological scholarship
in the United States. Nonetheless I find several problems with it, both in
general and in detail. Let us begin with two preliminary observations. First,
most biblical exegetes would not contest the claim that the biblical text
must be understood in its context. But the greater the contextualization, the

---

[31] Browning et al., *From Culture Wars*, p. 136.
[32] Browning et al., *From Culture Wars*, p. 137. Based on an unpublished seminar presentation.
[33] Browning et al., *From Culture Wars*, p. 142.
[34] Browning et al., *From Culture Wars*, p. 141.
[35] Browning et al., *From Culture Wars*, pp. 145–6.
[36] Browning et al., *From Culture Wars*, p. 147.

greater the cession of interpretation to the historians. This is not to deny the immense importance of history to theology: nonetheless, liberal Protestantism has much to learn from the partial ceding of interpretation of the Gospels to the form critics for the last 150 years or so. The critics are unlikely to agree, and their disagreement seriously impairs authoritative use of the texts. While historians will profitably debate further the experience and forms of families in the very early church, a hermeneutic is needed which can be relied on while historians continue to argue. Although I am no historian, I do not think the historical case for egalitarian marriage is nearly as strong as Browning's team (and I myself) would like it to be.

The second problem is a similar one: the more the meaning of a text is derived from its context, the less likely are conservative readers to accept it. Contextualization has the effect of rendering a text *strange*. The strangeness sometimes effects surprise and response which in turn aid understanding. But another consequence of rendering a text strange is that the distance is initially increased between it and its readership. The strange, contextualized biblical text will never satisfy the stronger, conservative, battalions in the culture wars about families, because they have already staked everything on the text meaning "what it says." Impatience with the "referential view of language"[37] is another symptom of the condition of postmodernity that conservatives will not share. I have no problem with contextualization, or with rendering a text strange to modern readers. Those millions of conservative Christians who believe that the Bible is "a perfect treasure of divine instruction" (above, 1.3) are already inured against revisionary understandings of texts. But there is a higher hermeneutical card to play, for prior to historical analysis and contextualization there must be an antecedent recognition of what God's self-revelation is: the Christ to whom the New Testament communities bear their diverse witness. However, these are preliminaries. There can be no objection to historical investigation, or with following arguments to surprising conclusions. The real difficulties lie in whether the evidence for egalitarianism and equality can be regarded as established, and if it is not, what happens to both.

Egalitarian marriage?

Let us examine the nest of assumptions that early Christianity was egalitarian, and that it practiced an ethic of equality and a discipleship of equals.

---

[37] Vanhoozer, "Theology and the condition of postmodernity," p. 10.

John Elliott has terminally savaged these assumptions (at least to his own satisfaction).[38] While conceding the importance of households to the early
Jesus movement he argues that Christian households were "organized on
stratified, not egalitarian, lines." Contrary to critical familism he avers that
"no discipleship of equals was founded by Jesus, so none was introduced following his death."[39] The "egalitarian argument" is said to be "fatally flawed
in several respects." The key terms are not defined. *All* texts put forward in
support of it are susceptible to different interpretation. The "egalitarian
theorists" provide "no evidence of actual concrete economic and social
equality established by Jesus among his first followers," whereas they are
accused of ignoring the actual contrary evidence. "An especially disastrous
element of this theory is its obscuring or misconstruing the prominence of
the household/family in the teaching of Jesus," and "the manner in which
the household/family is employed by Jesus" to illustrate many aspects of his
teaching, including "its significance as chief metaphor for clarifying the
divine-human relationship and life under God's rule (as, for example, obedient 'children' trusting in a heavenly 'father') . . ."[40] And the rout of the
egalitarians continues. There was no "'abandonment' of equality" and no
"'reversion' to patriarchalism," as Schüssler-Fiorenza claims, because there
was no equality in the first place. The early baptismal formula preserved in
Galatians 3:28 says nothing about equality among church members, nor
how this might have been organized or worked out in a patriarchal society.
In Elliott's judgment

> The statement, "You are all one in Christ," affirms the ethnic and social inclu-
> siveness of the Jesus movement and the unity of all who are in Christ but says
> nothing about any equality of those included. The statement speaks not of
> being "equal" in Christ, but of being "one" in Christ. The Greek employed
> here is not *isos*, "equal," but *heis*, "one." "One" denotes inclusion and unity,
> not equality.[41]

The point is: scholars again disagree (which occasions no surprise). But the
problem for Browning's team is that they try to justify, by historical argument, that early Christian life was of such a type; that this type is expressed
in a trajectory or historical movement; that this trajectory was curtailed; and

[38] See John H. Elliott, "Jesus Was Not an Egalitarian. A Critique of an Anachronistic and Idealist Theory," *Biblical Theology Bulletin*, 32/2, 2002 [75–91]; and his "The Jesus Movement Was
Not Egalitarian but Family-Oriented," *Biblical Interpretation*, 2003, 11/2 [173–211].
[39] Elliott, "The Jesus Movement," p. 173.
[40] Elliott, "The Jesus Movement," pp. 175–6.
[41] Elliott, "The Jesus Movement," p. 178.

that the insights of critical familism help to put the trajectory back on track, albeit in a vastly different cultural context. They are still possibly right about the historical detail, but if they are not, is not the whole project imperiled? The recommendations and conclusions of critical familism are far too important to rest on these historical (and logical) assumptions alone. Elliott speaks for too many embarrassed egalitarians when he confesses, "With every fibre of my egalitarian being I wish it were demonstrable that the Jesus movement had been egalitarian, at least at some point in its early history." And they have no alternative but to take seriously his judgment that

> this well-intentioned theory is an unhappy example of anachronism and ideal-ist thinking that must be challenged not just because it is indemonstrable [sic] or an example of flawed interpretation but also because it is so seductive. The notion that the Jesus movement ever formed a "community of equals" founded by Jesus is a phantasm, a *fata morgana*, a wish still awaiting incarnation.[42]

"Servant leadership?"

Unfortunately there are other deceptively awkward problems lurking in the detail of critical familism. A key series of terms in its revision of masculinity is "servanthood," "servant leadership," and "servant responsibility."[43] Jesus' teaching about the reversal of ordinary relations of power within the Reign of God is undoubtedly original and radical, but it has become molded into a conservative language-game played by those many Christians who, having re-affirmed the biblical principle that men lead women, then qualify (or mask?) their power advantage with the proviso that their style of leadership is (or ought to be!) one of service. Leaving aside the disingenuousness that is likely to accompany such discourse, there must be doubt whether, even within the scriptures themselves, this series of oxymorons can be regarded as authorized. In the Household Codes, slaves really are slaves. But in other places the institution of slavery becomes a root-metaphor for believers, the metaphorical "servants of God," to characterize their relationship to the divine. But the current language-game of male servanthood is almost wholly discontinuous with that unjust and cruel institution of slavery. Has it not become a domesticated, voluntarized, and romanticized discourse that fails to capture the radicalness of the teaching of Jesus about the reversal of power in the Reign of God? It also fails to capture the sheer horror of that

---

[42] Elliott, "The Jesus Movement," pp. 205–6.
[43] Browning et al., *From Culture Wars*, p. 132.

institution whether in ancient or modern households. It is another product of the discontinuities discussed earlier in this chapter.

Jennifer Glancy, having attended to the historical institution of slavery in the Roman Empire of the first century CE, warns against attempts among contemporary Christian exegetes "to subsume relationships of slavery within the warm circle of the family." She shows that the "natal alienation at the heart of the ancient slave experience is ultimately intertwined with the forms of alienation inherent within families themselves."[44] In common with Elliott her analysis also "disrupts the optimistic picture that we would like to have of Christian origins as a time of egalitarian relations." This picture (she calls it a "family plot") "distorts the reality of slavery as an anti-kinship structure, a structure of domination contingent on natal alienation." Once again we are brought back to an historical impasse, this time about the improved status of slaves in the Christian household.

A further problem with the weight Browning and his co-authors place on "servanthood" is the connection between the teaching of Jesus in the Gospels about slaves and the advice on gendered relations in the Letters. The Gospels leave us in no doubt that Jesus preached and practiced the reversal of hierarchical values. What is surprising is that this teaching does *not* obviously appear in the New Testament Letters. This is a further example of plurality. The slaves in the Ephesian Household Code (Eph. 6:6–8) are real slaves, not powerful husbands pretending to be slaves. It is of course true that Ephesians gives husbands the example of Christ to follow, and that He "loved the church and gave himself up for it." But the identification of Christ's self-surrender with metaphorical servanthood in this passage is far from obvious even with the help of a favorite, mediating text that describes the self-emptying of Jesus as a descent into slavery (Phil. 2:7). The idea that husbands in biblical times thought of themselves as servants to their wives and households is based on association, nothing more, with texts such as Matthew 19:30 (which Browning's team quotes).

A nagging doubt remains regarding the use made in *From Culture Wars to Common Ground* of the appeal to husbands to love their wives. Remarkable though it is, it is conjectural to suppose a link with the commandment of Jesus to love our neighbors as the co-authors do. That a wife is to be loved as "oneself" because she is a "neighbor," and that the commandment to love one's neighbor applies to husbands vis-à-vis their wives, is not an argument that the text uses. "Neighbors" do not feature in the Household Codes. A

[44] Jennifer A. Glancy, "Family Plots: Burying Slaves Deep in Historical Ground," *Biblical Interpretation*, 10.1, 2002 [57–76], p. 75.

husband is to love his wife because together they are said to form a single body (Eph. 5:31b). The love of a husband for a wife is an extension of his own self-love as the text plainly says. One supposes this is a lesser reason than the greater reason of imitating the love of Christ for the church!

There is also selective omission in the way the Browning team constructs its case. For example, while Paul is commended for his view that the bodies of husband and wife belong *to each other* (1 Cor. 7:3–4), the sexism in the same Letter which allows Paul to deny that women are made in the image of God, is unnoticed and unrebuked (1 Cor. 11:7–9). The argument that Ephesians 5 provides "a genuine reversal of ancient heroic models" is easily supplanted by a counter-argument that it provides an *intensification* of such models. There is a considerable list of heroic actions that Christ performs – consecrating the church, cleansing it, presenting it, and so on (Eph. 5:26–7) – while the passivity of wives in the face of all this heroic activity is undisturbed. Almost all revisionary commentators upon this passage simply fail to notice that loving is something that the heroic Christ and, following him, heroic husbands do, or are enjoined to do, while wives do not, and are enjoined instead (three times) to be submissive.

The trajectory hypothesis?

The idea that there existed a trajectory in early Christianity toward equality of the sexes and equal regard marriages is especially attractive to liberal Protestants whose seminary education is likely to have proposed similar doctrinal developments, within and beyond the New Testament with regard to, for example, the full divinity of Jesus Christ, or later the Holy Trinity. A continuous development toward a particular conclusion is posited, and in the present case the particular conclusion is full equality of the sexes, with the proviso, of course, that the development was unfortunately (and very early) interrupted. There has been steady episodic advance and critical familism identifies itself in this revisionary stream. Carolyn Osiek, in a symposium volume on critical familism, carefully qualifies the support she gives to this construction. She says "The best way to be faithful to a biblical vision is to do what they did, to continue the early Christian movement toward something like what Don Browning and others call 'equal regard.'"[45]

---

[45] Carolyn Osiek, "Did Early Christians Teach, or Merely Assume, Male Headship?," in David Blankenhorn, Don Browning, and Mary Stewart Van Leeuwen (eds.), *Does Christianity Teach Male Headship? – The Equal-Regard Marriage and Its Critics* (Grand Rapids, MI/Cambridge, UK: Eerdmans, 2004) [23–7], p. 27.

But we have already seen that the trajectory toward equal regard is a dubious hypothesis, and its dubiety is likely to damage the entirely laudable attempt to achieve, within and without the church, the full equality of women with men. If the original equality of the Jesus movement could be established, the next difficulty would be to establish what happened to it. The delayed *parousia*, the sheer weight of Greco-Roman patriarchy upon the growing church, the need for moral order, and so on, might all play their part. But in that case "trajectory" is quite the wrong metaphor to explain what went on. A trajectory is a curve that a body traverses (an example being a planet or comet in its orbit) as it moves through space. But where in the New Testament is the forward movement such as the metaphor "trajectory" implies? In relation to the context, there is no doubt that the early fledgling churches, in their theology and their practice, re-visioned human relationships. But if there is a trajectory in the New Testament, that trajectory appears at other times to travel *away* from the transformative unveiling of Godself in Jesus. Christians discern an intensification of divine power and love surrounding the life, teaching, death, and resurrection of Jesus, the implications of which are still being pondered by the present church. But even in New Testament times, as the cultural and chronological distance grew between the historical life of Jesus and the fledgling churches, the original fiery revelation glowed with a more distant hue.

Supporters of the trajectory hypothesis need to resort to increasingly sophisticated versions of it in the face of its broken core metaphor and its lack of clinching evidence. One such version suggests that Jesus, Paul, and the early church were all against patriarchy, and in favor of equality, but because of the cultural conditions within which they operated, they proceeded at only half their desired speed. Mary Stewart Van Leeuwen thinks Paul's deeply ambivalent attitude to women

> would seem to indicate that he supports women's freedom in Christ but that, for the sake of spreading the Gospel, he does not want women to let their freedom go to their heads. In the midst of a patriarchal society already inclined to see this new Jewish-messianic sect as at best somewhat weird and at worst subversive of the political order, some concessions to local gender norms were essential.[46]

Perhaps. But now we are in a further difficulty. We are obliged to attribute to the early Christian saints and writers a sophistication they might

---

[46] Mary Stewart Van Leeuwen, "Is Equal Regard in the Bible?," in Blankenhorn et al. (eds.), *Does Christianity Teach Male Headship?* [13–22], p. 20.

never have had. They must have understood both the direction of the transforming power of the Gospel and the demeaning influences of Roman
culture so well that they actually had a blueprint for penetrating it without
annoying it too much. Daniel Mark Cere is right to be sceptical about this
further qualification, doubting whether "the apostolic authors" could ever
have had such an "astute grasp of the underlying substructures of patriarchal
order and a remarkably prescient strategy for sabotaging this cultural
matrix."[47]

Where is Christian doctrine?

It is therefore not clear that the version of biblical history favored by critical
familism is the most plausible construction available. True it relies on sound
scholarship, but there are also partial readings, unproven assumptions, selective omissions, and misleading metaphors. Neither is it clear that, in the use
of the Bible the discussion gets beyond what one of the contributors calls
"proof text poker."[48] Let us take the hermeneutic of one more work in the
critical familism library, Stephen Post's *More Lasting Unions*. The "starting-
point" of this positive work is "the Judeo-Christian notion of a prophetic
ethics." This is said to combine "three distinct, though complementary,
social principles (in addition to the theological principle of faithfulness to
God). The *first* principle (as elaborated by Amos, Hosea, and Isaiah) is that
we give greater protection to the most vulnerable," and this is enunciated as
the principle of "Care for All Children."

> The *second* principle is that of creation, of fidelity in marriage to ensure for all
> children the benefit of having both a caring mother and a caring father . . .
> This second principle is metaphorically related to the Covenant of Sinai,
> which is likened to a marriage covenant; its hallmarks are fidelity, fruitfulness,
> love, and forgiveness. The *third* principle is that within the marriage covenant,
> women must be treated with equal regard.[49]

What is at once surprising is the omission of any reference to or sign of Jesus
Christ in this methodological statement. The first principle is said to provide
a "prophetic preferential option for the oppressed" and to be "somewhat

---

[47] Daniel Mark Cere, "Marriage, Subordination, and the Development of Christian Doctrine," in Blankenhorn et al., *Does Christianity Teach Male Headship?* [92–100], p. 97.
[48] Van Leeuwen, "Is Equal Regard in the Bible?," p. 16.
[49] Stephen G. Post, *More Lasting Unions: Christianity, the Family, and Society* (Grand Rapids,
MI/Cambridge, UK: Eerdmans, 2000), p. 29 (author's emphases).

captured by the natural-law theories that define those 'goods' which are absolutely essential for human flourishing."[50] The second principle turns out to be the advocacy of "Faithful Monogamy," which is affirmed because Jesus taught it, and because "on average," marriage is better for children.[51] But the justification for invoking the third principle is simply that it is found in critical familism. Post repeats the claims about "the egalitarian Christian ethos in church and family," and thinks the authors of *From Culture Wars* "make a persuasive argument that better New Testament exegesis points toward equal regard in both church and family. The task of nurturing and sustaining this equality is headed in the right direction but is still a work in progress."[52]

But Post buys uncritically into the ancient equality hypothesis and the trajectory hypothesis, and he clearly locates his work within the on-going trajectory. I have already dealt with these difficulties, and wish instead to draw attention to a hiatus in his description of his own methodology. Where exactly is Jesus Christ? The tradition of "prophetic ethics" is undoubtedly a gift of Judaism to Christianity, in which Jesus himself stands, while the second principle is an important item within Jesus' own teaching. But are we not now, and somewhat wearily, coming to the conclusion that the culture wars are being fought on territory that is insufficiently broad? Specifically, what difference is made to the flourishing of families and children by the coming of the Son of God who is himself the revelation of God? What difference does Christian *doctrine* make to Christian ethics? How might equal regard be promoted if ethics began instead with God, and in particular with the doctrine of the Triune God as a loving communion of Persons-in-relation? How much more contemporary sense might we be able to make of the biblical texts, strange yet familiar, sometimes oppressive, sometimes inspirational, if we gave methodological priority to God's gift of the Son, and to the Spirit as an aid to our poor discernment (as the Bible itself actually does)? How much easier would the task of interpretation be if due distinction were made between the Word of God among us in Person, and the words of scripture in the witness they bear to the Word?

---

[50] Post, *More Lasting Unions*, p. 30.
[51] Post, *More Lasting Unions*, p. 34.
[52] Post, *More Lasting Unions*, p. 35.

2.3 Family-Friendly Readings

Our analysis of the interpretative problems within critical familism leaves undiminished the goals of that movement, while underlining the need for a hermeneutic that more readily facilitates a Christ-centered contribution to the flourishing of families and children (whether within or beyond Christendom) and which grounds equal regard more centrally in the resources of Christian doctrine. That hermeneutic will be "post-critical." While it will "submit sources to dense historical readings . . ." critical analysis "is part of the act of interpretation, not its end or point." The point of such hermeneutics, as William Schweiker envisages it, "is to show the contemporary meaning and truth of the work. It is to open the text or symbol or event for renewed engagement within the dynamics of current life."[53] But it will also be more overtly theological. "The dependence of both the Bible and theology upon a prior revelation of God, and the denial that theology consists simply in deductions from the Bible, can be confirmed by recalling that Christian theology antedated the Christian Bible."[54] So, of course, did the church.

I do not accuse critical familism of making simple deductions from the Bible in proposing a Christian ethics of the family. But I look for readings of the Bible that are more informed by the church's doctrinal, creedal and theological commitments (to which of course, prolonged historical reflection on the scriptures gave rise). I also think the task of showing "the contemporary meaning and truth" of the biblical text is considerably more complex than Schweiker suggests, requiring much of the accumulated theological wisdom available to the community of readers (that is, the church). In this section I lay out several principles which drive my own attempt to think theologically of families and children in a more obviously Christocentric and theocentric direction. These will guide the response to the twin problems of plurality and discontinuity: they will provide an escape-route from "proof-text poker" and from entrapment in historical controversies; and assist in making a contribution to a Christian ethics which attempts to think directly out of whom and what Christians take their God to be. Each principle of course will demand much more space than can be provided here (so they must remain largely stipulative) but they will receive further elaboration and application in the chapters that follow.

---

[53] William Schweiker, *Theological Ethics and Global Dynamics in the Time of Many Worlds* (Malden, MA, and Oxford, UK: Blackwell, 2004), p. xx.

[54] Robert Morgan, "The Bible and Christian Theology," in John Barton (ed.), *The Cambridge Companion to Biblical Interpretation* (Cambridge, UK: Cambridge University Press, 1998) [114–28], p. 117.

Eight principles

First, God's revelation in Christ must be given priority over God's revelation in scripture. The gracious revelation of the Triune God is first of all the Word made flesh, not the written words of scripture, which bear witness to the living Word that is God. Grave distortions of the faith occur when the Bible is used as a source of revelation equal to the Personal revelation of God through the Son. Of course, when appealing to the teaching of Jesus, one appeals to the Gospels, and the Gospels are scripture. But the Church existed even before the Gospels. The insistence that Christ has precedence over scripture in the life of the Church is not intended to de-value scripture, but to prevent oppressive uses of it which run counter to God's self-gift in Christ.

Second, as a matter of theological method, Christology precedes ethics and shapes them. This is how the New Testament writers interpreted the Hebrew scriptures. A surprising source for a heightened Christological emphasis is in fact the Ephesian Household Code, which actually enjoins this priority upon us! In all the arguments about this Code I have not yet found anyone who has analyzed it methodologically. Beneath and beyond the undoubted asymmetry and sexism of the drawn analogies (husband/wife, Christ/church) lies a primordial, methodological, procedure. Everything to do with relations within households has to be sorted out by prior reference to Christ and his self-sacrificial love for the church. Yes, it is "a stunning idea" that the author of Ephesians tells husbands to love their wives: and yes, this injunction opens up visceral difficulties (generally evaded by all the warring factions) regarding the asymmetry of the love between partners, and (for us) the author's incipient sexism; but who has noticed what is going on in the text methodologically?

The re-thinking of household, marital, and family relations that Christian communities were undertaking has to be pre-determined by Christ's sacrificial death, understood as the revelation of divine love. The mutual subjection of spouses is actually grounded in the "reverence for Christ" that remains unexplicated, even though it starts to change everything (and is of course a source for the trajectory hypothesis). The injunctions governing the conduct of fathers, slaves, and masters are similarly imprinted on their recipients by these relations being "in the Lord." Slavery is not yet expunged from Christian households, but slaves are enjoined to regard themselves instead "as slaves of the Lord rather than of men" (Eph. 6:7b). Masters are sternly reminded that they and their slaves "both have the same Master in heaven; there is no favouritism with him" (Eph. 6:9c).

The diverse ethical landscape of the New Testament looks different if it is seen as a series of multiple attempts to relate then current ethical dilemmas to the divine love that is instantiated in the death of Jesus. Part of the value of the Ephesian Code lies in the pervasive Christological method which it demonstrates. It provides an exciting prospect for fresh thinking in contemporary ethics. It is not at all obvious to a reader of the Gospels that "Christ loved the church and gave himself up for it" (Eph. 5:25b). But the author of Ephesians interprets and applies what he believes to the meaning of Christ's death. Another Letter-writer undertakes a similar Christological reflection and concludes "My dear friends, let us love one another, because the source of love is God. Everyone who loves is a child of God and knows God, for God is love. This is how he showed his love among us: he sent his only Son into the world that we might have life through him" (1 Jn. 4:7–9). Here too, Christology precedes ethics and shapes it.

Third, scripture must be read in the light of the church's doctrinal commitments, not independently of them. This, of course, was one of the reasons for the Rule of Faith in the period of the Apologists. The creeds are a resource – why not use them? The Spirit of whom they speak is "the Spirit of truth" who "will guide you into all the truth" (Jn. 16:13). They tell us who Christ is, and who God is in the light of Him. There are no weightier considerations for Christians to ponder. A fresh argument for equal-regard marriages and for two-parent families might be mounted on this basis. The argument might run that Christians endorse particular family forms because those forms are more likely to embody the divine love that sent the Son into the world. Or even that the union of two persons "in one flesh" is an icon of the mutual love of the divine Persons within the unity of the one God?[55] Or again, that Christ, having secured the final victory over sin, has therefore also secured the victory over the entrenched social sins of patriarchy and sexism? These would be different arguments from the one that finds equal-regard marriage advocated or at least anticipated by the New Testament.

Fourth, the love commandments of Jesus take priority over Household Codes, and over all other ethical injunctions that are not derived from them. The authority of the teaching of Jesus is placed above the authority of the New Testament Letters, and the love commandments of Jesus (Mk. 12:28–34; Mt. 22:34–40; Lk. 10:25–37; Jn. 15:11–17) are allowed to inform our understanding of his ethical teaching. If, for example, there is any incommensurability between the father who, in the teaching of Jesus, forgives his wayward son and

---

[55] See, for example, Eugene F. Rogers, Jr, *Sexuality and the Christian Body* (Malden, MA, and Oxford, UK: Blackwell, 1999): Michael G. Lawler, "Perichoresis: New Theological Wine in an Old Theological Foreskin," *Horizons* 22.1, 1995 [49–66].

receives him joyfully (Lk. 15:11–32), and the patriarchal tone of the Household Codes, the teaching of Jesus has priority.

*Fifth, all ethical practice is subject to revision as the church reflects further on the love
commandments of Jesus.* The love commandments generate opposition to all
practices that compromise them. Schweiker, in a careful study of the *Didache*,
has shown how, in that second-century work, the love commands and the
Golden Rule shatter any limitations placed on them. The *Didache* begins
with an affirmation of the love commands, but operates within a dualistic
framework within which the "other" is characterized as evil. The community
responsible for the *Didache* practiced "inscription," the formation of members
of that community in its thought and action. But a tension is set up between
the love commands, expanded to include even the enemy, and the opposi-
tional logic between church and world which that community set up.
Commenting on this tension Schweiker observes how "The second great
command tears asunder any constriction on who the neighbor is, any limita-
tion of compassion, respect, and justice to members of one's own clan, race,
gender, community, or religion. In this respect, the presence of the command
within the *Didache* overturns the dualism of the way of life and the way of
death."[56] There is a "trap found in the practice of inscription,"[57] namely the
restriction on who the neighbor is, which places boundaries around the
Christian community, objectifies what is "other" than it, and places it beyond
loving communication.

While Schweiker is concerned with a global ethic, the process he
describes is identical in relation to families and children too. In fact his
global ethic is required at the systemic level of near-universal need already
described (above, 1.2). But church and family alike can place limits on their
love. The continued maintenance of patriarchy (whatever its historical justifications) is a failure of love because it renders women and children as not
simply "different," but "other" and inferior. The zeal for the holy life must
not alienate those it defines as beyond its boundaries. There are countless
people, single parents, divorced people, people of a particular class, people
of racial or sexual minorities, and so on, who feel they are placed beyond
the boundary within which the practice of accepting love supposedly takes
place.

*Sixth, it has become necessary to allow ethics to be much more obviously shaped
by, in particular, the doctrine of the Triune God* (below, 4.1). This is an extension
of principle 2. Being shaped by doctrine entails allowing insights into

[56] Schweiker, *Theological Ethics*, p. 100.
[57] Schweiker, *Theological Ethics*, p. 106.

human being that are derived directly from whom we take God to be, that is, a loving communion of Persons. While there are problems of analogy yet to be negotiated, this doctrine gives us priceless insights into our being as persons, and is able to raise "relation" to primordial status in family life. Our "relations" do not remain simply "kin," or other family members: we *are* relations in that being children, fathers, mothers, grandparents, neighbors, and so on, we also constitute ourselves. Pope John Paul II has pioneered the connection between the doctrine of the social Trinity and the Christian understanding of the human family (below, 4.2). These profound insights must be allowed to illumine human families without being dimmed by the shadows of less substantial or more peripheral material such as natural law, or by the darkness of historical androcentrism or "flat" readings of scripture which conflate revelation with context.

Seventh, all families are able to receive and embody the love of God whether or not they believe in or know God. This is possibly the most contentious of my hermeneutic rules, but the case for it is strong. The author of 1 John clearly teaches this. "God is love; he who dwells in love is dwelling in God, and God in him" (1 Jn. 4:8,16b, and cited above, 4:7–9). God's love is unbounded by those who call God Father, especially since some of those who do have not yet learned that God is love (1 Jn. 3:17). True there are boundaries in this Letter. The church has to define itself over against false prophets and their teaching (1 Jn. 4:4–5); against the unloving (1 Jn. 4:7–8); against "the whole world" that "lies in the power of the evil one" (1 Jn. 5:19b); against idolatry (1 Jn. 5:21). The trap of inscription is present in these very boundaries, but the love of God includes those outside the boundaries, however they are marked. Again the methodology is striking. The Christian life is one of love. "The message you have heard from the beginning is that we should love one another" (1 Jn. 3:11).

The quality of family life is not guaranteed by the religious faith of parents but by their love. Marriages which last and remain loving may be sacramental, or undertaken in faith, but they may not be. Their existential quality is not guaranteed by the outworking of religious faith or by the power of the sacraments in their lives. Leaving aside the tricky problems of measuring "happiness" in families or "success" in marriages, Christians generally do not appear to have the monopoly of either. But Christians name the sources of love, wherever these sources perform their sustaining, nurturing, transforming work. They know how to access them, and can testify to their efficacy. Openness to the teaching that divine love is universal is akin to the realization in the New Testament that the Gospel is universal, that, yes, even Gentiles can receive it too. On this view evangelism is the task of showing people without faith that their love for one another and for their children is already a sharing in the love of God, by whom it may also be deepened. This is an intimate relational God, manifest in relations of love, already involved in the lives of those yet to discern the identity of the One who lives between and within them.

The tenor of narrative ethics, currently fashionable, stresses the distinctiveness of Christian ethics, over against other kinds, and the Christian virtues over against the lack of them. "Those outside the church are defined as what is not-church – call it the 'world,' or, worse yet, the Enlightenment!"[58] Relations between church and world can then slip into mutual incomprehension, indifference, opposition, or even violence. What is required is not simply a universalism of reason whereby church and world are subsumed by a rational or idealist thought-world, but a universalism of God whose omnipresence takes form in the cradling and nurturing that is human love.

Eighth, living tradition grows and changes. As Denys Turner shows, the "faith rediscovers itself in the debate with tradition." This debate with tradition, he explains, "ought to be less an appeal to, or an authoritative repetition of tradition, but rather a reworking of tradition in the context of contemporary questions and problems."[59] Cere is alone among the critics of critical familism to suggest an enhanced role for tradition. He borrows from John Henry Newman the "principle of continuity," arguing that "the job of the theologian is to sift through the tradition to try to identify certain principles or methods that are consistently applied in the exploration of a particular subject matter." This is well said, but there is little excitement in the activity of "sifting through" tradition (as if it were débris?), because there is little sense of tradition as an escalating and developing relation of the Church to Jesus Christ. And his conclusion, albeit reluctant, that "The question of authority relations in marriage is essentially a political-ethical issue that is to be resolved by the culture," involving "'practical reason' rather than a theological proclamation,"[60] overlooks the possibility that our life in God may be able to shape all our relations especially those where power and intimacy are involved.

We cannot tarry over the problems with which the development of traditions presents us. We are tradition-makers, not just tradition-receivers, and if what we hand on to the next generation of Christians is not both continuous *and* discontinuous, we will have fossilized it. These principles require

---

[58] Schweiker, *Theological Ethics*, p. 139.
[59] Denys Turner, "Tradition and Faith," *International Journal of Systematic Theology*, 6.1 (January 2004) [21–37], p. 21.
[60] Cere, "Marriage," pp. 107–8.

much more justification than is given here. A whole book has recently been devoted to establishing "five hermeneutic rules."[61] A bigger book cultivates the reading of scripture as itself an art form,[62] governed by "Nine Theses on the Interpretation of Scripture."[63] I agree with most of the precepts of these volumes, but instead of drawing upon them, I have devised similar principles for using scripture in the construction of a theology of, and for, families and children. Their justification will lie partly in their use, and partly in whether they help to construct a theology that is faithful to the revelation of the Triune God, made known in Jesus Christ, and attested by scripture, tradition, and the Holy Spirit.

It is now time to take stock of the argument. The use of the Bible in support of families and children gave rise to two sets of problems: discontinuity and plurality. Critical familism was warmly welcomed but shown to be partially afflicted by both. Problems were also found to do with historical evidence, alleged connections between texts, selective omission, the organizing metaphor "trajectory" and method. The principles in the present section start to address these problems. They put the Person, teaching, and self-sacrifice of Christ above scripture. Where the plurality of the biblical witness is the problem, the teaching of Jesus about families and children is paramount (and the difficulty of arriving at it is also acknowledged). Scripture is the witness of the primitive churches to Christ. We need not worry too much about the status of women and children in ancient households. What matters is how Christ's love for them encompasses and redeems them now. It is not necessary to become committed to a particular historical view regarding the extent of the transformation of households that the first Christians were able to achieve. What is necessary is to access now the sources of love and grace that helped to make whatever transformations were made then.

Doctrine, especially Christology, shapes ethics (as the New Testament makes clear) and both licenses and demands extraordinary love for the neighbor, the stranger, the enemy. Within this schema, the love of spouse, children, parents, grandparents is also located. Not only is tradition open to revision: without revision there can be no growth in faith or practice. The practice of costly love provides continuity with Christ, even if it does not provide continuity with much that occurred in the history of the church.

---

[61] Charles H. Cosgrove, *Appealing to Scripture in Moral Debate* (Grand Rapids, MI/Cambridge, UK: Eerdmans, 2002).
[62] Ellen F. Davis and Richard B. Hays (eds.), *The Art of Reading Scripture* (Grand Rapids, MI/Cambridge, UK: Eerdmans, 2003).
[63] Davis and Hays, *The Art of Reading Scripture*, pp. 1–5.

Faith in the Triune God tells us much more about who we are, and in particular, that we *are* relations, just as we are persons. As we shall see, when faith is understood as a way of being "in Christ," or "abiding in God," or "abiding in love," much spiritual value is added to the immediacy and the minutiae of relationships within families.

Chapter Three

The Teaching of Jesus about Families and Children

In this chapter I continue to marshal together the sources for a theology of families. The teaching of Jesus about families will first be examined, and its lack of congruence with the late modern nuclear family will be noted. In the second section the astonishing teaching of Jesus about children will be examined and summarized in ten propositions. These will be utilized in Part II of the book. But fidelity to the teaching of Jesus about families and children brings with it a moral conundrum. In the Reign of God the ties of family are relativized over against the ties of discipleship, and the teaching of Jesus about children is about children generally, not about those particular children who are our daughters and sons. So what priority is to be given to our kin, as opposed to our neighbors? The third section probes this dilemma, and considers two possible answers. The first is kin altruism, the belief that kin preference is justified for reasons to do with evolutionary psychology and natural (or neo-natural) law. The second is that children are to be classified as near neighbors. The fourth section settles the dilemma. It revisits the lawyer's question "But who is my neighbor?" (Lk. 10:29b) and concludes that parents of children cannot simply regard them as near neighbors. The impasse reached at the end of the chapter is resolved by the revised Trinitarian anthropology that is the subject of chapter 4.

3.1 The Teaching of Jesus about Families

The synoptic Gospels clearly and repeatedly depict Jesus as relativizing the kinship group, and emphasizing the priority of the family of God over the family of kin. Scholars have studied these passages intensively in recent years but neither the passages themselves nor the scholarly findings are well lodged in Christian understanding, probably because they run counter to modern and cherished assumptions about "the family." Yet contemporary accounts of the teaching of Jesus on families are vital for the present work, and according to our rules for a family-friendly reading of scripture, the teaching of the Word made flesh in scripture is to be given priority over scriptural teaching elsewhere.

Kingdom above kin?

What does Jesus say about families? Mark intentionally contrasts obligations to kin with obligations to God. He has the family of Jesus attempt to "take charge of him. 'He is out of his mind,' they said" (Mk. 3:21). Later when his mother and brothers are unable to get near him because of the crowd, they send a message "asking for him" (Mk. 3:32). Jesus then asks a question that goes to the heart of his own identity and that of his kin: "Who are my mother and my brothers?" (Mk. 3:33). Without waiting for a reply, he looked around "at those who were sitting in the circle about him" and said, "Here are my mother and my brothers. Whoever does the will of God is my brother and sister and mother" (Mk. 3:34–5). When Peter reminds Jesus that his disciples had "left everything" (Mk. 10:28) to follow him, he replies "Truly I tell you: there is no one who has given up home, brothers, or sisters, mother, father, or children, or land, for my sake and for the gospel, who will not receive in this age a hundred times as much – houses, brothers and sisters, mothers and children, and land – and persecutions besides; and in the age to come eternal life" (Mk. 10:29–31). Following Jesus, Mark's Gospel warns, turns family members against each other: "Brother will hand over brother to death, and a father his child; children will turn against their parents and send them to their death" (Mk. 13:12).

Jesus' calling of the earliest disciples "requires leaving behind occupation, possessions and family"[1] (Mk. 1:16–20). The Jesus of Mark's Gospel, says Stephen Barton, relativizes household and kinship ties,

> by belief in the breaking in of the kingdom of God with the coming of Jesus the Son of God, who establishes the nucleus of a new covenant community open to the Gentiles. This new covenant community is understood as the eschatological family of Jesus constituted, not on the basis of inheritance and blood ties, but on the basis of active obedience to the will of God.[2]

[1] Stephen C. Barton, *Discipleship and Family Ties in Mark and Matthew* (Cambridge, UK: Cambridge University Press, 1994), p. 122.
[2] Barton, *Discipleship and Family Ties*, pp. 121–2.

Matthew's Gospel retains and develops the radical relativization of household and kinship ties. The breaking-in of the Reign of God has "absolute precedence," Barton says: "Indeed, so high is the precedence given to following Jesus that only so fundamental an issue as family, household and occupational ties is adequate to make the point."[3] Carolyn Osiek and David Balch are wary of egalitarian readings of this Gospel, but they concede that Matthew pushes Christian households in a more egalitarian direction. The parable of the landowner who pays the same wage to the workers who begin work in his vineyard at different times uses the word *isos* ("equal") (Mt. 20:12),[4] and the chapter moves quickly to a discussion of authority in the Kingdom of Heaven. Jesus' teaching is perhaps too radical ever to have been properly assimilated:

> You know that, among the Gentiles, rulers lord it over their subjects, and the great make their authority felt. It shall not be so with you; among you, whoever wants to be great must be your servant, and whoever wants to be first must be the slave of all − just as the Son of Man did not come to be served but to serve, and to give his life as a ransom for many. (Mt. 20:25b-28)

Once again we notice the grain of the Christological thinking. Like the authors of Ephesians and 1 John (above, 2.3), Matthew too assumes that Christology precedes ethics and shapes it (our second hermeneutic principle). Following Jesus is worked out in relation to his sacrificial death on the Cross, and here the implications are noted, not for spousal relations as in Ephesians or for general ethical conduct as in 1 John, but for relations of power, not simply in Christian households but in the churches that met within them and to some extent replicated them. This is a very different milieu from that of the Household Codes.[5] In the Syrian context of Matthew's Gospel, after the Judean-Roman war, Matthew probably thought that "the hierarchical and androcentric pattern of the surrounding society has not been sufficiently abandoned, and the new structure, which the presence of the Reign of God required, was not properly visible."[6] Chapters 19 and 20 of the Gospel make "new proposals for new family relationships, which oppose divorce followed by remarriage; present eunuchs, children,

---

[3] Barton, *Discipleship and Family Ties*, p. 217.

[4] Carolyn Osiek and David L. Balch, *Families in the New Testament World: Households and House Churches* (Louisville, KY: Westminster John Knox Press, 1997), p. 134.

[5] Osiek and Balch, *Families*, p. 134. See above, 2.1.

[6] Osiek and Balch, *Families*, p. 132. They quote Warren Carter, *Households and Discipleship: A Study of Matthew 19–20* (*Journal for the Study of the New Testament* Supplement 103) (Sheffield, UK: JSOT Press, 1994), p. 213.

and slaves (and in 21:31 prostitutes) as models; and encourage the abandonment of houses, that is, of status based on wealth."[7] Nonetheless, patriarchy is not removed from these proposals. The discussion of divorce is a discussion about what husbands unilaterally may do (Mt. 19:3–9).

Luke removes the reference to Jesus' family thinking him mad, but with Mark and Matthew he too depicts Jesus as stressing the priority of the Reign of God over the ties of kin. The incident where the family of Jesus are prevented by the crowd from reaching him, elicits from Jesus the reply, "My mother and my brothers are those who hear the word of God and act upon it" (Lk. 8:20–1). Luke adds "wife" to the list of items that disciples may be expected to leave behind (Lk. 18:29). Even the bonding of a baby with his or her mother at the breast cannot match the bonding of a disciple with God's revelation in Jesus: "While he was speaking thus, a woman in the crowd called out, 'Happy the womb that carried you and the breasts that suckled you!' He rejoined, 'No, happy are those who hear the word of God and keep it'" (Lk. 11:27–8). Turid Seim thinks Luke redefines motherhood in the Reign of God because he associates the mother of Jesus with responding to the Word of God rather than with child bearing.[8]

The best known of the stories in Luke's Gospel, the parable of a "prodigal" father,[9] confirms Jesus' relativization and subversion of the values of the patriarchal household. The son has dissipated the family's honor along with his share of the family's wealth. Osiek and Balch say the parable would have been received as

> an alienating, offensive, implausible, potentially transforming metaphor of the kingdom of God clashing with centuries of domestic, didactic wisdom. The goal of the household is to increase property, against which the younger son sins. By its extravagant ending, Jesus' parable collides with this ordered world, and evokes the protest of the elder brother. The story . . . is a parabolic metaphor that breaks through and contradicts the order and righteousness of the household.[10]

I am concerned in this work to develop a contemporary Christian family

[7] Osiek and Balch, *Families*, p. 135, again citing Carter.
[8] Turid Karlsen Seim, *The Double Message: Patterns of Gender in Luke and Acts* (Nashville, TN: Abingdon Press, 1994), pp. 113–16, 200–7, 252, 256–7.
[9] The parable of "the Prodigal Son" is an unfortunate title. Since "prodigal" means "recklessly extravagant," the title assumes the reckless extravagance of the son in squandering his father's resources. More pertinent, surely, is the reckless extravagance of the father in forgiving the son and killing the fatted calf in celebration of his return?
[10] Osiek and Balch, *Families*, pp. 139–40.

ethic which is faithful to Jesus, to his teaching, and especially to his teaching about families. But how are Christians to use this teaching? Faithfulness to Christ and to scripture requires that these teachings are foregrounded in any theology of families. They cannot be ignored (because they appear to subvert modern nuclear families) or rendered vacuous (by being spiritualized). Most theologians invoke the historical-critical method at this point, that is, they deal with the relativization of the family by Jesus by relativizing it further and sinking it deeply into its early Mediterranean context. While this might make us more comfortable, the question arises whether it is likely to make us more faithful? A post-critical hermeneutic can still redound upon its users with life-changing force.

Lisa Cahill explains that "the family in Greco-Roman culture of the first century is a highly important social institution organized to favor the prerogatives of male elders and the élite classes and to favor access to material and social goods for their inferior dependents."[11] It is this institution that Jesus subverts. The "father's house" in ancient Israel is "the strongest source of identity and inclusion for the Israelite. It is an extended family, comprising all the descendents of a living ancestor, except for married daughters, who become part of their husbands' families."[12] We have already noted that up to 100 persons might comprise this family, while within this large group there might be smaller "core" groups, and that these may approximate rather more to the nuclear family of modern times.[13] Some of its members would be patrons, and patronage was a "mutual relationship between unequals for the exchange of services and goods."[14] While the patron might call his suppliers his "friends," the language of friendship veiled the inequalities beneath it.[15] This larger structure, says Cahill, "is the nexus of relationships of social inequalities maintained by structures of precedence and subjugation."[16] In this social world, "each generation is socialized to obedience to the *paterfamilias* and to the social web, which exerts its own pressures on him via its criteria of prestige." These considerations are said to explain the apparent anti-family teachings of Jesus noted above:

---

[11] Lisa Sowle Cahill, *Family: A Christian Social Perspective* (Minneapolis, MN: Fortress Press, 2000), p. 23.
[12] Cahill, *Family*, p. 24.
[13] Halvor Moxnes, "What is Family? Problems in Constructing Early Christian Families," in Halvor Moxnes (ed.), *Constructing Early Christian Families: Family as Social Reality and Metaphor* (London and New York: Routledge, 1997) [13–41], p. 29.
[14] Osiek and Balch, *Families in the New Testament*, p. 48.
[15] Osiek and Balch, *Families in the New Testament*, p. 50.
[16] Cahill, *Family*, p. 27.

Their meaning comes into focus in the context of the first-century patriarchal family, where familial forms of faithfulness serve as demarcators of social
approbation and status and as structures through which material and social
well-being is assured for some and denied to others. Loyalty to one's own
group and dedication to the status of that group over all others and at the
expense of whoever stands in its way are incompatible with a life of mercy,
service, and compassion for the neighbor in need or for the social outcasts
and the poor existing on the margins of society.[17]

While the teaching of Jesus about families is importantly at odds with
modern appeals to family values, it is actually more congruent with antique
Jewish *and* pagan teaching. Osiek and Balch show that the Romans' highest
value was the state; the Stoics' highest value was moral, not domestic duty,
while in 4 Maccabees, love for parents, spouses, children, and friends is also
relativized; the Mosaic, divine law may not be broken even for the sake of
family.[18] Another, comparative, study of the Gospel of Mark assumes Mark
has what the author calls "a strategy of good living."[19] The strategy is inseparable from Mark's depiction of family relations. Stephen Ahearne-Kroll
compares Mark's strategy of good living with two literary expressions of
roughly contemporary movements, Cynicism and the Therapeutae.[20] All
three examples relativize family relations in their strategies of good living,
and all three adopt "family" as a metaphor for new life within each strategy
of goodness. Real households, then, become partially eclipsed when references to them are pressed into metaphorical duty to point beyond themselves to other arrangements.

A further instance where the radical character of this teaching may
impinge on contemporary family life has to do with the virtual *replacement*
of the earthly father by the Heavenly Father in the new hierarchy that
replaces the old one. Jesus unmistakably and repeatedly addresses God as
"Father," but this practice, Cahill claims, "shifts loyalty from the *paterfamilias*
to God alone." It

can challenge human fathers to forego prerogatives that derive from their
power over their dependents, if God's fatherhood is imbued with the divine
qualities of mercy, forgiveness, and perfection that Jesus urges the disciples to

[17] Cahill, *Family*, p. 29.
[18] Osiek and Balch, *Families in the New Testament*, pp. 124–5.
[19] Stephen P. Ahearne-Kroll, "'Who Are My Mother and My Brothers?' Family Relations
and Family Language in the Gospel of Mark," *Journal of Religion*, 81.1, Jan.2001 [1–25], p. 1.
[20] That is, Epictetus' and the Cynic Epistles' expression of Cynicism and Philo's expression of
the Therapeutae found in his *On the Contemplative Life*.

imitate. If God alone is "father" for the disciples (Mt. 23:9), then the author-ity and power of the human patriarchal fathers are vastly diminished or even rejected in the Christian community.[21]

It is possible to suggest a pattern of appropriation, in three phases, of the teaching of Jesus about families within the contemporary church. The first phase is the simple recognition of his teaching. The ties of kin are not ulti-mate and are to be exceeded by the ties of the Reign of God. A second phase, where the historical-critical method comes to our aid, enables us to locate these sayings within the appropriate contexts. Households may easily seek narrow advantage for themselves. The household system is not replaced but required to serve the wider family of God who is "Father" to all people (below, 7.1–7.2). But the third phase of this appropriation is still largely ahead of us. What does it mean for us now to believe that our ties with kin are transcended in the Reign of God? How does that transcendent claim map on to our experience of those congregations that claim to represent the Reign of God now? Does not this teaching of Jesus, in its new guise, intro-duce a new problem, how we are to weigh our love for our spouses and children with our love for our neighbors, friends, rivals, enemies? The issue of priorities in the Reign of God is now a crucial one (but it must be post-poned to section 3.3 after examining the teaching of Jesus about children).

3.2 The Teaching of Jesus about Children

While the historical Jesus remains in many ways an elusive figure, the Gospels preserve relatively straightforward accounts of some of his teachings about children and some of his encounters with them. His sayings about children have an extraordinary simplicity, directness and counter-cultural force. There is an immediacy about them, absent from the harsher-sounding observations about families and kin. On the basis of the various pericopes in the synoptic Gospels, beginning with Mark, I will advance ten fairly uncon-tentious statements about the attitude of Jesus to children in the next few pages. We shall need to refer to these again (below, 6.2) when considering the remarkable congruence between Jesus' teaching about children and the secular doctrine of children's rights.

First, Jesus touches and *blesses* children.

---

[21] Cahill, *Family*, p. 31, following Elisabeth Schüssler Fiorenza, *In Memory of Her: A Feminist Theological Reconstruction of Christian Origins* (New York: Crossroad, 1983), pp. 149–50.

They brought children for him to touch. The disciples rebuked them, but when Jesus saw it he was indignant, and said to them, "Let the children come to me; do not try to stop them; for the kingdom of God belongs to such as these. Truly I tell you: whoever does not accept the kingdom of God like a child will never enter it." And he put his arms round them, laid his hands on them, and blessed them (Mark 10:13–16; and see Matthew 19:13–15; Luke 18:15–17).

The efforts of the disciples to prevent Jesus from blessing the children indicate the counter-cultural character of his action. The texts do not tell us whose children they were, or what family background they came from, or whether their parents were practising Jews, or whether they under-stood what he was doing. They are not being rewarded for good behavior. He hugged and blessed them for no other reason than that they were children.

Second, Jesus teaches that the Kingdom or Reign of God belongs to chil-dren. "The kingdom of God belongs to such as these." Those who think they are entitled to it must move over to make room for the children. Third, children belong to the Reign of God because they are powerless and vul-nerable. This is an inference from the text, but soundly based on Jesus' teaching about who blessed people actually are (the Beatitudes, Mt. 5:3–12; Lk. 6:20–3), and about the Reign of God elsewhere in the Gospels: "chil-dren shared the social status of the poor, the hungry, and the suffering, whom Jesus calls 'blessed.'"[22]

Fourth, Jesus teaches that children are examples for adults to follow. "Whoever does not accept the kingdom of God like a child will never enter it." Judith Gundry-Volf sets out an argument which, in summary form, runs like this:

1   Children were not required to follow the law and fulfil it. But,
2   adults were under an obligation to follow the law and fulfil it. And,
3   adults who followed the law and fulfilled it thought themselves worthy to enter the Reign of God. But
4   Jesus teaches that it is necessary to enter the Reign of God as a child. Therefore,
5   Jesus accepts "those without obedience to the Law into the Reign of God."[23]

---

[22] Judith M. Gundry-Volf, "The Least and the Greatest: Children in the New Testament," in Marcia J. Bunge (ed.), *The Child in Christian Thought* (Grand Rapids, MI/Cambridge, UK: Eerdmans, 2001) [29–60], p. 38. I am indebted in these pages to Gundry-Volf for her fresh presentation of Jesus' teaching about children.

On this interpretation, obedience to the law is an "irrelevance" and Jesus' teaching about children is a deliberate "provocation" of complacent right-eousness. The pericope is one more "conflict story" which shows Jesus importantly at odds with scribes and Pharisees, and which Mark uses to indicate that the Reign of God is beyond their comprehension.

"Childness"

Fifth, Jesus teaches the "childness" of mature adulthood. The interpretation that children have entered the Reign of God just because they are children, and not because they have meritoriously fulfilled the obligations of the law may be exegetically and contextually probable, but I think a stronger and more prescriptive meaning can be derived from Jesus' words. There may be a danger in taking "like" or "as" (*hòs*) in the phrase "like a child" to license some imitative search for particular qualities of being a child that adults are then required to emulate. "Likeness" implies discontinuity between child-hood and adulthood, along with an attempt to re-introduce certain claimed similarities between them. Herbert Anderson and Susan Johnson have introduced a stronger concept, "childness," which is instead premised on the *continuity* of being between children and adults, with the proviso that what children already possess, adults are in danger of losing. They say

> What we mean is more than being "like a child." It is an enduring way of experiencing the world that continues to emerge as we move towards matu-rity. We will use the metaphor "childness" to identify qualities of being a child that continue in adult life: vulnerability, openness, immediacy, and neediness. We do not intend to suggest that these qualities exhaust what it means to be human. They are, however, necessary dimensions of an anthropology that is inclusive of children.[24]

Anderson and Johnson do not claim to have derived "childness" exegetically from the Gospels, but they assume it in their treatment of the Markan text. In their hands, childness is a *human* quality that children exemplify and adults are likely to compromise or lose. That is why adults need the example of children to remind them of what they may so easily forget. Of course it may be objected that the stated qualities of childness ("vulnerability, openness,

---

[23] Gundry-Volf, "The Least and the Greatest," p. 40.
[24] Herbert Anderson and Susan B.W. Johnson, *Regarding Children: A New Respect for Child-hood and Families* (Louisville, KY: Westminster John Knox Press, 1995), p. 10.

immediacy, and neediness") bring us back to the imitative search for ways in which adults are supposed to be "childlike." But there are good reasons for persevering with "childness" (below, 6.1–6.2). Not only are the qualities of childness derived in part from the Gospel narratives,[25] "childness" helps to present "a radically new and more inclusive vision of the community." It also helps "to challenge our assumptions of anthropology" and to expand "the norms for discipleship." It is fully consistent with the teaching of Jesus, and it helps us to re-appropriate that teaching for ourselves by providing new insights into it. That is why the statement "Jesus teaches the 'childness' of adulthood" firmly stands. While it also remains true that Jesus regards children as examples for adults to follow, there is a stronger sense in which there are *human* or *Kingdom* qualities that children better exemplify and adults need to regain.

Sixth, the teaching of Jesus about children in the Gospels is linked to questions of social power and reverses the structures of power within the Reign of God. Matthew records how

> the disciples came to Jesus and asked, "Who is the greatest in the kingdom of Heaven?" He called a child, set him in front of them, and said, "Truly I tell you: unless you turn round and become like children, you will never enter the kingdom of Heaven. Whoever humbles himself and becomes like this child will be the greatest in the kingdom of Heaven, and whoever receives one such child in my name receives me. But if anyone causes the downfall of one of these little ones who believe in me, it would be better for him to have a millstone hung round his neck and be drowned in the depths of the sea." (Mt. 18:1–6)

We have already noted how, in this Gospel, Jesus critiques the hierarchical and androcentric structures of households (above, 3.1). Those structures are reversed ("Whoever wants to be great must be your servant") in the Reign of God, and here that reversal is underscored. Again the adverb "like" (*hòs* again) should not lead us into a mimetic, and indefinite, search for particular child-like qualities to be imitated. Rather the *human* quality of humility is specified and again, children have it and adults are in danger of losing it. Children exemplify a *human* virtue, and the Reign of God is arranged around it. The counter-cultural, radical, anti-hierarchical, power reversal taught by Jesus has probably never yet been adequately practiced in any earthly institution. Perhaps it is so far from realization that the required feat of imagination to recognize it remains for the present beyond us, or, as

---

[25] Anderson and Johnson, *Regarding Children*, pp. 20–1.

theologians say, "in the *eschaton*." Nevertheless it prioritizes the position of children in the Reign of God, and does so simply and unambiguously. Any theology of families should rejoice in this elevation of children and seek to work out its far-reaching implications.

Seventh, receiving a child is receiving Jesus. "Whoever receives one such child in my name receives me." There seems to be a deliberate indefiniteness about this remarkable statement. The receiving or welcoming of a child entails also the receiving or welcoming of Jesus. The statement raises questions about the solidarity or identity between Jesus and children which themselves raise further questions about what ontology may be required to elucidate them. There is an even stronger identity claim between Jesus and children in Mark's narrative about power and influence within the Reign of God. Jesus "took a child, set him in front of them, and put his arm round him. 'Whoever receives a child like this in my name,' he said, 'receives me; and whoever receives me, receives not me but the One who sent me'" (Mk. 9:36–7). The solidarity of children with Jesus is a solidarity with God the Father also.

The interpretation of identity offered by Gundry-Volf requires first an identity not of Jesus himself with children, but of Jesus' sufferings with the sufferings of children. That is a different identity claim. Children's suffering may derive from their low status or from deliberate cruelty, and the forthcoming sufferings of Jesus are the subject of the immediately preceding pericope (9:30–2).[26] Children are to be welcomed by the church because Jesus suffers as they do. Second, "As suggested by Mark's larger narrative, welcoming children may also *enable* one to welcome the Jesus who became like a little child."[27] Welcoming children may predispose one to welcome the Christ in the response of faith. But the stronger claim available to Christians is that Jesus *was* a child: stronger still is the claim that God became a Child, God the Child, in Christ. But this last claim belongs not to Jesus' teaching about children but to the church's teaching about Jesus (below, 4.3).

Perhaps these weak forms of identity are the most that a historical, textual interpretation can justify. However I shall be proposing a stronger version of the identity claim that receiving a child is receiving Jesus, in the pages that follow. We have seen in the preference for "childness" over "childlikeness," that similarity does not do justice to the deeper anthropological and ontological issues at stake. The dilemma posed here is itself similar to that posed

[26] Gundry-Volf, "The Least and the Greatest," p. 45.
[27] Gundry-Volf, "The Least and the Greatest," p. 45 (author's emphasis).

by the more familiar claims within Christian theology that Christ is *really* present in the eucharist ("This *is* my body"), or that Christ is *really* God, as the Nicene and subsequent creeds affirm. While the claims may be difficult to explicate, it is better to live with the difficulties than to opt for a reductive memorialism or Arianism. When one receives a child, one receives Jesus. And one can expect to receive the ministry of Jesus through the welcomed child. Implications are waiting to be drawn.

Eighth, Jesus teaches that for adults to inflict harm on children is a horrendous crime. The deservedly lurid end of the offender against children is an expression of horror in the face of any harm to children deliberately inflicted by adults, not a cry for vengeance. The "little ones" (in Mt. 18:6) "believe in" Jesus. Is the reference then only to the children of Matthew's community or the community of disciples? Not necessarily. No such restriction is placed on the children of the immediately preceding verses. If the root reference to real children is metaphorically extended to vulnerable children of faith (including of course adults), perhaps that emphasizes its strength.

Ninth, children are shown to have an innate understanding of who Jesus is. Matthew records that

> In the temple the blind and the crippled came to him, and he healed them. When the chief priests and scribes saw the wonderful things he did, and heard the boys in the temple shouting, "Hosanna to the Son of David!" they were indignant and asked him, "Do you hear what they are saying?" Jesus answered, "I do. Have you never read the text, 'You have made children and babes at the breast sound your praise aloud'?"(Matthew 21:14–16)

The incident in the temple does not of itself invite the generalization that all children are able to recognize Jesus. What the scene does is present an ironic contrast between the chief priests and scribes who, their piety and learning notwithstanding, do not recognize Jesus, and the children who, their *lack* of piety and learning notwithstanding, do. Elsewhere in the Gospel Jesus thanks God for "hiding these things from the learned and wise" (11:25), and revealing them to infants (*nèpiois*). Gundry-Volf concludes "In the gospel tradition, children are not mere ignoramuses in terms of spiritual insight. They know Jesus' true identity. They praise him as the Son of David. They have this knowledge from God and not from themselves, and because they do, they are living manifestos that God is the source of all true knowledge about Christ."[28] The incident invites an association in the minds of contem-

---

[28] Gundry-Volf, "The Least and the Greatest," pp. 47–8.

porary readers with the extraordinary insights that children possess when they speak untutored about God or heaven. Children have a capacity for knowledge of God and Matthew knows this. He depicts them as intuiting who Jesus is, and he depicts their intuition as prophesied by scripture and warranted by Godself.

Tenth, Jesus had a particular and intense love for children. This is an inference from all the texts we have considered and from the rest of his teaching. He exemplified and fostered a counter-cultural adult attitude to them, awarding them first place both in the Reign of God and in social and household hierarchies. This is a simple conclusion to carry forward into our theology for families in Part II, with exhilarating possibilities. In the present chapter we have seen that Jesus relativizes households and family ties. We have just observed the inordinate and unconditional love of Jesus for children. But these conclusions raise further questions, at least for parents of children. Are they justified in putting *their* children first? That question persists and is not answered in the Gospels. But an answer is needed, and is begun in the last two sections of this chapter.

3.3 Parents, Children, and Priorities

The teaching of Jesus about children is about all children. It is not addressed in the first instance to parents. Adult priorities toward them are not specifically discussed. Thus we reach a surprising conclusion at the start of any utilization or appropriation of the teaching of Jesus in a theology for families, namely, parent–child and child–parent relationships are not addressed directly in the teaching of Jesus. They are however addressed in the Household Codes. Since family ties are relativized in the Reign of God, and there is a clear Gospel priority afforded to all children, not just some of them, how, if at all, are our responsibilities to our own children to be accounted for, articulated, given priority? "Our own"? Even this expression invites suspicion. Is it possessive? Is it exclusive? All that is intended here by that expression is that "our" children are "ours" if one or both parents are the biological parents, or we are wholly responsible for children whom we have adopted, or who have legally joined a new family.

There appear to be two standard theological answers to this problem. Neither do our family-friendly principles for Bible reading appear to help, for the Bible does not directly address the question. The first answer is "kin altruism." The second is the incorporation of children within the category of neighbor. Our kin are our nearest neighbors. One of the main themes of this book is to provide a more adequate and theologically satisfying answer to this root question. It will be done by rejecting the second answer and accepting the first, although with a large qualification: kin altruism requires a developed theological anthropology so it can be more deeply grounded in doctrinal sources. But that is to anticipate. First it will be necessary to present this problem in its sharpest form, and then to examine each of the answers.

Our own children have no particular claims upon us! That is, we should accord them no special priority in the care they receive. Rather we should love all children generally, including our own. That is the clear conclusion of several theologians, and of a detailed argument by Garth Hallett, who reopens A.C. Ewing's dilemma of 1953: "It is clear that the money spent by a man in order to provide his son with a university education could save the lives of many people who were perishing of hunger in a famine, yet most people would rather blame than praise a man who should deprive his son of a university education on this account."[29] The dilemma is, of course, a version of the conundrum of the nearest versus the neediest. "Virtue ethics" is useless in handling the problem – "To be sure, charity is a virtue; but what preferences does charity dictate?"[30] "In real life (as opposed to philosophers' imaginings), the distinction between self and others is clear-cut: there is no problem as to who is 'I' and who is not . . ." The nearness of another to "me" is immaterial: "Mere spatial proximity, in itself, lacks moral relevance."[31] Ties of affection can be stronger than ties of kinship. The assumption of critical familism that families "create unique obligations" is thrown back at them: the poor create unique obligations too.[32]

Preference for the poor over family is maintained in further arguments. After a survey of New Testament passages, Hallett concludes the evidence is "massively one-sided" in favor of the poor, and against the family. He concedes this may be "because family ties, being psychologically so strong, posed a special challenge to the claims of the gospel, not because such ties lacked validity."[33] A chapter is devoted to ravaging the *ordo caritatis* to which Aquinas gave respectability. This order takes the general form, "First, God is

[29] A.C. Ewing, *Ethics* (London: English Universities Press, 1953), pp. 37–8: in Garth Hallett, *Priorities in Christian Ethics* (Cambridge, UK: Cambridge University Press, 1998), pp. 1–2.

[30] Hallett, *Priorities*, p. 13.

[31] Hallett, *Priorities*, p. 14.

[32] Hallett, *Priorities*, p. 21. The author cited is Stephen Post, *A Theory of Agape: On the Meaning of Christian Love* (Lewisburg, PA: Bucknell University Press, 1990), p. 92. Post is one of the authors associated with "critical familism," but that term began to be used later. See above, 2.2. Post's position remains unchanged in his later *More Lasting Unions: Christianity, the Family, and Society* (Grand Rapids, MI/Cambridge, UK: Eerdmans, 2000).

[33] Hallett, *Priorities*, p. 53.

to be loved, second ourselves, third our parents, fourth our children, fifth members of our household, sixth strangers."[34] Especially problematic is the preference for self over others, and "the inclusion of kin within this preference."[35] Since self-love is unsupported by the scriptures, the inclusion of one's immediate dependents within the category is unjustified.

Hallett's arguments are powerful, especially when the teaching of Jesus about families and children explored in this chapter is added to them. It will take a new and major line of argument to counteract them. For the present, let us merely note some preliminary reliefs. First, the dilemma *is* a philosopher's imagining, albeit an uncomfortable one. Why limit the demands the starving make on the parents' resources to this one canceled obligation to this one offspring? Why not deprive other members of the family of many more relative goods in order to relieve famine as well? Where do these obligations end? Do they end? Second, the world is not structured as the example supposes. The calculated saving as a sum of money, invested in some way to relieve famine, may not certainly relieve it, and certainly will not relieve it directly without intermediaries or agents. In turn, that shows, third, the implied concept of agency ignores that social, political, and economic agency is required for famine to be relieved. Sure, personal giving is required, and political decisions are taken by groups of persons, but agency is required at different levels. The parents have a co-responsibility for the starving along with all who are fed.

But these reservations introduce graver ones, of an ontological character. In "real life" the distinction between self and others is not "clear-cut," especially if the other is, as in marriage, "one flesh" with oneself; or if the other is one's children who matter to their parents as much as, or more than, their own lives. Christian faith gives us a theory of the self (so, of course, does philosophy) where the boundaries between some selves are very permeable; where love becomes a relation between two or more individual persons, uniting them; where there is an intensification of intimacy unsustainable beyond an immediate, and therefore a definable and potentially excluding, circle. Granted, there are residual patriarchal assumptions about the hegemony of household and family heads that ought to have no place in contemporary families, where the "one flesh" of marriage is still the husband's (and the wife's is included in it), or where the householder has a property-owning relationship to his whole domain, including his wife, children, other kin, dependents, servants, and estate. Individualism exposes

---

[34] Hallett, *Priorities*, p. 68.
[35] Hallett, *Priorities*, p. 76.

these "corporatizing" frauds, where the patriarchal body includes everyone and everything else on its own terms, but individualism does not understand the relationality out of which intimate bonds emerge.

The notion that spatial proximity in itself lacks moral relevance is misleading. The "in itself" invites an abstract treatment of the term, and spatial proximity suggests the arrangements of objects, tools in a box, or buttons on a customized toolbar. But spatial proximity is a precondition of much that is highly morally relevant. Sexual and other relations like parenting *do* require proximity. The baby in the mother's womb refutes dogma about the boundaries of selves being markable: and the baby in the womb or at the breast is not merely proximate. There is a bonding here that individualism cannot fathom. Nearness is morally relevant, spatially and relationally, because it is those other people who are nearer and dearer to me that make me most aware of myself. Neither, we should add, is the indefinite comparison between the bonds of kin and the bonds of affection relevant to the fact that human beings bond.

When Hallett concedes the strong psychological ties that may exist within families, he appears to regard these as antipathetic to the Gospel. Indeed they may be, especially if the families operate as clans and enter power struggles with other clans. Abuse, fratricide, and incest belong within families, and so-called "Reality TV" shows convert the horrendous dysfunctionality of some families into entertainment for the rest of us. But there are other ways of explaining family ties which are pre-psychological and coincident with the Gospel, where the "ties" are ties of love, and where the love is a mingling of human and divine. Despite these criticisms of Hallett, I admire the consistency of his argument. In taking a different tack, and arguing for a different set of preferences it will be necessary to introduce a theological anthropology which can make better sense of family ties and which is grounded in that ultimate Subject and Object of Christian theology, the Communion that is Godself.

Kin altruism

A bold attempt to articulate, defend, and justify the priority of the bonds of kinship between children and parents has been made by Don Browning (and his co-authors), by means of the related ideas of "kin altruism" and the "male problematic." I admire this effort, but think that a Trinitarian anthropology would both bestow upon it a greater theological impact and provide further theological grounding for its empirical base. Kin altruism is "the preferential treatment people tend to give to their biologically related family members."[36] But the power of the idea is that it is a natural tendency common throughout the natural world which human beings inherit. "Kin altruism is the idea that all creatures, including humans, are more likely to invest in and sacrifice for those who share their own genes than they are for nonkin."[37] Running counter to kin altruism is "the *male problematic*," which is "the increasing tendency of men, partially due to the pressures of modernity and partially because of archaic evolutionary tendencies, to mate and procreate but live separately from their children and often relinquish their paternal responsibilities."[38] The male problematic, then, is also in part an inherited tendency of our species. Christianity, and indeed the Semitic faiths, have been a major socializing influence on male behavior in encouraging men to remain with their wives and offspring by emphasizing, indeed sacralizing, the social bonds between them. These ideas, from evolutionary biology and evolutionary psychology, are new to theology, and the novelty of the treatment they receive at Browning's hands deserves wider recognition.

Two further ideas will quickly establish the relevance of kin altruism to our earlier discussion about our priorities to our children – "inclusive fitness" and "parental investment." Inclusive fitness supplants earlier evolutionary theory which taught that it was individuals – or more properly their genes – that successfully reproduced themselves. According to the theory of inclusive fitness the "basic unit of evolutionary change" is not simply the individual who passes on his or her genes. Rather, the individual includes the genes that he or she shares with close kin. It follows that

> Individuals, according to this perspective, do not fight just for their own survival; they also work for the survival and flourishing of the biological relatives who carry their genes. They do this because these genetically related individuals are literally extensions of themselves. Inclusive fitness is not just the fitness of the individual, it is the fitness of the *extended family*.[39]

---

[36] Don S. Browning, Bonnie J. Miller-McLemore, Pamela D. Couture, K. Brynolf Lyon, and Robert M. Franklin, *From Culture Wars to Common Ground: Religion and the American Family Debate* (Louisville, KY: Westminster John Knox Press, 1997), p. 71. I have attributed the theological use of these ideas to Browning because he expounds them as a single author elsewhere. See also Don S. Browning, *Marriage and Modernization: How Globalization Threatens Marriage and What to Do about It* (Grand Rapids, MI/Cambridge, UK: Eerdmans, 2003), p. 77.

[37] Don Browning, "The Problem of Men," in David Blankenhorn, Don Browning, and Mary Stewart Van Leeuwen (eds.), *Does Christianity Teach Male Headship? – The Equal-Regard Marriage and Its Critics* (Grand Rapids, MI/Cambridge, UK: Eerdmans, 2004 [3–12], p. 10.

[38] Browning, *Marriage and Modernization*, p. 77 (author's emphasis). See Browning et al., *From Culture Wars*, p. 106.

[39] Browning et al., *From Culture Wars*, p. 108 (authors' emphasis).

The theory of kin altruism explains why "Under some circumstances, individuals are willing to sacrifice their own inclusive fitness on behalf of a relative, and they tend to do this in proportion to the degree of relatedness of the relative." These theories enable Browning to conclude that "Evolutionary psychology tells us why both biological parents and members of the extended family are so important to a child's well-being. It is kin who are most likely to contribute to the flourishing and defense of children. It is not just mother and father who are important to children but the whole crowd . . ." Finally, parental investment (or commitment) is "any investment by the parent in an individual offspring that increases the offspring's chance of surviving . . . at the cost of the parent's ability to invest in other offspring."[40]

The genius of Browning's use of evolutionary theory is the congruence he finds between some of its concepts and the teachings of Aristotle and Aquinas. Having carefully placed Aquinas in context and dissociated himself from Aquinas' patriarchy and misogyny, Browning finds that Aquinas too "made assumptions about humans' natural preference for blood-related family, ideas similar to the modern-day theory of kin altruism." Four features of his thought constitute the comparison: the dependency of infants on both their parents; the need for men to be sure of their paternity; the mutual assistance between husband and wife; and the limitations on sexual exchange.[41] These facts belong to nature, and so to the way God created it. According to nature, we love our children "because, as Aristotle also taught, we love the image of ourselves that we find in our children." But there is also a greater, theological reason why we love them, because the image of God is within them.[42] Both of these reasons for loving our children accord with the purposes of God.

Stephen Pope has shown how kin altruism can contribute to Roman Catholic moral theology, and especially its deliberations about the *ordo caritatis*. His argument, made independently of the critical familists, coincides with theirs in several points of detail. Pope reiterates how attachment theorists have shown how "human bonding at times is constituted and maintained by deeply biologically based affective capacities and inclinations that cannot be ignored by realistic attempts to understand love."[43] The parent–

[40] Browning et al., *From Culture Wars*, p. 109, citing Robert Trivers, "Parental Investment and Sexual Selection," in B. Campbell (ed.), *Sexual Selection and the Descent of Man* (Chicago, IL: Aldine Publishing Co., 1972), p. 139.

[41] Browning et al., *From Culture Wars*, pp. 115–18.

[42] Browning et al., *From Culture Wars*, p. 121.

[43] Stephen J. Pope, "The Order of Love and Recent Catholic Ethics: A Constructive Proposal," *Theological Studies*, 52.2, June 1991 [255–89], p. 262. He cites John Bowlby, *Attachment and Loss 1: Attachment* (New York: Basic Books, 1969); and M.D.S. Ainsworth et al., *Patterns of Attachment* (Hillsdale, NJ: Lawrence Erlbaum, 1978).

infant bond "is the prototypical case of this kind of love." Perhaps if Christian theology had had a more positive attitude to the body we would be less surprised by these important discoveries. Aquinas, Pope reminds us, advocated "gradations of affections" on the basis that "the affection of charity, which is an inclination of grace, is not less orderly than the natural appetite, which is the inclination of nature, for both inclinations flow from Divine wisdom."[44] The natural love of parents for children, then, also derives from, and is ordered by God. Sociobiology, or evolutionary psychology, provides theology with much empirically based information about it.

Thomas' conclusions regarding parental love were (as Pope explicates them):

> (1) parents love their children as "parts" of themselves, and therefore parental love, more than any other kind of love, is akin to self-love, (2) parents know better the biological origin of their children than children know their own biological origin, and this knowledge grounds a stronger love, and (3) parents love their children for a longer period of time, and therefore more strongly, than their children love them.[45]

Thomas was acutely aware (below, 8.2) of the apparent contrast between his claim that parents are to love their children as parts of themselves and the teaching of Jesus about families reviewed earlier in this chapter. He was able to reconcile these to his satisfaction by invoking the distinction between *caritas* and *cupiditas*. "Whereas caritas subordinates love of self to love for God, cupiditas reverses this order."[46] There is an improper self-love, and there is also an improper love of kin.[47] "Just as improper love of self in fact amounts to 'hatred' of self," continues Pope,[48] so, "by implication, disordered love of family entails a de facto 'hatred' of family, i.e., a disordered attachment that frustrates and undermines its own true good."[49]

Pope concludes that kin altruism is able to contribute to the treatment of

---

[44] Pope, "The Order of Love," p. 262, citing Thomas Aquinas, *Summa Theologiae* (tr. Fathers of the English Dominican Province), 3 vols (New York: Benziger Brothers, 1947), 2–2, q.26, a.6.

[45] Pope, "The Order of Love," pp. 264–5, citing Thomas Aquinas, *Summa Theologiae*, 2–2, q.26, a.9.

[46] Pope, "The Order of Love," p. 263.

[47] Pope, "The Order of Love," p. 263, citing Thomas Aquinas, *Summa Theologiae*, 2–2, q.26, a.2.

[48] Pope, "The Order of Love," p. 263, citing Thomas Aquinas, *Summa Theologiae*, 2–2, q.25, a.7;1–2, q.77, a.4, ad.1.

[49] Pope, "The Order of Love," p. 263, citing Thomas Aquinas, *Summa Theologiae*, 2–2, q.26, a.7, ad.1.

the ordering of love in Roman Catholic thought "in three primary ways: first, it highlights the multiplicity of objects of love and the problem of priorities; second, it helps us understand the natural basis of the ordering of love; and third, . . . it provides natural grounds for a moral justification of the gradation of love."[50] And, we might add, it provides a fresh perspective on the teaching of Jesus about families, perhaps providing the basis for the extension of families in the way the Reign of God requires.

I welcome the theological appropriation of kin altruism by Browning and Pope. It is grounded in contemporary social science; it provides a helpful explanatory framework for the crisis of fatherhood in many parts of the world. The science of course may be wrong, but that is no reason for not engaging with it. All knowledge is partial and provisional: there are no "No trespassing" signs around particular intellectual property sites to frighten theologians off. There are other difficulties to fend off. Is not the alarming increase in the absence of biological fathers from their children contrary evidence that kin altruism is false, or weak, or plain trivial? Not necessarily. The claim is that kin altruism is weak in any case, and it is possibly being undermined by contemporary social practices which do not reinforce it. And we may be a mass of contradictions anyway. Is there not a further contradiction between the male problematic and the socially desired goal of equal-regard marriages, for the steady erosion of patriarchy makes the withdrawal of fathers more, not less, likely?[51] Again, no. This is a charge that says absent fathers may return to their family homes, provided patriarchy is reassembled for them to reassume their mastery. But that is not a price worth paying: it isn't going to be paid; and even if it were to be paid, there is no guarantee it would purchase the desired result. My worry about kin altruism is only that when it is incorporated into theological analyses of humanity, it needs a stronger theological anthropology to engage it. How is it that we are beings who create other beings who are "literally extensions" of ourselves? What does this say about how we are constituted? Parents may be disposed to "invest" in their biological children because the bonds that bind them belong to their social nature. And that is how God has made them. They are in-relation before they are in-dividual. That is how we are made. To be in the image of the Triune God is already to be in-relation, and our relationality is at its most obvious in our care for the children who are God's gifts to us. More will be said about this in the next chapter.

Kin altruism provides an explanation and partial justification for giving

---

50 Pope, "The Order of Love," p. 274.
51 See John W. Miller, "The Problem of Men, Reconsidered," in Blankenhorn et al. (eds.), *Does Christianity Teach Male Headship?* [65–73], p. 67.

priority to our own children. At least it tackles the problem of kin priority. I wonder whether that problem is evaded in much theological writing about families, not just Hallett's. Michael Lawler, following John Wesley, rightly says "Since the love of God is universal and unrestricted, so also is Christian, neighbor-love universal and unrestricted. Christians are to love not just their spouses, not just their families, not just their neighbors, but all people."[52] Yes, but equally? Lisa Cahill frequently makes the criticism that "families tend to create solidarity around their own well-being, although the most distinctively Christian moral virtue is sacrifice for the well-being of others."[53] This criticism is expressed unfortunately. What about sacrifice (a problematic notion anyway, see below, 7.3–7.4) for our own children? Are they to be included in the amorphous "others" too? At several points in her analysis, the priority to be accorded to family members is occluded into the generalized notion of neighbor-love. Is there not then room for saying explicitly that love for one's children might be the paradigm for relations of love to external neighbors, an intensification of a Gospel norm, but not an implied exception to it?

Hallett's solution is to include our own children within the category of neighbor. "Not only are children, spouses, parents, and the like to be recognized as our neighbors, and as such to be preferred to oneself, but they are to be regarded as privileged neighbors."[54] Further questions need to be asked about the extent of the privileges assigned to them which clearly involves the ordering of priorities. Alternatively children are "strangers" to whom hospitality, albeit privileged, is due.[55] But these solutions are outright failures. The gift of a child to parents can evoke from them a response of joy and commitment that cannot be rivaled or shared with any other claimant on our love. The special relationship of parents to their children is demeaned if it is required to be assumed under a universal rubric of neighbor-love. Our children are far too special for that.

3.4 Loving Neighbors, Loving Children?

Our children, I just said, are too special to be classified as among our neighbors or special strangers. Our relation to them is more fundamental than

---

[52] Michael G. Lawler, "Towards a Theology of Christian Family," *INTAMS Review*, vol. 8.1, Spring, 2002, [55–73], p. 66.

[53] Cahill, *Family*, p. 48.

[54] Hallett, *Priorities*, p. 78.

[55] For a discussion of children as strangers see Rodney Clapp, *Families at the Crossroads: Beyond Traditional and Modern Options* (Leicester: Inter-Varsity Press, 1993), pp. 143–8.

either of these ethical categories suggests. That said, it is important to affirm the basis of Christian ethics in the Golden Rule of Jesus ("Always treat others as you would like them to treat you" – Mt. 5:12) and in the Great Commandments of Jesus to love God and our neighbors as ourselves (Mk. 12:28–34; Mt. 22:34–40; Lk. 10:25–37). The Great Commandments assume relations of love between the self and God, the self and the neighbor, the self with itself, and some balance between these relations. The parental love of children is able to be justified by an appeal to the Love Commandments and would of course conform to our fourth principle (above, 2.3) that they take precedence over the Household Codes. But what is at stake here is the possibility of a relation between parents and children which precedes the classification of children as neighbors. The relations assumed by the Great Commandments will provide our entry into a Trinitarian framework which, in turn, will generate fresh thinking about the relations between parents and children. Unfortunately, each of these relations (to God, neighbor, self) generates much theological disagreement, but as we will see, the controversies they generate provide a further reason for advancing a Trinitarian interpretation of the self.

I assume with Karl Rahner that, in loving our neighbor, we love God through our neighbor, whether explicitly as an expression of Christian practice, or implicitly, as a human act that promotes the Common Good. Rahner claims that "the 'God in us' is really the one who alone can be loved and who is reached precisely in the love of our brother and in no other way."[56] Loving another, then, is loving God in and through the other. Or again, Rahner observes

> most theologians today would still shrink from the proposition which gives our fundamental thesis its ultimate meaning, its real clarity and inescapable character, viz., that wherever a genuine love of man attains its proper nature and moral absoluteness and depth, it is in addition always so underpinned and heightened by God's saving grace that it is also love of God, whether it be explicitly considered to be such a love by the subject or not.[57]

I do *not* shrink from this proposition,[58] but in signing up to it, there is no

---

[56] Karl Rahner, "Reflections on the Unity of the Love of Neighbor and the Love of God," *Theological Investigations*, vol. 6 (London: Darton, Longmann and Todd, 1969) [231–49], p. 235.

[57] Rahner, "Reflections," p. 237.

[58] Paul D. Molnar explains this passage in Rahner by explicating a series of defects which, from his preferred Barthian perspective, invalidates Rahner's starting point. See his "Love of God and Love of Neighbor in the Theology of Karl Rahner and Karl Barth," *Modern Theology*, 20.4, October 2004 [567–99].

need to follow him in other emphases.[59] Loving a neighbor is loving the God who calls to us through, and is present to the neighbor. God, then, may be the source of neighbor-love, and the recipient. That is why at Holy Communion the congregation pray "Give grace to us, our families and friends, and to all our neighbors, that we may serve Christ *in one another*, and love as he loves us."[60] The neighbor may mediate the expression of our love for God, but this does not commit us to the proposition that the two loves are identical. The neighbor is not God: neither is the neighbor worshiped. Human love, however, is underpinned and intensified by the divine love who is God. This is surely preferable to the restricted, Barthian claim that neighbor-love is a necessary expression of our prior love of God.[61] Rather, through our love of neighbor, the God who is revealed there may also come to be known as the One who is completely revealed in Christ. In the love of parents for their children we may find the paradigm case of the love of God manifested through the parents' love of their child, and the parents' love a response to the God present to their child. But that is to anticipate.

In asking whether it is adequate to suppose that our children are first among our neighbors, that is, whether "neighbor" is an adequate category in relation to our children, we need to re-visit the lawyer's question to Jesus "But who is my neighbor?" (Lk. 10:27). Standardly the Parable of the Good Samaritan is thought to demonstrate to the Jewish questioner that the category of neighbor is to be extended, however reluctantly, even to a representative of the hated Samaritan race. Even Samaritans are capable of neighborliness when priests and Levites are not. This feature of the parable itself explodes the assumption that Christians, Jews, or religious people necessarily have anything original to contribute to the theory and practice of neighbor-love. Rather, being religious, in this pointed parable, was what prevented it. The Samaritan becomes a neighbor to the victim of robbery. William Schweiker draws attention to the way Jewish people would have understood the parable. Jews held strong beliefs about "the relation between righteous action and the human being as the image of God . . . The *imago dei* is hardly an attribute of the mind or soul, as many early and medieval

---

[59] For example, the "transcendental method," the "mutual conditioning" of the two loves, the conflation of the immanent and the economic Trinity and the alleged "false immanentism" of the latter. See Molnar, "Love of God and Love of Neighbor," pp. 568, 573, 579.

[60] Church of England, *Common Worship*, Prayers of Intercession at Holy Communion (my emphasis). www.cofe.anglican.org/worship/liturgy/commonworship/texts/hc/intercessions. html. Accessed 02.09.2006.

[61] Molnar, "Love of God and Love of Neighbor," p. 590, citing Karl Barth, *Church Dogmatics* 1, 2, p. 406.

theologians thought. It is manifest in actions that imitate God. 'Neighbor' is defined not by likeness but by the work of compassion."[62]

Children: more than neighbors

Schweiker's account of the practice of inscription well indicates the escalating character of neighbor-love and the nigh impossible extension of its scope (above, 2.3). In the time of globalization, he states, "the point of the second great commandment is to guide action in response to those radically different than self." I have no quarrel with this. But the more the understanding of who the neighbor is, is (rightly) allowed to escalate, the less serviceable is the concept of neighbor in relation to our children. As the range of neighbor-love expands in the Christian consciousness, and the more inclusive it becomes in the direction of the stranger and the enemy, the greater the urgency to locate the love of children within a different range of compassion altogether. It is not merely a matter of constructing a polarity of "near" and "distant" neighbors,[63] and locating children at the proximate end of neighborliness defined by degrees of distance: the category of neighbor will not suffice for the intimacy with one's children that being a parent requires.

The search for an alternative basis for parental love is given a further impetus by the apparent reflexivity of the command: "*as* yourself." Must "I" love myself in order to love my neighbor, or am "I" permitted to love myself as much as my neighbor? Against frequent exhortation to self-sacrifice, is self-*love* actually commanded here? These matters are investigated by Darlene Weaver in *Self Love and Christian Ethics*. Weaver begins with *caritas*, "God's love given to the self, by which the self properly loves God and others. In caritas, the human is given her highest good. Thus, the human endeavour to love God is simultaneously the pursuit of her own good."[64] The Reformation weakened the "co-ordination" of self-love and love for God. Weaver ably guides her readers through the varying fortunes of the self in Enlightened thought, and through its deconstruction, leading to the raging debate "whether there is any subject behind the discourses that con-

[62] William Schweiker, *Theological Ethics and Global Dynamics* (Malden, MA, and Oxford, UK: Blackwell, 2004), p. 100.
[63] See Elizabeth Stuart and Adrian Thatcher, *People of Passion – What the Churches Teach about Sex* (London: Mowbray, 1997), pp. 231–2.
[64] Darlene Fozard Weaver, *Self Love and Christian Ethics* (Cambridge, UK: Cambridge University Press, 2002), p. 4.

stitute its identity," or "some subject that precedes its construction."[65] There are two extremes to avoid: rampant individualism that absolutizes the self, and rampant deconstruction that "reduces the self to systems or the intersection of determining forces." The postmodern problem of the self, she claims, "indicates that a contemporary theory of self-love requires a complex account of the self who loves herself" . . .[66]

Writing as a Christian, Weaver identifies, as I have done, "the need for theological moral anthropology." A theological account of self-relation does more than speculate on or describe our being in the world; it orients our acting and relations with others and in the world.[67] I differ from Weaver over what a theological moral anthropology is taken to be. She provides a typology of self-love drawn from twentieth-century ethicists all of whom have written illuminatingly about self-love. But if the moral anthropology offered is to be a theological one, why start there? Why not begin with the God in whose image we are made? If our relation to God, the neighbor, and ourself is the issue, why not begin with the prior category of relation? If the anthropology is *theological*, why not begin with the Triune God and the relations *there*?

Weaver rightly berates theories of self-love which "begin and proceed according to some account of love rather than some account of the self who is to love."[68] But instead of beginning with the self-in-relation or, say, with ourselves as *lovers* (of God, neighbors, and ourselves), she takes the crucial indicator of selfhood to be the self's reflexivity, the relation of the self to itself. Thus a relational theory of the self is offered which is not situated in relationships (and especially not in family ones)! A crucial step is taken when she says "The activity of understanding is central to what it means to be human, and to what it means to be a moral creature."[69] So she concentrates on self-understanding as *the* basic human activity. "The basic activity of self-understanding or interpretation is central to self-relation."[70] But this is almost Cartesian! The "turn to self-understanding"[71] successfully relocates the problem of self-love with the self rather than with love, but this merely replicates the individualized modern self whose relation to itself is the insurmountable problem. The self is now established as some one separate from

[65] Weaver, *Self Love and Christian Ethics*, p. 28.
[66] Weaver, *Self Love and Christian Ethics*, p. 29.
[67] Weaver, *Self Love and Christian Ethics*, p. 41.
[68] Weaver, *Self Love and Christian Ethics*, p. 46.
[69] Weaver, *Self Love and Christian Ethics*, p. 79.
[70] Weaver, *Self Love and Christian Ethics*, p. 81: and see p. 93.
[71] Weaver, *Self Love and Christian Ethics*, p. 82.

others and so from relationships with them. I want to see relation as the primary category, not self-understanding, and to include parents, siblings, members of the extended family, friends, etc., among the many relations that have gone into the making of "me."

It will become apparent that much so-called "theological anthropology" is child-exclusive. It is essentialist, and sketches theories about human beings in which children have no part. That being assumed, our relations to them fall outside its restricted scope as well. A child-centered focus, such as that provided by Jesus, is a necessary antidote to this anthropology. Schweiker has a different worry about interpreting neighbor-love "through some idea of reflexivity." Loving one's neighbor as oneself has invited the charge that Jews and Christians are in danger of reducing the neighbor to the self, to the degree that "the other is simply an object within my self-understanding, something that exists in some odd analogy to myself."[72] He acknowledges the tradition of reflexive consciousness in Western philosophy, but in his desire to respond to Emmanuel Lévinas and others, he is in danger of removing self-love from the command to love the neighbor altogether:

> For a Christian interpretation of the double love command, the clause "as yourself" does not mean that we love others as we naturally care for ourselves. The command does not warrant some kind of extended egoism or benevolent self-interest! Rather, one is to love as one has first been loved by God, a love manifest in creation, in Christ, and in the reign of God. Christian self-love is grounded not in the self but in God. One's being as a Christian is *in* Christ. There is an "otherness" at the very core of any Christian conception of consciousness and the self.[73]

But there is an unintended consequence of this account of the love commands. Self-love is removed from the triangle of God, neighbor, and self. Clearly, in Christian faith "one is to love as one has first been loved by God." This formulation of the meaning of the command comes close to the Johannine version: "This is my commandment: love one another, as I have loved you" (Jn. 17:12). But while God's love is manifest in creation, in Christ and in God's reign, that does not account for Jesus saying "You shall love your neighbor as yourself," instead of saying "You shall love your neighbor as God has loved you." Schweiker tells us that Christian self-love is grounded in God, but he does not tell us how. I think in his desire to overcome the objection that Christian ethics is reducible to self-love, he

---

[72] Schweiker, *Theological Ethics*, p. 100.
[73] Schweiker, *Theological Ethics*, p. 103 (author's emphasis).

minimizes self-love in relation to God and neighbor. And the concept of the self that he minimizes is the reflexive self.

Schweiker's treatment of the love commands, like Weaver's treatment of self-love, requires a concept of the self that is as equally, fundamentally and ontologically related to others as it is to itself. He moves toward this concept in saying that one's being as a Christian is *in* Christ. To be "in Christ" is to be a member of Christ's body, and so to belong socially to it. He is right to say there is an "otherness" at the very core of any Christian conception of consciousness and the self. But what is this otherness at the core of the self? The untried but essential answer lies in an account of the self that is relational. That is, a self may be so enmeshed, intertwined with, or involved in another self or selves that it is not possible to say where the boundaries of oneself end and the boundaries of the other begin. Parent–child relations are like this. Loving one's neighbor as oneself proceeds neither by reducing the neighbor to the self, nor by reducing the self to the neighbor.

A relational self, as opposed to an individual self, is one whose identity is inevitably bound up with those nearest to him or her. And that is why finally our children are not to be counted among our neighbors. They can be so close to us that they *are* us, as much they are separate from us, and we cannot begin to identify who we are without referring to them and our relation to them. In the next chapter we connect with a Trinitarian anthropology which extends kin altruism and provides an alternative to the assumption that our children are our neighbors.

Chapter Four

Relations, Families, and the Triune God

In this chapter we begin the task of constructing a theological anthropology where children and families are central. The relation of parents to children has required a theological exposition that does not treat children only as strangers or neighbors, that takes kin altruism seriously, that remains faithful to the teaching of Jesus about children *and* households, and that is not entrapped within the hierarchical relations assumed by the Household Codes. The requirement is met partly by an understanding of persons and relations, a "theological anthropology," which derives from the being of God as Trinity. The first section sets out in what way the Trinity is able to be the basis for a Christian family theology. In particular it draws on the medieval theologian Richard of St Victor. The second section analyzes how the doctrine of the Trinity has been utilized by two twentieth-century theologians in their contributions to a theology of family. They are Karl Barth and Pope John Paul II. The third section grounds the gift of children within the bounteous provision of "the Gifting God." And it seeks further application of the traditional doctrine that God the Word became a child, the Christ-Child. The fourth section situates families and children firmly within the range of the idea of the "image of God": we are made *in imagine dei*, and we image God not merely as persons, but as couples and families. The fifth section reminds us, after the sublime thoughts of this chapter, that universal, structural sin causes havoc in our relationships, especially within families. Detailed consideration of a "theology of parenting" must await chapter 7.

4.1 Relations and Families

A relational self, as opposed to an individual self, is one whose identity is inevitably bound up with those nearest to him or her. And that is why finally our children are not to be counted among our neighbors. They can be so close to us that they *are* us, as much they are also separate from us, and we cannot begin to identify who we are without referring to them and our relation to them. This relational self was extensively described by John Macmurray (but without reference to children) in his famous Gifford Lectures of 1953–4.[1] His portrait does not appear in Weaver's gallery of theorists of the self (above, 3.4). Alistair McFadyen provides an excellent theological account of the relational self. He saw clearly that "we become the people we are through our relationships with others; it is other people who enable us to become persons who, as such, may exercise a degree of autonomy . . ."[2] Working in a psychiatric hospital he quickly learned that patients were presenting themselves as "people whose identities and capacities for relation appeared to be distorted in some way . . ."[3] thereby demonstrating the degree to which they and we are shaped by others for good or ill. Convinced that a "third option" is necessary between individualist and collectivist theories of the "self," he outlines a "basic conception of the person" which is "both dialogical (formed through social interaction, through address and response) and dialectical (never coming to rest in a final unity, if only because one is never removed from relation)."[4]

McFadyen's "basic position" is "that persons have to be understood in social terms – if only because they are somehow the product of their relations. Individuality, personhood and selfhood do not . . . refer to some internal and independent source of identity, but to the way one is and has been in relation."[5] I adopt a similar method to McFadyen in drawing analogies of relation and participation between human and divine persons. He advocates an orthodox understanding of the Transcendent as a unique community of Persons in which Person and relation are interdependent moments in a process of mutuality. Each Person is a social unity with specific characteristics unique to Him or Her but whose uniqueness is not an asocial principle of being. The terms of personal identity within the Trinity identify not just unique individuals but the form of relation peculiar to them. "Father," for instance, denotes both a specific individual and the form of relation existing between Him and the other Persons.[6]

[1] John Macmurray, *The Self as Agent* (London: Faber & Faber, 1957), and *Persons in Relation* (London: Faber & Faber, 1961).
[2] Alistair I. McFadyen, *The Call to Personhood: A Christian Theory of the Individual in Social Relationships* (Cambridge, UK: Cambridge University Press, 1990).
[3] McFadyen, *The Call to Personhood*, p. 2.
[4] McFadyen, *The Call to Personhood*, p. 9.
[5] McFadyen, *The Call to Personhood*, p. 18.
[6] McFadyen, *The Call to Personhood*, p. 27.

I agree wholeheartedly with this approach to persons and relations, an approach by now "so much in vogue in recent decades as an antidote to 'individualism.'"[7] I will incorporate further insights into its method and content through the medieval theologian Richard of St Victor, and the late Pope John Paul II, before pressing the analogy between the relations between parents and children and the relations between the divine Persons. McFadyen did not develop his argument in this direction, even though attention to relations between parents and children would have strengthened his thesis. This is the ground on which it will be clearly shown that our children are more than neighbors; that, if we have them, our selfhood is incomplete without them.

The recovery of the doctrine of the Trinity in the last 30 years is a great achievement of theology:[8] its "next wave" must demonstrate its significance within Christian ethics and practice.[9] This will not be easy. First, the neglect of the Trinity within the churches continues. The legacy of modernity still has it that the doctrine is more of a liability than an asset in dialogs with people of the non-Christian faiths, or with scientists or philosophers. Consequently whether one speaks about the Trinity from the pulpit or to non-theologians in interdisciplinary fora, the inevitable look of surprise reveals non-verbal disbelief at what is being undertaken. Second, there is now emerging a polarization among Trinitarian theologians themselves. Sarah Coakley leads a team of distinguished authors, "a significant portion" of whose work "is involved in the tolling of the final funeral bell on a *misreading* of Gregory's Trinitarianism that has been peculiarly long-standing and pernicious for ecumenical understanding . . ."[10] But Gregory, whether or not he is mis-read, is one of the sources of the social model of the Trinity on which the revival of that doctrine largely rests. The danger looms that disagreement among theologians will undermine the confidence in the doctrine that ethical application requires. A similar, more familiar situation arose when theologians handed over to historical criticism the job of sorting out which bits of the New Testament could be really believed. While dis-

---

[7] David Ford, *Self and Salvation* (Cambridge, UK: Cambridge University Press, 1999), p. 34. Ford wisely distinguishes between "relationality" and the thought of Emmanuel Lévinas, Emmanuel, 76, 80 (pp. 36–44).

[8] See David S. Cunningham, *These Three Are One – The Practice of Trinitarian Theology* (Malden, MA, and Oxford, UK: Blackwell, 1998), Appendix 1, "Recent Works in Trinitarian Theology," pp. 339–42.

[9] See Cunningham, *These Three Are One*, p. ix.

[10] Sarah Coakley (ed.), "Introduction – Gender, Trinitarian Analogies, and the Pedagogy of *The Song*," *Re-Thinking Gregory of Nyssa* (Malden, MA, and Oxford, UK: Blackwell, 2003), [1–14], p. 2 (author's emphasis).

agreement may be the fuel of innovation, it must not paralyze application in the process.

Third, it is essential not to lose sight of the analogical character of any comparisons between human relations and the relations within the Persons of the Trinity. Unfortunately semi-popular theological writing reveals such a tendency. Scott Hahn's book on finding the family within the Trinity contains a chapter entitled "The God Who Is Family." Hahn claims "When God revealed His name, He revealed Himself fully – and He revealed Himself as family: as Father, Son, and Holy Spirit."[11] God for Hahn is the primordial Family, and real human families are so, only as they temporally resemble the primordial family that God eternally is. "God is not *like* a family. He *is* a family. From eternity, God alone possesses the essential attributes of a family, and the Trinity alone possess them in their perfection. Earthly households have these attributes, but only by analogy and imperfectly."[12] All traces of embodiment, sexuality and gender are expunged from how we are to think of the Trinity. There are no "masculine or feminine qualities within the Godhead," and "no bodily features of gender and sexuality in the Trinity." At most, "human forms of physicality and sexuality are reflections of the purely immaterial relations unique to each member of the Trinity. It is in the relations of the human family that the life of the Trinity is reflected more truly and fully than anywhere else in the natural order."[13]

I have drawn attention to Hahn's use of the Trinity/family analogy in order to indicate how the analogy can quickly become over-extended. While there is clear parental and filial imagery in the doctrine, there is no systematic exposition of the Trinity as a family within the Christian tradition. Pope John Paul II's discussions of the topic are more nuanced (below, 4.2). John Chrysostom urges parents to love their children as the Father loves the Son,[14] but that is far from believing the Trinity to be a family. The unity of the Three is expressed by words translated as "being," "essence," or "nature," not "family." Father, Son, and Spirit are Persons, or rather Relations, not brothers and sisters. If God is a family, it is hard to see how tritheism is to be avoided. Second, families are called "families" for historical reasons (above, 1:1), not because, within Christian theology, they replicate

---

[11] Scott Hahn, *First Comes Love: Finding Your Family in the Church and the Trinity* (London: Darton, Longman, and Todd, 2002), p. 42. He attributes this view to Pope John Paul II. The Holy Father, however, was considerably more subtle.

[12] Hahn, *First Comes Love*, p. 43.

[13] Hahn, *First Comes Love*, p. 138.

[14] Vigen Guroian, "The Ecclesial Family: John Chrysostom on Parenthood," in Marcia J. Bunge (ed.), *The Child in Christian Thought* (Grand Rapids, MI/Cambridge, UK: Eerdmans, 2001)[61–77], p. 64.

analogically and imperfectly the divine Family of God. Third, since relations within the Trinity are immaterial, whereas embodiment, sexuality, and gender permeate life together in real families, it is hard to see how the analogy is sustained. The perfect family, then, is neither sexed nor gendered. Hahn may wish to say (i) there are relations within God; (ii) there are relations between parents and children; (iii) there is a "communion of persons" or *communio personarum* both within the Triune God and within families; (iv) careful comparisons may be made between each set of relations, or *personae*, which are mutually illuminating; and, (v) within and beyond families, relations of human love may resemble relations of divine love, and even participate in it. All this may, can, and must, be fruitfully pursued, but without the claim that there is a divine Family. Further work remains to be done on the Trinity/family analogy before it is able to yield these results.

4.2 Love as a Relation

The Athanasian creed

Already then, there are three reasons for avoiding a theology of families that tries to build on the doctrine of the Trinity: unfamiliarity, disagreement, and the danger of false starts. But they must not be allowed to veto our explorations. Lack of familiarity must be addressed by patient exposition; disagreements can be left to the specialists; and false starts are made by eager runners who go on to win races. That said, there is much to commend setting as the start of any Trinitarian ethic the definition of the Trinity contained in the *Quicunque vult*[15] or Athanasian Creed. Here is part of it:

> And the Catholick Faith is this: That we worship one God in Trinity, and Trinity in Unity;
>   Neither confounding the Persons: nor dividing the Substance.
>   For there is one Person of the Father, another of the Son: and another of the Holy Ghost.
>   But the Godhead of the Father, of the Son, and of the Holy Ghost, is all one: the Glory equal, the Majesty co-eternal . . .
>   And in this Trinity none is afore, or after other: none is greater, or less than another;
>   But the whole three Persons are co-eternal together: and co-equal.

---

[15] Named after the first two words, "Whoever will . . ." Almost certainly not written by Athanasius, the earliest known copy of the creed was included in a preface to a collection of homilies by Caesarius of Arles (d. 542).

So that in all things, as is aforesaid: the Unity in Trinity, and the Trinity in Unity is to be worshipped.

He therefore that will be saved: must thus think of the Trinity.[16]

There is currently much discussion about the "Unity Model" (beginning with the Godhead or divine substance) and the "plurality model" or "social model" (beginning with the three Persons and moving from them to the one divine nature).[17] It is still conventional to suggest that the West, at least as typified by Augustine and Aquinas, favors various unity models, which all share the same psychological emphasis with God understood as a single person, whereas the East favors the social model and begins with the three *hypostaseis*, or Persons. We have seen how Coakley attempts to undermine some of these assumptions. But I have chosen the Athanasian Creed as my starting point for reflection on the Trinity *precisely because it does not require us to opt for one or the other, but to maintain both in tension with one another.* Let me explain.

The Creed maintains as an indispensable requirement for the Catholic faith that Christians "worship one God in Trinity, and Trinity in Unity." Now "one God in Trinity" and "Trinity in Unity" may not exactly map historical (and indeed contemporary) preferences for the unity model or the social model of the Godhead, but the Creed *does* map that difference sufficiently closely to suggest that something very like the unity and social models are required for thinking about God. The Catholic faith does not require one or the other, but both. It requires the worship of God who is one in Trinity, and Trinity in unity. The Creed licenses, indeed insists, that the God who is beyond knowledge and understanding must be thought of by means of both unity and social models. I am prepared to stipulate, if necessary, that that is how I will attempt to think of God in the remainder of this book. However, I think that much of the unfamiliarity with Trinitarian language and the use of this in Christian ethics, is due to the undoubted prominence in the West of the unity model. My use of the social model may help in a small way to counteract the overwhelming use of the unity model. But another reason for using the social model is that it helps us to think about the personal relations which constitute ourselves. In order to illustrate the point, I shall draw, not on the Cappadocian Fathers, but on a Western theologian, unjustly eclipsed by Thomas Aquinas, Richard of St Victor (d. 1173).

[16] From the *Book of Common Prayer* (1662), where it is appointed to be read (or sung) on certain feast days at Morning Prayer.

[17] A landmark in the discussion was David Brown's *The Divine Trinity* (London: Duckworth, 1985). See in particular p. 243.

Richard of St Victor

Richard utilizes the human experience of loving and being loved for the task of thinking about the God who is pure Love. This starting point is itself methodologically significant. Beginning with inter-personal love may be sharply contrasted with Augustine's use of reason and states of individual consciousness for his Trinitarian analogies. As Dennis Ngien aptly states, for Richard

> The effulgence of the divine is reflected in the creaturely phenomenon of loving. Interpersonal love is an analog of the Trinity. Instead of looking at the inner soul for his clues to the nature of God, Richard looks at human persons in relation. To penetrate into the inner life of the Trinity, he moves through human love to divine love, uniting these two poles, seeing in this union an interpenetration in experience. For in the perfection of human love, where one person transcends himself in the love of another, Richard sees a reflection of the infinite self-transcending love of the Trinitarian existence.[18]

In Richard's view love cannot keep itself to itself. Within God there can be no such thing as an *amor privatus*, for the obvious reason that love reaches out beyond itself to an other. Richard argues that God is supremely perfect, so that in the particular case of divine love, another divine Person is required who, unlike a human person, can perfectly love God in return and is an appropriate object for the divine Love. As Richard says

> as long as anyone loves no one else as much as he loves himself, that private love which he has for himself shows clearly that he has not reached the supreme level of charity. But a divine person certainly would not have anyone to love as worthily as Himself if He did not have a person of equal worth. However a person who is not God would not be equal in worth to a divine person.[19]

It is important to concentrate more on the vision of the Trinity that emerges from Richard's writings than on the particular historical argument for the threefoldness of the Persons which is a concern of the *De Trinitate*. So far Richard has arrived at a "binity" of Persons: only two are needed for mutuality, reciprocity, and equality to be established. A third Person, however, is needed to avoid the possible mutual absorption and complacency

---

[18] Dennis Ngien, "Richard of St Victor's Condilectus: The Spirit as Co-Beloved," *European Journal of Theology*, 12.2, 2003 [77–92], p. 79.

[19] Grover A. Zinn (tr. and Introduction), *Richard of St Victor* (New York: Paulist Press, 1979), p. 375: cited in Ngien, "Richard of St Victor's Condilectus," p. 81.

that could afflict the couple. As Ngien explains, "selfishness or complacency may surface in the mutual love of only two persons, and only when a third is introduced into a circle of love is love perfected."[20] Richard observes "in mutual love that is very fervent there is nothing rarer, nothing more excellent, than that you wish another to be equally loved by him whom you love supremely and by whom you are supremely loved."[21] The Spirit is the *condilectus*, the One with whom the other two Persons share their love. "Shared love is properly said to exist when a third person is loved by two persons harmoniously and in community, and the affection of the two persons is fused into one affection by the flame of love for the third."[22]

Richard's analogy from human to divine inter-personal love moves from self-love to other-love and thence to shared love. The Holy Spirit is not the mutual love between Father and Son, but the co-Beloved of them both. We cannot stop to consider Richard's ingenious account of the processions of the Persons, nor whether, having posited a single *condilectus*, he ought to posit some greater number of Persons than just three, according to the same premises. Nor can we pursue the implications of Marilyn McCord Adams' provocative treatment of Richard's Trinitarianism as an intimate community of same-sex lovers.[23] Richard gives us a profound and highly illuminating account of the "Trinity in Unity" which resonates well with the themes of this book and complements the more familiar "Unity in Trinity." I agree with Ngien's conclusion that this social view of the Trinity

> has profound implication (*sic*) for understanding humanity, in view of which human personhood is not to be understood in purely individualistic terms, but in concrete, communitarian, and relational terms. That which defines personhood is indeed its reciprocity and relationship. Divine existence, thus, is the ideal of personal existence.[24]

The "big shift": from attitude to relation

We will therefore take forward several features of Richard's doctrine of the Trinity to our theology of families (while refusing to be side-tracked by

[20] Ngien, "Richard of St Victor's Condilectus," p. 82.
[21] Zinn, *Richard of St Victor*, p. 384.
[22] Zinn, *Richard of St Victor*, p. 392.
[23] Marilyn McCord Adams, "Trinitarian Friendship: Same-Gender Models of Godly Love in Richard of St Victor and Aelred of Rievaulx," in Eugene F. Rogers, Jr (ed.), *Theology and Sexuality* (Malden, MA, and Oxford, UK: Blackwell, 2002), pp. 322–42.
[24] Ngien, "Richard of St Victor's Condilectus," p. 88.

other, open issues, such as: Can the ancient *persona* and *hypostasis* be translated "person"?[25] Is the "immanent" Trinity the "economic" Trinity?). First, and in accordance with 1 John 4, God is Love: God is Love in God's own nature or essence. Second, the method for thinking about God is to begin *both* with God's own self-revelation through Christ and the Spirit, *and* with the human experience of love. Third, love is inter-personal: love cannot be love without relation. Indeed love *is* a relation. The basis of families for Christian thought has to be a sharing in the inter-Personal love of God.[26] The unique contribution that theology is able to make to the practice of family life is to deploy this theological vision of divine love, stress its availability to people of all faiths and none, and proclaim it as an alternative to the imitation of particular historical family forms, especially patriarchal ones.

There is a considerable implication which has not so far been adequately noticed with regard to the notion of love that is integral to descriptions of God, of divine and human persons, communion, and so on. This is what I have called elsewhere "the big shift," i.e., the shift from understanding love as a quality or a virtue, to love as itself a relation.[27] The rediscovery of the person as a person-in-relation assisted in the renascence of the doctrine of the Trinity in the final quarter of the twentieth century. I am awaiting *a similar transformation of the concept of love*, i.e., from love as a property inhering in a subject, to love as the quality of a relation *between* subjects. This is what I mean by the "big shift." In the doctrine of the Trinity there is no need for a shift, for love is the relation between the subjects already.

Within the diverse interpretations of love in Christian thought there is likely to be agreement that love is the property or quality of a subject, human or divine. It is often described as an "attitude." As such it has a subject, the agent who expresses the attitude, and an object of the attitude, which may or may not be another person. As an attitude it is a property of an agent who displays it in his or her actions. Love is the supreme Christian attitude, a virtue which we realize fully only with the help of God. The difficulty I am raising with this basic understanding of love is not that it is wrong, but that it is one-sided, and that the other side is rarely, if ever, put. The alternative approach to love is as a relation, where both lover and beloved are equally subject, and love is the relation between them.

[25] David Cunningham thinks not. See his *These Three Are One*, pp. 26–9.
[26] See Karl Rahner, "Experience of Self and Experience of God," *Theological Investigations*, 13 (New York: Crossroad, 1974), p. 128.
[27] Adrian Thatcher, *Marriage after Modernity: Christian Marriage in Postmodern Times* (Sheffield, UK: Sheffield Academic Press, and New York: New York University Press, 1999), pp. 225–8.

Balance may be restored to Christian treatments of the concept of love by seeing love as a quality of the relation between the lover and who or what is loved. So an anonymous act of love toward a beneficiary may be capable of being understood as embracing donor and recipient. More importantly and simply, loving partnerships between people also *require* to be treated as a relation. For example, when marital breakdown occurs, both accounts of love may be needed to make phenomenological sense of the breakdown, that is, one partner may continue to love the other, but since the other no longer loves, love continues as an attitude (of one of the partners) and terminates as a relation (between the two of them). Under these circumstances it is hard to see how a marriage can survive (whether or not it ends in divorce).[28]

The big shift is further suggested by the renewed emphasis on the social Trinity. The image of the God who loves the world (and sends the Son) should not be allowed to suggest a one-sided picture of a single divine Subject or Individual, who possesses the virtue of love *modo proprio*, and because of which the world is redeemed. The communion of the Three suggests a different but complementary picture. God *is* Love, and the Relations within God constitute the divine Communion. Human relations are offered a participation in the divine Relations. Families offer the possibility of relations of love which also convey the Love that God is. There are fairly obvious links to be pursued between the social model of the Trinity, the relational concept of the self, and the configuration of love as the dynamics of personal relations, instead of being a property of one of the relation's subjects.

There are obvious theological gaps that the relational concept of love can fill. It helps to make sense of the enigmatic "God is love" without resorting to abstractions. God is no "Individual with attitude": rather is God the mutual love of Persons for one another in a communion where each is also distinct. The relational concept of love restores to love the ontological primacy that properly belongs to it. If love is an attitude of an individual subject, it is related to it as a property to an individual. The individual is clearly primary – the subject with a property. If love is a relation, then love is primary, embracing both subjects. Love, then, belongs fundamentally to being. It is not a mere property that a subject might possess or lack. Relational love is phenomenologically necessary in explicating human love: it is fundamental also to the love that is divine communion.

---

[28] On the issue of the necessary limitations of our commitments, even our marital commitments, see Margaret Farley's perspicuous "Marriage, Divorce, and Personal Commitments," in Adrian Thatcher (ed.), *Celebrating Christian Marriage* (Edinburgh and New York: T&T Clark, 2002), pp. 355–72.

4.2 Families and the Trinity

Karl Barth and domination

Karl Barth discusses parent–child relationships in the light of the relations within the Trinity.[29] His treatment of them has been called "perhaps the finest theological discussion of parenting available in the English language."[30] The discussion is complex, and woven into the grander themes of Barth's theology, so I will select particular elements of it, all of which have a bearing on his use (inconsistent, I will urge) of the doctrine of the Trinity. Care will also be needed to respect his dialectical method for dealing with these matters: what looks to be a clear statement of his view can turn out to be controverted later. First, parents act *in loco dei*. "From the standpoint of children parents have a Godward aspect, and are for them God's primary and natural representatives."[31] God is Father of all, but the being and acting of human parents corresponds finitely to the being and acting of the infinite God who is and acts as Father to "His" people. It follows, second, that being a father ("fatherhood") is always secondary to and derives from God's absolute Fatherhood. "No human father, but God alone, is properly, truly and primarily Father . . . But it is of this Father's grace that, in correspondence to His own, there should exist a human fatherhood also."[32] On the basis of the Hebrew scriptures Barth can say "human fatherhood is set alongside and compared with the incomparable fatherhood of God, and human parents stand in the light of this analogy. It is this which entitles them to receive honor from their children."[33]

Our primary interest is in the analogy that Barth draws between divine and human parenthood, and, as might be expected, it derives directly from the being and action of God in Christ. So, third, there is an analogy of relation, an *analogia relationis*, between a human father and his children, and the divine Father and "His" children. There is a

> relationship of primary to secondary, of God to his creatures, being reflected in the relationships among his creatures . . . It has a real basis in our being-in-

---

[29] Karl Barth, *Church Dogmatics* III/4 (Edinburgh: T&T Clark, 1961), Chapter XII, section 54, part 2.

[30] Gary W. Deddo, *Karl Barth's Theology of Relations – Trinitarian, Christological, and Human: Towards an Ethic of the Family* (New York: Peter Lang, 1999), p. xv.

[31] Barth, *Church Dogmatics*, III/4, p. 245.

[32] Barth, *Church Dogmatics*, III/4, p. 245.

[33] Barth, *Church Dogmatics*, III/4, p. 246.

relation to God's own being-in-relation. This, of course, is not only revealed but made actual, i.e. takes ontological shape, in Jesus Christ. Thus, parents only represent or bear witness to this deeper actual truth. They are not, in their relationships, identical to it.[34]

God's fatherly relation to the people of God is transformed by God being Father also to the Son. The identification of God the Son with us enables God's Fatherhood to be shared among all people as brothers and sisters of Jesus Christ. Christians then experience God's Fatherhood primarily through Jesus Christ for whom God is supremely Father, while they are the brothers and sisters of Christ in the family of Church. Fourth, for Barth, the divine–human relation is always primary (the *analogans* or what makes the analogy): the parent–child relation is always secondary (the *analogatum* or what is analogized). The direction of the analogy is vertical and downwards, from divine to human, and is deliberately asymmetrical. The direction of the parent–child relation is both vertically downwards (parents command; children obey), *and* horizontal, parents and children alike are creatures, all under the authority of God. God commands: we obey. Parents command: children obey. God has authority over God's children: parents have authority over their children.

There are three further elements of Barth's discussion of parenthood relevant to any theology of families: the highly hierarchical framework within which family relations are conducted; the problem for his theology of poor or abusive parenting; and his extraordinary use of the eschaton in relation to filial disobedience. So, fifth, the hierarchical framework, already noted, is sustained by a narrative of dominance and submission which Barth locates both in the relation of adults to God and of children to parents. The vocabulary of relations within the Barthian family is striking. "Children are directed to assume a very definite attitude of subordination in relation to their parents."[35] The children "are invited to adopt this attitude," and "must be content to accept this leading from their parents." Children are to be "challenged to submit themselves," and if they resist their parents they resist the grace of God.[36] Parents have a "superiority," a "seniority," an "authority,"[37] which children must honor. Children are also responsible "to Him who as the true and proper Father is also the true and proper Commander before whom the child is answerable." A young child "will need simply to

[34] Deddo, *Karl Barth's Theology of Relations*, p. 199.
[35] Barth, *Church Dogmatics*, III/4, p. 243.
[36] Barth, *Church Dogmatics*, III/4, p. 245.
[37] Barth, *Church Dogmatics*, III/4, pp. 246–7.

accept as such the instruction and guidance offered by its parents and therefore to heed and obey their words literally."[38] Such instruction will direct the child to the "higher court" of God, and adolescents are required to accept "uncomplainingly" the "heteronomy" of their parents.[39]

It will be obvious, sixth, that poor or abusive parenting will not fit well into this hierarchical scheme. Barth concedes there are "weak, foolish, self-seeking, flippant and tyrannical parents,"[40] but, however bad they are, a grown child cannot be dispensed "from a faithful observance of the command, since it is not within his competence absolutely and definitively to decide that they are failures and nothing but failures in regard to their duty as parents."[41] Children may be entertaining "illusions" about the failures of their parents. Children are "in no event authorised to make a judgment upon them." But what "if a man really cannot rid himself of the impression that his parents have failed in their duty"?

> The answer is plain and immediate. They must see to it that they for their part make good that which in the behaviour of their parents they rightly or wrongly regard as less good. They must see to it that in so doing they remember their place and preserve their humility. And they must also see to it that, if their human parents really fail, their heavenly Father becomes all the greater, dearer and more authoritative.[42]

Finally Barth asks what happens if someone receives a call from the heavenly Father, and the earthly father disagrees with the call, causing a crisis of obedience? Predictably enough, the heavenly Father is to be obeyed: less predictably is the reason given. At the eschaton and in eternity obedience will no longer be required. When all is restored, obedience will no longer be necessary. The call from God represents a prolepsis of the end times and obviates the obligation of obedience to the earthly father.[43]

Barth is right to say, sin notwithstanding, that parents represent God to their children. They are the principal human agents of God's divine care for them. This, so far, is a structure for families written into any monotheistic view of the world. Assuming God's will is for children to flourish, who else is better able to ensure it, given the right social and economic environment, than parents? Welcome too is the Christological transformation of the

[38] Barth, *Church Dogmatics*, III/4, p. 253.
[39] Barth, *Church Dogmatics*, III/4, p. 254.
[40] Barth, *Church Dogmatics*, III/4, p. 255.
[41] Barth, *Church Dogmatics*, III/4, p. 257.
[42] Barth, *Church Dogmatics*, III/4, pp. 255–6.
[43] Barth, *Church Dogmatics*, III/4, pp. 258–65.

symbol "Father." While "Father" was a common name for God among the Jews at the time of Jesus, the Son makes clear who the Father is. I concur with Barth's grounding of parent–child relations in the Trinitarian relations, and in the use of the device of *analogia relationis* in order to set these relations out. But after these agreements, points of disagreement unfortunately pile up.

We might begin with the insistence that fatherhood is derived from God's incomparable fatherhood. In an important sense everything derives from God: in practice, human parents derive their parenting skills from attending to their children. They may pray to the heavenly Father to be loving and wise parents, and if they try to love their children as God loves the world, they will doubtless please God. But those desired outcomes are unlikely to be realized if their exercise of parenting is secondary in *any* sense. The *analogia relationis* is unidirectional, flowing from greater to lesser, solidifying the asymmetry on both sides of the relation. The analogy reinforces hierarchies, divine–human, and parent–child, whereas the prospect of a non-hierarchical, reciprocal set of relationships, grounded in and inspired by the Trinity is passed over.

Barth's analysis of human fatherhood is heavily influenced by the Household Codes. Our principles for family-friendly readings of scripture (above, 2.3) suggest a hermeneutic for moving beyond them. Indeed the language of domination and submission, however qualified, is best left in the pagan world of New Testament times. If this section of the *Church Dogmatics* were shown to a children's welfare officer, or a professional social worker, they would surely be appalled that the section was ever written, and still more appalled that it continues to be believed and practiced among Christians today. Of course, Barth knew less when he wrote it about the sheer scale of parental cruelty to children, and we know more than he did about the fatal contribution of patriarchal, masculinist theology to the abuse of children.[44] A fresh start is needed in thinking through parent–child relations, by means of a different paradigm.

Similar worries attend Barth's recommendations to children whose parents have failed them. To accuse a child of entertaining illusions about bad parenting is to invite the child, who may have insuperable difficulties in getting adults to believe him or her, to doubt or disbelieve their own shocking testimony. What psychological scars may await those adults seeking to "make good that which in the behavior of their parents they rightly or wrongly regard as less good"? The path from cruelty by a human father to

---

[44] See, for example, Janet Pais, *Suffer the Children: A Theology of Liberation by a Victim of Abuse* (New York/Mahwah, NJ: Paulist Press, 1991); Hilary Cashman, *Christianity and Child Sexual Abuse* (London: SPCK, 1993).

the dearer love of the heavenly Father is a tortuous one even for those who are prepared to tread it. The possibility of abuse aside, a further problem runs through the section. Barth lays on children the capacity and the obligation to work out for themselves that they are in all cases to submit to their parents as the command of God. In this he assumes a maturity of thought (and of faith?) that children simply do not have. He does not honor their "childness" (above, 3.1). Rather he "adultizes" them by ascribing to them the prudential power to work out that submission to parents is in their interests and what God requires.

In the light of the dominance–submission framework of both sets of relations it is clear why the conflict of obedience remains a problem for Barth. But his solution, that the call from the final Reign of God neutralizes filial obedience, is surely capable of extension. If the breaking-in of God's call or of God's reign to a daughter or son overrides filial obedience, then presumably God's reign is actualized in the prevention of all mistreatment of, or cruelty to, children? And, in that case, the entire framework of compliance and obedience is undermined whenever mistreatment is rightly questioned.

So despite the enormous influence of Barth on twentieth-century theology, I think Richard of St Victor's model of the Trinity is more useful to theology in the present day. His starting point is human love, and he finds divine Love in its depths. There is divine Love between the Persons, which because of its desire to share itself, issues in the *condilectus* by means of whom the creative, reciprocal Love of the Persons is realized and more widely shared. Here is the Trinity without the heavy masculine bias, without the asymmetry of relation, and we might add, without the pneumatological deficiency. The Spirit perfects the circle of love which the other Persons have for one another, providing a powerful analogy which in the human case unites the parents in the love for their child. We shall probe these distinctions further in chapter 7. The difficulties we have uncovered in Barth's *analogia relationis* do not require the abandonment of his method. But they do require a different model of divine *and* human relations, based instead on mutuality and reciprocity.

Pope John Paul II and communion

Our second example of a theologian who draws an analogy between the human family and the divine Trinity is the late Pope John Paul II. In his writings and talks, the Pope drew many times, before and after his papal election, on section 24 of *Gaudium et Spes*: "Indeed, the Lord Jesus, when He prayed to the Father, 'that all may be one . . . as we are one' (John

17:21–2) opened up vistas closed to human reason, for He implied a certain likeness between the union of the divine Persons, and the unity of God's sons in truth and charity."[45] Mary Shivanandan describes how the passage opened up new horizons even for the Pope himself in his intention to speak "in a new way to contemporary married couples."[46] The same text teaches that people resemble God in their "spiritual *and* social nature,"[47] and not simply in their individualities or souls. People are made for communion (*communio*) with one another, and in this respect they image the Triune God whose being is Communion. *Communio* is not specifically reserved for marriage, but is one of the terms used to describe it. While still Cardinal Wojtyła, the Pope wrote "Christ himself suggests to us this resemblance, or metaphysical analogy, as we may call it between God as person and community (i.e., the communion of Persons in the unity of the Godhead), on the one hand and, on the other, man as a person and his vocation towards the community."[48] These reflections were developed in The Wednesday Catecheses[49] and elsewhere, until a developed Trinitarian "anthropology," embracing marriage and the family, is expressed in e.g., *Familiaris consortio*, *Mulieris dignitatem*, and *Letter to Families*.[50]

In *Familiaris consortio* there is a direct vertical relation between communion in God and communion among the beings who are created in God's image.

> "God is love" and in himself he lives a mystery of personal loving communion. Creating the human race in his own image and continually keeping it in being, God inscribed in the humanity of man and woman the vocation, and thus the capacity and responsibility, of love and communion. Love is therefore the fundamental and innate vocation of every human being.[51]

---

[45] The quotation is from *Gaudium et Spes* (1965), section 24. www.vatican.va/archive/hist_councils/ii_vatican_council/documents/vat-ii_cons_19651207_gaudium-et-spes_en.html. Accessed 02.09.2006.

[46] Mary Shivanandan, *Crossing the Threshold of Love – A New Vision of Marriage* (Edinburgh: T&T Clark, 1999), p. 78.

[47] Shivanandan, *Crossing the Threshold of Love*, p. 79.

[48] Shivanandan, *Crossing the Threshold of Love*, p. 79, n. 36, citing Karol Wojtyła, *Sources of Renewal: The Implementation of the Second Vatican Council* (tr. P.S. Falla) (San Francisco, CA: Harper and Row, 1980), pp. 61–2.

[49] Subsequently published as *The Theology of the Body according to John Paul II: Human Law in the Divine Plan* (Boston, MA: Pauline Books, 1997): see Shivanandan, *Crossing the Threshold of Love*, p. 94.

[50] Shivanandan, *Crossing the Threshold of Love*, p. 94.

[51] *Familiaris consortio*, section 11, "Man, the Image of the God who is Love."

While marriage is not necessary to the purposes for which God created us, communion is. Communion is an inclusive human vocation: marriage is a particular and intense form of communion; and so is the family. The *Catechism of the Catholic Church* describes the Christian family as "a communion of persons, a sign and image of the communion of the Father and the Son in the Holy Spirit."[52] In the *Letter to Families* the family is explicitly

> a community of persons whose proper way of existing and living together is a communion: *communio personarum*. Here too, while always acknowledging the absolute transcendence of the Creator with regard to his creatures, we can see the family's ultimate relationship to the divine "We." Only persons are capable of living "in communion." The family originates in a marital communion described by the Second Vatican Council as a "covenant," in which man and woman "give themselves to each other and accept each other."[53]

These are the fundamental values, derived from the very being of Godself, that "constitute the foundation of the institution of the family" (above, 1.3). There can be no doubt that the personalism of John Paul II developed earlier forms of Catholic personalistic philosophy[54] and brought them to a wider and more general audience. In this history is likely to see him as a genuine innovator. Recent criticisms of his personalism come to nothing (below, 8.2). The problem for papal personalism is its uneasy synthesis with other areas of Catholic moral thought about persons. It is hard to see how, if marriage is a communion, it continues indissolubly when the communion no longer exists. Again, a community of persons modeled by "the divine 'We'" cannot permit gender hierarchy or androcentrism, for, as we noted earlier, "in this Trinity none is afore, or after other: none is greater, or less than another; But the whole three Persons are co-eternal together: and co-equal." And since some persons clearly enjoy personal communion with other persons of the same sex, and the Persons in God are not sexed, the proscription of homosexual relations becomes harder still to defend. But our present concern is with families and children so these matters are not pursued here.[55]

---

[52] *Catechism of the Catholic Church* (London: Geoffrey Chapman, 1994), section 2205.
[53] John Paul II, *Letter to Families*, section 7, "The Marital Covenant" (author's emphases). The quotation is from *Gaudium et Spes*, section 48.
[54] For example, the work of Dietrich von Hildebrand and Heribert Doms.
[55] See Adrian Thatcher, "Marriage and Love: Too Much of a 'Breakthrough'?," *INTAMS Review*, 8.1, 2002, pp. 44–54.

4.3 The Gift of a Child

Richard of St Victor's handling of the doctrine of the Trinity connects mutual love with fruitfulness or fertility. It indicates that love is generative. The human experience which provides the materials for thinking about the Trinity is, in part, a realization of the limits of coupled love, however mutual, until each party shares his or her love more widely with a "third." The analogy does not require that the "third" is a child, but if it is, and its identity derives directly from his or her biological parents, then it is the expression of their love. And the one "flame of love" for the child enriches both the child and the mutuality of the couple's love.

Another fruitful way of linking the having of children with the encompassing of the divine Trinity is through the notion of "the gift."[56] Let us notice, first, how the language of giving and receiving is linked liturgically to the experience of having children; second, how, according to some theological analysis, the practice of giving is corrupted in modern societies; and third, how the restoration of giving, which is our salvation, is located in the divine Life. Christians acknowledge that life itself is a gift from God. The Son is God's gift to the world (Jn. 3:16), and the Christian virtues are the gifts of the Spirit (Gal. 5:22). Prayers of thanksgiving are appropriate responses to God's gifts: indeed the Christian life itself is plausibly described as the state of "being-in-gratitude."[57] The language of the gift is prominent liturgically in the marriage service. Couples who marry[58] pray that the Holy Spirit will pour into their hearts "that most excellent gift of love." They hear in the Preface that marriage is "a gift of God in creation;" and that "The gift of marriage brings husband and wife together in the delight and tenderness of sexual union and joyful commitment to the end of their lives." They may thank God in prayer "for your gift of sexual love,"[59] as well as for its fruitfulness ("by your gracious gift the human family is increased").[60] The priest may ask for "the gift of children" which they receive as a blessing ("Bless

---

[56] A similar approach is taken by Todd Whitmore. See Todd David Whitmore (with Tobias Winwright), "Children: An Undeveloped Theme in Catholic Teaching," in Maura A. Ryan and Todd David Whitmore (eds.), *The Challenge of Global Stewardship: Roman Catholic Responses* (Notre Dame, IN: University of Notre Dame Press, 1997), pp. 161–85.

[57] McFadyen, *The Call to Personhood*, p. 21.

[58] At least according to the Marriage Service of the Church of England's *Common Worship*. www.cofe.anglican.org/worship/liturgy/commonworship/texts/marriage.html. Accessed 02.09.2006. Most, if not all, marriage liturgies use language of this kind.

[59] Common Worship Marriage Service, Additional Prayer 14.

[60] Common Worship Marriage Service, Additional Prayer 24.

this couple with the gift and care of children").[61] The introduction to the special non-baptismal service of Thanksgiving for the *Gift* of a Child (which may also be used publicly or privately on the occasion of the adoption of children) observes how "many people are overcome by a sense of awe at the creation of new life and want to express their thanks to God."[62] The parents must answer the question "Do you receive these children as a gift from God?," and in thanksgiving they pray "God our creator, we thank you for the gift of these children."

The language of giving and giving thanks is fundamental to the church's liturgies and is particularly apposite in the case of the marriage service, where marriage itself, sex, love, and the expression of shared human love in the birth and care of children are all enveloped within it. Children, says Pope John Paul II, are a "priceless gift."[63]But there is a strong case for saying that we who live in late modern societies may largely have forgotten what is involved in giving and receiving. John Milbank plans a series of works where "the gift" is basic.[64] Creation, grace, and incarnation are gifts, whereas the fall, evil, and violence are refusals of God's gifts, requiring atonement as "the renewed and hyperbolic gift that is forgiveness."[65] Our loss of understanding of gift may be due to certain major developments in Western thought, or as Stephen Webb avers, to the invasive and insidious effects of economic models of the person upon our self-understanding (which amounts to the same thing). Webb thinks our present "linguistic climate" may make giving unreinstatable, and that is because "modern Western culture has undertaken a prolonged and massive rehabilitation of the terms egoism and selfishness, while the very purity of the ideas of altruism and sacrifice has become the easy target of ridicule and rejection." In this climate "the logic of economics has successfully colonized and thus presently regulates what can and cannot be said about giving," so that even talk of responsibility and reciprocity in giving "more likely permits the cunning of self-interest to dominate every social interaction."[66] If our experience of giving and receiving has been so

---

[61] Common Worship Marriage Service, Additional Prayer 4.

[62] *Common Worship*: "Thanksgiving for the Gift of a Child." www.cofe.anglican.org/worship/liturgy/commonworship/texts/initiation/thanksgiftchild.html. Accessed 02.09.2006.

[63] Pope John Paul II, *Letter to Families*, 9.

[64] The first of these is *Being Reconciled: Ontology and Pardon* (New York and London: Routledge, 2003). See also his "Can a Gift Be Given? Prolegomena to a Future Trinitarian Metaphysic," *Modern Theology*, 11.1 (January 1995), pp. 119–62.

[65] Tracey Rowland, "Divine Gifts to the Secular Desert," *Reviews in Religion and Theology*, 11.2, April 2004 [182–8], p. 182.

[66] Stephen Webb, *The Gifting God: A Trinitarian Ethics of Excess* (New York: Oxford University Press, 1996), p. 7.

seriously corrupted, the metaphorical value of speaking of children as gifts may also have been seriously damaged. Perhaps that is why there is more than a suggestion of cliché conveyed by the phrase? We shall pursue what Bonnie Miller-McLemore calls "the market-driven eclipse of children as gift"[67] (below, 8.4). At present we will remain with metaphysics, in an attempt to regain a more primordial sense of giving. But the metaphysics has a particular practical point: to help us to appreciate the wondrous gift of children.

In the metaphysics of John-Luc Marion, giving precedes being. When I wrote *The Ontology of Paul Tillich* back in 1978, I was then prepared to hold, albeit critically, to a version of Tillich's fundamental *dictum* that God is Being, or Being itself. "What ontology calls 'being-itself', theology calls 'God'. The relation between ontology and theology is to be elaborated in two separate approaches to the same putative reality, being-itself or God."[68] Whatever the merits of this accommodation (or John Macquarrie's use of Martin Heidegger's thought in refining it),[69] Marion savages all theology and metaphysics that obscures that God is first of all, and prior to all attributions, *Giving*. When Marion distinguishes between the biblical God and the God of metaphysics, he puts a "ø" or cross through the "o" of the word "God" in order to distinguish between iconic and idolatrous uses of that Name. No word, especially not the word "God," can bring to thought the One beyond all thought. But this One beyond all thought is not apprehended or reinstated according to some version of the ancient *via negativa*. What is unthinkable rather is the outpouring of love for us upon the Cross. Marion asks "does the name of the Gød, who is crossed because he is crucified, belong to the domain of Being? . . . We are speaking of the Gød who is crossed by a cross because he reveals himself by his placement on a Cross, the Gød revealed by, in, and as the Christ."[70]

The crossing out of the word "God" is also "the 'crossing' of being," or the erasure of all speculation or ontologizing about being. This is dissipated by the light of Christ's sacrificial death. It is the elimination of all metaphysical speculations by and in favor of the God who gives Godself in Christ.

---

[67] Bonnie J. Miller-McLemore, *Let the Children Come: Reimagining Childhood from a Christian Perspective* (San Francisco, CA: Jossey-Bass, 2003), p. 88.

[68] Adrian Thatcher, *The Ontology of Paul Tillich* (Oxford, UK: Oxford University Press, 1978), pp. 161–2.

[69] John Macquarrie, *Principles of Christian Theology* (London: SCM Press, 1966).

[70] Jean-Luc Marion, *God Without Being* (tr. Thomas A. Carlson) (Chicago, IL, and London: University of Chicago Press, 1991), p. 71.

Metaphysicians ancient and modern have used God's revelation to Moses in Exodus 3:14 ("I Am That I Am") in order to found ontological language within the text of the Bible. Marion asks

> whether the name indirectly implied by Exodus 3:14 inevitably precedes other names, like the one that 1 John 4:8 insinuates, ho theos agape estin, "God is love" . . . What makes God God is loving, not being, and even if Exodus 3:14 did deliver "one of the divine names," we still would have to determine whether it is a question of the first. No exegesis, philological fact, no objective inquiry could accomplish or justify this step; only a theological decision could do so.[71]

We have already noted the Parable of the Prodigal Father as a powerful biblical model of fatherhood (above, 3.1). Marion makes much of the fact that the term *ousia* or "being," which appears in only one passage in the New Testament, occurs twice in this parable. The son demands "Father, give me my share of the property (*ousia*)" (Lk. 15:12). Jesus narrates how the share is turned into cash, and the son then dissipates his goods (*ousia*). Marion's mischievous meditation on this parable leads him to comment on the disposability of "being." The son wanted possession of his "goods." He was not content to receive them as a gift but to demand them as an entitlement. But this exegesis of the parable serves, of course, another teasing agenda: the priority of love over being, and the dissipation of ontotheology by the divine love that gives and for-gives. *Ousia* in the parable "is inscribed in the play of donation, abandon, and pardon," and these contrast absolutely with being or beings. "The gift is the primary category that orients all our living."[72] "*The gift delivers Being/being.*"[73] Whereas for Tillich there was an infinite difference between God and the "God above God," for Marion the infinite difference is between God or Being and the God who "strictly does not have to be, nor therefore to receive the name of a being, whatever it may be. *God gives.* The giving, in allowing to be divined how 'it gives,' a giving, offers the only accessible trace of He who gives."[74]

Many criticisms might be made of Marion's prioritization of giving over being. Even gifts must be. The Crucified Christ does most certainly belong to the domain of being. Neither does God reveal Godself without a name. Despite these reservations I think Marion's analysis valuably enables us to recover what is most fundamental to the Christian understanding of life, and

---

[71] Marion, *God Without Being*, p. 74.
[72] Marion, *God Without Being*, p. 100.
[73] Marion, *God Without Being*, p. 101 (author's emphasis).
[74] Marion, *God Without Being*, p. 105 (author's emphasis).

of the world: they are gifts before they are analyzable in any other terms such as the natural and human sciences provide. Since the Word made flesh has priority over the written word of the Bible (principle 1, above, 2.3), it has greater priority still over metaphysics. We wanted to say something more about "the gift of a child." Marion enables this even though children do not appear in his metaphysics. That is because he foregrounds "givenness" over all of our other, derived apprehensions. A child is not bought, not possessed, is not an object, does not exist for another's end. Of all the gifts the Giving God gives, surely the gift of a child is supremely the greatest, next to the gift of one's life-partner, and of life itself. The wonder and joy at the birth of a child is confirmation of the givenness of all things along with the child. Such joy, the second of the Spirit's "fruits" after love, is given phenomenological articulation by means of this mischievous metaphysic. And that joy of course is the fundamental human experience by which God's own self-revelation enters human thinking. It is the joy of the angels, the shepherds and the *magoi* in the Christmas story. The giving God has given the Son.

The "gifting" God

There is, then, something of a theological treasury for thinking about our children which is rarely deployed in contemporary theological discussion about families and children. Another resource is the combination of a theology of the gift with a Trinitarian understanding of the Giving, or rather, the "Gifting" God. The Father is "God the Giver," the Son is "God the Given," the Spirit is "God the Giving." So argues Stephen Webb. His concern in *The Gifting God* is with the transformation of economic life, but much of his analysis of the Trinitarian dynamics of giving is applicable to the dynamics of families too. "Gifting," an admitted neologism, stands for the giving that makes further giving possible:

> God makes possible our giving by an activity that precedes, surpasses, and sustains all of our gifts. God's special economy provides a contour that shapes and empowers our own antieconomic acts. I have chosen to call this process, by God's giving and our own, *gifting*, in an attempt to synthesize both the activity of giving, its verbal form, and the idea that giving begins with a prior giving and with something already given, its nominative form. The neologism *gifting* should remind us that the gift precedes and empowers giving, and that giving is always in response to a prior gift.[75]

---

[75] Webb, *The Gifting God*, p. 93.

But this analysis of gifting quickly issues in a Trinitarian dynamic into which all the people of God are summoned. "God the Giver" is Father.[76] "God the Given," following Barth and Marion, is Jesus. "God's giving in Jesus Christ makes sense of all of God's other gifts; this gift, then, orders and organizes God's giving." In Christ, Webb writes, "we have a Christian version of squandering, a lavishing that both shocks and consoles."[77] Webb, like Richard of St Victor, takes issue with the narrowness of the classical doctrine of the Holy Spirit as the mutual love between Father and Son. God the Giving inspires further giving. The work of the Spirit is to take the gift of the Son, and inspire those who receive the gift into acts of further giving. The Spirit thereby inspires further love and completes the work of the gifting God Who, in giving, inspires the giving of further gifts. Webb claims the authority of Aquinas for his account of the Spirit. "Aquinas is reaching toward the idea that God is the First Giver, not in the sense of causing all other giving but in the sense that God gives the love that is the action of the gift . . . The Spirit is of God and ourselves, belonging only to the dissemination that is grace."[78]

The gift *of a child* is one of God the Giver's greatest gifts. Parents who receive the gift of a child joyfully are, by that very experience, better able to understand the central claim of Christian faith. For God the Son is also a gift. God the Son is God the Given. The gift of a child to parents calls forth an endless response of freely-given love. This too, is Giving, in response to the Gift. There are several other ways in which parents can locate their mutual loving, conceiving, birthing, and nurturing in the life of the life-giving God, who generates, processes, inspires: who is Giver, Given, and Giving. The Trinitarian insights we have collected in this chapter cry out for application in our task of a theology for families. We will come to that in Part II.

God the Child

There is, of course, another equally important, equally central doctrine vital to the construction of family theology: the incarnation of God in Christ, or, still more specifically, in the Christ Child. To contemplate the Christ Child is to move away from the teaching of Jesus about children into different territory: to the theological fact that God became a Child in Christ Jesus and

---

[76] Webb, *The Gifting God*, p. 91.
[77] Webb, *The Gifting God*, pp. 141–2.
[78] Webb, *The Gifting God*, p. 155.

to its implications. Once again Pope John Paul II applies classic Christian doctrine in his concern for families. At the start of his *Letter to Families* he writes

> The only-begotten Son, of one substance with the Father, "God from God and Light from Light," entered into human history through the family: "For by his incarnation the Son of God united himself in a certain way with every man. He laboured with human hands . . . and loved with a human heart. Born of Mary the Virgin, he truly became one of us and, except for sin, was like us in every respect." If in fact Christ "fully discloses man to himself," he does so beginning with the family in which he chose to be born and to grow up. We know that the Redeemer spent most of his life in the obscurity of Nazareth, "obedient" (Lk 2:51) as the "Son of Man" to Mary his Mother, and to Joseph the carpenter.
>
> The divine mystery of the Incarnation of the Word thus has an intimate connection with the human family. Not only with one family, that of Nazareth, but in some way with every family . . .[79]

This is of course standard Christian teaching. John Paul allows that Jesus may have been shaped by his family. He is clear that there is an "intimate connection" with the human family and with every family. But what, more precisely, is this connection, and how is it to be understood?

For Herbert Anderson and Susan Johnson, the connection is that "In the birth of the Christ child, God took on all the powerlessness, weakness, and neediness of human childhood for the sake of our salvation. What is remarkable about that story is that the truth of God is embodied in a child."[80] For Janet Pais "A theological understanding of the child and of God the Child will enhance the possibility of a change in adult attitudes toward, and in adult relationships with, both external children encountered in the world and adults' internal child-selves."[81] All three writers derive from the theological fact of the incarnation an identification of God the Son with all children, and consequently a possible transformation of adult attitudes toward them. The argument seems to be that since God became a particular Child, both the personal worth and the social status of all children are now somehow different. Such an argument does not limit the

---

[79] Pope John Paul II, *Letter to Families* (1994), section 2. www.vatican.va/holy_father/john_paul_ii/letters/. Accessed 02.09.2006.

[80] Herbert Anderson and Susan B.W. Johnson, *Regarding Children: A New Respect for Childhood and Families* (Louisville, KY: Westminster John Knox Press, 1995), p. 20.

[81] Janet Pais, *Suffer the Children: A Theology of Liberation by a Victim of Abuse* (New York/Mahwah, NJ: Paulist Press, 1991), p. 16.

blessing of God to the sex that God in Christ became, or to the age group to which Christ belonged, since that would exclude the elderly, women, and girls. It is rather that in the ancient world childhood was probably considered "as pure prelude, an unfortunate, because *incomplete* state of being that was to be left behind – discarded – in the acquisition of adulthood, the acknowledged state of human perfection."[82] After and because of Jesus, childhood is included in what counts as perfect humanhood. There is nothing incomplete, imperfect, or preliminary about it. Whatever childhood is, God the Word becomes it.

Robin Maas claims that "from the very moment the Word takes flesh and comes to dwell among us, even *in embryo*, all reality is altered at its root, that is, in its *significance*."[83] The incarnation then, changes our attitude even to pre-sentient human life. But for Hans Urs von Balthasar, the fact of the incarnation of God in the Christ Child is matched by the manner of his *receiving his life from another*:

> It takes the Incarnation to show us that being born has not just an anthropological, but also a theological, eternal significance, and that to be from the generative, birth-giving womb of another is the ultimate, unsurpassable beatitude. The "meaning-logos" that is "with God" is the product of a love which is prior to anything else we can think and which is always wanting to give itself away; it is the fullness which owes its origin to an infinite emptying of the paternal womb.[84]

Balthasar's insight further emphasizes the work we have already done in this chapter on the Trinity as a source of overflowing generativity and love. It speaks of a relational account of the person even in the unique case of the Son of God who has his being from another. Maas' comment on the passage is that

> Jesus, the eternally generated Son of the Father, is a revelation of what it truly means to be a "child." In him, we find the secret of our own mysterious origins and the path of return to the Father's house. The human child, vulnerable, utterly dependent and trusting, now becomes the *real presence* of Christ – a living sacrament of the kingdom of heaven.[85]

---

[82] Robin Maas, "Christ as the Logos of Childhood: Reflections on the Meaning and Mission of the Child," *Theology Today*, 56.4 (January 2000) [456–68], p. 457 (author's emphases).

[83] Maas, "Christ as the Logos of Childhood," p. 456 (author's emphasis).

[84] Quoted by Maas ("Christ as the Logos of Childhood," p. 457) from Hans Urs von Balthasar, "Jesus as Child and His Praise of the Child," *Communio*, 22 (1995).

[85] Maas, "Christ as the Logos of Childhood," p. 458.

These are reflections which we will, I hope, enjoy taking into the heart of imminent discussions about children and parenthood in Part II.

4.4 Our Families and Ourselves in God's Image

Is it possible to claim that the doctrine of our being made in the image of God both confirms and contributes to a theology of families? I think so. It would add considerably to our assemblage of insights about persons, relations, love, gifting, and so on developed in this chapter. The text of Genesis 1:26–7 has been enormously influential throughout the history of Christian theology. In his deep reflection on the text, Pope John Paul II mused how "before creating man, the Creator withdraws as it were into himself, in order to seek the pattern and inspiration in the mystery of his Being, which is already here disclosed as the divine 'We.'"[86] A lengthy, major study of the topic has recently been made by Stanley Grenz. His *The Social God and the Relational Self* "seeks to extend the insights of contemporary trinitarian thought to theological anthropology, with the goal of developing a social or communal understanding of the concept of the *imago dei.*" He calls this "social personalism."[87] Grenz thinks it is now a "widely accepted philosophical conclusion that 'person' has more to do with relationality than with substantiality and that the term stands closer to the idea of communion or community than to the conception of the individual in isolation or abstracted from communal embeddedness."[88] He finds two basic approaches to the image of God within the tradition: the substantial or structural view, which understands the *imago dei* as consisting of certain attributes or capabilities lodged within the person, and the relational view, which sees the divine image as referring to a fundamental relationship between the human creature and the Creator.[89]

The relational view is very much the "minority view"[90] but, perhaps surprisingly, Grenz opts for a third alternative, "The *Imago Dei* as Goal."[91]

Grenz' survey of the biblical exegeses of the *imago dei* and of the uses made of it by historical theology indicates raging controversy and bewildering diversity. There is no essential, fixed, obvious, or authoritative meaning

---

[86] Pope John Paul II, *Letter to Families*, section 6.
[87] Stanley J. Grenz, *The Social God and the Relational Self: A Trinitarian Theology of the Imago Dei* (Louisville, KY, and London: Westminster John Knox Press, 2001), p. 3.
[88] Grenz, *The Social God*, p. 4.
[89] Grenz, *The Social God*, p. 142.
[90] Grenz, *The Social God*, p. 173.
[91] Grenz, *The Social God*, p. 177.

that scholarship might be expected to uncover regarding the image of God.[92] The image of God is connected to the making of humankind as male and female which in turn prompts Grenz to say that in God's creative work "humans are fundamentally incomplete in themselves. Human sexuality not only participates in this incompleteness but also spurs individuals to seek community through relationships."[93] But, he claims, the "New Testament focus on the community of Christ marks a radical step beyond the Old Testament understanding of the nature of the primal human community."[94] The step is from "familial" to "spiritual ancestry." Jesus "promised to his loyal disciples a larger, spiritual family to compensate for the loss entailed in leaving one's natural family for the sake of discipleship."[95] The relational self or version of *imago dei* that Grenz is finally able to commend is the participation of Christians in the body of Christ who is Himself the image and likeness of God (Col. 1:15). He presents "an ecclesial ontology of persons-in-community" which he sets out "for the sake of the construction of the relational self as the ecclesial self."[96] Thus the re-established social self ends up lodged in the ecclesial community where its sociality anticipates the communion of saints in heaven.

This erudite survey of the *imago dei* does not quite provide the endorsement of the relational self that a Christian theology of family requires. Of course that is not what Grenz set out to do. But then a general criticism to be made of almost all theological anthropology is that it is firmly essentialist in character, method, content, and tone: the human essence is an adult one and children feature nowhere within it (including in Grenz' index). Here then is another example of childless theology. The discussion of sexuality operates at an essentialist level as well. Male and female may be created in the image of God, but a theology for families needs to hear more about real parent–child relationships, not simply the archetypal man–woman relationship. Although the man and woman are to "Be fruitful and increase" (Gen. 1:28b), the relation to their fruit counts for nothing.

There are other problems with Grenz' account of the relational self. His depiction of the New Testament community does not sound like a radical step forward, since it requires loss, and compensation for the loss. Having

---

[92] He describes "The Royal Image," the Image as "Similarity," as "Counterpart," as "Dominion," as "Representation," as "True Human," and so on (pp. 190–203).
[93] Grenz, *The Social God*, p. 280.
[94] Grenz, *The Social God*, p. 281.
[95] Grenz, *The Social God*, p. 282.
[96] Grenz, *The Social God*, p. 305.

shown how important pair bonding is for understanding the *imago dei*, the early church was called to renounce it. We are back, of course, with the teaching of Jesus about families (above, 3.1) but with none of the contextuality that makes discipleship with regard to that teaching even possible. And once relationality is mapped along ecclesial and eschatological lines, the problems of kin altruism and kin preference re-appear. Once we are back in the family of the church, how are we to account for our special connectedness to those children who are the fruit of our pair-bonded love? A concept of the relational self is required that takes care of this, as well as the corporate familial activity of growing up into the image and likeness of Christ.

African indigenous thought already possesses a concept very similar to the relational self, *ubuntu*.[97] One classical theologian who links the image of God with parenthood and childhood is John Chrysostom. In *On Marriage and Family Life* he observes "When we teach our children to be good, to be gentle, to be forgiving (all these are attributes of God), to be generous, to love their fellow men, to regard this present age as nothing, we instill virtue in their souls, and reveal the image of God within them."[98] The image of God is already to be found within the child, and the nurture of the child by the parents draws it out and imprints it on the child's character. I remain confident that the doctrine that people are made in the image of God is highly serviceable in a theology of, and for, families. God is Love: this we know because of God's self-gift in Christ, Christ's self-gift in his death, and the Spirit's self-gift in enabling us to love one another as the one God in three Persons has loved us. Christ "is the image of the invisible God" (Col. 1:15). But He is "one in being with us in all things except sin," and so completely identifies with us in childhood and adulthood. We look to Genesis 1 not just to tell us that we are made in the image of God, but to provide deep confirmation of who and what we believe we are in the light of Jesus and who and what He is. The indefiniteness and variability of the content of the divine image in historical theology provides an opportunity to develop it in a relational direction. We are lovers. We are made for love. That is how we image God, and attend to the elicitation of the divine image in our children. There can be no love without relation. Trinitarian theology and social philosophy converge on that point. And as Christian doctrine faithfully seeks to explicate the saving mystery of God's love, its

---

[97] See Desmond Tutu, "Restoring Justice," *The Tablet*, February 21, 2004, p. 14.

[98] John Chrysostom, *On Marriage and Family Life* (tr. Catherine P. Roth and David Anderson) (Crestwood, NY: St Vladimir's Seminary Press, 1986), p. 44: cited in Guroian, "The Ecclesial Family," p. 66 (emphasis added).

signs and symbols are drawn from the relations between parents and their children.

"Three-in-one flesh"?

There is another obvious means of support for the relational concept of the person, and that is the teaching of Jesus about marriage. In the well-known passage where Jesus appeals to the creation narratives of Genesis 1 and 2 in order to counteract the practice of the easy divorce of women by men, he cites in full Genesis 2:24 ("That is why a man leaves his father and mother, and is united to his wife, and the two become one flesh") (Mk. 10:7–8a), and for emphasis, he adds "It follows that they are no longer two individuals: they are one flesh. Therefore what God has joined together, man must not separate" (Mk. 10:8b–9; and see Mt. 19:5–6). The "one flesh" of course has historically been patriarchally understood. "Her" flesh has been subsumed in his, and this practice has generated a storm of justified feminist protest. One such moderate voice is that of Karla Hackstaff who points out that in stifling marriages with domineering husbands, more, not less, individualism is required of hard-pressed wives:

> Because we proceed from a history of male dominant marriages, individualism does not *mean* the same thing to women and men. For men, putting the self first remains a way to sustain male dominance in marriage. For women, putting the self first is a way to counter male dominance in marriage . . . In the context of divorce culture, women's individualism may be inevitable, if not crucial for redefining marriage in an egalitarian direction.[99]

If some women's individualism is necessary on the road to egalitarian marriages, so be it. But counter-patriarchal readings of essential texts can also provide important signs on the same road. Jesus' interpretation of the Genesis text is itself counter-patriarchal because he uses it in his teaching against the practice of unilateral divorce of wives by husbands. But marriage for Jesus is clearly a one-flesh unity (however the metaphorical elements of that phrase are drawn out). I have suggested that two powerful models of marriage, those of "covenant" and "one-flesh union" counterbalance each other, "for 'covenant' clearly maintains the separate identities of the spouses

---

[99] Karla B. Hackstaff, "How Gender Informs Marital Fragility," *INTAMS Review*, 10.1 (2004) [33–47], p. 43.

as they undertake a common project, whereas the one-flesh union clearly maintains their oneness, 'a union of hearts and lives.'"[100]

Again it is to Chrysostom that we must turn for an interpretation of the "one flesh" model of marriage in a way that deliberately encompasses the children of the marriage. In *On Marriage and Family Life* he wrote

> How do they become one flesh? As if she were gold receiving purest gold, the woman receives the man's seed with rich pleasure, and within her it is nourished, cherished, and refined. It is mingled with her own substance and she then returns it as a child! The child is a bridge connecting mother to father, *so the three become one flesh* . . . And here the bridge is formed from the substance of each! Just as the head and the rest of the body are one, so it is with the child. That is why Scripture does not say, "They shall be one flesh." But they shall be joined together "into one flesh," namely the child. But suppose there is no child; do they then remain two and not one? No; their intercourse effects the joining of their bodies, and they are made one, just as when perfume is mixed with ointment.[101]

This is a remarkable passage which links, as I am attempting to do, families and children with incarnation and Trinity. We have just seen that for Chrysostom, parents draw out the image of God in their children. Here he makes at least three points about the one flesh model which are transposable to a contemporary theology of families. First, the language he uses to describe the sexual intercourse that makes the couple one expresses wonder, joy, and delight. He did not understand the physiology of conception as we now do, but he is unreservedly positive about the process that leads to it, whether or not a pregnancy results. Second, the metaphor "bridge" does not simply unite the couple as a bridge would unite, say, two sides of a river: the ontological union of the couple is extended to include the child. What was two in one flesh, is now three in one flesh, and without diminution of the union. Chrysostom emphasizes this point when he compares the union of head and body in a single individual with the union of the parents with the child. There is a new union in which all share. Third, by interposing a point of grammar, the meaning of "one flesh" is converted from the joining of the couple in sexual intercourse to the fruit of that union. In this second account of the one flesh, the child, not the parents, is the one flesh who comes from the love-making of the two.

We have already seen how in the case of kin altruism a state of affairs in

---

[100] Thatcher, *Marriage after Modernity*, p. 213.
[101] Chrysostom, *On Marriage and Family Life*, p. 76: cited in Guroian, "The Ecclesial Family," p. 67 (emphasis added).

nature is supplemented and fulfilled in grace. A parallel and yet more primary case may be found in the human bonding, prior to the bonding of parents and children. Paul Peachey rightly discerns in the "leaving and cleaving" of Genesis 2:24 the historical and universal persistence of the human pair bond, the significance of which, he thinks, is ontologically and experientially prior to the duty or end of marriage understood as the pro-creation of children.[102] In his terms, "conjugality" precedes "procreativity." Consanguinity, or the ties of blood, are not ultimate in the meaning-making which is marriage. Rather, "the germ of society lies, not in kinship as bio-logical descent, but in the leaving and clinging archetype that is the human pair-bond, the conjugal union." Peachey thinks that "the pair-bonding pro-clivity arrived with the species, and thus is to be taken as a given in the human condition."[103] Pair-bonding with a stranger is more fundamental to the human condition even than "the biologically-grounded bond between mother and infant,"[104] and childhood is described as "a covenanting appren-ticeship under two biologically unrelated strangers, bound by a deliberate covenant."[105] Although he does not say so, what he calls the "pair-bonding proclivity" of the species is a further example of our created nature ground-ing us in relationality, of which marriage is but the most intense and intensified example.

4.5 Families and Structural Sin

The ideals in this chapter will only ever be partially realized on earth, but we can pray, and work, that "Your kingdom come, on earth as in heaven"! The relational self still practices "selfishness" (that concept is better able to explain why selfishness is wrong): our love is often no more than *amor priva-tus* because it is not widely shared. Children often arrive not as the expression of covenant love, but sometimes unwanted and resented, the very opposite of the gift that they are. We do not always keep the covenants we make with our spouses and children, and often we and especially our children suffer as a result. If the analysis of Webb (and others, below, 8.4) is sound, the ideals of the global economic system in which we are entrapped, have corrupted us insidiously in favor of egoism. Having argued in favor of

---

[102] Paul Peachey, *Leaving and Clinging: The Human Significance of the Conjugal Union* (Washing-ton, DC: University Press of America, 2001), p. 5.

[103] Peachey, *Leaving and Clinging*, p. 22.

[104] Peachey, *Leaving and Clinging*, p. 76.

[105] Peachey, *Leaving and Clinging*, p. 94.

the legitimate preference for the love of our children, we doubtless exercise the preference in a way that restricts the love of other children who are straightforwardly neighbors. The social personalism of this chapter explains how we are inevitably in relation, but it says nothing about the quality of those relations which, without much virtue and resolve, will lack love. The closer the intimacy, the greater the vulnerability; the greater the vulnerability, the greater the likelihood of actual hurt. A relation, like marriage, may be socially and ecclesially approved, while being a source of constant distress. As Rowan Williams warns, "an enormous number of 'sanctioned' unions are a framework for violence and human destructiveness on a disturbing scale . . ."[106] The name for all this is, in Christian tradition, sin. God's reign is the redemption from sin through Christ. And redemption is needed at the individual-relational level, at the social level, and at the structural levels. Currently 150 million children suffer from malnutrition (above, 1.2). Faced with these and other numbing statistics, structural sin needs no further explication.

Parents, especially fathers, need to supplement their bonding to their partners and children, which is embedded in nature, with the further grace of commitment to them. Kin altruism is precarious. Many men (and a few women) do not bond permanently, or even at all, with the children they help to create. Those who stay have often remained aloof from their children and disciplinarian with regard to them. Browning and his co-authors write sympathetically also of a *female problematic*, the tendency of females under some conditions to suppress their own needs and raise children without paternal participation, sometimes under great stress and at great cost.[107]

That "private family matter," and scourge of nuclear families, domestic violence, blights the lives of countless partners and their children. Children themselves, warns Miller-McLemore, are capable of being "deceitful, manipulative, and even malicious."[108] She advances several reasons for persisting with the grain of theological analyses about the sinfulness of children. She wants to counter the conservative use of it and to promote an understanding of children that leads to compassion in the face of inappropriate

---

[106] Rowan Williams, "The Body's Grace," in, for example, Rogers, *Theology and Sexuality* [309–21], p. 316.

[107] Don S. Browning, Bonnie J. Miller-McLemore, Pamela D. Couture, K. Brynolf Lyon, and Robert M. Franklyn, *From Culture Wars to Common Ground* (Louisville, KY: Westminster John Knox Press, 1997), p. 106.

[108] Bonnie J. Miller-McLemore, *Let the Children Come: Reimagining Childhood from a Christian Perspective* (San Francisco, CA: Jossey-Bass, 2003), p. 59.

behavior: "it especially speaks to the moral and spiritual complexity of the teen years without pathologizing them." And, she thinks, the expectation that children are sinful provides a mean between Augustinian notions of depravity and liberal romantic notions of innocence.[109]

We will need to examine the origin of the tendency of couples to have fewer, or no children (below, 8.4). It is possible that here too private selfish attitudes and materialistic values, themselves social in origin, merge with what Anderson and Johnson call cultural "indifference" to children.[110] The ending of nearly half of all marriages in divorce, and the detrimental impact of these on children, point not only to a lack of communicative skills in negotiating and recovering from inevitable disagreements, but to a lack of commitment to a common life together which itself renders exiting a marriage more plausible and likely.

Miller-McLemore shows how many children are *victims* of narcissistically needy parents, and of a popular culture which peddles poisonous myths to girls (about their appearance, sexuality, availability) and to boys (about bravado, denial of feelings, violence).[111] This too is structural sin. There are strong socio-cultural tendencies which diminish spousal commitment, trivialize love, exploit mothers and children, disrupt families, instill greed, consumerize and commodify relationships. Even the strident advocacy of family values can turn out to be "advocacy for one's own kin group or 'social class.'" "The pro-family agenda," warns Cahill, can "motivate rationalizations against class-spanning love of neighbor, care for the poor, and table fellowship with the stranger, those moral duties that distinctively mark the Christian life."[112] Above all, children are victims of poverty and hunger.

Families and children are fairly obviously potential and real victims of social and structural sin. They can be its perpetrators too. The essentialism of almost all Christian thought about families and children ("*the* family" as a substantive, "children" as a sub-class of person) has led to a paucity of thinking about relations within families, and the most central of these are between parents and children. There are no children in the abstract.[113] We will examine these relations in later chapters, for these are the *loci* equally of sin and of grace. While personal, social, and structural sin is pervasive within and around families and children, our emphasis will remain upon the oppor-

[109] Miller-McLemore, *Let the Children Come*, pp. 64–6.
[110] Anderson and Johnson, *Regarding Children*, p. 13.
[111] Miller-McLemore, *Let the Children Come*, pp. 33–5.
[112] Lisa Sowle Cahill, *Family: A Christian Social Perspective* (Minneapolis, MN: Fortress Press, 2000), p. 6.
[113] Pais, *Suffer the Children*, p. 30.

tunities for the creation of strong and loving relationships within families, grounded in the divine love made known in Jesus Christ and, embryonically at least, at the heart of all families already.

Having reached the end of Part I we have uncovered many resources and insights for a theology of families. To the practical side of family relationships we must now turn.

Part II

Relations

We have now examined a range of Christian doctrines out of which a theology for families is capable of being constructed. In Part II, we examine relations: between spouses and partners; between parents and children; between wider family members; between families and churches; and between families, children, and the wider society.

Chapter Five

Spouses and Partners

What does the Gospel tell us about family form? Is there an abiding historical form for families? Or is the form of a family relative to its function? If so,
is there agreement about what the function is? The questions sound a little
arid, yet the answers could scarcely be more important. In section 5.1 the
more liberal view, that form is relative to function, is identified and criticized. In section 5.2 empirical evidence about marriage, used to support the
case for critical familism, is found to be sound. Theology and empirical
sources are used to advance a suggestion – a "theology of liberation for children," and to mount a critique of the secular "optimists." But supporters of
marriage have to deal with the problem of exclusivism and the apparent
condemnation of alternative forms. Section 5.3 offers a solution to the
problem with the more controversial hypothesis that marital or conjugal
values are not confined solely to married couples.

5.1 Do Families Need Marriages?

Families: is form still important?

Yes: families need marriages, and form is just as important as function. But
since the cultural understanding of marriage is changing, and there is
disagreement about what constitutes a family and what its function is, that
unambiguous "Yes" can only be arrived at via much theological and
sociological argument, all of it, of course, contested. Let us begin with those
theological advocates of families who insist that families are to be defined
and evaluated by the functions they perform. Anderson and Johnson think
that "there are a variety of family structures that can nurture children
effectively if there is sufficient personal commitment and environmental

support."[1] Deteriorating environments, such as poor schools and health services, have a negative impact on families. Having two parents is not enough for a child "if one holds the view, as we do, that it takes *more* than two parents to raise children." While their analysis of children and families clearly assumes and advocates deep commitment of partners to each other and of partners to their children, they do not advocate any priority to the marital family form as the means of achieving it. Instead, they make the form of families relative to their function:

> Considering the purpose of the family also introduces questions about the relationship between family form and function. The family has endured in part because it has adapted to changing needs and circumstances. Moreover, structures of the family have changed over centuries and will continue to change while its purposes have remained more constant. We assume that a family is what it does. This idea that form follows function is a theological reality as well as an architectural principle. *Christian teaching has more to say about what families must do than what they should look like.*[2]

Here, then, is a theological version of the secular view we have already met (above, 1.1), that family practices are to be preferred to family forms. If it is true that form follows function, then disagreement about function might be expected to show itself in disagreement about forms. If there are diverse understandings of family functions, there will be a diversity of family forms. Anderson and Johnson go even further. The actual diversity of family forms is said to be evidence of God's always surprising creativity, and the plurality of family forms, whatever their function, becomes sacralized:

> The pluralism of family structure in our time is not so much an instance of decline as it is an extension of the diversity inherent in the creation that God has labeled good. The diversity of family structures over history is not just an accommodation to necessity; it is the result of physical, social, and psychological changes that are built into the process of human growth towards maturity.[3]

While "having both a father and a mother involved in the childrearing process remains the ideal," what matters more than family form or function is "what families believe and seek to transmit to the next generation."[4]

---

[1] Herbert Anderson and Susan B.W. Johnson, *Regarding Children: A New Respect for Childhood and Families* (Louisville, KY: Westminster John Knox Press, 1995), p. 18.
[2] Anderson and Johnson, *Regarding Children*, p. 49 (authors' emphasis).
[3] Anderson and Johnson, *Regarding Children*, p. 65.
[4] Anderson and Johnson, *Regarding Children*, p. 66.

Clearly there are theologians among the "optimists" (above, 1.3) about families. John and Olive Drane maintain a similar level of optimism about the shape of the new family emerging from the breakdown of more traditional family forms. They say "Whatever happens next, we can be sure that the redesigned family will feature in the emerging social landscape. But the shape of the new design is not yet clear, nor is it likely to be for some time to come. As a culture we are still at the drawing board stage."[5] The challenge for Christians is "whether we can think creatively enough to make a positive contribution to the process." It is not enough to be "constantly bemoaning the disappearance of the industrial nuclear family." Rather "to see the situation as an opportunity will require careful discernment to enable us to identify those new emerging values that reflect God's will . . ."[6]

Other practical theologians hold that advocacy of one particular family form is inseparable from stigmatizing the growing number of people in other family forms. Lisa Cahill advocates "an inclusive and supportive approach to family life, one that can hold up ideals such as male–female co-parenting and sexual fidelity without thereby berating and excluding single-parent families, divorced families, gay and lesbian families, blended families, or adoptive families." She thinks, with Anderson and Johnson, that "the ideals of Christian family life should focus more on function (fostering Gospel-informed commitments and behavior) than on regularity of form," and defends the thesis "that strong family, spousal, and parental relationships are important, but that these ideals are undermined by condemnatory and punitive attitudes and policies toward nonconforming families."[7] Pamela Couture, similarly, worries that the commendation of a particular form stigmatizes all other (uncommendable) forms. "In a misguided attempt to strengthen the forms of family life, some popular movements today seek to stigmatise fragile families." They have failed to see that "theologically, fragile families are of equal worth and have often become a means of God's grace."[8]

These arguments are not entirely convincing. I take issue especially with Anderson and Johnson's treatment of the form versus function dilemma. Yes, children need supportive environments, and more than just two parents, if they are to thrive. But this need not inhibit pointing out that if children are nurtured by their two biological parents, they are more likely to

[5] John Drane and Olive M. Fleming Drane, *Family Fortunes: Faith-full Caring for Today's Families* (London: Darton, Longman, and Todd, 2004), p. 40.

[6] Drane and Drane, *Family Fortunes*, p. 41.

[7] Lisa Sowle Cahill, *Family: A Christian Social Perspective* (Minneapolis, MN: Augsburg Fortress Press, 2000), p. xi.

[8] Pamela D. Couture, *Seeing Children, Seeing God: A Practical Theology of Children and Poverty* (Nashville, TN: Abingdon Press, 2000), p. 99.

thrive than if they are not. If children need the commitment of both parents, why not commend the family form that encourages and institutionalizes this? Families change over time, they say, while the purposes of families remain more constant. But the fact of change does not entitle us to dispense with caution in the face of *every* change. Several of the "family functionalists" are remarkably sanguine about historical change as if it were both morally neutral and unshaped also by our freedom to choose. And what is the ground for saying that the function or purpose of the family has remained constant? Just as there is no longer a single substantive, "the family," so there may no longer be a single purpose to inform it. Why should form follow function? If function has changed little, why then should form have changed so much?

Perhaps the biggest *lacuna* in the argument is the assumption that diversity of family form is the work of the diverse, creative God. Why suppose this? The diversity within a given form is no reason for suspending judgments about which items within it might be preferred to others, and for diverse reasons, because, for example, they work better, hold the road better, run faster, look more beautiful, fly further, and so on. Several further premises need to be worked into an argument that the fact of diversity in the case of family form, is evidence of divine creativity. Of course, it might be, but it is also explicable by the social sciences which refer to circumstances closer to home. This hypothesis also overlooks the fact that the increased freedom of choice that goes into the making of the variety of family forms might be bad choice. If Anderson and Johnson advocate a world-view within which the human race is growing to maturity (and breaking out of family forms that impede its progress?), then this seems like the familiar liberal optimism that two world wars shattered, and which remains hopelessly vulnerable to standard conservative critique. And how can "what families believe" be more important than family form? There is a strong connection between what we believe, at any rate about families, and the family form to which we aspire.

Drane and Drane's sensitive approach to families is also weakened by the liberal optimism behind some of their assumptions. They use the extended metaphor of the drawing board to build an unargued thesis about the shape of future families. On this drawing board "the redesigned family" sits, awaiting completion and eventually cultural adoption. Their analysis is too sophisticated for them to imply, and us to infer, a divine designer of the new family in waiting (although Anderson and Johnson come very close to this). But there are several unsatisfactory design features of this design metaphor. If God is not designing the new family, who is? The answer is: the *culture* is; and the task of Christians is to contribute to this creative cultural task. But there is no sign at all that the culture is designing *anything* with regard to new social arrangements for families. The suppositions of agency, purpose, and social co-operation in relation to these supposed goals, remain suppositions, which sit uneasily with the diversity and fragmentation that the social sciences describe (and explain by hypotheses which assume social *reaction*, not purposive social action). The culture is, rather, letting things happen to families which are not all good for them, and with little if any thought at all about the consequences of its *laissez-faire* attitude to emerging family trends. For all we know, culture may be more like nature in neo-Darwinian evolutionary theory. Without denying the possibility of human freedom in relation to cultural pressures, culture might show features of design which turn out to be blind and purposeless, like the apparent design of *The Blind Watchmaker*.[9] Theology might do better to analyze the trends from its own resources, instead of contributing, on the basis of flawed premises, to a design process that isn't happening.

Having just provided a comprehensive account of the diverse families in Britain today (above, 1.1) Drane and Drane assume that diversity will issue in a new unity when the newly designed family is unveiled. But there is at least equal evidence that the growing diversity of family forms will issue in rank chaos, not some putative new standard form. (Presumably when this new form arrives, it will take precedence over function?) It will take more than faith to discern in the depths of this social ambivalence "new emerging values that reflect God's will." In any case the theological task is a different one: to affirm *Gospel* values which will help to transform whatever form families will take in the direction of love and grace.

Cahill's "inclusive" approach to family life is surely commendable, but her worries about the "berating" of non-traditional family groups and about "condemnatory and punitive attitudes and policies," which may too often accompany pro-marriage advocacy, are not going to be salved by blurring the distinction between form and function. What is needed rather is a different kind of inclusivism. Why should "Gospel-informed commitments and behaviour" remain confined to function, not form? If, say, there were agreement among Christians about a particular form which, on balance, was thought to express Gospel-informed commitments better than others, should Christians remain silent about it, for fear of causing offence?

[9] Richard Dawkins, *The Blind Watchmaker* (London: Penguin Books, 1988).

5.2 Disputes about Evidence

Clearly there is as yet no truce in the "culture wars" of the United States. Very similar trends, as we have seen, operate in many other countries, where the discussion follows similar, but less polemicized, contours. Those practical theologians who cannot accept all aspects of conservative evangelicalism or fundamentalism, or official Roman Catholicism, differ among themselves on how they read and evaluate certain empirical evidence about families, and what they should do about it. The evidence and the conflict over it must now be examined more closely. In order to do this I will use a recent and reliable summary of findings of social science research (2002), and then join in the fray about how to read them.

The summary is contained in a report of thirteen renowned family scholars, prepared for the Institute for American Values, *Why Marriage Matters: Twenty-One Conclusions from the Social Sciences*.[10] It has a British counterpart, *Does Marriage Matter?*[11] The American work covers much of the ground already traversed in Linda Waite and Maggie Gallagher's *The Case for Marriage* in 2000.[12] The report deals with four areas. With regard, first, to family relationships it concludes that "Marriage increases the likelihood that fathers have good relationships with their children;" that "Cohabitation is not the functional equivalent of marriage;"[13] and that "Growing up outside an intact marriage increases the likelihood that children will themselves divorce or become unwed-parents." Divorce is twice as likely among children whose parents have divorced. They also conclude that "Marriage is a virtually universal human institution."[14]

Second, with regard to family economics, the team concludes that "Divorce and unmarried childbearing increase poverty for both children and mothers." They warn that "Parental divorce (or failure to marry) appears to

---

[10] Institute for American Values, *Why Marriage Matters: Twenty-One Conclusions from the Social Sciences* (New York: 2002) [1–28]. Its authors are a team of eight male and five female American family scholars, chaired by Norval Glenn. There is a voluminous supporting literature detailing the research which must be consulted through the copious endnotes provided.

[11] CIVITAS, *Does Marriage Matter?* (London: undated) [1–51]. Rebecca O'Neill, who prepared the text, acknowledges that the work is "inspired" by *Why Marriage Matters*, which she describes as having been used as a "model" for its production. In fact long sections of text of the American version appear without further acknowledgement in the British work.

[12] Linda J. Waite and Maggie Gallagher, *The Case for Marriage: Why Married People Are Happier, Healthier, and Better Off Financially* (New York: Doubleday, 2000).

[13] For a long review of evidence about cohabitation see my *Living Together and Christian Ethics* (Cambridge, UK: Cambridge University Press, 2002), chapter 1.

[14] *Why Marriage Matters*, pp. 7–9.

increase children's risk of school failure," and has "a significant, long-term negative impact" on children's "educational" and "socioeconomic attainment."[15] Third, with regard to physical health, the team concludes that "Children who live with their own two married parents enjoy better physical health, on average, than do children in other family forms"; and that "Parental marriage is associated with a sharply lower risk of infant mortality," around 50 percent in the case of children of unmarried mothers. Marriage is associated with "reduced rates of alcohol and substance abuse for both adults and teens," and with "better health and lower rates of injury, illness, and disability for both men and women." Married people live longer than single people.[16]

Fourth, there are, according to the team, similar benefits with regard to the mental health and emotional well-being of members of intact families. Children of divorce have higher rates of psychological distress and mental illness, and of suicide. And divorce can contribute to crime and domestic violence. "Boys raised in single-parent homes are about twice as likely (and boys raised in stepfamilies are three times as likely) to have committed a crime that leads to incarceration by the time they reach their early thirties."[17] Families where parents stay married provide a safer environment for men, women, and children. Adults are less likely to be "either perpetrators or victims of crime," and "Married women appear to have a lower risk of experiencing domestic violence than do cohabiting or dating women." "A child who is not living with his or her own two married parents is at greater risk of child abuse."[18]

These conclusions confirm earlier, and extensive, British studies.[19] The tone of these studies was polemical, alarmist, and conservative, but I do not think they can be dismissed simply as pessimism. Despite much sand in the engine of political correctness, I am unaware of any successful attempt to refute their conclusions. The association between changing family forms

---

[15] *Why Marriage Matters*, pp. 9–11.

[16] *Why Marriage Matters*, pp. 11–14.

[17] *Why Marriage Matters*, pp. 15–16.

[18] *Why Marriage Matters*, pp. 16–17.

[19] The Health and Welfare Unit of the Institute of Economic Affairs (London), an educational charity, published an influential series, "Choices in Welfare," in the 1990s. The following are relevant to this discussion: Jon Davies (ed.), *The Family: Is It Just Another Lifestyle Choice?* (1993); Norman Dennis, *Rising Crime and the Dismembered Family: How Conformist Intellectuals Have Campaigned Against Common Sense* (1993); Norman Dennis and George Erdos, *Families without Fatherhood* (1993); Patricia Morgan, *Farewell to the Family? Public Policy and Family Breakdown in Britain and the USA* (1995): Robert Whelan (ed.), *Just a Piece of Paper? Divorce Reform and the Undermining of Marriage* (1995); Miriam E. David (ed.), *The Fragmenting Family: Does It Matter?* (1998).

and the variety of miseries for children has led directly to "critical familism" as a positive theological and social response. A problem for writers supporting marriage is that the positive benefits of being and remaining married are little understood even among the professionals dealing with marital breakdown. (I have had a similar experience myself. A booklet I wrote for a church organization praising marriage was dismissed by some as ideological and exclusive. Its rehearsal of some of the social facts about the advantages of marriage was frankly disbelieved by several clergy. Even in the churches marital pessimism is deeply ingrained.) So in *Marriage, Health, and the Professions*,[20] the critical familists again set out the health benefits of marriage[21] and the personal and social costs of divorce,[22] and it is again shown that "the widespread prevalence of divorce probably has been a major contributor to the continuing decline of child-centeredness in modern times."[23] John Witte, Jr, is quick to point out that what he calls "the health paradigm of marriage" is "both very new and very old"[24]; new because it is validated by empirical secular research, old because "the West had had a long and thick overlapping consensus that marriage is good, does good, and has goods both for the couple and for the children."

With the "health paradigm" of marriage we reach the basic ground on which the commendation of lifelong marriage as the preferred family form is based. It is now being claimed, on empirical grounds, that marriage is more likely to be better than alternatives to marriage, both for spouses and for children. Marriage need no longer be favored on grounds of social convention, religious teaching or ideological proclamation alone. It can be shown to provide positive benefits for couples, and especially for their children, irrespective of faith or political commitments. *Marriage, Health and the Professionals* seeks to familiarize professionals, including theologians and clergy, with the evidence, inviting them to change their practice in the light of the confirmation that the marital form receives from years of research. How might their practice be changed? Muller Davis, a family lawyer, shows

---

[20] John Wall, Don Browning, William J. Doherty, and Stephen Post (eds.), *Marriage, Health and the Professions: If Marriage Is Good For You, What Does This Mean for Law, Medicine, Ministry, Therapy, Business?* (Cambridge, MA: Eerdmans, 2002).

[21] Linda J. Waite, "The Health Benefits of Marriage," in Wall et al. (eds.), *Marriage, Health and the Professions*, pp. 13–32.

[22] David Popenoe and Barbara Dafoe Whitehead, "The Personal Costs of Divorce," in Wall et al. (eds.), *Marriage, Health and the Professions*, [33–46].

[23] Popenoe and Whitehead, "The Personal Costs of Divorce," p. 46.

[24] John Witte, Jr, "The Goods and Goals of Marriage: The Health Paradigm in Historical Perspective," in Wall et al. (eds.), *Marriage, Health and the Professions* [49–89], p. 86.

how current legal practice favors spouses seeking divorce, and not concilia-
tion. He gives suggestions to family lawyers about how to enhance marriage
with their clients[25] and argues that in law, "There needs to be more of a
balance established between the individual and the collective parts of the
family."[26] Health care professionals are urged to "openly discuss the health
data on marriage with patients, who then, in their patient autonomy, can
make the life choices that they will. Indeed, a truly informed choice about
marriage or divorce must take into account all the facts."[27] Given the lack of
social awareness about these matters, that is the least contribution professionals can make.

A professor of medicine shows how "the family doctor of the future is
challenged to practice medicine *of* the family as much as family medicine for
its presenting member."[28] Marital therapists are urged to address the "profound crisis in the core professional identity of marital therapy, that is, it
promotes '*individual*' well-being" while also having to recognize that these
individuals "chose to commit themselves to marriage and family as *social
institutions*."[29] Two Christian feminists explain their support for "the growing movement to reinstitutionalize marriage, especially in light of recent
research showing the generally negative effects of divorce and nonmarital
cohabitation and childbearing, and the generally positive effects of marriage
for both individuals and society."[30] Marital therapists offer a new "model of
marital health" which does not just promote the partnership but operates at
"four ecological levels" – individual, family, community, and society. Each
level "comprises various moral stakeholders whose well-being both influences and is influenced by the marriage relationship."[31] Even business
professionals are urged to rediscover "the wider covenantal fabric of the civil

---

[25] Muller Davis, "Is the Genie out of the Bottle?," in Wall et al. (eds.), *Marriage, Health and the
Professions* [90–107], pp. 105–7.
[26] Davis, "Is the Genie out of the Bottle?," p. 107.
[27] Stephen G. Post, "Health, Marriage, and the Ethics of Medicine," in Wall et al. (eds.), *Marriage, Health and the Professions* [108–29], pp. 128–9.
[28] Edmund D. Pellegrino, "The Family as a Clinical Entity," in Wall et al. (eds.), *Marriage,
Health and the Professions* [130–45], p. 140.
[29] John Wall and Bonnie Miller-McLemore, "Health, Christian Marriage Traditions, and the
Ethics of Marital Therapy," in Wall et al. (eds.), *Marriage, Health and the Professions* [186–207],
p. 186 (authors' emphases).
[30] Christine Firer Hinze and Mary Stewart Van Leeuwen, "Whose Marriage Whose Health?
A Christian Feminist Ethical Response," in Wall et al. (eds.), *Marriage, Health and the Professions*
[145–66], p. 145.
[31] William J. Doherty and Jason S. Carroll, "Health and the Ethics of Marital Therapy and
Education," in Wall et al. (eds.), *Marriage, Health and the Professions* [208–32], p. 225.

society on which good business depends," and this "entails a strengthening of the family."[32] These writers engage in a task familiar to practical theologians. They want to encourage change to practice, except that the practice is for the most part secular and the drive for change is led by the findings of social scientists, rather than the analyses of theologians.

Can the research findings be trusted? Are they durable? There is an impressive array of caveats introducing the research, designed to fend off the critics. First, it is explained that social science is better at documenting whether certain alleged social facts are true than at saying why they are true. Second, the team are experienced social scientists who can be expected to avoid the familiar trap of turning an association between social factors into causal explanations of one by the other. "We can assert more definitely that marriage is *associated* with powerful social goods than that marriage is *the sole or main cause* of these goods."[33] Third, the research takes into account "selection effects" (the "pre-existing differences between individuals who decide to divorce, marry, or become unwed parents"). The conclusions reached are based mainly on "large, nationally representative samples that control for race, family background, and other confounding factors," particularly poverty. Fourth, the researchers confined themselves to "general questions," not to "individual circumstances." They do not say that all marriages are equally good, and they *do* say that "divorce or separation provides an important escape hatch for children and adults in violent or high-conflict marriages."[34] Fifth, it hardly needs to be said that all empirical knowledge is provisional, subject to verification, falsification, and the general rules of induction.

Critical familism and other advocates of marriage are caught between conservative critics in the churches who don't like its progressive theology, and liberal critics who don't like its apparent conservatism over the marital form of family. Christian ethics in liberal hands is likely to be based on versions of justice and rights, an advantage of which may be congruence with secular campaigners who adopt a similar language and goals. But there is also a greater disadvantage in this tactic: the resources and heritage of Christianity, with its distinctive vocabulary and rootedness in basic doctrines, are

---

[32] Max L. Stackhouse, "Familial, Social, and Professional Integrity in Relationship to Business," in Wall et al. (eds.), *Marriage, Health and the Professions* [233–53], p. 247. And see Shirley J. Roels, "Reconstructing Home: Business Responsibility for the Family," in Wall et al. (eds.), *Marriage, Health and the Professions* [254–82].

[33] *Why Marriage Matters*, p. 4 (authors' emphases).

[34] *Why Marriage Matters*, p. 5.

sidelined. One side accuses the other of "open inclusivism,"[35] that is, of supporting all families without discrimination between family forms; the other side accuses its opponents of being élitist because it holds "that one family form fits all and should be privileged in church and social policies."[36]

I think the burden of evidence, and the theological arguments, favor the critical familists, although the charge of élitism still needs to be firmly dispatched (below, 5.2). It would be rational to advocate lifelong marriage as a preferred family form if the evidence pointed only to the *probability* that marriage was, on balance, better for children, for spouses and wider families, and for society. This procedure would invoke Bishop Butler's maxim, "To Us, probability is the very guide of life."[37] Of course there will be healthy debate about what standards of probability are to be invoked, but the dilemma about family form is akin to other weighty international dilemmas that confront us. What standard of proof is required to clinch the probability that global warming is occurring as a result of human actions? For Butler the link between probability and changed behavior was more direct: even "in questions of difficulty . . . where more satisfactory evidence cannot be had . . ." probability "determines the question, even in matters of speculation; and in matters of practice, will lay us under an absolute and formal obligation . . ."[38] There may be some medical scientists who still deny a causal link between smoking cigarettes and a raft of fatal diseases. Evidence of the kind summarized in *Why Marriage Matters?* cannot be dismissed so easily. If probability is to be our guide, then there is a strong case to answer (as well as a strong case for accruing further evidence which confirms the hypothesis or requires it to be modified, or even eventually abandoned).

Since the case for critical familism is strong, and its case is more likely to be ignored instead of answered, some notes of caution might be sounded from a friendly source. First, there is a risk that familism becomes too closely associated with a politically conservative ideology. Outside the United States, the name "Society for American Values" sounds hopelessly implicated in wealth, class, and republicanism. Second, in controlling for selection effects, one must ask whether the many deleterious effects of

---

[35] That term was used by Don Browning in his criticism of the report of the Presbyterian Church of the United States of America, presented to the General Assembly of that Church in 2003. See Don Browning, "Empty Inclusivism," *Christian Century*, vol. 120, issue 13 (June 28, 2003), pp. 8–9.

[36] Gloria Albrecht, "A Comment in Defense of 'Living Faithfully with Families in Transition'" (2003). www.witherspoonsociety.org/03-may/albrecht.htm. Accessed 02.09.2006.

[37] Joseph Butler, *Analogy of Religion Natural and Revealed* (1736) (London: Religious Tract Society edition, 1855) Introduction, para. 3, p. 5.

[38] Butler, *Analogy of Religion*, Introduction, para. 3, p. 5.

poverty can ever be sufficiently weighed in the balance of advantage and disadvantage. Lisa Cahill is right that "failure to marry and provide a two-parent home for children is, for the disadvantaged, due less to individualism or lack of conviction about the desirability of such a home in principle than it is to realistic hopelessness about the prospect of achieving it, given poor education and joblessness."[39]

Third, there is a widely held view that the pro-marriage movement is "simplistic, biased, and nonempathic toward people divorcing."[40] It is undoubtedly true that marriage is often defended in ways that condemn non-marital unions and alternative family forms. But that is merely an argument for commending the goods of marriage in a better, more charitable and more effective way. Fourth, I worry that the undoubted advantages that accrue to the family form of marriage may dissipate in the coming years, as a result of the changes to family form since the 1970s. Where the practice of divorce is widespread and affordable, the expectation that marriages do not last grows inexorably. The social understanding of marriage itself changes, with the paradox that high expectations of marriage lead to quicker disappointments, and divorce is used as a means of terminating conflict. But these notes of caution hardly comprise a single dissonant chord. It is necessary to follow arguments wherever they lead, even if political or religious adversaries are traveling to the same destination by a different route. In any case, many of the great issues of our time require solutions which extend beyond the bipolarity of left and right. The point that poverty makes life more difficult for families is intuitively obvious. Poverty is as morally unacceptable as rich people moralizing about the morals of the poor. But if we were to refrain from the advocacy of marriage, because some sectors of a society found it more difficult to achieve than others, we would not be helping anyone. Liberal Christians just don't want to hear that their politically correct endorsement of all family types, both renders advocacy of *any* family form superfluous (since the fiction is maintained that they all function equally well), and ignores the mounting body of evidence that some family forms function better than others. The weakening of marriage provides no argument at all for its abandonment. Not every social change can be commended, and some require reversal.

---

[39] Lisa Sowle Cahill, *Family: A Christian Social Perspective* (Minneapolis, MN: Augsburg Fortress, 2000), p. 5.
[40] J.H. Harvey and M.A. Fine, *Children of Divorce: Stories of Loss and Growth* (Mahwah, NJ: Erlbaum, 2004), p. 19.

A theology of liberation for children?

The theological doctrines advanced in the last two chapters also assist the case made by critical familism. We saw there how kin altruism helps to explain why children are more likely to be cared for by their biological parents: why our children are closer to us than the nearest neighbor; how our family relations may image the God who is Three; how the marital covenant of the couple extends to the "three-in-one flesh" of themselves and their children; how the "relational self" is itself through the other selves to whom it is connected; how children call forth from us the deepest possible intimation that they, and we ourselves, are given; and how relations within families can participate in the loving communion which is God. But the teaching of Jesus about children is also highly applicable within this context. It cannot be claimed that the teaching of Jesus honors nuclear families, for we have seen how it is persistently suspicious of any family structure not rooted in the values of God's Reign. The teaching of Jesus puts children first, and reverses all power structures around children which compromise the priority that is to be afforded to them. The teaching of Jesus supports whatever arrangements best assist the thriving of children, and that is treated in the social research as a largely *empirical* matter. If lifelong marriage best serves the interests of children, then the promotion of lifelong marriage is the promotion of the teaching of Jesus about the blessing and flourishing of children.

A very simple theological argument is available which consists of two uncluttered premises and a simple conclusion. It goes like this:

Premise 1   Jesus Christ wills the flourishing of all children.
Premise 2   Children are more likely to flourish within marriage.
Therefore: Jesus Christ wills marriage for bringing up children.

I think this argument is sound. There will always be exceptions. The conclusion does not pretend to be a direct intuition of the mind of Christ. It does however follow inductively from the premises. Premise 1 is derived from the teaching of Jesus about children. Premise 2, long believed by the church, is now given further (and massive) empirical support. The conclusion is highly congruent with the better known teaching of Jesus about marriage and divorce, and supports the traditional interpretation of it. We can therefore conclude confidently: the combined testimonies of scripture, tradition, and reason powerfully merge in favor of the marital form.

Before attending to the problem of élitism implicit in the commendation of marriage, a further defense is available to it, which might well be designated a theology of liberation for children. In the mid-1990s, as I was writing my book *Marriage After Modernity*,[41] it was becoming increasingly necessary to digest unpalatable British research findings regarding the relative well-being of children of divorced parents compared with the children of so-called "intact families."[42] One such study in Britain, published in 1993, anticipated many of the conclusions of the contributors to *Why Marriage Matters*. Its author, the distinguished socialist A.H. Halsey, observed

> that the children of parents who do not follow the traditional norm (i.e., taking on personal, active and long-term responsibility for the social upbringing of the children they generate) are thereby disadvantaged in many major aspects of their chances of living a successful life. On the evidence available such children tend to die earlier, to have more illness, to do less well at school, to exist at a lower level of nutrition, comfort and conviviality, to suffer more unemployment, to be more prone to deviance and crime, and finally to repeat the cycle of unstable parenting from which they themselves have suffered.[43]

Many similar studies with similar conclusions were becoming available in the United States.[44] I noted that the plight of some children in northern and Western societies was that they were "victims" of their parents' fickleness which was itself capable of being analyzed by means of an excessive economic and moral individualism.[45] Many of the concepts and features of the theology of liberation, forged in the poverty and oppression of the South, appeared applicable to the plight of many of the children of the North. A "preferential option" not just for the poor, but for children, seems fully justified. Just as liberation theology begins with "the marginalized" and seeks the transformation of their existence, so many children in rich countries appear marginalized and the transformation of their existence becomes an urgent matter.[46]

Children need to be liberated from parenting which does not put their interests first. Liberation theology starts with "practical measures for human betterment [which] have embraced theologians as co-workers in practical

---

[41] Adrian Thatcher, *Marriage After Modernity: Christian Marriage in Postmodern Times* (Sheffield, UK: Sheffield Academic Press/New York: New York University Press, 1999).
[42] See note 19 above.
[43] A.H. Halsey, "Foreword," in Dennis and Erdos, *Families without Fatherhood*, p. xii.
[44] Some of it was summarized by Stephen Post in his *Spheres of Love: Toward a New Ethics of the Family* (Dallas, TX: Southern Methodist University Press, 1994).
[45] Thatcher, *Marriage after Modernity*, pp. 142–9.
[46] Thatcher, *Marriage after Modernity*, pp. 149–54.

expressions of Christian commitment."[47] In the present case it is the betterment of children that is the primary concern. Liberation theology "is distinctive in its emphasis on the dialog between Christian tradition, social theory and the insight of the poor and marginalized into their situation, leading to action for change."[48] Many children are poor and marginalized and some of them are poorer and more marginalized through their parents' actions and inactions. When their insights into the desirability of their parents' prospective divorces are sought, they are almost always against them.

Again, a "preferential option," originally for the poor, "represents today a point of orientation for the pastoral activities of the Church and an important guideline for being a Christian."[49] A preferential option for children is one way of taking forward the teaching of Jesus about them. Theology, we are reminded, is "critical reflection" on practice. Theologians are told to expect a guilty conscience if they are preoccupied with the intellectual challenge of the European Enlightenment, that is with unbelief, at the expense of the moral and spiritual challenge of those "'non-persons,' those who are not recognized as people by the existing social order."[50] But that is precisely what much Christian theology and almost all "theological anthropology" does. Its agenda is fixed by modernity and children may get an odd reference in an index.

A key device in liberation theology is the analysis of social relations by means of the idea of "structural sin." It has already been introduced in order to contrast an ideal family world with the actual world of real families. In liberation theology structural sin operates like an analytical power tool. It shows

> how personal evil can be simultaneously strengthened and disguised by social relationships. A particular economic structure (a historical system of relationships between people) can easily create a series of situations which make necessary – and thus apparently reasonable – that conduct which favours one's own greed or that of one's family at the expense of the life and dignity of many others.[51]

[47] Christopher Rowland, "Preface," in Christopher Rowland (ed.), *The Cambridge Companion to Liberation Theology* (Cambridge, UK: Cambridge University Press, 1999), p. xiii.

[48] Rowland, *Cambridge Companion*, p. xiii.

[49] Gustavo Gutierrez, "The task and content of liberation theology," in Rowland, *Cambridge Companion*, [19–38], p. 27.

[50] Gutierrez, "The task and content of liberation theology," pp. 28–9.

[51] Valpy Fitzgerald, "The economics of liberation theology," in Rowland, *Cambridge Companion*, [218–34], p. 224.

But this concept of structural sin or "sinful structures" awaits application in the northern context where "social relationships" include relationships between parents and children; where the "historical system" increasingly incorporates non-standard forms of family life; where the raising of children by single parents becomes "necessary"; where "greed" may be a possible and unspoken reason why many couples avoid having children at all, and where "the life and dignity" of many children, including the unborn, is seriously at risk.

Children first

The evidence regarding the impact of family breakdown on children cannot remain a morally neutral matter for theology. Neither can theology avoid taking sides in the argument over family structure between "pessimists," "optimists," and "democrats" (above, 1.3).[52] A scene is set which, on the basis of the work we have considered in this chapter, can now be seen to be misleading. In this setting *any* bad news about alternative families can be pejoratively labeled as pessimism and ideological motivation disdainfully assigned to it, without reply. On the other hand, optimism requires no sustained analysis, despite the weight of the evidence against it. But commentators who point out the impact of divorce on children need not be influenced by some meta-narrative, religious or social, historical, or moral, which compels them to make carping judgments. They might just be advocates for children. This is not pessimism: in affirming that staying together is often better for everyone concerned, attention is drawn to springs of hope, springs which run counter to cultural pessimism about the ephemerality of lifelong commitments and the need for their regular re-negotiation. Neither are the "pessimists" making the category-confusion between association and causality. If an unmarried couple with children splits up, the pessimists do not claim that the cause of the split is the unstable relationship that was unlikely to last. There will be many causes which in individual cases could probably never be finally enumerated. The familists are drawing attention to statistical probabilities, and pointing out that, in general, relations of that kind are more likely to end than marriages are. Since many cohabiting couples may be largely unaware of the public information about what is likely to happen to

---

[52] Fiona Williams, ESRC CAVA Research Group, *Rethinking Families* (London: Calouste Gulbenkian Foundation, 2004), pp. 26–56.
[53] See William R. Garrett, "The Protestant Ethic and the Spirit of the Modern Family," *Journal for the Scientific Study of Religion*, 37.2, June 1998 [222–34].

people like them, there is a simple fact-imparting job to do. Indeed to refrain from it, and to entertain the falsehood that any structure is as good as any other, is woefully to misrepresent social realities as they are.

The move from patriarchal to egalitarian marriage which began at the Reformation[53] and has taken a further decisive step forward in the last 50 years will surely be welcomed by everyone except very conservative male Christians. Indeed the process needs to extend further still into a fairer sharing of domestic responsibilities. The preference for egalitarian, companionate marriage is the development of a religious tradition, not one that has replaced or run counter to it. It indicates that marriage itself is capable of change within a framework of lifelong commitment. The assumption that advocates of Christian marriage cannot accommodate egalitarian or companionate marriage is ideological, like the tying of the label "harmism" on familists who seek to point out the real harm done to many children in family breakdown, and who are not "harmist" or alarmist at all. Williams concludes that

> our empirical research on changes in parenting and partnering shows that the picture of self-actualising pioneers or selfish individuals fails to capture the moral texture of family lives and personal relationships in Britain today. Instead, it finds people to be energetic moral actors, embedded in webs of valued personal relationships, working to sustain the commitments that matter to them.[54]

She finds that people are making "morally informed responses to changes in their circumstances," and drawing "on repertoires of values about care and commitment in order to work out what, in practice, would be the 'proper thing to do.'" The diversity of response to new circumstances "should not be read as moral decline."[55] Indeed unabashed optimism attends these new arrangements and the new values accompanying them. "Commitments extend beyond blood and marriage to households linked through dissolved marriages, cohabitations, through new step-relations and friendships . . ." Many people do not share "agreement on a set of abstract moral imperatives, but a weighing-up of the given situation." People contemplating divorce consider "the effect on other close relationships (especially children but also grand-parents); whether it is the right time (for example, in terms of ages of children); the extent of harm/benefit to all those involved."[56]

---

[54] Williams, *Rethinking Families* p. 41.
[55] Williams, *Rethinking Families*, p. 42.
[56] Williams, *Rethinking Families*, p. 43.

Perhaps the most striking conclusion of the research is that commitment remains constant throughout these changes.

> Divorce does not therefore inevitably spell rupture. Post-divorce kin relation-ships show the *changing shape* of commitments as they extend across households no longer linked by marriage. The practical ethics which are important in these situations are based on attentiveness to others' needs, adaptability to new identities, and a spirit of reparation.[57]

This is a remarkable analysis, based on careful empirical research, like *Why Marriage Matters* (although its focus, on how families cope with divorce, is different). But it is bursting with moral assumptions. Before exposing these let us draw attention to its positive features. It is positive about people. It recognizes and honors people's commitments, and finds these in new config-urations of families, relations, and friends. It is honest in recognizing the disappearance of traditional moral frameworks that would once have inhib-ited adults from taking many of the decisions they now make about having sex, staying together, and remaining committed to their children. That said, the analysis is surely deficient in its assumptions about morality, about the meaning of commitment, and about the adequacy of any process of weighing up alternatives. How are people's decisions to split up "morally informed"? Their lack of use for abstract moral imperatives is depicted as a rejection of moral concepts and principles on the ground of irrelevance, but these same concepts and principles were only ever important insofar as they exerted their power to shape the characters and choices of people who affirmed them. Married people promise fidelity for life to one another and to their children. These are moral imperatives (keeping promises, keeping faithful) which are far from abstract even as they are set aside. It is beyond the scope of *Rethinking Families* to examine some of the likely causes of marital breakdown, how some breakdowns might be prevented, and how the honoring of life-com-mitments can contribute to this. But the alleged practical wisdom involved in abandoning or re-negotiating old commitments and entering into new ones may turn out to be a postmodern disdain for all moral frameworks. This disdain is not intellectually considered or defended, however. Neither is the possibility that the side-lining of moral principle may be an effect of the very selfishness Williams is keen to minimize.

What does commitment mean after lifelong commitments are termi-nated? Since commitments to partners and children are no longer absolute, but revocable, revisable, and re-negotiable, without fault, what is this dimin-

---

[57] Williams, *Rethinking Families*, p. 45 (author's emphases).

ished commitment actually worth? Serial monogamy is consistent with it, and since abstract principles have been dumped, what is left to discourage it? Once commitment becomes a relative matter, how can it inspire security, encourage the growth of love? It is remarkable that the abandonment of commitment is misleadingly depicted as a passive change in circumstances, or a change of the "shape" of commitment, when what is done is actively willed. It is yet more remarkable that the processes are uncritically described in a way that shows their consequentialist character. Divorce is right or wrong in terms of the calculation of consequences. How are the consequences of divorce on children going to be calculated (especially when the likelihood of harm to them is discounted or suppressed)? What felicific calculus[58] will be invoked in determining the right time to go? How does the calculation of "harm/benefit" differ from any other cost/benefit analysis? The name for this type of rational calculation is consequentialism: the rightness of actions is to be decided by right consequences. Unfortunately, because human agents are not God and lack omniscience, they are rarely capable of foreseeing the full and actual consequences of their actions. They are also persuadable to the point of deep self-deception that the calculation of consequences will be benign on all others who are affected by them. That is one of the reasons why any morality, Christian, or otherwise, defines and relies on principles. These help us to govern our actions when we are least capable of governing ourselves.

5.3 'Marital Values' and the Problem of Commitment

In the present chapter we have taken mild issue with those theologians who reduce family form to family function, and seen that other kinds of reduction are involved in this false move. What is required is a form where all members of a family, especially children, are more likely to thrive, and at this juncture, theology has to deal with empirical evidence which is itself contested. I have argued that, on the basis of probability, the evidence points to the need for children generally to be brought up by their biological parents whenever possible. The different evidence in *Rethinking Families* brackets out most of the moral considerations that are implicit in the processes it describes. My problem, at this point of the argument, is how to avoid the "empty inclusivism" of the liberals which regards all family forms as morally

---

[58] The idea that it is possible to quantify the overall value or disvalue of particular acts or policies was introduced into British philosophy by Jeremy Bentham (see his *An Introduction to the Principles of Morals and Legislation* (1780)), and has been attacked as inadequate ever since.

neutral, while also avoiding the clear implication of more conservative approaches to families, that it appears to, and often does, harshly judge all family forms not based on the married couple paradigm. That is the task of the present section.

Marital values beyond marriage?

Since only about half of households (in Britain) consist of or contain married couples, churches will need to get better at welcoming "non-traditional" families. They need a theology of marriage which assumes that marriage is normative, while at the same time accepting without reservation alternative relationships and family forms, and providing encouragement and support for them. Critical familism in its advocacy of marriage says little about alternative family forms (except that they are generally worse): mainline Protestantism, in its drive for inclusivism, is (at least in the United States) lukewarm about marriage. A bold theology of marriage is available that would strengthen each.

First, it is necessary to distinguish marriage as a legal, social, and religious institution, and marriage as an arrangement that embodies certain values, values for the sake of which it is upheld as an institution and held in esteem as a covenant, sacrament, holy estate, and so on. This distinction is used, not to hasten the unwelcome trend toward the treatment of marriage as a purely personal relationship unrelated to any sense of the common good, but rather to ask *all* Christian defenders of marriage why marriage is so important to them, especially when the New Testament is ambivalent about it. My answer is that in marriage, at its best, a woman and a man pledge to love one another as Christ loves the church and gave himself up for her as his bride (Eph. 5:25–33).[59] But that is a development of the Ephesian Household Code in accordance with principle 2 (above, 2.3) (and not an attempt to say that the Code says what it plainly does not.) Alternatively, the new covenant between God and God's people, sealed by the giving of the life of Christ, his blood, for us (Mk. 14:24; Mt. 26:28), and acknowledged at every eucharistic celebration, is also instantiated, and finitely enacted in the sacrament of marriage. Married partners are aided by grace to set forth this covenanted love as an icon of the Triune God who is Love and, in particular, to envelop their children with it. That is the vocation of marriage. The values lived out in this iconic relationship may be variously described but include deepening

---

[59] For a commentary on the exegetical moves involved in coming to this conclusion, see my *Marriage After Modernity*, pp. 90–5.

love, life-long fidelity, and mutual commitment – "to have and to hold from this day forward; for better, for worse, for richer, for poorer, in sickness and in health, to love and to cherish, till death us do part; according to God's holy law."[60] Let us call these values "marital values."

Now it is very clear that some marriages are lacking in marital values, and some non-marriages possess them. Marriage, then, is no guarantor of the provision of marital values (any more than the valid administration of a sacrament is the guarantor of faith in its recipients). Rowan Williams has rightly decried "the insistence on a fantasy version of heterosexual marriage as the solitary ideal, when the facts of the situation are that an enormous number of 'sanctioned' unions are a framework for violence and human destructiveness on a disturbing scale." Sexual union, he declares, "is not delivered from moral danger and ambiguity by satisfying a formal socioreligious criterion."[61] Wherever marital values are found churches should commend and name them, drawing the holders of them toward the self-giving source of all values, revelling in the prevenient grace of God among the millions of men and women who may still be ignorant of any Christian teaching about marriage.

Let us see how this suggestion works in practice, in relation to some of the alternative family forms. The churches will always want to commend marriage as better for married couples and their children, in most circumstances, than alternative family forms. But this advocacy cannot rest on the priority of the marital form alone, however attractive the theological packaging, especially since some marriages are miserable. However, its advocacy can rest on the promotion of the marital values just described. First, let us make the convenient distinction between pre-nuptial and non-nuptial cohabitors.[62] Since the former (but not the latter) are sufficiently one already, to intend to solemnize their relationship in a future marriage ceremony, earlier generations would have expected them to have become betrothed, and may have arranged a betrothal service for them, secular or religious.[63] The right pastoral approach to the increasing number of Christian couples who live together before marriage is to thank God for the marital values their togetherness already expresses, and to guide them to the

---

[60] From "The Vows" of the *Common Worship* Marriage Service of the Church of England. www.cofe.anglican.org/worship/liturgy/commonworship/texts/marriage/marriage.html. Accessed 02.09.2006.

[61] Rowan D. Williams, "The Body's Grace," in Eugene F. Rogers, Jr, *Theology and Sexuality: Classic and Contemporary Readings* (Malden, MA, and Oxford, UK: Blackwell, 2002) [309–21], p. 316.

[62] Thatcher, *Living Together*, pp. 45–63.

[63] I argue this at length, and discuss the details, in Thatcher, *Living Together*.

solemnization and deepening of those values in the sacrament of Christian marriage. Expressions of disapproval, accusations of living in sin, insistence even on separation prior to the wedding (what could be more daft?) are pointless and destructive, themselves a sin against the prevenient grace that is bringing the couple to a lifelong commitment. Increasingly, unmarried couples are bringing their children to church for baptism. With appropriate counseling for the parents, priests are wholly right to baptize these children, and to express the joyful solidarity of the church with the demanding tasks facing young parents.

Second, single parents with children. There are several possible entry points into this particular family form. One is the death of a spouse or partner; another is a non-nuptial cohabitation that ended; another is divorce or annulment; another is pregnancy in an uncommitted relationship, perhaps where the termination of the pregnancy has been offered and courageously refused. Popular media present distressing cases of obvious promiscuity, of the failure of sex education, of the burgeoning cost of child support and welfare, of the neglect of children by inexperienced or reluctant mothers, or the pressing of older children into premature responsibility for their younger siblings, and so on. Single-parent families are far from ideal, yet probably no family corresponds to the ideal in every way. It is likely that the single parent, the mother in over 90 percent of cases, is doubly committed to her child or children, trying to be both mother and father to them, and placing them and their needs before her own. These are heroic examples of commitment, often requiring emotional, economic, and physically exhausting self-sacrifice which ought to be honored by the churches, even as they are honored by the Father of all. They are every bit marital values, probably maintained at considerable cost outside the marriage relationship. This is where *Rethinking Families* scores. Understanding, acceptance, and support are needed to strengthen the mother's resolve and efforts. So are efforts which may lead the family to greater stability in the future. Any lingering sense of stigma merely contributes to a sense of isolation and rejection. Any attribution of blame is already too late, even if it is useful. And if the mother refuses sexual intimacy or cohabitation with a potential new partner until she has the promise of commitment to her and to her children, she acts in her own and her children's interests.

For similar reasons, there are, third, marital values in stepfamilies or blended families which must be acknowledged and encouraged. Parents and children may not find blending to be quite as they expected to find it, and, once new configurations of relationships are established, everything must be done to create commitment and stability in changed circumstances. According to the argument of this book many family break-ups are preventable and should not happen, but that is no argument for withholding support, friendship, fellowship, or encouragement from blended families as they become established (below, 8.1). It is not inconsistent both to advocate that many families which break up should, in their own interests, stay together, and to advocate marital values in the case of recombined families who have undergone pain through separation and further union.

Fourth, that marital values exist in the case of many thousands of lesbian and gay couples is undeniable. I have argued elsewhere that the case for extending the rite and the right of marriage to couples of the same sex is overwhelming.[64] (That is not to say, of course, that all lesbian and gay couples want, or ought, to marry.) If they promise to try to love one another as Christ loves the church, then marital values are present. Thank God that there are many people of the same sex who desire to promise themselves to each other in this way! Where the couples are free (and willing) to adopt or foster children, their love extends to and embraces them as well, and in many cases strengthens the union. The informal blessings of same-sex unions, and indeed, the writings of lesbian and gay theologians themselves, indicate that such blessings display more than an analogical resemblance to heterosexual marriage. It is sad that out of deference to Christian teaching the registration of civil partnerships by same-sex couples throughout the United Kingdom is not permitted in religious premises.[65] That drives a further wedge between the recognition of marital values and the institution that solemnizes, encourages, and supports them.

A final example of marital values outside of institutional marriage is an elderly, childless, cohabiting couple (known to me) where one is the carer of the declining and dying partner. Without the public promise to love her partner for better, for worse, in sickness and in health, till death them do part, such love is willingly given; the pain is shared, and an easier life sacrificed for the good of the loved one. It is difficult even to entertain the question whether marital status is important to the couple, to their community and to God. What matters is the presence of marital values in a non-marital relationship, and these are present abundantly.

Extending the marital norm

If readers are unhappy with the extension of marital values to relationships that are not formally marriages, and remain to be persuaded, a parallel

---

[64] Thatcher, *Marriage after Modernity*, pp. 294–302.
[65] The Civil Partnership Bill became law in Great Britain in December 2005.

argument may be advanced. The argument is that marriage is the norm for sexual behavior among Christians, but as soon as the norm is converted into a rule, and the rule applied to every occurrence of heterosexual sexual intercourse, then the point and purpose of the norm is lost. The confusion between norms and rules, claims Joseph Monti,[66] is an "analytic mistake" that is constantly being made. A major flaw in denominational conversations in the United States about sexual relations is said to be the "collapse" of "the distinction and distance between norms and rules." Norms, he says, become operational for the Christian community in metaphor, symbol, and sacrament. Norms disclose and generate values which shape the moral life: rules are "proximate," providing guidance "in particular situations and circumstances." When the two are confused, confusion in moral thought and action soon follows. There are three levels to moral discourse. Level one consists of norms. These are foundational, and are embedded in the deep history of religious traditions. Level two consists of principles. Principles mediate between general norms and the third level which consists of rules, that operate in particular circumstances.

An example of a norm (see above, 3.3) is "You shall love your neighbor as yourself." Any conduct inconsistent with this norm should not be countenanced in Christian ethics. But the norm needs application in real circumstances. When the lawyer asks Jesus "But who is my neighbor?" (Lk. 10:29), prompting the telling of the parable of the good Samaritan, we could say he wanted Jesus to translate the norm into a rule. Jesus didn't do this, but instead told a parable that illustrated it. The lawyer's reply to Jesus' question, "The one who showed him kindness," might be said to generate the rule, "It is always right to act kindly." Even so a rule does not materialize. The lawyer is told to "Go and do as he did," leaving the circumstances and application of the norm to the lawyer to work out for himself.

An example of the possible confusion between norm and rule is the principle "Always tell the truth." This is a norm so deep that it helps to form character and promote moral goodness. However if the norm is appropriated "as an absolute rule of literal speech − a regulation of literal behaviour in any and all circumstances," the norm becomes dysfunctional. Since preference for a literal understanding of moral norms has become "a modern idolatry," the dysfunctional collapse of the difference between norms and rules is difficult to prevent. Marriage is so embedded in Christian understandings of covenant, sacrament, personal union, and so on, that it too is a

---

[66] Joseph Monti, *Arguing about Sex: The Rhetoric of Christian Sexual Morality* (New York: State University of New York Press, 1995).

fundamental norm for sexual relations. But a norm it remains, rather than a rule – "in upholding the norm of heterosexual marriage as a rule of behaviour in any and all situations and circumstances, many denominations are making the same analytic mistake of confusing ethical norms and moral rules."[67]

This analysis has obvious relevance to the appropriateness of the extension of marital values beyond the institution of marriage. Presumably there is agreement among Christians that sexual relations among them are condoned by and confined to marriage. At least that remains official teaching, where it has certainly functioned in the past as a rule. Well, suppose the rule is relocated as a norm, on a different level of discourse, so that marriage remains "norm-ative" in a Christian sexual theology and the norm is allowed to generate different rules in different circumstances? While marriage remains the "official" norm of sexual behavior for Christians, the embodiment of the values of the norm may, it turns out, reside in relationships other than marriage. This is a further important feature of Monti's argument. The "orbit of the norm is flexible enough to sometimes change what has traditionally been included and excluded." Using marriage as an example of a norm, he claims

> It is possible to argue that in principle, and on the basis of abiding and effective values of love and commitment revealed by the norm of marriage, that sexual intimacy may be morally responsible in certain material conditions and situations other than marriage and heterosexuality because the same values are being effected as goods. In these cases, the sacramental effectiveness of the Church's norm has been extended functionally to these states of affairs.[68]

Something else needs to be said about rules. In some cases rules are obvious, in others less so. "Never rape another person" seems to me a good rule, whether or not it is derived from the principle "Honor vulnerability" or directly from the norm of neighbor-love. Rules have to be applicable to situations, or they won't be applied: they won't be recognized as relevant. What Christian sexual ethics generally has been reluctant to face is the explosion out of the closet and in the public domain of novel personal "situations" which, *prima facie*, are simply not covered by rules that were formulated for different situations and different times. These situations include the circumstances of adults remaining unmarried until their thirties; of postmarried people lacking the gift of celibacy; of cohabiting couples

---

[67] Monti, *Arguing about Sex*, pp. 115–16: 160: 121.
[68] Monti, *Arguing about Sex*, p. 154 (emphasis added).

before, after, and without reference to marriage; of lesbian and gay people forsaking the closet and presenting themselves to the churches for their blessing, and so on. All such people are likely to be alienated by being told that if they are not married the church cannot condone their sexual behavior, their sexualities or themselves. If, however, the values generated by the norm of marriage are allowed to permeate to them, through principles, to rules that do make sense in these situations, then the marital norm is upheld, and contact between Christian teaching and those who are marginalized by it, is rebuilt.

If these arguments carry conviction it follows that the hallowed contrasts made between marriage and celibacy, or marriage and singleness, so beloved of writers of church sexuality reports, will require modification. Stephen Post, for example, in his commendable haste to include single people in his theology of the family, does not consider that the distinction between marriage and singleness may not serve him well in today's circumstances. "The single Christian should appreciate the opportunity that singleness offers to free him or her from anxious concern about spouse and children in order to serve all of humanity."[69] Perhaps. But singleness is not the same as celibacy, and single Christians may have other anxious concerns to attend to in the absence of spouse and children. Neat conceptual distinctions in any case never replicate reality as it is or as it might be. If celibacy is a rare gift, and only about half or less of adults are married, there will be sexual relationships galore which, whether they are right or wrong, plainly resist the cosy dual categorization of marriage or singleness, but will be found somewhere along the murky continuum between these demarcated states. The operative value here is chastity. Chastity is not the requirement of abstention from sexual relations, even though some chaste people choose abstinence as its appropriate form. It is the exercise of appropriate restraint in the relations one has. "All Christ's faithful are called to lead a chaste life *in keeping with their particular states of life*."[70] But there are several "states of life." Married couples are required to be chaste. That means they cannot have sexual relations with anyone but their partners. That is the restraint to which they voluntarily subscribe. Chastity for people who are heterosexual, fertile, and unmarried may mean abstaining from full sexual relations with a loved one until both are ready for mutual commitment to one another, and to any children the couple might have.

---

[69] Stephen G. Post, *More Lasting Unions – Christianity, the Family and Society* (Grand Rapids, MI/Cambridge, UK: Eerdmans, 2000), p. 36.
[70] *Catechism of the Catholic Church* (London: Geoffrey Chapman, 1994), section 2348 (p. 502) (emphasis added). My use of this quotation would of course be anathema to its authors.

I hope in this section to have shown that there can be marital values in non-marital relationships; that unconditional commitments to partners and children exist within and without the marital institution. The reality of marital values, wherever they are found, is to be preferred to the rhetoric of family values, which must be practiced by traditional nuclear families. The pastoral care of non-traditional families is likely to include the acknowledgement and praise of marital values, to deepen understanding of these, and in some cases to nudge couples toward the solemnization of their relationship when their commitment goes unconditional. Marital values build a solid bridge between an empty inclusivism and a prescriptive traditionalism by celebrating marriage and extending its goods.

Chapter Six

Children, Parents, and Rights

In the previous chapter it was argued that the marital family form be favored, not just because the Christian faith has always assumed this, but because it can be shown, on balance, to benefit children better than other forms. The teaching of Jesus requires us to assume family forms which suit children best. But millions of children do not have the benefit of the marital family form and some of those who do may be victims of cruelty or neglect within it. In such cases the rights of children serve to protect them, and children's rights, it will be argued, deserve the support of all Christians. However, rights present a complex problem for theology, and in this chapter that problem is grasped. I ask first why, given the rich theological sources for families, children have been neglected in theology. Second, a recent defense of children's rights in *Honouring Children*[1] is considered and endorsed. But, third, the chapter diverges from that work by grounding children's rights in the teaching of Jesus about children and in his human identity as the Christ Child.

Because this chapter engages with rights, it is largely theoretical, so a brief justification is needed as to why it appears in the second part of the book entitled "Relations." There are two main reasons. Rights entail duties, and children's rights entail duties to children whose relations with their parents are impaired, perhaps by cruelty, or by parental death, or by physical or economic incapacity. Rights come into play when relations with parents are seriously impaired or curtailed. But a second reason has to do with the teaching of Jesus Himself. We have seen how that teaching addresses children universally or generally but does not address their relationship to

---

[1] Kathleen Marshall and Paul Parvis, *Honouring Children: The Human Rights of the Child in Christian Perspective* (Edinburgh: Saint Andrew Press, 2004).

parents. But in its sheer universality it overlaps considerably with children's rights which, if they exist at all, exist universally. So while parent–child relations are of the utmost importance for the theology of families which is building in this book, the rights of children protect their interests in the wider family of humankind. It will be shown that the function of children's rights, namely the protection of vulnerable children, encapsulates and extends part of the teaching of Jesus about children, in our present global context.

6.1 Where Are the Children?

Why, then, is there a dearth of theological reflection about children, both historically and in the present? The temptation to include our children under the rubric of neighbor was resisted. The bond between parents (especially mothers) and children was explained by means of kin altruism, and by a theological anthropology which assumes a basic relatedness, to God and to other people, of the human person. God becomes a child, the Child Jesus. God's joyful gift of the Son to the world is reflected in the joy of parents in the gift of a child. Why have these doctrinal themes largely failed to inform Christian teaching about children?

Drawing on the suggestion in the last chapter that a theology of liberation for children is overdue, we do well to note that another key concept in that theology is "hiddenness." This is not the hiddenness or *lètheia* of the God who is subsequently disclosed in the "unhiddenness" or *alètheia* of "the truth." No, these are the ones who are hidden by the preoccupations of dominant discourses (including theological ones); who do not feature in dominant world-views or influential anthropologies; who have no representation among the powerful, whether they be women, or slaves, or ethnic minorities, or the poor. One of the disturbing features of much theology is the hiddenness of children. "Systematic theologians and Christian ethicists have said little about children, and they have not regarded serious reflection on children as a high priority."[2] But that is true of historical theology as well. Feminist theology wants liberation for women, but while there is much "carping about feminist oversights" in relation to children from the theological mainstream,[3] its record on children is poor (but no worse than

[2] Marcia J. Bunge, "Introduction," in Marcia J. Bunge (ed.), *The Child in Christian Thought* (Grand Rapids, MI/Cambridge, UK: Eerdmans, 2001), p. 3.
[3] Bonnie J. Miller-McLemore, "'Let the Children Come' Revisited: Contemporary Feminist Theologians on Children," in Bunge, *The Child in Christian Thought* [446–73], p. 446.

more mainstream branches of theology). Sexual theology, lesbian and gay theology, and queer theology, for all their liberatory intent, generally collude with the hiddenness of children. It is no defense for these theologies to argue that their interests are elsewhere for that is precisely the charge against them. It would take a major investigation to inquire into the reasons why, "although the church has highly developed teachings on other issues, such as abortion, economic justice, and moral conduct in war, theologians have not offered sustained reflection on the nature of children or on the obligations that parents, the state, and the church have to nurture children."[4] There is no higher authority for a theology of childhood than the teaching of Jesus: in order to hear it afresh, some of the interference on our listening wavelengths needs to be filtered out.

We asked earlier, in order to engage with the difficulties, how the New Testament views children (above, 2.1), and noted three substantial qualifications to the teaching of Jesus: the ambiguity surrounding marriage which is extended to children; the harder tone of the Household Codes when compared with the Gospels, regarding children, and the possible usurpation of teaching about children in conceptualizations of adults as children of faith, in relation to the heavenly Father. More details might be added to this ambiguous picture. The author of *Calling God "Father"* has gamely attempted a "biblical" picture of human fatherhood, but even he has to admit that "in fact, the paucity of New Testament texts that speak explicitly to or about fathers regarding their duties as fathers *of their own children* is a little surprising."[5] He acknowledges that the Hebrew scriptures and the Talmud are more fruitful in this regard (and is so troubled by "the lack of attention in the teaching of Jesus to the role of fathers as caretakers of their own children," that he finds a "partial explanation" in the apparent alienation of Jesus from his biological family[6]). The author of Ephesians contrasts "the full stature of Christ" with the gullible state of childhood which Christians are to eschew (Eph. 4:14). The author of 1 Timothy thinks that having children is how women overcome the gendered consequences of the fall of Eve (1 Tim. 2:15). Having children is a way of atoning for the responsibility for bringing sin into the world. He also thinks that raunchy young widows are to deal with their renascent desires by further marriage and having children (1 Tim. 5:14). Hugh Pyper says that in the New Testament "childbearing is

---

[4] Bunge, "Introduction," p. 4.
[5] John W. Miller, *Calling God "Father": Essays on the Bible, Fatherhood and Culture* (New York/ Mahwah, NJ: Paulist Press, 1999), p. 73 (my emphasis).
[6] Miller, *Calling God "Father,"* p. 77.

if anything discouraged," citing this verse as "the one justification for it."[7] Paul's inspirational poem about the greatest of the Spirit's fruits, love, is less positive about the provisional and immature state of childhood: "When I was a child I spoke like a child, thought like a child, reasoned like a child; but when I grew up I finished with childish things" (1 Cor. 13:11). These verses are an aside, an illustration of a more important point, yet in the process they reveal an element of Paul's thinking about children. In the same letter he complains that when he came to Corinth "I had to deal with you on the natural plane, as infants in Christ. I fed you on milk, instead of solid food, for which you were not yet ready. Indeed, you are still not ready for it . . ." (1 Cor. 3:1b–3a). The model of childhood he uses rather assumes that being a child is an unenviable, provisional, and ignorant state to be left behind quickly and gladly. When the child/adult distinction is made into an analogy by being compared with the natural/spiritual distinction, the dismissive attitude to children becomes clearer.

The Gospel of John models the adult relation to God on the basis of being a child. To believers is given "the right to become children of God, born not of human stock, by the physical desire of a human father, but of God" (Jn. 1:12b,13). John is more interested in the second birth, the birth "from above" (*anòthen*) (Jn. 3:3). "Flesh can give birth only to flesh; it is spirit that gives birth to spirit" (Jn. 3:6). It is not suggested that the metaphor of regeneration or second birth is in any way intended to eclipse the generation and "first" birth of children, or that giving birth in the flesh is to be disparaged. However, consequences are often unintended. While the preaching of the Gospel will stress the importance of the new birth in baptism and in spirit, the church's proclamation of these matters must not create the impression that the birthing and raising of children is not also a vital matter.

Clement of Alexandria

So the first reason for the child-shaped hiatus in theological thought may be the paucity and diversity of views about children in the New Testament itself. In these circumstances, according to our principles for family-friendly readings of scripture, the teaching of Jesus has clear priority. The diversity of attitudes to children is another reason why these rules are necessary. A second reason for child neglect in theology may be due to the continuing

---

[7] Hugh Pyper, "Children," in Adrian Hastings, Alistair Mason, and Hugh Pyper (eds.), *The Oxford Companion to Christian Thought* (Oxford, UK: Oxford University Press, 2000), p. 110.

legacy of this diversity in patristic and subsequent thought. Clement of Alexandria, Augustine, and Aquinas will be our examples.[8] Clement of Alexandria is closest to the spirit of the teaching of Jesus. Unfortunately he is also the least influential. Christian adults are the children of God in faith, and they are to imitate the simplicity of real children in the practice of their faith. Clement reminds his readers that it was children who shouted "Hosanna to the Son of David!" in the temple, offering perfect praise (Mt. 21:14–16).[9] Clement's allegorical reading of scripture allows him to say that when Jesus refers to people as lambs (a reference to Mt. 25:33) "he alludes to the simple children, as if they were sheep and lambs in nature, not men; and the lambs He counts worthy of preference, from the superior regard He has to that tenderness and simplicity of disposition in men which constitutes innocence." Scriptural references to calves and chickens receive similar treatment, pointing to children's innocence and simplicity. Clement explains Moses' prescription of the sacrifice of two pigeons or doves as a sin offering by explaining "that the harmlessness and innocence and placable nature of these tender young birds are acceptable to God."

Clement does not simply extrapolate an ideal element of childhood and demand its imitation by adults. The youthfulness of the colt on which Jesus entered into Jerusalem stands allegorically for the eternal youth of the new covenant, of the new life in Christ "which shall know no old age." Children are "the fairest and most perfect objects in life." When Jesus used children as an example for adults to follow, Clement explains, it was not because they were without understanding or learning, but because children "know Him who is God alone as their Father, who are simple, and infants, and guileless, who are lovers of the horns of the unicorns." Clement was able to derive the Greek for infant (*nèpios*) from the word "gentle" (*èpios*), and to conclude that "the child (*nèpios*) is therefore gentle (*èpios*) and therefore more tender, delicate, and simple, guileless, and destitute of hypocrisy, straightforward and upright in mind, which is the basis of simplicity and truth." Finally the whole Christian community is itself when it behaves with a child's tenderness:

> And we are tender who are pliant to the power of persuasion, and are easily drawn to goodness, and are mild, and free of the stain of malice and perverseness, for the ancient race was perverse and hard-hearted; but the band of infants, the new people which we are, is delicate as a child.

---

[8] Bunge's *The Child in Christian Thought* may be consulted for many more.
[9] *Paidagogos* [*The Instructor*], 1.5. All references are to Book 1, Chapter 5, in Roberts-Donaldson's English translation. www.earlychristianwritings.com/clement.html. Accessed 02.09.2006.

Augustine and Aquinas

Clement's view of the child has much in common with the idea of "child-ness" (above, 3.2), but it was eclipsed by the towering authority of Augustine. Augustine's view of children is much better known, even if it is not well understood. If Clement's over-idealization of childhood is barely recognizable among today's parents and child psychologists, hardly anyone today can prefer Augustine's view of children to his. In her positive and sympathetic essay on Augustine's theology of childhood Martha Ellen Stortz charges him with "overly theologizing and moralizing childhood. What we regard as developmental issues he examined for evidence of the burden of a sin that had infected all of Adam's progeny."[10] She shows how, in his furious argument with Julian of Eclanum, two different Latin translations of Romans 5.12 ("sin came into the world") were put to radically different interpretations. Julian's translation contained the verb *introire* ("come into"): Augustine's version had *intrare* ("penetrate"). "For Augustine the word *intrare* dripped with sexual meaning: the contamination spread from Adam's semen! Goaded by Julian of Eclanum into further specifying the site and circumstances of Adam's sin, Augustine did not disappoint . . . The sin of Adam penetrated all of human nature, even the newborn baby."[11]

Stortz shows how this theology, albeit unwittingly, extended the attribution of sin even to the unborn child in the womb. The doctrine of the goodness of all created things was maintained but fatally compromised: "creatures possessed a good creation but a corrupt propagation." Because sin begins in the act of conception, "from conception the creature was trapped in a second nature penetrated by sin and driven by a vitiated will."[12] The "non-innocence" which Augustine had observed in the behavior of very young children extended to the foetus *in utero*. Only Christ himself, being conceived without sexual intercourse, escaped the doom of original sin, and can save us from it. Baptism is needed for the cleansing from sin. Without it eternal damnation follows the premature death of a child. This, decided Augustine, was the fate of the Holy Innocents (Mt. 2:16–18). The baptismal rite contained an exorcism of Satan. "Belief that the newborn lay in the grasp of Satan undergirded these practices, and the rite of baptism signified first and foremost Christ's repossession of the child." The argument with the

[10] Martha Ellen Stortz, "'Where or When Was Your Servant Innocent?': Augustine on Child-hood," in Bunge (ed.), *The Child in Christian Thought* [78–102], pp. 99–100.
[11] Stortz, "Where or When Was Your Servant Innocent?," p. 93.
[12] Stortz, "Where or When Was Your Servant Innocent?," p. 94.

Pelagians and Julian of Eclanum led to further clarification of this belief: "all the unbaptized, including newborns, were 'under the power of the devil.'"[13]

My reason for rehearsing Augustine's dismal view of children is not simply to repudiate it but to suggest that it further inhibited a positive theology of childhood thereafter. Theologians wishing to sound a sweeter note were denied the breadth of vision by the sheer hegemonic power of Augustine's pessimistic synthesis. Even Chrysostom, who is praised for his theology of parenthood and childhood,[14] was also known for less positive attitudes to children.[15] Christina Traina suggests "the history of the theology of childhood might well be cast as the history of the struggle to preserve and express Augustine's doctrine of original sin without eroding beliefs in both divine justice and divine mercy toward the weak and vulnerable."[16] Aquinas, she says, adopted a "curious hybrid solution" to the problem, synthesizing the two "contradictory theological anthropologies" of Augustine and the newly rediscovered Aristotle. Aquinas upheld the doctrine of original sin, but against Augustine, he also upheld "the manifest actual innocence of the unbaptized child."[17] His solution for the case of unbaptized *older* children (who have begun to acquire the faculty of reason) and adults is the "baptism of desire." "Rational persons who by God's grace genuinely wish to be baptized but are prevented from participating in the sacrament receive all the grace of sacramental baptism, including the remission of original and actual sin, simply through this wish."[18] This solution is unavailable to infants, so the *limbus puerorum* is created specially for them. In limbo "they are denied intimate union with God but spared the physical, spiritual, and psychological pain of hell." Traina comments that

> the chilling implications of this interpretation of the inexorable logic of divine justice are unmistakable in its bizarre psychology . . . Thomas argues matter-of-factly that in limbo, unbaptized children – then possessing the natural perfection of reason – will recognize but not protest their separation from God: "If one is guided by right reason one does not grieve through being deprived of what is beyond one's power to obtain, but only through

---

[13] Stortz, "Where or When Was Your Servant Innocent?," p. 96, citing Augustine, "On Marriage and Concupiscence," 1.11.

[14] Vigen Guroian, "The Ecclesial Family: John Chrysostom on Parenthood," in Bunge, *The Child in Christian Thought* [61–77].

[15] See Chrysostom, *Homily 1 on Marriage*, in Eugene F. Rogers, Jr (ed.), *Theology and Sexuality* (Malden, MA, and Oxford, UK: Blackwell, 2002) [87–92].

[16] Christina L.H. Traina, "A Person in the Making," in Bunge (ed.), *The Child in Christian Thought* [103–33], p. 105.

[17] Traina, "A Person in the Making," pp. 113–14.

[18] Traina, "A Person in the Making," p. 114, citing *Summa Theologiae*, 3.68.8–9.

lack of that which, in some way, one is capable of obtaining." Innocent bearers of original sin, they neither deserve nor expect heaven.[19]

Our subject in this section is the inattention ceded to children in the theological tradition. It has not been demonstrated that children have received scant attention in the tradition (though they have not). It has been suggested that the tensions surrounding the topic of children in the tradition are sufficiently severe for positive writing about them to have been impeded by the very tensions the tradition generates. In contrast the teaching of Jesus about children is unreservedly positive about them. The earliest church did not have time, because of the imminent parousia, to develop a theology of childhood. The later New Testament church was preoccupied more with matters of persecution and fundamental doctrine. It adopts and adapts Household Codes, probably without even noticing the changing tonal contrast with the teaching of the Lord, which, even then, was just being written down in the Gospels. The view of childhood as a state of immaturity lacking value in itself, found in the asides of St Paul, is not yet re-shaped. The voice of Clement on children was untypical of the third century, and his near adulation of children may actually have more to do with a distanced romanticism than with serious theological analysis. Childhood is caught up in divisions, often bitter, about other matters. Peter Brown describes the growing tide of asceticism and attempted sexual renunciation from St Paul to St Augustine.[20] The sense of the universality and inevitability of sin associated with sexual intercourse, even in marriage, impacts inevitably on the means of conception and on the meaning, efficacy, mode, and administration of Christian baptism. The unintended consequence of the argument with Pelagius was a heightened emphasis on baptism as God's means of washing it away. The eternal damnation of unbaptized infants, however theologically odious and ruinous it might seem to us, is a perfectly correct inference from this unfortunate historical nexus of theological ideas, and the fiction of the *limbus puerorum* is actually a daring attempt to modify them. From our contemporary perspective, we are likely to say that this child theology is perverse. It cannot be modified. It should be abandoned altogether.

Having identified this theology as an inhibitor of positive appreciation of children, it is important to mention the moral enormity of a theology that assigns unbaptized children to hell (and even leads to the sanctioning of

---

[19] Traina, "A Person in the Making," p. 115, citing *Summa Theologiae*, Appendix, 1,1.2.
[20] Peter Brown, *The Body and Society: Men, Women and Sexual Renunciation in Early Christianity* (London: Faber and Faber, 1989).

instruments for baptizing children in the womb.[21]) This is not to say that
our theology does not suffer from equally grievous flaws: only that it should
not continue to suffer from these particular ones. Neither does it follow
that a grievous theology of childhood issues in the grievous treatment of
children. It can generate compassion toward them, and, "within a rich theological context, [it] can provide a kind of positive, egalitarian framework of
thought that opens a door to responding creatively and effectively to the
needs of poor children . . ."[22] It is one thing to side with Augustine against
Pelagius over the universality and effect of sin. It is quite another thing to
locate this in the body, or sexuality, or sexual intercourse, and to extend
damnation to small human beings whose capacities for agency, conscience,
and reason are minimal. Augustine's assumptions about children do not
appear to be compatible with the teachings of Jesus about children. They
represent too formidable an obstacle to negotiate for any Christian who
wants to regard children as Jesus did and to see them as precious gifts of
God. That they are conceived in sin and arrive in the world damned, are
two premises which poison the theology of childhood. Indeed "poisonous
pedagogy" is now a well-used term which describes some of the perverse
practices that appeal directly to it.[23]

Other possible reasons for the neglect of children in the tradition must
be mentioned more briefly. One is undoubtedly gender. Men are more
distanced from their children than women are, yet men have controlled
theology for two thousand years. Who looks after the children? The answer,
of course, is that mothers generally bond more closely to their children than
do fathers, and are more involved in their upbringing, especially in the early
years. And women, historically, have had much less access to theology, being
mainly ineligible for ministry until the end of the last century. In churches
run entirely by men, where mothers do not preach, teach, or administer the
sacraments, is it surprising that childhood is a neglected topic? Where theological reflection is male reflection, and men are distanced from children, is
it surprising that there is little reflection about children, and what there is, is

---

[21] Stortz, "Where or When Was Your Servant Innocent?," p. 94.
[22] Bunge, "Introduction," p. 16, referring to her essay, "Education and the Child in Eighteenth-Century German Pietism: Perspectives from the Work of A.H. Francke," in Bunge
(ed.), *The Child in Christian Thought* [247–78].
[23] For the distressing poisonous pedagogy thesis see Philip Greven, *The Protestant Temperament,
Patterns of Child-Rearing, Religious Experience, and the Self in Early America* (New York: Alfred A.
Knopf, 1977). Also his *Spare the Child: The Religious Roots of Punishment and the Psychological
Impact of Physical Abuse* (New York: Alfred A. Knopf, 1991), and Alice Miller, *For Your Own
Good: Hidden Cruelty in Child-Rearing and the Roots of Violence* [tr. H. and H. Hannum] (New
York: Farrar, Straus, and Giroux, 1983).

poor? There were almost no married theologians until the Reformation, so much of the extant writing about children in the tradition has been undertaken by men who have not fathered children at all. Questions must be asked about the experience of childhood of some of those theologians. What would it have been like for a child to have been given away, at the age of six, to a monastery? That was Aquinas' experience of childhood. Questions must also be asked about the experience of fatherhood of some of the theologians who had children, for example, Augustine. His son was illegitimate, and the effect of his liaisons with two different partners on his subsequent theology of sexuality can hardly be overestimated.

And questions must be asked about the role of experience in theological writing. In the Anglican Communion references are sometimes made to "the three-legged stool" (scripture, tradition, and reason) and to the issue whether, with the addition of the category of experience, it may become a "four-legged" one. While empiricism embraced the evidence of the senses as a secure source of knowledge in the seventeenth century, there has been no such move in theology until the late twentieth century, when the experiences of exclusion, oppression, poverty, or discrimination were rightly claimed by theologians of liberation as a source for doing theology. A theology for children has to listen to the experience of children, and to those who raise them.

Finally, the use of children and childhood as an extrinsic metaphor for bringing into speech aspects of the adult relationship to God can end up demeaning real children, pushing them off stage. Since most theological language about children is metaphorical, real children are in danger of being overlooked. The very mention of children in the tradition is normally taken to refer metaphorically to adults. It is easy to assume, mistakenly, that a purpose of childhood is to provide adults with convenient conceptualizations of their adult relationships with God. The assumption is unavoidable to anyone reading Clement, notwithstanding his view of real children. The language-game of childhood in Christian discourse is, paradoxically, an adult one. Adults call *themselves* children of the Heavenly Father, with overwhelming biblical endorsement; no-one on earth is to be called "father"; and many Christians learn to speak of their church as their Mother. There can be little doubt that real childhood suffers displacement whenever this language-game is played. The needs of real children are in danger of being supplanted by the spiritual needs of the adult children of God. Worse, this language can be appropriated for political purposes. A reason for treating adults as children is to demand obedience from them, or, the same thing, to exercise power over them. Whatever the reasons for the lack of emphasis on children in the tradition, the emphasis on children in the teaching of Jesus is unmistakable, and to this, with much relief, we now return in the next section.

6.2 The Defense of Children's Rights

Honoring children

The title of the book by Kathleen Marshall and Paul Parvis, *Honouring Children*, already signifies a reversal of the emphasis of the fifth commandment, "Honour your father and your mother" (Ex. 20:12; Dt. 5:16). Filial devotion to parents is not the only requirement of families informed by biblical faith: children too are to be honored. Marshall and Parvis aim "to show that promotion of the rights of vulnerable people, especially children, is an effective way of promoting the Christian agenda."[24] Much of their work is helpfully descriptive, bringing to theology important material more familiar to lawyers and child protection specialists. We are reminded that the United Nations Universal Declaration of Human Rights (1948) rests on the premise that "recognition of the inherent dignity and of the equal and inalienable rights of all members of the human family is the foundation of freedom, justice and peace in the world." In 1989 the United Nations General Assembly passed the Convention on the Rights of the Child. In 2004, only two countries, Somalia and the United States, had failed to ratify the Convention, the latter due in part to "questions raised by Christian politicians about the potential impact of the Convention on the stability of family life and the authority of parents."[25] Human rights language is said to be used "to denote conditions for the realisation of human dignity justified with reference to moral, religious or legal authority or reasoning."[26] John Locke derived "natural" rights from "natural law." This derivation is partly responsible for the sympathy of the Catholic tradition toward human rights. On the fiftieth anniversary of the Declaration, the Pontifical Council for the Family stressed "the convergence between this Declaration and Christian anthropology and ethics, despite the fact that the document makes no reference to God." The Vatican made clear that the Declaration "recognises the rights it proclaims, it does not grant them."[27]

---

[24] Marshall and Parvis, *Honouring Children*, p. 3.
[25] Marshall and Parvis, *Honouring Children*, p. 1.
[26] Marshall and Parvis, *Honouring Children*, pp. 95–6.
[27] Marshall and Parvis, *Honouring Children*, p. 109, citing Pontifical Council for the Family, *The Family and Human Rights*, December 9, 1999, para. 2.

Children's rights are a sub-species of human rights. Children are human beings, so if there are human rights, they cover children. So what is covered by rights? The "characteristics of the human rights" proclaimed by the 1948 Declaration are that they recognize the *inherent* dignity of all members of the human family; apply *equally* to all; and are *inalienable*.

In terms of content, the rights proclaimed include:

> life; freedom; equality; dignity; justice; property; freedom of thought, conscience and religion; freedom of opinion and expression; freedom of peaceful assembly and association; protection of family; participation in civil society; work; rest and leisure; an adequate standard of living; education; freedom from want.[28]

But children's rights are additional to human rights. The 1989 Convention on the Rights of the Child contained 54 Articles. On these Marshall and Parvis say

> There are a number of possible ways of analyzing the rights contained in the Convention; perhaps the most common of these refers to the three "Ps;" that is to say, the Convention proclaims the rights of children to:
> * protection – from abuse, neglect, and exploitation;
> * provision – of services to promote survival and development;
> * participation – in decisions about matters that affect them.[29]

When rights are ascribed to children problems arise over the relationship between parents and the child, the child and parents, and over the tripartite relationship between child, parents, and the state. Children, especially young children, do not have duties associated with their rights. Regarding the vexed question

> Who should decide what is in a child's best interests? The Convention is clear that that right and responsibility to decide on the child's best interests belongs *primarily* to the child's parents. However, such determination cannot be left *exclusively* to parents. There must be some mechanism for the broader society of which the child is a member to intervene in the face of inappropriate parental behaviour . . .[30]

---

[28] Marshall and Parvis, *Honouring Children*, p. 101 (authors' emphasis). They stress that their summary is "a selective and simplified list" (note 31).
[29] Marshall and Parvis, *Honouring Children*, p. 13.
[30] Marshall and Parvis, *Honouring Children*, p. 207 (authors' emphases).

What happens when parents fail, or are unable, to fulfil their responsibilities to their children? According to the Convention their rights over the child exist to enable them to fulfil their responsibilities. They are therefore secondary to the rights of the child to the three Ps. "It is therefore appropriate for the state to act as advocate or supporter of the rights of the child where these are being undermined by the parent."

> On the one hand, the rights of parents provide the bulwark for the child and the family against the kind of totalitarianism seen during the twentieth century. On the other hand, the rights of children are a bulwark against the reality of parental abuse and neglect of children, whose extent has become more evident in recent years.[31]

Marshall and Parvis make the case for children's rights overwhelmingly. Readers interested in the legal and philosophical minefields surrounding the rights of children will want to consult the book directly. Its authors are aware of the association of rights with excessive individualism. They counter the modern scepticism about rights (from Bentham through McIntyre). The UN Charter and the Universal Declaration are outstanding achievements by and for humanity. Rights language, while a "secondary framework" in relation to the religious and moral thought of different cultures, is nevertheless "a common language that will help different cultures, and different groupings within the emerging multi-cultural societies, discuss their differences in the light of the impact their disagreement may have on what all hold dear."[32] "In our 'fallen' world, all power is liable to abuse, and much of that abuse will come to pass. Communities that acknowledge the rights of their members to challenge oppression, and provide mechanisms for it, are doing themselves a favour." And, as strongly, "children need rights to counter the potentially abusive power of adults."[33]

Once we have applauded the defense of children's rights in *Honouring Children*, the question remains how rights can be incorporated into Christian theology and ethics. What contribution might they make to a theology of childhood, and of the family? Here I think the book may be less successful (below, 6.3). The authors record that successive Assemblies of the World Council of Churches affirmed basic human rights[34]: so did Pope John

---

[31] Marshall and Parvis, *Honouring Children*, pp. 209–10.
[32] Marshall and Parvis, *Honouring Children*, p. 142.
[33] Marshall and Parvis, *Honouring Children*, pp. 366–7.
[34] Marshall and Parvis, *Honouring Children*, p. 157.

XXIII.[35] The origin of modern rights language in the Enlightenment is not allowed to compromise its effectiveness – "We may deplore an individualism that fractures society and still feel that individuals need protection." That people appeal to their rights in "confrontational and self-regarding" ways, does not vitiate the case for rights: rights may no more cause aggressive self-assertion than lifeboats cause ships to sink.[36] Justice for the poor is a clarion call in the Hebrew scriptures, much as rights language is intended to sound today.[37] The charge that human rights are extrinsic to the Christian tradition is answered by three examples where extrinsic ideas are happily accommodated (the logos of John 1, the Aristotelianism of the Latin West, and the influence of the new humanism on Calvin).[38] The charge that human rights are unbiblical is answered by a reflection on the Golden Rule and the Love Commandments. Even these are contextual, and operate on a level different from rights language. "The two simply do not occupy the same moral space."[39]

On the relation between rights and theology the authors explain that rights have a considerable "theological payoff":

> First, rights have a force and a focus that can sharpen and toughen up a general appeal to duties and obligations. Secondly, rights language shifts the focus from the stronger party in a relationship to the weaker. And thirdly, rights language gives the Christian community at this point in time access to the wider world – a way of engaging with the secular society in which we live and a way of becoming involved in a global conversation and a global enterprise to extend protection to the needy and oppressed.[40]

These are vital advantages convincingly defended. Within the internal debates of academic Christian ethics, Marshall and Parvis convincingly critique the influential communitarianism of Stanley Hauerwas. Hauerwas does not think rights are attributable to children, or to people generally, because relations between people are determined primarily by the communities to which people belong. Rights language extrapolates from families, and is the pretentious product of reason. Instead of rules, we need virtues. "The language of 'rights,' especially as it is displayed by liberal political theory, encourages us to live as if we had no common interests or beliefs.

---

[35] Marshall and Parvis, *Honouring Children*, p. 161.
[36] Marshall and Parvis, *Honouring Children*, p. 165.
[37] Marshall and Parvis, *Honouring Children*, p. 168.
[38] Marshall and Parvis, *Honouring Children*, pp. 170–2.
[39] Marshall and Parvis, *Honouring Children*, p. 177.
[40] Marshall and Parvis, *Honouring Children*, p. 181.

We are thus trained to regard even our children as potential strangers from whom we need protection."[41]

Against Hauerwas it is pointed out that children need protection, even in religious communities. The very widespread acceptance of human rights indicates that a moral consensus is possible that is much broader than anything found in religious communities as Hauerwas understands them. Virtues and rules operate at different levels of moral discourse. All this is well said, and the strongest point against any communitarian ethic is itself a theological one, derived from a core belief about who the broad Christian community thinks Jesus is: "The story of Jesus of Nazareth, as it has been understood in Christian tradition, is the story of the Word of God – the Logos, the one who is the meaning of all things – coming into our world of time and space to live an authentically human life, a life that has significance for the whole of humankind."[42] The widest human community is the human race itself.

I think the appeal to the Logos is crucial to the universal application of the teaching of Jesus about children in the present time and is supported by the analysis of that teaching undertaken above (3.2). It follows from the belief that the Christ is the Logos of all humanity: and it is a vital component of the church's mission. There is what might be called a "thread of universality" running through the teaching of Jesus on children. That teaching has universal application. Nothing he says about children depends on them being Jewish or Christian children, even though the Jewishness of his teaching is the indispensable context for all he says about them. Brief reference to the ten statements which summarized Jesus' teaching about children (above, 3.2) should remind us of the astonishing inclusiveness and breadth of this teaching. "The kingdom of God belongs to such as these." "Such" automatically widens the application. It is not just in the children that Jesus touches that the Reign of God is manifested. Part of the blessedness of these children (statement 1) is perhaps that they represent children more widely. It was an inference from this text that the children belonged to the Reign of God (statement 2) because they were powerless and vulnerable (statement 3). There are millions of powerless and vulnerable children, whose plight traverses religious, ethnic, cultural, and class boundaries, whose presence in any community is a heart-rending scandal.

---

[41] Marshall and Parvis, *Honouring Children*, p. 276, citing Stanley Hauerwas, *Suffering Presence: Theological Reflections on Medicine, the Mentally Handicapped, and the Church* (Notre Dame, IN: University of Notre Dame Press, 1986), p. 130.
[42] Marshall and Parvis, *Honouring Children*, p. 281.

That same thread of universality runs through the remaining items of our summary of the teaching of Jesus about children. The preferred interpretation of accepting "the kingdom of God like a child" (statement 4) was that Jesus accepts "those *without obedience to the Law* into the Reign of God." If this is correct then it follows clearly that where God reigns, the religion of anyone, adult or child, is not a condition of citizenship. In these vital respects, the language of rights is able to encapsulate the sheer openness of membership of the Reign of God, and to percolate, on behalf of vulnerable children, into the world's political fora where it can be used to advocate their assistance and protection, as no other language can (especially theological language). This same universal thread runs through Jesus' teaching about childhood and about the reversal of power. Childness was used to name certain qualities of living that children possess and adults are in danger of losing (statement 5). While childness may have Jewish or Christian forms, it is a characteristic that is required, according to Jesus, to live a fully human life in community with others, baptism or circumcision notwithstanding. The example of children in illustrating "the counter-cultural, radical, anti-hierarchical power reversal" taught by Jesus (statement 6) is, again, a teaching whose universal relevance is demonstrated wherever power is oppressively used and becomes "power-over."[43]

The thread of universality also runs through Jesus' teaching about his identification with, and his proscription of harm to, children. It will take Christian eyes to discern the presence of Christ in the child, and in the welcome a child receives (statement 7). In this respect Christ's presence may be like the discernment of children's rights. States and authorities do not grant people rights: they recognize them as already there. Harm deliberately inflicted on all children, not just Christian children, is and remains a horrendous crime, worthy of the millstone metaphor (statement 8). The boys in the temple shouting "Hosanna" reveal their Jewish origins, but Jesus' reply ironically reveals that the children's knowledge of his identity is unmediated by the official guardians of Jewish tradition (statement 9). This depiction of the faith of children is not far from contemporary notions of "implicit faith," or "fundamental trust,"[44] where faith is assumed to be present prior to its object becoming further defined. The love of Jesus for children extends to them all (statement 10).

But the affirmation of Jesus as the Logos of God is not just consistent

---

[43] See Pamela Cooper-White, *The Cry of Tamar: Violence against Women and the Church's Response* (Minneapolis, MN: Fortress Press, 1995), p. 31.

[44] See Hans Küng, *Does God Exist?* (New York: Vintage Books, 1981), pp. 438–77.

with what Jesus teaches about children. God makes Godself known in a child, the Christ Child. That child is Jewish. The Word became human flesh, and that flesh was Jewish. But the "enfleshment" or incarnation of God is not simply the identification of God with a Jewish person, but with all people universally. The universal range of the Logos is clearly set out in the Prolog to the Fourth Gospel. Nothing came into being without the Logos. The Logos is the source of all life, and the source of the universal moral life. "In him was life, and that life was the light of mankind" (Jn. 1:3). The light that is Christ is "The true light which gives light to everyone" (Jn. 1:9) even before it manifests itself in the Child Jesus.

The universal reference of the Logos symbol towers above narrower distinctions between church and world, believer and unbeliever, sacred and secular. It reminds us that all life comes from the Gifting God. The "heavenly Father" "causes the sun to rise on good and bad alike, and sends the rain on the innocent and the wicked" (Mt. 5:45). "Every family in heaven and on earth takes its name" (Eph. 3:15) from the same Father. And God the Wind, the Breath, the Spirit, "blows where it wills" (Jn. 3:8). The basic distinction between peoples in the New Testament is between Jew and Gentile, and the wall of partition between them is now broken down. "Gentiles and Jews, he has made the two one, and in his own body of flesh and blood has broken down the barrier of enmity which separated them . . . so as to create out of the two a single new humanity in himself, thereby making peace. This was his purpose, to reconcile the two in a single body to God through the cross . . ." (Eph. 2:14,15b,16a). The whole of humanity has been reconciled to itself and to God through Christ, the meaning of whose Ascension to the Father's right hand is that all humanity is taken into the divine radiance through its Brother and representative.

It would take another book to outline where the trajectory of this particular argument might end. Theology needs to address the world beyond Christendom, and beyond churches. But it must recognize that the Triune God is also present beyond Christendom and the churches, as the source of life and love. Like rights, discerned rather than granted, so it is with the divine presence. The missionary task after Christendom is to help everyone to discern the movement of the Triune God among the nations and in particular the world's children already. The church will point finitely to these glorious and transcendent realities and name them. But she does not own them, and the more she maintains the fiction that they are hers alone, the more the open secret of God's redemptive purpose will remain closed.

6.3 The Christ Child and the Rights of All Children

The foundations of rights

I strongly agree with Marshall and Parvis' claim that "if we are to talk of rights in the proper sense, we have to make sure that we are not just address-ing Christian children or the children of Christians and then thinking of some way of letting others slip in under the wire."[45] In part, rights language does this. However, it is when they "try to find a secure grounding for talk of children's rights somewhere within central concerns of the Christian theological tradition"[46] that I entertain some minor disagreements. The concept of person is said to be fruitful, but its association with the possession of reason from Boethius on might suggest that young children and handi-capped people who lack reason are not persons. On the other hand, the relational concept of person might suggest that relationships and interac-tions are necessary for "fully developed personhood" to be assigned to a human being.[47] The concept of covenant is also rejected, and for perhaps surprising reasons. God's covenant with Israel was less than universal, whereas rights, because they apply to everyone, *must* be universal, and "that means that we have to have a *universal* covenant to start from."[48] Calvin's understanding of the new covenant is still partial. "So Muslim parents, for example, clearly have no obligation to present their children for baptism. And yet we need to be able to say that, if children's rights are based on some sort of covenant, all children have rights and all parents – Christian, Muslim, whatever – have obligations."

The search for a grounding of universal rights comes to rest in the idea of the *imago dei*. If our concern here is with the rights of the child, we want to start by affirming the basic human dignity of all children. And that means that we want to be able to talk about the way in which God is imaged forth even by those who are too young to exercise the power of reason or to make moral choices or consciously to shape their patterns of relationship.[49]

We have already seen (above, 4.4) that "the image of God" has been vari-ously interpreted in the tradition. Irenaeus' well-known treatment of the

---

[45] Marshall and Parvis, *Honouring Children*, p. 273.
[46] Marshall and Parvis, *Honouring Children*, p. 273.
[47] Marshall and Parvis, *Honouring Children*, pp. 300–5.
[48] Marshall and Parvis, *Honouring Children*, p. 308 (authors' emphases).
[49] Marshall and Parvis, *Honouring Children*, p. 320.

image of God is affirmed, co-opted, and thought to yield four characteristics, all of them relevant to children's rights. It is

> (1) something bodily and physical in which all human beings share. It is (2) not lost at the Fall but rather remains as a locus of God's saving activity in the world. It is (3) modelled after the flesh of Jesus Christ, in which God became visible in the world he had made. And it is (4) the subject of a process of growth and transformation that will reach its culmination only when our human God-likeness is restored and we come to see God as he is, face to face.
>
> It is that idea of image that we would like to adopt and make our own. It is that that we would like to put forward as a theological basis of the concept of children's rights.[50]

Marshall and Parvis think the Irenaean treatment of the image of God gives them what they are looking for. It is inclusive (everyone has bodies): in particular it includes the most vulnerable, and it "has a dynamism that looks beyond our world as it is to what it will become."[51] But at this point the doubts start piling up. Why not start with the Christ Child instead of the theological anthropology of Irenaeus? If the advantages of the image of God are embodiment, inclusivity, and hope, the Christ Child is better able to deliver these than the *imago* doctrine. The Christ Child had a body too (in fact Irenaeus emphasized the bodiliness of Jesus more than most theologians). The Logos became "flesh." The Christ Child was a real child: the image of God is an "idea," albeit a significant one. The assumed connection between the vulnerable and the image of God is tenuous (no clear argument is provided for it), whereas the connection between the Christ Child and vulnerable children is immediate and obvious. Christ *becomes* vulnerable and weak, identifies with them and with their suffering. As we have noted, children may be called "blessed" on account of their inclusion in the category of poor, hungry, and suffering people, the very people contemporary rights language is intended to protect. If being made in the image of God suggests a process of growth into the divine likeness, either by the individual person, the church, or the human race itself (in Irenaeus' view) why cannot reflection on the Christ Child who, as a child, was "one being with us in all things except sin" also deliver these things? If there is growing up to do, why not "grow up into Christ" (Eph. 4:15b)? Of course Irenaeus derives his account of the image of God from his dynamic Christology, and *Honouring Children* draws on this. That is why the lack of a Christological starting point is more of a surprise.

---

[50] Marshall and Parvis, *Honouring Children*, p. 324.
[51] Marshall and Parvis, *Honouring Children*, p. 325.

The dismissal of "person" and "covenant" appears over-hasty. Terms which are important to theology easily become polysemic: further use of them requires their users to stipulate which meanings operate. The meanings of these terms that disqualify them could just be disavowed. That would not render them unserviceable for the sought-after foundation for rights. There is a better alternative. The dismissal of terms shows that Marshall and Parvis may be looking in the wrong category, in theological concepts instead of in the Word made flesh. Perhaps the difficulty is that an appeal to the identity of Jesus of Nazareth as the revealed Logos of God compromises the required universal range of language that is aimed at protecting children. The notion of covenant did not pass this test: Muslims could not agree to it, and so for similar reasons it might be assumed that they could not agree either with an appeal to the Christ Child as a basis for the rights of all children. But in that case how might they be expected to agree with the idea, however promising, of a second-century Christian theologian? Is the idea of being made in the image of God sufficiently bland to circumvent the doctrinal differences between the two faiths? Hardly, since it is Trinitarian through and through. How might Buddhists and other non-theists be included within the universal range of this idea?

There is a further difficulty over the chosen theological method in *Honouring Children*. The theological method of the work aims to do different things. It seeks to examine how the legal material "fits in to the evolving Christian theological tradition";[52] or, how children's rights "fit into the Christian scheme of things."[53] Or again, a chapter is devoted to "a theological look at children's rights."[54] Or again, there is a quest for "a solid foundation within the central traditions of Christian theology for the notion of children's rights."[55] On the one hand, "fitting in" and "taking a look at" beg big hermeneutical questions, principally about the assumed relationship between Christian and secular thought, and about what kind of theological analysis is being undertaken. On the other hand, the quest for the solid foundation makes two assumptions: one, that it is possible for secular thought to be "grounded" somewhere in Christian theological traditions; and two, that the relationship between them is analogous to the relation between the foundation and superstructure of a building. Why not honor children by starting with the Christ Child as this "solid foundation," together with his own avowed solidarity with the world's children?

---

[52] Marshall and Parvis, *Honouring Children*, p. 153.
[53] Marshall and Parvis, *Honouring Children*, p. 156.
[54] Marshall and Parvis, *Honouring Children*, p. 267.
[55] Marshall and Parvis, *Honouring Children*, pp. 297–8.

The Christ Child as the foundation of rights

Can there be a Christian theological foundation for the notion of universal children's rights? Yes, there definitely can. But this unambiguous answer depends on further clarifying how "foundation" and "universal" are understood in the question. When Christians look for foundations, they surely look to Jesus Christ? As Paul said (but with reference to the factions in the church at Corinth), "There can be no other foundation than the one already laid: I mean Jesus Christ himself" (1 Cor. 3:11). To say this is to refuse the help of a metaphysic which provides the rational "grounds," or the "underpinnings" for some of the more dubious truths of faith. It is also to refuse the help of any secondary doctrinal theme when a primary theme is available. In the particular case of a foundation for children's rights, the turn to Christ Himself is greatly aided by his identification of himself and the Father, with children in his teaching, and by his coming among us as a Child.

It may be helpful to observe that claims to universality are not undermined by being tradition-specific. It is hard even to imagine a universal claim that was tradition-exempt and, as it were, free-floating. Now Christians make many universal claims which derive from the particularities of Jesus. Here are three from Paul. "God was in Christ reconciling the world to himself" (2 Cor. 5:19a). " . . . at the name of Jesus every knee should bow – in heaven, on earth, and in the depths – and every tongue acclaim, 'Jesus Christ is Lord', to the glory of God the Father" (Phil. 2:10–11). "There is no such thing as Jew and Greek, slave and freeman, male and female; for you are all one person in Christ Jesus" (Gal. 3:28). All I am wanting to notice about these momentous statements at the moment is that (i) they are made on the basis of the identity and achievement (or "Person" and "Work") of Jesus Christ: (ii) they are advanced by the church in her proclamation of the good news to everyone without exception; and (iii) they will not be universally accepted, and for several reasons. The understanding of the identity and achievement of Jesus Christ belongs to the church, and the language of Christian faith is not yet spoken by everyone. And these universal claims, when they *are* understood outside the church conflict with other universal claims advanced by other faiths.

Now rights language is clearly thought to have achieved universal application already. Rights are universally understood, it is claimed, and the universal range of rights language can be empirically confirmed. National governments and international organizations understand it and governments have promised, with markedly contrasting degrees of resolve, to implement it. Now, if I understand Marshall and Parvis aright, Christian theological language is in trouble because, however much it makes universal claims, it cannot match the universal acceptability of rights language because it derives from particulars which in a universal context are bound to be contested.

If this is the test, then no religious claim from any religion can pass it. All religious claims are advanced from local origins. But this need not negate religious claims, for rights have local origins too (among them, natural rights, natural law, and secular Western philosophy). Rights lack an ultimate rational foundation, since philosophers from Bentham onward have been able to justify their verdict that they represent "nonsense on stilts." There will always be disagreement about which rights claims are allowable as rights. And an appeal to their rights has not yet halted the conscription of young children in African militias, the widespread exploitation of child labor, particularly in India, or the appalling crime of clitoridectomy on millions of young girls. But these failures of rights provide no reason for failing to endorse them theologically. As Marshall and Parvis point out, the extent of the acceptance of human rights among governments, politicians, lawyers, and child advocates is very remarkable. The spread of rights language might be considered to be one of the greatest achievements of that most violent of all centuries, an outpouring of hope after the shattering effects of two world wars. There is no other aspirational declaration of comparable influence or scope. Rights language intends the protection of the vulnerable, which alone should secure the support of all Christians. Christians wary of human rights might consider the possibility that God the Spirit operates throughout creation and may have inspired the people of good will who labored to formulate and implement them.

To return to our question: Can there be a foundation for children's rights in theology? Christian theology will ground its support for children's rights principally in the teaching of Jesus about children, and in its core conviction that God in Christ became a Child. Neither of these claims is invalidated by being locally sourced. We have seen the very strong identity claim between Jesus and children in Mark's statement that Jesus "took a child, set him in front of them, and put his arm round him. 'Whoever receives a child like this in my name,' he said, 'receives me; and whoever receives me, receives not me but the One who sent me'" (Mk. 9:36–7). The text emphasizes solidarity between Jesus and children, and between Jesus and the Father in the receiving of children. I suggest this text provides very strong support for endorsing children's rights theologically.

So how would the argument go? Jesus identifies himself with "a child like this," not just this particular child, but *any* particular child. The New Testament describes many ways by which the body of Christ is extended, made present, and identified not just with the church or with the eucharistic bread and wine, but also with people in need (Mt. 25:31–46). We should not then be surprised that in the case of children we find another example of the extended identity of Christ. Now in the cases of the doctrines of incarnation and eucharist a moderate realism is appropriate. That is to say, the church teaches that God really became a human being: to say "Jesus Christ is God" is an expression of the significance he came to have for his followers is truthful, but not enough, for Christ's deity is grounded in his very being, not simply in pious value-judgments about him. I propose a similar interpretation of moderate realism with regard to the identification of Jesus with children. If one claims to behold the face of Christ in the face of a child, the claim is not a maudlin sentimentalism. It is to see how the very heart of Godself extends in love toward that child. Or, to see how close (to the point of identity) the Father is to all children. Or, to acknowledge Christ in the child by loving Christ through the child, and the child through Christ. Or, to recognize the solidarity of the suffering, risen Christ with the suffering of children, mindful that the suffering of Christ proleptically secures a world where all suffering through a combination of divine and human action, will one day cease. And so on.

In this respect the teaching of Jesus is confirmed by the church's teaching about Jesus, that He is God incarnate, and so God the Child. The contingencies and exigencies of growing up in a large family, in a politically insecure and religiously plural environment, were all directly experienced by him. Even the cry of the woman in the crowd, "Happy the womb that carried you and the breasts that suckled you!" (Lk. 11:27b), while rebuffed by Jesus, is allowed to make the point that the Messiah was a vulnerable embryo requiring the very suckling that adult metaphor has claimed for itself in its articulation of being fed spiritually by God. In the first case Jesus identifies himself and the Father with children. In the second case, the Triune God becomes a Child, making the identity a literal and precarious one, in flesh and blood, in vulnerability and weakness.

How does the connection look between children's rights and the Christian tradition when it is grounded in the teaching of Jesus, and the church's belief in him as God Incarnate, God the Child? Secure. Where there is doctrinal development there is continuity and discontinuity through time. That there is no exact equivalent of children's rights is a discontinuity between biblical times and our own, but that causes no problem. There is a deep continuity springing from the teaching and being of the Christ who manifests himself in children and their needs. The protection that rights afford children could hardly be in greater accord with the teaching of Jesus, and its universality is a great gain for theology.

Parents and rights

There are no children without parents. A major theme of this book is to provide strong support for good, enabling relations between parents and children. Relation is fundamental to being a child, an adult, a person. But relations between parents and children sometimes break down, and the relative security of the enduring marital household commended in the previous chapter becomes unavailable to the child. The conviction that children have rights entails that when their parents are unable to provide for them, then others should, and local or state intervention is justified.

The day I write this paragraph British newspapers report the trial and conviction, in Angers, France, of 65 adults for child abuse. These adults had raped and prostituted children, including their own. One man was found guilty of raping his daughter, son, and four grandchildren. Two other men were accused of raping 15 and 14 children respectively. The *Guardian* newspaper reported that "the case revealed stories of incest and rape going back several generations. More than a dozen of the defendants had suffered sexual abuse themselves as children."[56] The victims, 26 girls and 19 boys, had been "demolished," their lawyers said. "Some barely speak, or scream when approached by strangers; one girl was forced to perform oral sex so often that she cannot eat in the company of adults."

These crimes against children are unspeakable, horrendous evils. Even the condition of sin, social, structural, or original, cannot fully explain the appalling, surd character of these horrific crimes. The victims are now "in care," that is, in institutions which have often failed children terribly, or are with foster parents. In such cases, no one doubts that alternative arrangements for these children must be found. And there are many other less extreme but less desperate situations where the "three Ps" of protection, provision, and participation are denied to children, requiring legal intervention to ensure, as far as possible, that they receive them. Some of the cases discussed in *Honouring Children* include children whose parents are drug addicts; young children who are sometimes left alone by a single mother when she leaves for work; children who cannot be controled by their parents; a 13-year-old girl placed in a children's home where she receives the attentions of three sexually active teenage male residents.[57] In all such cases the exercise of the rights of these children becomes a responsibility more widely shared. The rights of children legitimize intervention on their behalf

---

[56] The *Guardian*, 28 July, 2005, p. 2.
[57] Marshall and Parvis, *Honouring Children*, p. 5.

by the legitimate authorities when parents are failing to cope, often to provide them with support. Families can be pernicious, evil places for children. Perhaps that is why we find little endorsement of them in the Gospels. The family, thankfully, cannot be isolated from wider, caring influences.

The rights of parents over their children, against external intervention, are often asserted (and are the reason why the USA has not ratified the United Nations Convention on the Rights of the Child). But the examples above show that some procedure must exist to intervene "in the face of inappropriate parental behavior." Some place *must* also be accorded to parental rights to protect against the encroachment of totalitarian regimes (above, 6.2), and in many cases where intervention is required (both in support of, and against parents), there will be disagreement about how the child's rights are to be best interpreted. Theology has a particular problem when parents use religious justifications for suspending the rights of their children.

Two well-known cases are parents who practice Christian Science and who assert the right to withhold medical treatment from a gravely ill child, and Jehovah's Witnesses who refuse blood transfusions even to prevent a child's death. Each sect proclaims a version of Christianity that is plainly heretical. One is Gnostic and dualistic. The other is extreme in its literalism. Both deny orthodox belief in the Incarnation and the Trinity. A more difficult case is the alleged parental right of chastisement extended to teachers of Christian schools *in loco parentis*. The case here is usually based on the advocacy of beating children in the book of Proverbs (13:24; 22:15; 23:13–14; 29:15), and on the alleged need to enforce the obedience of children enjoined by the Household Codes. Our family-friendly rules for the interpretation of scripture (above, 2.3) already proscribe these lamentable arguments. There is a different theological vision of parent–child relationships, in which physical punishment has no place, and to that we now turn.

Chapter Seven

God, Parents, and Children

Chapter 7 returns to intimate family relationships and attempts a serious contribution to a theology of parenthood. Section 1 critiques the identification of God with maleness in an attempt to separate the fatherhood of God from its familiar role in endorsing male authority over wives, children, and household. Section 2 welcomes attempted revisions of the depth grammar of divine fatherhood, but notes that they manage to leave intact the association of the Father with the male gender. A recent, far-sighted attempt to deal with the oppressive masculinity of God and priesthood by a renewed emphasis on God's Mother[1] is welcomed but reluctantly resisted. Section 3, the heart of the chapter, situates human parent–child relations in the Triune Relations that constitute the Communion of Persons Who are God. It sketches two ways by which the tradition licenses the situatedness of families in God, and introduces a term for each of them: the analogy of sacrifice, and the analogy of mutuality. While the first of these is not abandoned, the second receives most emphasis. Section 4 adds the testimony of theologians who are mothers to the growing sense of mutuality between parents and children. Finally the Trinitarian account of mutual love within families is preferred to the biblical defense of mutuality within critical familism.

7.1 God the Father and Human Parenting

How does belief in God the Father contribute to the practice of human parenting? That question is hard even to pose, given the undoubted

---

[1] Tina Beattie, *God's Mother, Eve's Advocate* (London and New York: Continuum, 2002).

reinforcement of patriarchal power and practice, inside and outside the church, by means of the divine Father symbol. My concern with God the Father is sharply at odds with mainstream debates about the gender of God. How in Christian faith might the heavenly Father inform, inspire, and assist mothers and fathers in their care for their children? In pursuit of an answer to that question, the arguments about gender cannot be ignored. I am concerned with the dearth in Christian tradition about parenting, and with the inevitable cultural relativism of what can be discovered there. "Surprisingly, despite all the attention social science has recently paid to fatherhood, theology has said very little. The lack of reflection on what it means to be a father is even more surprising given the fact that father is the central metaphor for God in the Christian tradition."[2] As often as not, the symbol "Father" is a barrier to effective parenting because of its association with exclusively male power and gender.

God the Father: patriarchal reactions

John Miller is an advocate of patriarchal fatherhood and its legitimation by a male, monotheistic God. Influenced by the child psychology of Antoine Vergote, he explains the distant, secondary role that fathers have in the upbringing of their children.

> When fathers are "effectively present to their families," they "insert themselves into the bond between mother and child as a 'second other' by an initiative very much like that of adoption." Where this initiative is energetic and winsome, developmental psychology teaches us, an essential autonomy from the mother is fostered and children of both sexes are significantly helped in orienting themselves to the cultural universe outside the home with its laws and ethical norms.[3]

There is an inevitable distancing of the father from his child because he does not experience the bonding of the mother and child through pregnancy, birth, and breast-feeding. The practising of paternal care-at-a-distance,

---

[2] Julie Hanlon Rubio, *A Christian Theology of Marriage and Family* (Mahwah, NJ: Paulist Press, 2004), p. 138.
[3] John W. Miller, *Calling God "Father": Essays on the Bible, Fatherhood and Culture* (New York/Mahwah, NJ: Paulist Press, 1999), p. 47. The quotation within the quotation is from Antoine Vergote, *The Religious Man: A Psychological Study of Religious Attitudes* (Dublin: Gill and Macmillan, 1969), p. 161.

although it may "embrace feminine or maternal attributes," enables the father to behave with "firmness and directive action."[4]

Miller has in his sights those feminist theologians who seek to depatriarchalize the God of the Bible. He answers them with the double claim "that the biblical representation of God is more, not less patriarchal than generally recognized," and that they miss the real problem that God the Father poses for daughters: "insofar as women, in contrast to men, must at a certain point move beyond the father to complete their identity, the evocation of God as father, in their case, could have an inhibiting effect at this stage in their development."[5] The patriarchal God of the Hebrew scriptures encouraged the involvement of fathers in their families. The androgynous depatriarchalized God of the feminist theologians is incapable of inspiring anyone.

> There is simply no solid basis in human experience for relating to a *personal* reality that is both male and female, or neither, or fluctuates between the two. If God is "person" and that person is one, only two figures have an analogous "ultimacy" in actual human experience to that of God, mother and father. And while these personages overlap, they are not the same . . .[6]

Human fathers need a Father God!

This is an extraordinary handling of both the concepts "father" and "Father God." Miller selects certain cultural elements of being a father, distance and detachment, blames them on biology, and assumes these are essential for the exercise of paternal discipline and authority. Once the analogy is set up in this way, the heavenly Father is seen to endorse particular paternal practices. But plenty of fathers-in-waiting are closely involved in the mother's pregnancy and in the nurturing of their children, and when they act gently and tenderly toward their children, they can do this as the men they are without psychologizing explanations that they are being motherly or exercising their supposed feminine side. The ironic truth of Miller's approach is that throughout the Common Era, at least until the Reformation, it is male *theologians* in all traditions who have been distanced from human fathering. Their lack of intimate contact with wives and children makes it hard for them to discern meaningful connections between human parenting and the divine Parent. It is therefore not surprising that

---

[4] Miller, *Calling God "Father,"* p. 47, citing Antoine Vergote, "The Parental Figures: Symbolic Functions and Medium for the Representation of God," in Antoine Vergote and Alvero Tamayo (eds.), *The Parental Figures and the Representation of God: A Psychological and Cross-Cultural Study* (The Hague: Mouton, 1981), p. 220.

[5] Miller, *Calling God "Father,"* p. 106.

[6] Miller, *Calling God "Father,"* p. 106 (author's emphasis).

distance and authority are the supposed paternal qualities that the heavenly
Father is thought to validate and encourage in "His" earthly counterparts.

Miller's concept of "Father God" is equally unhelpful. He is Unitarian in
his concept of God as one Person. Much popular Christian thought frankly
does not understand the centrality of the doctrine of the Trinity for every
aspect of faith: even so, the casual, one-person monism still comes as a surprise. When he moves to the assertion that God must be either male or
female, he loses touch altogether with the need to speak of God by means of
symbols, and so with the infinite distinction between the creature and the
Creator. To be created is to be sexed: to be the Creator is to exist beyond the
sexed distinctions of creatures as the author of both. Miller fails to grasp the
opportunity provided by the doctrine of the Trinity to understand God's
being Father through God being Father to the Son, through whom the
Father is supremely known. His "biblical" account of fatherhood relies
heavily on the Hebrew scriptures, and that most promising of New Testament models of parenthood, the Parable of the Prodigal Father, remains
uninvoked.

A group of theologians, led by Alvin Kimel,[7] has attacked the attempt of
feminist theology to depatriarchalize the God of the Bible. But by concen-
trating on poor arguments and undoubted excesses within that movement,
these theologians manage to beg many of the questions that feminist theologians rightly raise. We are told that "the Bible uses masculine language for
God because that is the language with which God has revealed himself."[8] It is
a divine *fait accompli*, whether we like it or not, so we had better get used to it.
If we stop calling God "He," "him," and so on, we "would subvert belief in a
personal God."[9] The "sexual emphasis" has no place in deity.[10] Why then is it
essential that God be addressed in masculine terms if the sexual emphasis in
relation to God is so incongruous? Later we hear that "the matter of the
Fatherhood of God is a matter not of maleness but of ontological discontinuity: of otherness."[11] But if otherness is the issue, would not an impersonal
Absolute suffice? Other poor arguments depend on God's unrevisable name.
God "announces himself to us and names himself as *Father, Son, and Holy*

---

[7] Alvin F. Kimel, Jr (ed.), *Speaking the Christian God: The Holy Trinity and the Challenge of Feminism* (Grand Rapids, MI: Eerdmans/Leominster, UK: Gracewing 1992).
[8] Elizabeth Achtemeier, "Exchanging God for 'No Gods,'" in Kimel (ed.), *Speaking the Christian God* [1–16], p. 5.
[9] Roland M. Frye, "Language for God and Feminist Language," in Kimel (ed.), *Speaking the
Christian God* [17–43], p. 25.
[10] Frye, "Language for God," in Kimel (ed.), *Speaking the Christian God*, p. 26.
[11] Colin Gunton, "Proteus and Procrustes," in Kimel (ed.), *Speaking the Christian God*,
[65–80], p. 78.

Spirit." This is "a revelation of what he really is in his own eternal nature apart from us. God *is* Father, Son, and Holy Spirit."[12] Is not God's name "I AM" (Ex. 3:14)? Is the divine self-communication not the Word made flesh? Is the Triune name God's only name? What exactly is resolved by italicizing the copula here? If it is to assert the "'is' of identity," the claim merely begs many other questions. I *am* Adrian Thatcher, but there are vast differences between me and the name to which I answer. The relation between God's eternal nature and God's names is precisely the issue at stake.

Other contributors invoke similar versions of epistemological realism. The names "God the Father" and "the Son of God" are "transparent equivalents to the divine reality" . . . They "function as structural metaphors," and "to ignore or deny such structural metaphors can cripple the whole body of theological meaning that they articulate."[13] While metaphors can hint at the deeper mysteries that come to the surface in them, there is apparently no mystery about the sex of God. "Father" and "Son" say it all. Another, audacious, argument for divine maleness has to do with divine self-emptying. Since men possess social power, God must be incarnate in a man, or God's self-abandonment would not make sense. A powerless woman therefore could not be the vehicle of such self-emptying. She would be empty already! Feminists thereby "seem generally to have missed the irony of patriarchy."[14] If this argument were sound one could easily imagine matriarchal societies where God would thereby be required to become incarnate as a woman. Yet a principal argument of these writers is that God is eternally Father irrespective of the constructions and contingencies of all human communities and their social arrangements.

None of the authors get to grips with the contextuality of theological knowledge. Some of them however admit that theology must "correct the distortions of male-centred misreadings,"[15] or "seek a way by which the language of divine fatherhood may be detached from the male idol of patriarchal religion."[16] None of them has much to say about how this situation might be addressed. None of them deals with the problem (to be considered next), that bad *biology*, in the form of spurious beliefs about the power of fertility belonging exclusively to the human male, underwrites the use of the symbol

---

[12] Thomas F. Torrance, "The Christian Apprehension of God the Father," in Kimel (ed.), *Speaking the Christian God* [120–43], p. 121 (author's emphasis).

[13] Frye, "Language for God," p. 42.

[14] Garrett Green, "The Gender of God and the Theology of Metaphor," in Kimel (ed.), *Speaking the Christian God* [44–64], p. 63.

[15] Green, "The Gender of God," p. 59.

[16] Janet Martin Soskice, "Can a Feminist Call God 'Father'?," in Kimel (ed.), *Speaking the Christian God* [81–94], p. 87.

"Father." The consequence is that re-assertion of divine maleness, after the facts of human reproduction are well known, introduces a new masculinism which lacks even the specious biological support enjoyed by the old patriarchy. All the contributors want to protect the Trinity from revisionary feminist proposals, yet none of them recalls the basic point about the sex of God, grasped by Gregory of Nyssa, that the term "mother" may be applied to the Person of the Father, because, as he says, "Both terms mean the same, because the divine is neither male nor female."[17] To be sexed is to be part of the created order, which God is not. Since then God cannot be male (or female), asymmetrical male language constitutes a fundamental problem for theologians who want to be heard beyond the pulverulent confines of historical and conservative theology. The essays soar far above the experience of human parenting from which all talk of God being "Father" and being "in-relation" ultimately springs. Relationality in God is all-important, but there is no attempt to link this lofty matter to human relations. The anthropology is generic (and childless), and we are left to guess how these polemics against Christian feminism have any practical relevance for the faith of real mothers and fathers and their relations with children.

Another strategy is to say that the problem of the maleness of God the Father will go away if we concentrate on more important matters. Rob Palkovitz comes into this category. Urging "the more central biblical principles" on us, he says, "Simply stated, if we took seriously the 'greatest commandments,' that is, if we were committed in our relationship to God and to others, the details of parenting and masculinity/femininity would fall into place."[18] If only this were true. There are very sincere, very committed patriarchs in all the religions, and few if any of them are ready to surrender their power over women. Miller's God will encourage them to remain where they are.

7.2 God the Father: Revisionary Proposals

An equally serious problem for theology is not the endlessly debated gender of God the Father (important though that is), but the neglect of human fathers and mothers. Just as Christian discourse about children can divert

---

[17] Verna E.F. Harrison, "Male and Female in Cappadocian Theology," *Journal of Theological Studies*, 41.2 (Oct.1990), [441–71], p. 441, citing *Cant.*7.
[18] Rob Palkovitz, "The 'Recovery' of Fatherhood?," in Anne Carr and Mary Stewart Van Leeuwen (eds.), *Religion, Feminism, and the Family* (Louisville, KY: Westminster John Knox Press, 1996), p. 322.

from and displace real children in its concern to present *adults* as children in their relation to God, so Christian discourse about parenting can divert from and displace the concerns of real mothers and fathers in its understandable preoccupation with the gendered fatherhood of God. The problem of gender is eased, but not removed, by the insistence of virtually any Trinitarian theology that to call God "Father" is to name a divine Relation, that of the Father in relation to the Son and the Spirit. While there are countless references in the Bible to God being Father, this tradition culminates not in itself but in naming the One whose Fatherhood is disclosed by being Father of the Son whom the Father sent. To risk a truism: a man or woman is a father or a mother when they have a child. Their child is what makes them parents: nothing else. They are parents *in relation to* their child. In a similar way, what finally makes God "Father" is God the Son: nothing else. The Father is Father in relation to the Son and the Spirit. It would be impossible for the Father to be deemed Father without them.

Real parents experience the grace of God when their relations to their children and to each other embody the Love that the divine Trinity discloses and is. The analogy between parents and children and between the divine Father and the Son is an analogy of relation. I have suggested that re-emphasis on the divine Relations is a partial solution to the gender problem. The language does not primarily name Individuals: it points to Relations. Since it has no individual subject or subjects (apart from Relations), that subject cannot be a male subject. But the language remains masculine, and, lest I too am seen to dismiss the problem, something further about the gender of the Father needs to be said. The very character of *human* parenting is at stake here. The entire biblical period and the first 18 centuries of the Common Era assume a theory of conception which assumes that fathers do it all. The sperm of the father provides the form of the embryo: the *mater* provides the *materia*, the physical matter on which form impresses itself. Conception, then, is an ovum-less affair. As Janet Soskice notes, "In a scheme where only males are truly generative then, in a sense, only males can truly give birth. The only true parent is the father, source of seed which it is the female task to nurture." She reminds us how Aquinas thought the first person of the Trinity could not be called "Mother" for that reason, because "God begets actively, and the role of the mother in procreation is, on the other hand, passive."[19] God is the active principle of creation, and in relation to children, the active principle is the

---

[19] Janet Martin Soskice, "Trinity and 'the Feminine Other,'" *New Blackfriars*, 75, January 1994 [2–17], p. 8.

father. That is why Aquinas can say "Wherefore since our father is related to us as principle, even as God is, it belongs properly to the father to receive honor from his children . . ."[20]

We need only call to mind the influence of biological ideas on human understanding at the present time to guess their influence in the past. Human evolution transforms our understanding of ourselves and our belonging in the universe, and the infant science of genetics offers prospects (however hyped and misrepresented) for cures of diseases, explanations of complex behaviors, increased crop yields, and so on. But there is no reason to think that the influence of biological ideas on pre-modern peoples was any less than in our own time. No one had reason to question the generativity of fathers and the passivity of mothers, despite the falsity of these suppositions when judged by our present (and highly relative) knowledge. The "father" symbol has its roots in generation, conceiving, creativity, life-giving-ness: only secondarily, contingently and as it turns out, falsely, is the miracle of life and new life associated with men alone. When the Apostles' Creed and subsequent Creeds affirm "I believe in God the Father, Almighty, Maker of heaven and earth," the transition from "Father" to "Maker" is smooth and natural, flowing from the undisturbed and unchallenged belief that fecundity and generativity are exclusively male properties. Theology must strive to avoid the error that creating anything is a male activity alone. The creation of a child is *shared*. It is the father who, after impregnation, contributes nothing further (at least until after the birth). But the connection between maleness and conception has lasted ever since the discovery, far from uniform, that pregnancy occurred as a consequence of insemination.[21] By comparison the full contribution of mothers to the generation and gestation of a child has only been understood for a few seconds of anthropological time (since the discovery of the human ovum by Karl Ernst von Baer in 1827).

Other theologians concede that the ideal of the heavenly Father continues to reinforce male power in church and family, but seek to revise and modify the central paternal symbol. It seems fair to call them "revisionists." Jürgen Moltmann has spoken of "the Motherly Father" who brings forth the "only-begotten Son,"[22] and Leonardo Boff of "The Trans-Sexist Theol-

---

[20] Thomas Aquinas, *Summa Theologiae* (Benziger Bros edition, 1947: tr. Fathers of the English Dominican Province), 2.2.q26a9. www.ccel.org/a/aquinas/summa/SS/SS026.html. Accessed 02.09.2006.

[21] For the history of this see Miller, *Calling God "Father,"* chapter 1.

[22] Jürgen Moltmann, *History and the Triune God* (London: SCM Press, 1991), p. 19.

[23] Leonardo Boff, *Trinity and Society* (Tunbridge Wells: Burns and Oates, 1988), p. 120.

ogy of the Maternal Father and the Paternal Mother."[23] These welcome cross-gender symbols combine attention to the continued power of the heavenly Father to legitimate patriarchal attitudes and practices, with a constructive contribution to arresting them. They take several of the criticisms of feminist theology very seriously. However a possible weakness of these revisionary proposals is that "the male simply absorbs and ingests the 'otherness' of the female, reinforcing the dominance of the male and continuing to exclude feminine language for the divine."[24]

Another revisionist of divine fatherhood is Pope John Paul II. Fathers, he teaches, can image the Father God by loving their partners and children as the heavenly Father loves us all. There is a short section of *Familiaris consortio*, "Men as Husbands and Fathers," where the late Pope teaches "love for his wife as mother of their children and love for the children themselves are for the man the natural way of understanding and fulfilling his own fatherhood."[25] I call this conservative work "revisionary" because of its insistence on the rights of women and children, the equal dignity of women with men, its teaching that men should image God the Father by loving, not controlling their families, and much else. But John Paul also goes on to say "In revealing and in reliving on earth the very fatherhood of God, a man is called upon to ensure the harmonious and united development of all the members of the family." Even here we hit gender trouble, for as Julie Rubio points out, "The choice of God the father as model is telling, for women are not told to model God for their children. Rather, like Mary, they should mother their children and teach them devotion to God."[26] We might add that "to ensure development" is surely a shared responsibility of *mothers and* fathers. So while *Familiaris consortio* seeks in its own way to correct much gender bias in the tradition, the religious meanings of the "God the Father" metaphor must surely be made available to men and women if, in their nurturing of their children, they are also to be nurtured in the love of God.

John Paul II returns to the theme of divine Fatherhood in *Mulieris dignitatem*. After drawing attention to familiar passages in the Hebrew scriptures which predicate feminine images of God,[27] he ponders the deep question how biblical language "*points indirectly to the mystery of the eternal 'generating'*

[24] David S. Cunningham, *These Three Are One – The Practice of Trinitarian Theology* (Malden, MA, and Oxford, UK: Blackwell, 1998), p. 48.

[25] Pope John Paul II, *Familiaris consortio* (1981), section 25. www.vatican.va/holy_father/john_paul_ii/apost_exhortations/. Accessed 02.09.2006.

[26] Rubio, *A Christian Theology*, p. 138.

[27] Is. 49:14–15; Is. 66:13; Ps. 131:2–3; Is. 42:14; Is. 46:3–4.

which belongs to the inner life of God."[28] In a rich passage (which must be quoted in full), he continues

> Nevertheless, in itself this "generating" has neither "masculine" nor "femi-nine" qualities. It is by nature totally divine. It is spiritual in the most perfect way, since "God is spirit" (Jn. 4:24) and possesses no property typical of the body, neither "feminine" nor "masculine." Thus even *"fatherhood" in God is completely divine* and free of the "masculine" bodily characteristics proper to human fatherhood . . .
>
> All "generating" among creatures finds its primary model in that generat-ing which in God is completely divine, that is, spiritual. All "generating" in the created world is to be likened to this absolute and uncreated model. Thus every element of human generation which is proper to man, and every element which is proper to woman, namely human *"fatherhood"* and *"mother-hood,"* bears within itself a likeness to, or analogy with the divine "generating" and with that "fatherhood" which in God is "totally different," that is, com-pletely spiritual and divine in essence; whereas in the human order, genera-tion is proper to the "unity of the two": both are "parents," the man and the woman alike.

There is much here for which to be thankful. The author has explained that men and women equally share the image of God, both as bearers of reason and freedom and in relation to one another. Here then is another reason why God cannot be masculine: the truth about who images God forbids it. The oblique-sounding "elements of generation" proper to male and female acknowledge the existence of both sperm and ovum and therefore the full genetic contribution of the woman to a new human being. Since there are elements of generation "proper to woman" women are acknowledged to contribute at least equally with men to the human comprehension of what the "spiritual generation" of the Father might mean. Motherhood, like fatherhood, is rooted analogically in the divine generation of God the Father.

But there are disappointments too. Why is the Father wholly free of bodily characteristics, especially since the Father enters the world through the embryo that already was (in some sense!) the divine Son? If God's fatherhood really is "totally different" from human parenthood, then why mess about with analogies at all? Divine parenthood is not associated with male (or female) bodily characteristics, but the price to be paid for placing

---

[28] Pope John Paul II, *Mulieris dignitatem* (1988), section 8, "The anthropomorphism of biblical language" (author's emphasis). www.vatican.va/holy_father/john_paul_ii/apost_letters/index.htm). Accessed 02.09.2006.

the divine Father beyond the distinction between the sexes is a heavy one: identification with the divine Parent is impossible (and pointless) for human mothers and fathers alike. Unfortunately questions of gender cannot be resolved by an appeal to biology. Overwhelmingly, the male "Father" endorses male power in theology, culture, history, society, family, and church. We might just be persuaded by *Mulieris dignitatem* that the divine Father cannot be identified with human maleness. Sadly much Christian theology assumes exactly this. The heavenly Father sacralizes earthly male order, and that issue remains to be addressed in dogmatic and practical theology alike.

David Cunningham has made an original attempt to speak of the generation of the Son and the procession of the Spirit in ways that include the full feminine contribution to real gestation and incorporate those "elements of human generation proper to woman.' "The formation of a child in a woman's womb is a good example of 'going forth from oneself,' which is the notion behind the divine processions: the mother gives her own self to the 'other' within her, becomes 'other' to herself, yet does not thereby diminish herself."[29] Indeed the analogy of a "woman carrying twins . . . would in fact be very useful in describing the account that developed in Eastern Christianity, in which the two processions are described as identically related to that from which they come."[30] These analogies presuppose modern knowledge of the process of conception and so provide a genuine development of the tradition. Unabashed, Cunningham provides a further analogy derived from the female body. The "Trinitarian virtue of participation" is expressed in the eucharist, and in order to intensify the human sense of participation in the divine, in the eucharistic event, he adds "One of the most obvious ways that we 'are nourished by the body' of another human being is through breastfeeding. Because our culture does not tend to hold this activity in pride of place, we rarely attend to its theological significance. But nursing mothers (and their children) know what a profound experience of mutual participation breastfeeding can be."[31]

I applaud these analogies. Not only do they rehabilitate the female body within theology and further modify the masculine images of God that sustain patriarchy, they illuminate compellingly the very ultimate foundations of who and what we take God to be. I think their value can be enhanced further if they are seen to work in both directions: indeed, Cunningham's emphasis on participation prompts this suggestion. When they

---

[29] Cunningham, *These Three Are One*, p. 60.
[30] Cunningham, *These Three Are One*, p. 61.
[31] Cunningham, *These Three Are One*, p. 175.

work in the reverse direction they illustrate some deep truths about *human* creation, conception, and birth, for a theology for families. The formation of a child in a woman's womb is itself the fruit of a couple's creativity and fecundity and can be the occasion of much delight and wonder. In these experiences, the Trinitarian God is also at work, creating new life through the Spirit from the mutual self-giving of the father and the mother to one another. Perhaps the creative presence of God in these occasions is the phenomenological truth behind the joy surrounding the newly conceived, a strong intimation of the hallowed processes that have been set to work (above, 4.3) ? Can the mother's "giving of herself to the other" as the child grows in her womb not be a further intimation of the self-giving of God, as God goes out from Godself in creation, and again in redemption? In its handling of the generation of the Son from "the womb of the Father" (as one Church Council put it),[32] theology has already overstepped the limits of anything that can be said about the eternal Persons of the eternal God. It perseveres with that assertion in order to express something of the superabundant creativity of the divine Source. That same Source gives to human parents the power to be sources of new being, as together from them both, the third, the *condilectus*, arrives as the fruit and the subject of their love. Their unity with their child, and their child's unity with them, invites an ontology that only a full doctrine of God can authorize.

The Mother of God and human mothering

How might the Virgin Mary inspire and aid mothers in their task of mothering? I shy away from this near-impossible question. I am a father, and a Protestant. I cannot know the extent of the religious succor that the Holy Virgin has given to many millions of Roman Catholic mothers; nor the extent to which, as Marxists say, this might be a product of false-consciousness. I know a little of the anger of feminist theologians who see her as the creation of a patriarchal church, imposing on womankind through her, its own fantasized and fearful view of the feminine as necessarily submissive, and honored for her sexual abstinence. Respect for historical study requires confirmation that Mary was the real mother of an unknown number of sisters of Jesus as well as his brothers James, Joses, Judas, and Simon (Mk. 6:3). Helvidius was right to remind the church (around 383) of these facts, and so of the real humanity of Jesus, and the polemicism of Jerome's

---

[32] The 11th Council of Toledo, 675 CE. See Cunningham, *These Three Are One*, p. 47.

reply[33] draws attention to the weaknesses of the latter's arguments. On the other hand, the Councils of Ephesus (430) and Chalcedon (451) uphold the Virgin Mary as the *Theotokos*, the Mother of God. If the crucial developments in the doctrines of the Person of Christ and the Trinity during this period are to be upheld (and many Protestants are surprisingly acquiescent about this), then this quintessentially non-Protestant item of Christian faith must convey something profound that the inheritors of the Reformed faith have yet to fathom.

Several ideas in this book compel a veneration of the Virgin beyond the normal limits of Reformed mind-sets (like mine!). It was argued that we are who we are through our relations with others, especially our parents and our children. It was argued that in these relations we are capable of imaging the Trinitarian God: it was suggested that the ontological union between parents and children goes some way toward explaining why kin altruism works as an explanation for our preference for love of kin. Given these premises, Mary is both an ordinary and an extraordinary mother. Since Jesus Christ is, in the tradition, both fully divine and fully human from the moment of his conception, Mary, in a comprehensible and straightforward sense, gives birth to God. Her body not merely hosts the divine Son: the flesh of Christ is her flesh. "God sent his Son, born of a woman," says Paul (Gal. 4:4), unable to contain his surprise that God should become revealed through the whole risky, bloody, ceremonially unclean, business of giving birth. Our Lord is as nurtured, influenced, shaped, by His mother, as any of us have been in our mothers' care. Mary's motherhood is a refutation of the patriarchal "dis-ease" about the bodies of women. She gives birth to God, and without her our salvation through Christ could not have occurred. A woman's body has brought forth God, and suckled and cared for God. There could hardly be a more positive affirmation of women's bodies than this.

Tina Beattie has recently combined a restatement of the Catholic belief in the Virgin Mary with a devastating critique of her elevation in a phallocentric and phallocratic church.[34] Beattie sees masculinity "as a non-negotiable feature of God's fatherhood"[35] in Catholic theology, which is why Catholic women theologians must accept "that there is no other symbolic resource for the construction of a narrative of women's salvation within the Christian story, but also recognizing that before the symbols can become expressive of

---

[33] Jerome, *The Perpetual Virginity of Blessed Mary: Against Helvidius*. In *Nicene and Post-Nicene Fathers*, series II, vol. VI (undated). www.ccel.org/fathers2/NPNF2–06/. Accessed 02.09.2006.
[34] Beattie, *God's Mother*, see pp. 80–3 and throughout.
[35] Beattie, *God's Mother*, p. 81.

the realities and hopes of women's lives they have to be divested of their masculine fantasies and idealizations."[36] Mary's virginity is not to be compromised, as liberal Protestantism attempts to do, because only one who is a virgin can resist the phallus. The wonder of the Annunciation is that

> God disinvests fatherhood of its phallic power by reaching out beyond the intrusion of the phallus to create the world anew through the loving co-operation of a virgin mother. In the annunciation, God excludes the phallus from the act of (pro)creation, so that in so far as one can talk of the fatherhood of God, one has to recognize that this is a form of fatherhood that initiates a new symbolic world of non-phallic fecundity and creativity.[37]

Beattie's work is profoundly original, and deserves much reflection. The argument I am about to develop is a standard alternative: it denies that God the Father is masculine. That argument, however, is open to serious objection. It does not operate at, or deal with, the all-important symbolic level of apprehension. It needs to face the historical reality that masculine symbols have been continually utilized to accentuate androcentrism and bolster a patriarchal priesthood. And it may be insufficiently robust to deal with the pain of exclusion still felt by millions of Catholic women. My (typically Protestant) worry is that Mary, in Beattie's exciting reclamation as well as in Catholic tradition, may distract theologians from overcoming the masculinity of God, and even become a kind of compensation for, and retreat from, the overwhelming maleness of the patriarchal church and its use of the symbolic order. Jesus, not Mary, is God Incarnate. I want to avoid the temptation to commend God the Father to men, and the Mother of God to women, whether in the outworking of faith or of real parenthood. But Beattie's solution may be the right one, especially for Roman Catholic women, and, since this work is practical in its concern for families and children, it cannot engage further with her provocative and timely defense of the Holy Virgin.

7.3 Parenting, Divine and Human

In order to discern the action and grace of God in earthly parenting it is necessary to make the use of analogy clearer. The term *analogia relationis* compares two relations. Every analogy compares relations but "relations" is

---

[36] Beattie, *God's Mother*, p. 83.
[37] Beattie, *God's Mother*, pp. 128–9.

used here in a strong sense: these relations are relations of participation or inherence. They can be "unpacked" in two divergent ways. Tentatively I shall call these alternatives "the analogy of sacrifice" and "the analogy of mutuality." Both, I think, endow the task of parenting with holy significance, though the arguments in this book favor the second. In this section we will examine the basic analogy before considering the divergent implications that derive from it.

According to the basic analogy the relations compared are between the Father and the Son in the divine Trinity, and between parents and children in the human family, mediated by the Spirit. The inexhaustible love of the Father that the Son reveals in the divine self-giving is the basis of all Christian faith, and of any analogy between the divine Trinity and human families. When parents try consciously to love their children as God in Christ loves them and their children, there lie the points of participation, situated in the quality of each relationship, the divine and the human. In the loving and the caring of human parents, God's own loving and caring is plainly manifested, experienced, known, and reciprocated around the relational circle. The *analogia relationis* becomes an *analogia participationis*. There is a real participation, a real sharing of the infinite divine love in the giving and receiving of human love.

The name "Father" names God as God is known in the biblical traditions. After the church came to the conclusion, derived from the biblical witness to Jesus, that God is a Trinity of Persons, "Father" names the first Person of the divine Trinity. More precisely, "Father" names the Relation that makes God "Father": God is now known as Father through the Son. Christians continue to use "Father" in a straight monotheistic sense to name the one God, whether or not the divine reality is simultaneously understood in its Triune revelation. There will always be space in Christian prayer for the Father to be intimately addressed as "Abba," following the cry of surrender of Jesus in Gethsemane (Mk. 14:36). But recent biblical scholarship has destroyed the widely held view that Mark has Jesus uniquely addressing the Father as "Daddy." Indeed the view that this form of address was unique to Jesus, that is, absent from the Judaism of Jesus' time, is identified with the anti-Semitic scholarship of 1930s Germany.[38] "Abba" does not lie behind Jesus' use of *Patèr*. "'Abba' isn't 'Daddy.'"[39] Mary D'Angelo says "There can

[38] Mary Rose D'Angelo, "Abba and 'Father': Imperial Theology and the Jesus Traditions," *Journal of Biblical Literature*, 111/4 (Winter 1992) [611–31], pp. 612–13.
[39] James Barr, "'Abba' isn't 'Daddy,'" *Journal of Theological Studies*, 39, 1988 [28–47], and see also his "'Abba' and the Familiarity of Jesus' Speech," *Theology*, 91 (1988) [173–9]: both cited in D'Angelo, "*Abba* and 'Father,'" p. 614.

be little doubt the development of Christology was the most significant factor in the importance of 'father' in Christian theology."[40] That is a judgment that can be supported on theological, as well as on the historical-critical grounds which she presents. The loss of the sense of "Abba," as spoken diminutively by a young child, paves the way for a more adult sense of parenthood, as when an adult child, fully equal to his or her parents, speaks intimately to them. As we have noted with Barth (above, 4.1), the Father is known through the gift of the Son: through whom, in faith men and women are the brothers and sisters of Christ and thus children of the heavenly Father by adoption (below, 8.2). The Spirit brings to humanity the mutual love of the Father and the Son. At the micro level, human parenting is (for Barth) a secondary function, derived from the will of the divine Father of all. If we extend the analogy further, we may want to say that, as the Spirit is located in the relation between the Father and the Son, so is the Spirit also located in the love that is the relation between parents and their children.[41]

Problems begin to arise over the direction of the analogy. The action is always downward, from God to humanity, and at the human level, there is further downward action, from parent to child. It follows that there will always be an asymmetry in the analogy. Any analogy which derives from the basic divine/human relationship (for example God/world, Christ/church) will be asymmetrical (for divine and human are in asymmetrical categories). The problem arises when the divine/human relationship extends to model human/human relationships (for example, husband/wife, parent/child). The asymmetry is always going to be passed on with the consequence that inequalities on the human side will be reinforced, or, if they are not already there, introduced. There will always be a tendency for wives and children to be losers in these analogies. Wives and children alike will be submissive, passive, and obedient to the all-powerful husband/father.

This problem with the basic analogy is enmeshed with several others, including of course divine power and gender. The symbol "heavenly Father" compounds power (God is omnipotent) with gender (the symbol is masculine). Any vertical analogy therefore generates the necessity of con-

---

[40] D'Angelo, "*Abba* and 'Father,'" p. 622. See also Mary Rose D'Angelo, "Intimating Deity in the Gospel of John: Theological Language and 'Father'" in "Prayers of Jesus," *Semeia*, 85 (1999) [59–83].

[41] For a more technical mapping of Barth's use of Christological and parental analogies see Elizabeth A. Frykberg, "The Child as Solution: The Problem of the Superordinate–Subordinate Ordering of the Male–Female Relation in Barth's Theology," *Scottish Journal of Theology*, 47.3 (1994) [327–54].

stant qualification. One such qualification is the commendable attempt to introduce mutuality into the husband/wife relationship, against the asymmetry of the Christ/church relationship. Another qualification: it may be gamely stated that the Father need not always be associated with issues of power, discipline, or control, for divine power is most adequately understood in the powerlessness of the Cross. Any emulation of divine authority by human paternal authority just doesn't get validated after all. Again this is correct, but qualified. Another qualification: the heavenly Father is not really masculine, but generative, and so masculine/feminine after all. Such an argument has just been attempted. But it is a further qualification, and these qualifications, cumulatively, lose the immediacy of the symbol's impact upon the religious mind. The masculine God is imprinted too deeply on the religious consciousness. That is a further reason why the analogy of mutuality is required: mutuality will remove much of the requirement for qualification of God's paternal Name.

Sacrificial or mutual love?

The issue of qualification is serious but is eclipsed by the issue of sacrifice. When the expectation of sacrifice enters unequal power relations between people, oppression becomes inevitable. Several theologians who are mothers claim this is what has happened to motherhood in patriarchal cultures (below, 7.4). The analogy of sacrifice can encourage the expectation that, in the flow of human love, love is most like the love of God when it is expressed in the form of sacrifice. Our second principle of procedure for Christian ethics was that everything has to be sorted out by prior reference to Christ and his self-sacrificial love (above, 2.3). Now we face the difficulty that the expectation of sacrifice may not produce a "family-friendly reading of scripture," but may distort it by reproducing dominance/submission narratives at the heart of family life. It is almost a truism to say that, central to Christian faith, Christ lays down his life for the rest of us. The eucharistic wine is "my blood, the blood of the covenant, shed for many for the forgiveness of sins" (Mt. 26:28). Jesus lays down his life for his friends (Jn. 15:13) and "there is no greater love than this." The sacrificial death of Jesus is a central theme in the Letters of Paul, John, and Peter. "Christ died for us while we were yet sinners, and that is proof of his love towards us" (Rom. 5:8). "This is what love really is: not that we have loved God, but that he loved us and sent his Son as a sacrifice to atone for our sin" (1 Jn. 4:10). "He carried our sins in his own person on the gibbet, so that we might cease to live for sin and begin to live for righteousness" (1 Pet. 2:24). Since the sacrificial death of Jesus is the guarantor of the belief that the Father of Jesus is a self-giving God, any shifting of its central place in theology and faith is certain to be resisted.

On the other hand, that very death is interpreted in the New Testament by means of available Jewish sacrificial theories which for late modern Gentiles may read bizarrely both in their meanings and practices. The Abelardian theory of the process of at-one-ment, whereby that death reveals the extent of the divine love, or more modern kenotic theories which emphasize the self-emptying of God on the Cross, cope better with these frank discontinuities between the early church and the church now. A different (and primitive) voice is heard in the Letter to the Hebrews according to which the sacrifice of Christ abolishes the entire system of sacrifice on which His own sacrifice is predicated (Heb. 7:28; 10:9–18). On this view, suffering *in our place* means suffering so that *we do not have to.* To love one another as Christ first loved us indicates the lengths to which that love may go. But replicating the suffering of Christ for its own sake as a good is to nullify the very sacrifice that frees us from the very religious pointlessness symbolized by the religious system that according to Hebrews has been abolished and replaced. Dangers arise when Christ's sacrifice becomes a norm that parents, and particularly mothers, are expected to follow in their love for their children.

The argument is not about replacing the analogy of sacrifice with the analogy of mutuality, but about showing (here and in 7.4 below) how one complements the other and successfully draws the sting of criticism from it. The ontological grounding of the human family in the depths of Godself sacralizes its being. The eclipse of the social Trinity in Western thought has, as one of its consequences, the dropping away of the profound sense of family relations being held together in God through the Spirit. With Richard of St Victor, and the Fathers of the East (at least as they are presently understood) the combined unity and plurality of God serve better the attempt to model the human family. In order to get his analogy going Richard conceives the Spirit as "the Third," insofar as the First and Second Persons required a Third to share the fullness of divine Love. Richard did not need a lesson on the limitations of human language in relation to the divine Being in this regard. He believed in the eternal procession of the Spirit from the Father and the Son. But he was prepared to risk the human detail of lovers sharing their love with a third in order to enable the Trinitarian doctrine to resonate with human experience. It is time to take advantage of his legacy.

The analogy of mutuality, with due acknowledgement to Richard, sees the child of human parents as the *condilectus*, the one who is the expression of the parents' love. In the human detail of his depiction of the Trinity the child's mother and father together are the "source," the "origin," the "generative power," the "begetters," the co-creators of their child. If we look tentatively for correspondence between analogates, the Son in this analogy does not correspond to the human child: the Spirit does. The Spirit is the third, the *condilectus*, the one jointly loved, the one that issues from the co-generativity of the Father *and* the Son. The direction of the analogy is different. The Relation that is Father – Son is not vertical and downwards, but first horizontal, bringing forth from itself in its self-giving and breathing out from itself in the Spirit. This analogy does not require asymmetry. Indeed it requires that there be full symmetry for the Persons are fully equal and fully eternal. Given this full symmetry, no asymmetrical power relations can be loaded on to it without misrepresenting and doing violence to it. Once the divine life is understood as the doctrine of the Trinity requires, the "descending" action of God in Christ, culminating in his sacrifice on the Cross, is given the context of divine mutuality. The divine love issues in mutuality *and* sacrifice.

The analogy of mutuality has as a basic orthodox premise that all the Persons are for each other, and from each other. On the human level, this analogy provides much greater scope for mutuality not simply between partners but between couples and their children. Relations here can be horizontal too. The analogy is bi-directional. On the Godward side the Relations co-inhere. They are a "perichoresis" (which according to one derivation is a "dance"). The analogy encourages mutual interactive relations between family members and generations in a way the vertical analogy finds difficult. And the horizontal analogy makes sacrifice mutual too. While God the Son suffers and dies when Jesus Christ suffers and dies, Christ's death also shows us the suffering love of the Father and the Spirit. The Son in the divine outpouring of Love is not the only One who suffers. Christ suffers: God suffers.[42] Christ suffers *for* God as Christ also suffers for us, to bring us to God.

Gone from this analogy is the baleful influence of inadequate biology on our understanding of the divine Source of all: the divine Persons are Lovers whose Love cannot but be ever more widely shared. In their divinity the Father and the Son exist eternally beyond the sexed distinctions of creatureliness, Source of both of them in the created world. Gone too is the baleful influence of unexamined gender assumptions about males exercising "power-over," dominating, controlling, requiring obedience and submission, as we found in Barth's explication of parenthood (above, 4.2). The

---

[42] I won't be troubling to refute divine impassibility here. It can be confined to history.

divine Life is a dynamic, interactive flow, a Communion of Love, as John Paul II stressed. Grace happens, not when human relations are hierarchically ordered, but when they share in the Communion of Love which God is.

Parents epitomize the relational theory of the self as they care for their children (above, 4.4). There is no better illustration of parental love than the Parable of the Prodigal Father. *Human* love is able to express, however finitely, the ontological structures that the Athanasian Creed tersely articulates in relation to the Trinity. That Creed does not mention love, divine or human, but it speaks of divine Persons who must not be "confounded" and of a Substance that must not be divided. But there are human ways of living where the bonds of commitment constitute a profound unity among persons, stronger than all those influences that would divide it. Equally important is the avoidance of "pouring together" or "confusing" the beings of persons, a feat perhaps finally prevented only in the divine Trinity. The experience of many mothers is precisely of this pouring together, of their being continually without a break with their children, with negative results for each. To be confounded is not just to be puzzled or confused: it is (in an archaic sense) "to be brought to ruin." With good reason we pray "Let me never be confounded."[43] The analogy can be taken into the very heart of the parenting experience, where paradoxically over-identification with children or of couples with each other inhibits the flourishing of all parties. But it is equally important to insist that children are of one substance with their parents. John Chrysostom was very aware of this when he saw that the ontological union of parents could not be contained by them alone but was extended to the "three-in-one flesh" that embraces them all.

The analogy of mutuality comes into view as a consequence of the recent re-emergence of the social Trinity. The analogy of sacrifice derives from the belief in the one God who descends and condescends in Christ. We might also add that the mutual analogy derives from an understanding of the Trinity *ab intra*, from the inner divine Relations. The sacrificial analogy derives from an understanding of the Trinity *ad extra*, from the external relations of the Godhead to the world. In the next section we will see how the analogy of mutuality is enhanced by the forgotten contribution children make to the lives of their parents.

---

[43] The last petition of the ancient prayer *Te Deum Laudamus*.

ix¹¹

1	2	3	4	5	6	7	8	9	10	11	12	13	14	15	16	17	18	19	20
21	22	23	24	25	26	27	28	29	30	31	32	33	34	35	36	37	38	39	40
41	42	43	44	45	46	47	48	49	50	51	52	53	54	55	56	57	58	59	60
61	62	63	64	65	66	67	68	69	70	71	72	73	74	75	76	77	78	79	80
81	82	83	84	85	86	87	88	89	90	91	92	93	94	95	96	97	98	99	100
101	102	103	104	105	106	107	108	109	110	111	112	113	114	115	116	117	118	119	120
121	122	123	124	125	126	127	128	129	130	131	132	133	134	135	136	137	138	139	140
141	142	143	144	145	146	147	148	149	150	151	152	153	154	155	156	157	158	159	160
161	162	163	164	165	166	167	168	169	170	171	172	173	174	175	176	177	178	179	180
181	182	183	184	185	186	187	188	189	190	191	192	193	194	195	196	197	198	199	200
201	202	203	204	205	206	207	208	209	210	211	212	213	214	215	216	217	218	219	220
221	222	223	224	225	226	227	228	229	230	231	232	233	234	235	236	237	238	239	240
241	242	243	244	245	246	247	248	249	250	251	252	253	254	255	256	257	258	259	260

7.4 Parents, Children, and Sacrificial Love

The growing theological literature on motherhood presents in an acute form the problem of sacrificial love. When linked to Protestant understandings of *agapè* as sacrificial love, the expectation is that the love of mothers for their children most approximates to the divine love when it too is sacrificial. Critical familism is commendably sensitive to these issues. Several theological accounts of motherhood will shortly be examined and I will try to show how the theological work undertaken so far in the present volume can extend and further strengthen them.

The language of sacrifice carries with it extreme connotations, for example, the act of offering to a deity something precious, the killing of a victim on an altar, and in Christian faith, Christ's offering of Himself on the Cross. The very notion of sacrifice in Christian discourse, even when used metaphorically of giving up something for the sake of something else, is saturated by associations with violence, extreme pain, and death. Theology must thread a way between the conviction on the one hand, that God has given Godself for us in the life, death, and resurrection of Christ, and the uncomfortable realization on the other hand that the expectation of sacrifice, reinforced by the formidable power of the Cross as a symbol of total submission, is a perverse, albeit common, interpretation of the significance of Christ's death. From its opening pages, the authors of *From Culture Wars to Common Ground* turn away from sacrificial love and toward a love ethic of equal and mutual regard. They construct a theory of family love that makes equal regard or mutuality central and then makes self-sacrificial love an essential but subordinate moment of love that is mainly in the service of equal regard.[44] This is done on theological grounds (and it accorded well with the results of an opinion poll conducted on behalf of the authors, of over a thousand respondents, a clear majority of whom thought that mutuality within marriage was more likely to make a good marriage than either self-sacrifice or self-fulfilment). The authors claim the United States is undergoing a profound revolution in its image of good marital and family love. Mutuality is being perceived more positively; self-sacrifice is being perceived more negatively.[45]

[44] Don S. Browning, Bonnie J. Miller-McLemore, Pamela D. Couture, K. Brynolf Lyon, and Robert M. Franklin, *From Culture Wars to Common Ground: Religion and the American Family Debate* (Louisville, KY: Westminster John Knox Press, 1997), pp. 22–3.
[45] Browning et al., *From Culture Wars*, p. 20.

They think the expectation of sacrificial love is in large measure responsible for the "*female* problematic, the tendency of females under some conditions to suppress their own needs and raise children without paternal participation, sometimes under great stress and at great cost."[46]

The testimony of mothers

One of the key influences on Browning's team, in wishing to relativize sacrificial love,[47] was Christine Gudorf's essay, written in 1985, "Parenting, Mutual Love, and Sacrifice."[48] Gudorf had brought her theological expertise to bear on her experience of being mother to three children, two of whom were adopted and disabled. While she does not deny the need for sacrifice in the service of mutual love, she asks why, if parenting is essentially sacrificial, so many people universally desire it and find it a joyful and life-enriching experience.[49] In any case, sacrifice is only sacrifice if there is no return accruing from the personal cost entailed by it, whereas in parenting there are great returns to be had. If self-denial becomes the principal maternal value, then mothers are reduced to the mere means to an end: that of meeting all their children's needs. Motherhood, like all relationships, is developmental. Children, continues Gudorf, *contribute to their parents'* development in an under-acknowledged reciprocity. Further, "the parental role is a constantly diminishing one in the life of a child."[50] Parents, then, must work not only to make their children less dependent on them. They must attend to themselves in preparing to become less dependent on meeting the needs of their growing children. The sacrificial model of parenthood is thought to impede these processes. It inhibits parental growth and makes the inevitable disengagement from adult children more difficult to achieve.

A decade later Gudorf wrote a further essay which reinforced these criticisms and introduced new ones. She candidly admits she and her husband had to stop seeing their children "as extensions of ourselves who must par-

---

[46] Browning et al., *From Culture Wars*, p. 106 (authors' emphasis). And see the section "The Complaint against Sacrificial Love," pp. 283–5.

[47] Browning et al., *From Culture Wars*, p. 179.

[48] Christine E. Gudorf, "Parenting, Mutual Love, and Sacrifice," in Barbara Hilkert Andolsen, Christine E. Gudorf, and Mary D. Pellauer (eds.), *Women's Consciousness and Women's Conscience: A Reader in Feminist Ethics* (New York: Harper and Row, 1985).

[49] Gudorf, "Parenting, Mutual Love, and Sacrifice," p. 299.

[50] Christine E. Gudorf, "Dissecting Parenthood: Infertility, in Vitro, and Other Lessons in Why and How We Parent," *Conscience* 15.3 (Autumn 1994), p. 21: cited in Browning et al., *From Culture Wars*, p. 179.

ticipate in our search to prove our own worth."[51] The perception of parent-hood as primarily sacrificial "serves as ideological support for patriarchy." When women and children are characterized as innocent and good, they are also characterized as needing, and therefore justifying, protection and control by husbands and fathers. "The assumption that parental power is used in the interests of children . . . disguises the extent to which parental power is used in the interests of parents rather than children." Patriarchal domination can encourage women "to sublimate their desire for autonomy in the more socially acceptable domination of children." More obviously and devastatingly, "a principal function of the romanticization of parent-hood as sacrificial has been to mask the extent of parental abuse of children."[52] Heavy-handed parenthood is implicated in yet more woes. It is used "to justify relationships in which one partner has power, while the other is rewarded with social approval for accepting lack of power." It "prevents children from ever reaching equality with parents," yet this is an essential task for children to achieve, and an essential task for parents to bring about.[53]

Finally, historical conceptions of the Father-God have served to rein-force an unhealthy self-understanding of ourselves as dependent children who do not need to, indeed must not, grow up.[54] Religious infantilism is a dangerous phenomenon, which involves "viewing the God/human rela-tionship in terms of (parent/child) control and dependency."[55] However, as many theologians have pointed out, humanity perhaps as never before needs to act in an adult, mature, and responsible way in discharging its vocation as the co-creator of the world. But Gudorf does not advocate the abandonment of parent/child imagery in the context of the human rela-tionship to God. Instead she draws attention to the longevity of parents in the developed world whose children, inevitably, *have become adults.* "We will not need to abandon God as Parent in order to be responsible adults, and we can cease relying upon a model of divine Fatherhood that justifies parent/child domination."[56] Parents of adult children remain their parents,

---

[51] Christine E. Gudorf, "Sacrificial and Parental Spiritualities," in Anne Carr and Mary Stewart Van Leeuwen (eds.), *Religion, Feminism, and the Family* (Louisville, KY: Westminster John Knox Press, 1996) [294–309], p. 298.

[52] Gudorf, "Sacrificial and Parental Spiritualities," p. 300.

[53] Gudorf, "Sacrificial and Parental Spiritualities," p. 302.

[54] Gudorf, "Sacrificial and Parental Spiritualities," p. 304, citing Rosemary Radford Ruether's criticism of God as "a neurotic parent who does not want us to grow up." See her *Sexism and God-Talk: Toward a Feminist Theology* (Boston, MA: Beacon Press, 1983), p. 69.

[55] Gudorf, "Sacrificial and Parental Spiritualities," p. 305.

[56] Gudorf, "Sacrificial and Parental Spiritualities," p. 306.

but adjust their roles considerably. The human passage from being provider and carer to being friend and helper becomes a vital element in the God/human relationship.

Several of these themes can obviously be grounded in the analogy of mutuality outlined in the previous section. Children are gifts. Many people want them. The unidirectional model of love does not fit within the family this mother describes. It does not rejoice in, or accommodate, the contribution children make to the lives of their parents. Children grow, and contribute to the growth of their parents. Adult children have a different relation to their parents than they had when they were younger, and their arrival at adulthood within families, as within the family of faith, entails a new mutuality where patriarchy and its associated vocabulary of submission and obedience have no place.

A second theologian-mother deals with the mutuality problem by relocating and further qualifying what parental sacrifice entails. Julie Rubio accepts much of the feminist case against sacrificial love but perseveres with it, endowing it with bodily meanings. The paradigmatic case of parental sacrifice is pregnancy, "for the child takes over the mother's body (eating from her food, drinking from her drink, moving within her, causing her pain and discomfort, and distorting the shape of her body). If this is not self-sacrifice, what is?"[57] Disturbed sleep, changing diapers, forfeiting leisure activities, and so on, confirm the need to sacrifice oneself for one's children. Another mother, Carrie Heiman, associates the sacrifice of Christ on the Cross directly with her pregnancy. Comparing both what she had to give up to become a mother, and the changes in her body while pregnant, with what Christ gave up, and the changes in the body of Christ on the Cross, she discerns how "He gave and gave until his body was changed almost beyond recognition – as it hung on the Cross. And finally he gave his very body and blood in order to bring me to spiritual birth."[58] Rubio finds the supreme example of connectedness between people in a mother's *nursing* of a child. "Women's experience of having their milk 'let down' when they hear the cry of an infant leads them to a deeper knowledge of the connection among human beings."[59]

Sally Purvis, another theologian-mother, finds that "my richest and most

---

[57] Rubio, *A Christian Theology*, p. 92.

[58] Carrie J. Heiman, *The Nine-Month Miracle* (Liguori, MO: Liguori Publications, 1986), Week 24, cited in Rubio, *A Christian Theology*, p. 95.

[59] Rubio, *A Christian Theology*, p. 95, summarizing observations of the theologian Bonnie Miller-McLemore, *Also a Mother: Work and Family as Theological Dilemma* (Nashville, TN: Abingdon Press, 1994), p. 143.

powerful experience of agape, of unqualified, unconditional love for another, has come with my experience of being a mother."[60] She recalls and reproves Kierkegaard's formulation of Christian sacrificial love. For love to be Christian it must be disinterested, and his notorious test for appropriate disinterest is loving someone who is dead! Purvis explains: "Kierkegaard claims that in order to purify love of all of the complications that ordinarily surround it, to eliminate the dizzying diversity of life in which love is found, we focus on the practice of 'remembering one who is dead' as a model for Christian agape."[61] Loving someone who is dead is disinterested in three ways. There is no possibility of reciprocation or return. There is "nothing in the beloved that calls forth our love." And, third, "this love is the most faithful. The dead do not change . . . therefore if change occurs, it must occur in the living."

Purvis harries the assumption that *agapè* is best unpacked by means of detachment. At this point her experience of mothering her two sons is brought to bear upon what is involved in the real love of real people, or as she says, "the nursery might better replace the graveyard as agape's school room"![62] "A mother's love for her children" might provide a better "experiential model and foundation for agape."[63] Mother-love is "inclusive."[64] "There is a disposition on the mother's part to devote herself to the well-being of the child from birth and for its lifetime without knowing the particular talents or future achievements of that small person." Second, a mother's love "is both intensely involved and other-regarding." Indeed "the needs of the child as expressed in cries of different volume and tone are experienced by the mother as in some sense internal to her own being."[65] Third, "mother-love is unconditional. It is not dependent upon nor can it be canceled by the behavior of the child." The Kierkegaardian model of disinterested *agapè* and the "mother-love model" are assessed in accordance with the qualities of *agapè* shown by the Parable of the Good Samaritan, and the careful conclusion is drawn that "mother-love can provide an excellent model for the content of agape."[66] Mother-love, like the love shown by the Samaritan, responds to need, is other-regarding, even when it "interferes

---

[60] Sally B. Purvis, "Mothers, Neighbors and Strangers – Another Look at Agape," in Adrian Thatcher and Elizabeth Stuart (eds.), *Christian Perspectives on Sexuality and Gender* (Leominster, UK: Gracewing, and Grand Rapids, MI: Eerdmans, 1996) [232–46], p. 232.

[61] Purvis, "Mothers, Neighbors and Strangers," p. 233.

[62] Purvis, "Mothers, Neighbors and Strangers," p. 235.

[63] Purvis, "Mothers, Neighbors and Strangers," p. 236.

[64] Purvis, "Mothers, Neighbors and Strangers," p. 237.

[65] Purvis, "Mothers, Neighbors and Strangers," p. 238.

[66] Purvis, "Mothers, Neighbors and Strangers," p. 242.

with some agenda of her own," is focussed on "the immediacy of the demands that she attempts to meet," and is intensely involved. Relevant to our work on the "social self" (above, 4.1) she notes "If the 'self' that the mainstream agapic tradition has described as the model for agape is remote, distant, detached, the self that expresses mother-love is present, connected, involved, intensely caring."

These contributions to a theology of parenthood, from theologians who are mothers, are profound, comparable to the contribution to theology of married male theologians at the time of the Reformation who wrote experientially about love, marriage, and children. I remain uncertain, however, whether, in some otherwise outstanding contemporary theological achievement, the sacrificial death of Jesus for us is itself being sacrificed, lest it be found offensive to modern sensibilities. If there is a ring of truth to this suspicion, the analogy of mutuality must be allowed, not to replace the analogy of sacrifice, but to complement it. And I think all the theologies of parenthood discussed here would be yet richer if they drew on the analogies and Trinitarian sources brought to attention in this book. To these two matters we now turn.

Mutual love: mutual sacrifice?

The theory of family love advocated by critical familism appears to sideline *agapè*. There is no need to rekindle the nagging doubt about the egalitarian interpretation of scripture within critical familism (above, 2.2). However, if mutual regard is to be established as a Christian theory of family love, it is important to inquire how such establishment might be achieved, and for this we need not only scripture, but tradition and a strong hermeneutic confidence in developing both. In order to show that scripture itself will *not* suffice to validate theories of equal regard, it will be necessary to examine briefly the attempt to do so in *From Culture Wars*.

The authors make a renewed appeal to the Ephesian Household Code in seeking to establish their theory. "Equal regard" is found in the injunction, "Even so husbands should love their wives as their own bodies."[67] (5:28a) "Natural self regard" is found in the immediately following two sentences: "He who loves his wife loves himself. For no man ever hates his own flesh." (5:28,29) The authors comment "In contrast to the views of Christian love which make self-sacrifice its end, the Ephesians passage seems to see love as

---

[67] Browning et al., *From Culture Wars*, p. 284.

mutuality as the goal, with sacrificial love working to maintain Christ's relation to the church and the husband's relation to the wife." They then import into the interpretation a commendable principle of their own, that "*if Ephesians has validity for today, it must be interpreted reversibly in all respects – as applying to the wife as profoundly as it does the husband.*"[68] They believe they can illustrate this principle from the famous passage in 1 Corinthians where the apostle allows divorce in the cases where a believer is married to an unbeliever, and the unbelieving partner seeks one. If a believer and an unbeliever are married and wish to remain married, they are unsurprisingly encouraged do so. Paul gives them an additional ground for staying together – "For the unbelieving husband is *made holy through his wife*, and the unbelieving wife is made holy through her husband."[69]

This additional ground given to these couples, both in divorcing and in staying together, is given to the husband and the wife. It is therefore "reversible," applying to each. But Browning's team make much more of it than this. Paul is said here to imagine "the possibility of wives being to their husbands as Christ was to the church." The passage is said to communicate "the revolutionary idea that the wife can 'make holy' (some translations say 'sanctify') the unbelieving husband." It "suggests that Paul could imagine how women can mediate Christ's transforming and self-giving love to the family. Women too can participate in the Christic drama, not as subservient recipients but as active leaders performing the work of Christ." The authors conclude, almost triumphantly,

> Even in this Ephesians passage, it is assumed that humans have a natural inclination and right to cherish and nourish their own bodies. Even in these verses, considered to be the great passage in the Christian heritage that calls for sacrificial love in marriage, we have a full legitimation of the right of self-regard. Hence, self-regard is intrinsic to the logic of equal regard, and it applies to both the husband and the wife as humans made in the image of God.[70]

Unfortunately the argument claims more than the premises can support, and the premises themselves are weighed down by what the authors want these verses to say. Equal regard is not a valid inference from "Even so husbands should love their wives as their own bodies." The meaning of that verse is probably derived, as the authors acknowledge, from the familiar statement (in Genesis 2:24, and repeated by Jesus) that in marriage the two

---

[68] (authors' emphasis).
[69] 1 Cor. 7:14a, as cited by Browning et al., *From Culture Wars*, p. 284 (authors' emphasis).
[70] Browning et al., *From Culture Wars*, p. 285.

"become one flesh." There is no suggestion of reversibility in this statement: wives are not told to love their husbands as their own bodies (indeed, as we have noted, they are not told to love their husbands but to submit to them). The one flesh or body which is the husband-and-wife is traditionally understood to be the husband's body into which the wife's body is incorporated. When the husband loves his own body, he loves his wife's body *as an extension to his own*. Unfortunately this is not equal regard: it is assimilation of the wife's body by that of her husband in the one flesh of marriage. Yes, there is "a place for natural self-regard" in the passage, but it does not work in the way the critical familists assume. The argument *intensifies* self-regard. In loving his wife the husband is actually loving himself all along.

These premises, regrettably unestablished, support the extraordinary conclusion that "the Ephesians passage seems to see love as mutuality as the goal." We have already noted the heroism of the husband who is to love his wife as Christ loves the church, and that love is not mutual, but sacrificial ("Christ loved the church and gave himself up for it.") (Eph. 5:25b). The direction of love is one way: Christ – church: husband – wife. That is why the authors need to appeal to their principle of reversibility which is not, of course, justified by the text itself. The authors believe that they have found an instance in Paul's thought of genuine mutuality which supports their interpretation of Ephesians 5: it is his observation, in response to a specific marital dilemma for the church, that an unbelieving husband is sanctified by his believing wife, and reversibly, that an unbelieving wife is sanctified by her believing husband. Unfortunately there are exegetical problems here as well. When Paul wrote 1 Corinthians he was unwilling to acknowledge even that a woman was made in the image of God (11:7b). His argument for marital sanctification is based on the two convictions that a husband and wife are one flesh (even the prostitute and her client constitute "one flesh" – 1 Cor. 6:16), and that each individual Christian belongs as "limbs and organs" to the body of Christ (1 Cor. 6:15). A believing spouse sanctifies his or her unbelieving partner, because the believer represents in the body the body of Christ. That is why the act of Christian men having sex with prostitutes is hideous. It brings Christ's body into contact with the body of the prostitute and defiles it. Men and women necessarily represent the body of Christ. That is why there are striking consequences, in home and brothel. But that is some way from the conclusion that "Women too can participate in the Christic drama, not as subservient recipients but as active leaders performing the work of Christ." It says little about mutuality or equality between the members of the body.

The communion of love

The position is similar to that in 2.2 above. I agree with Browning's conclusions, but not with his premises. There is no "full legitimation of the right of self-regard" in Ephesians 5. That would be a curious thing to look for. What we find is an extension of self-regard to embrace a wife and her body within what is to count as self-regard. There is no equal regard either: the principle of reversibility is an import. And the model of love the author of Ephesians uses is not mutuality first, and sacrifice second. It is sacrificial love through and through, and the wife is to submit to it. I have drawn attention to these difficulties not to enter a fruitless argument with Browning's team, or score a few minor exegetical points, but to point to the need for a different route to establish his sound conclusions. The best way to establish a Christian family theory of equal regard is to root it in the Triune God: to situate families within the Trinity; to model family relations along the lines of Trinitarian relations. That will require a renewed grasp of that priceless doctrine, especially in its "social" form, and a bold use of material drawn from the human experience of creation, generation, nurture, and care, and especially from those human beings who know the most about such things, and have the most to contribute.

This doctrine is able to clarify, support, and develop the insights of the women theologians who have reflected on their experience of motherhood. It is able also to provide the ultimate theory of mutual love. Among the Three there is complete equality. The church has been swift to proscribe as heresy any attempt to subordinate any of the Persons to one another. "The whole three Persons are co-eternal together: and co-equal." The Persons are uniquely co-equal in a way that popular theological analogies often fail to capture. There is an inevitable asymmetry in any analogy between infinite and finite terms. A relation, such as a covenant, between God and the world or between Christ and the church, cannot fail to replicate the Creator/creature distinction, however lowly the Creator is depicted and however exalted the creature becomes. Within the Christian redemptive story, there is sacrificial love but little mutuality. And of course this qualitative distinction has been consistently and erroneously mapped on to the male/female distinction, replicating sexist asymmetry and skewed power relations between men and women.

In the relations that are internal to God there is no such skewing. "None is afore, or after other: none is greater, or less than another." The incarnate Son is undiminished in divinity in his conception, birth, life, and death. His sacrifice on the Cross reveals the nature of God as self-giving Love. To say

Jesus reveals the nature of God is to say He shows us not what God is like, but what God *is*. And what God is, God is in all the Persons of God's being. God's gracious summons in the Gospel is to *participate* in the loving Communion that is God's divine life. The asymmetry between God and ourselves is preserved. We are not divine Persons but human beings in need of divine grace. But as persons we cannot separate ourselves from the relationships that make us who we are. This is the crucial fact for our participation in God. It is our relationships that participate in the loving relationships which are God, and it is through our relationships with our spouses and children that our being "in" God may be most manifest.

Our treatment of self-love (above, 3.4) encouraged us both to begin the study of self with the category of relation, and to be wary of any theological anthropology which excludes children. Once again the analogy of mutuality provides gains in each case. The symbol "heavenly Father" will not for some time be dissociated from its exclusive masculinity and so from its function of endorsing and legitimizing particular constructions of fatherhood. But, as it has been constructed here "Father" assumes its place in Christian thought and prayer as the over-flowing Source of creative, generative, life, and so is actually unthinkable in human terms without the contribution of both sexes, just because they are both necessary to the creation of life.

Since it is the relations we are that share in the divine Relations that are God, it may not be helpful to press the analogies in such a way as to identify the divine and human relations too closely. That inevitably encourages us to look for individual subjects and to adopt the assumption of a one-to-one correspondence between them (Father is to Son, as parent is to child, and so on). The direction is two-way, vertically downwards and upwards. It is important to forget verticality for the present, to bracket it out and think instead of parallel lines. There are Relations that are wholly and entirely divine, that are horizontal, and do not "descend." They envelop and embrace. And there are relations between human persons which are also horizontal, sustained by God yet conducted "according to nature," without obvious reference to the divine. Only when the parallel lines are established can the connections between them be explored. God has broken revealingly into the human world and lifted it into the Life of God. The self-giving Love that makes and redeems the world, and which for Christians "spirates" or breathes out through the divine Spirit, spirates the love we come to share between ourselves. Within marriages and families, where life is intimately shared, the possibility exists for real participation in the divine life in the form of sacrificial love. Yet because intimacy is unknown without vulnerability, the possibility of physical and psychic injury can never be eliminated. Even here the image of the crucified Christ is able to offer healing.

However, let us press the analogies as far as we helpfully can. The "Father" in God stands for the aboriginal, uncreated Source of all things (from whom even the Son and Spirit eternally come forth!). Human fathers and mothers share equally in creating homes, families, children. They share in the creativity of the Father. They bring forth children as the Son is eternally brought forth from the Father. When we say the Father loves the Son, we say God loves God. When parents love their child, they love themselves, the one who is "consubstantial" with both of them, yet other than them. When the analogy moves this way it invites further extension: the love of the parents for the child parallels the mutual love of the Father and the Son which, in some Western thought, is the Spirit. The "gift" of the child extends the love of the parents to new horizons, just as "the gifting God" goes on giving, thereby making yet more giving possible. The mutual love of the man and woman resembles the mutual love of the eternal Father and the eternal Son. And the resemblance extends further (as it does for Richard of St Victor). That love requires a third for it to be generative, to extend beyond itself, to embrace what is other than itself in its compulsion to share itself. In this case, the "third" is the child who is held in the love that spirates from both the parents. As the Spirit is the *condilectus* in Richard's Trinity, the third in this analogy is the child, fruit of the relation of mother and father.

The basic thought that familial relations share in the divine Relations enables a sharper account of several of the insights borrowed earlier in this section. There are undoubtedly great rewards in being parents, as Gudorf reminds us, not least in the contribution children make to the moral and spiritual becoming of their parents. Children, as John Paul II observed, "offer their own precious contribution to building up the family community and even to the sanctification of their parents."[71] That is, always in the long term, and proleptically in the short term, there may be, and should be, mutuality in parent–child relations. Once the mind-set of power, control, domination, submission, obedience, punishment is excised from the Christian understanding of God's fatherhood, mutuality settles in, both in relations between spouses and in those between spouses and their children. Critical familism says little about mutuality between parents and children, seeking to make its own theological contribution to the politics of gender in the United States. A child will move from almost complete dependence on his or her parents, and especially on the mother, to almost complete independence from them in adulthood. Within this complex process, myriad

---

[71] John Paul II, *Familiaris consortio* (1981). www.vatican.va/holy_father/john_paul_ii/apost_exhortations/. Accessed 02.09.2006.

problems about appropriate behavior and the need for appropriate discipline arise (and are preferably dealt with by both parents). But it is a travesty of fatherhood to suggest that the primary role fathers play in relation to their children lies within the area of discipline and punishment. Worse still, when unexamined notions of heavenly Father are invoked to support it, theology becomes idolatry.

Indeed the picture of the dominating Father is useless and dangerous. It is never far from the thousands of cases of child abuse and it validates stereotypes of fatherhood that are a perversion of the Gospel.[72] It seems essential to continued belief in the Father God that that Name be located both as the Source of male/female attraction and differentiation and in relation to the Son. Without that relation, what God is as Father is void of content. Rubio's use of the experience of nursing a child is surely the closest human example of loving connectedness that can be found. The divine Relations respond to dangerous tendencies in real relations between people and God and between children and parents. The danger is that we are frozen as little children in our relation to the Divine when the Divine would draw us out to our full personhood, which of course will express our continuing "childness" (above, 3.2). The parallel danger is that our children will be frozen as children when they grow up and away from us as they must. The divine Relations can be our guide in both cases. Humanity is summoned to reach its full stature "measured by nothing less than the full stature of Christ" (Eph. 4:13b). And in the latter case parental love is directed toward the child achieving full independence, for this is what continued mutuality requires. Gudorf's invocation of the adult child who enters a different phase in the relation with parents, when parents become the closest of friends, is valuable here.

Purvis' achievement in providing a model of *agapè* based on motherhood cuts through the tortuous replacement of *agapè* by mutuality. There is little reason to modify the biblical witness to *agapè*. She has described the kind of sacrificial love that is required of a mother, so the expectation of sacrifice in this regard is not oppressive but gladly undertaken. Children need to be loved, whether or not this is to be regarded as agapic. Some of the practical consequences will be considered in the final two chapters.

---

[72] For a chilling account of this wretched process, see Janet Pais, *Suffer the Children: A Theology of Liberation by a Victim of Abuse* (New York/Mahwah, NJ: Paulist Press, 1991).

Chapter Eight

Open Families and Chosen Childlessness

Readers may well think that the argument so far has privileged nuclear families. I have found kin altruism a cogent social doctrine. It is a partial, but cogent, answer to the vexed and neglected problem of preference in Christian ethics. Support for it was found in the idea of the social self, the doctrine of the "social" Trinity, a renewed understanding of the *imago dei*, and a careful analogy between human family relations and divine Trinitarian relations. The care of children is an over-riding imperative for any reputable family theology, and their care cannot be separated from their relations with the parents who brought them into the world. It is now time to respond to critics who will think this analysis accommodates the nuclear family far too conveniently and even breaches our earlier principles for prioritizing the teaching of Jesus.

In section 1 I attempt to show that while the couple is often the nucleus of the family form, "nucleus," as that term conveys, may be the central point around which much gathering, concentration, or accretion takes place. In section 2 I defend the concept and the practice of "open" families or households. This will be done by friendly engagement with David McCarthy's *Sex and Love in the Home*,[1] since my version of the open family is very different from his. In section 3 I attend to the obvious criticism of the book that, so far, it fails to accord with the disruptive teaching of Jesus that the Reign of God, not ties of kin, constitutes the only, or the principal, viable family form for his disciples. In sections 4 and 5 I attempt the postponed examination of the growing phenomenon of voluntary childlessness in church and state.

---

[1] David Matzko McCarthy, *Sex and Love in the Home* (London: SCM Press, 2001).

8.1 Extending Families

When Pope John Paul II wrote to families in the Year of the Family (1994) he spoke of them as a "communion of generations." Although he does not use the term "gene" he speaks warmly of the "*gene*alogy of persons," acknowledges the biological origins of families, and teaches that "through the genealogy of persons, conjugal communion *becomes a communion of generations.*" In and through prayer, the late Pope hopes, "the family discovers itself as the first 'us,' in which each member is '*I*' and '*thou*'; each member is for the others either husband or wife, father or mother, son or daughter, brother or sister, grandparent or grandchild."[2] He regrets that too few families have "several generations living together," but does not advance the boundary of the family any further. "A man and a woman united in marriage, together with their children, form a family."[3] There is no further extension. Disciples of Jesus must accept "the invitation to belong to *God's family*,"[4] but nothing is said about the interaction between the human family and God's family.[5] For example, nothing is said about the adoption of children or the inclusion of friends or more distant relatives into families. Doing the will of the Father in heaven may require the relinquishment of a family member for the consecrated or priestly life, but not, apparently, extending the boundaries of families beyond the genealogies of their nuclei.

Grandparents and godparents

The communion of generations may be more in evidence now than it was a decade ago. Certainly households with three generations ("3G homes" – in the trade) are more common in Britain now than they were then. The high cost of housing keeps increasing numbers of prospective house-purchasers longer in the parental home, while increasing numbers of pensioners find their savings cannot cope with rising healthcare, heating, and tax costs and so move back to be with their children. A total of 800,000 homes are "3G."[6] Grandparents, whether or not they live in separate households, play an increasing part in the care of their children's children. In Britain many of

---

[2] Pope John Paul II, *Letter to Families* (1994), section 10 (author's emphases). www.vatican.va/holy_father/john_paul_ii/letters/documents/. Accessed 02.09.2006.
[3] *Catechism of the Catholic Church* (London: Geoffrey Chapman, 1994), section 2202, p. 475.
[4] *Catechism of the Catholic Church*, section 2233, p. 482 (authors' emphasis).
[5] See chapter 9 below for a discussion of the domestic church.
[6] According to research conducted for the organization Economic Lifestyle, and released 11.14.05. www.economiclifestyle.co.uk/?s=Events&AID=22. Accessed 02.09.2006.

them are likely to be under 60 and in fulltime work. Their help with child care can be inestimable, provided they do not become principal carers, or feel pressurized to take on more child care than they actually want.[7] Daughters are better at involving their parents with grandchildren than are sons. Two out of three grandparents see their grandchild or grandchildren every week. Sixty percent of childcare in Britain is provided by grandparents.[8] Grandparents are particularly useful during school holidays, and are likely to have wisdom to impart to new parents. But the place of grandparents within family networks is not defined simply by their utility. One way adult children may honor their parents is by accepting the contribution these parents are able to make to the new household. We have seen how relations between generations have a dynamic of their own: parents who provided care will soon need care, whether or not their children provide, or merely help to ensure, it. Whether an ageing parent should be admitted to a household, especially if he or she has special needs, is a particularly sensitive dilemma for increasing numbers of families to negotiate.[9]

The genealogical route extends backwards to encompass grandparents, but does it extend sideways to aunts, uncles, cousins? They too are surely family members, whether or not they occasionally become temporary or permanent members of another household unit. Historically the existence of godparents ensured the extension of a child's family. The diminished role of godparents in the sacrament of baptism[10] in the contemporary churches should not allow students of the family within Christian faith to overlook the special bonds that were created between families by the spiritual affinity sealed at infant baptism. The role of godparent probably arose from the practice of the sponsoring of candidates for adult baptism.[11] The sponsors would vouch for the candidates' sincerity and probity. When the practice of baptizing infants became almost universal, the role of godparent changed. The godparent "became a spokesperson for the godchild and assumed a vicarious

---

[7] See L. Clarke and C. Roberts, "The meaning of grandparenthood and its contribution to the quality of life of older people," in A. Walker and C. Hagan Hennessy (eds.), *Growing Older: Quality of Life in Old Age* (Milton Keynes: Open University Press, 2004), pp. 188–208.

[8] Statistics issued by the Grandparents' Association. www.grandparents-association.org.uk/. Accessed 02.09.2006.

[9] For a highly sensitive and helpful discussion of this, see Stephen G. Post, *More Lasting Unions: Christianity, the Family and Society* (Grand Rapids, MI/Cambridge, UK: Eerdmans, 2000), chapter 6, "The Challenge of Intensive Family Caregiving" [151–76].

[10] See, for example, Rachel Harden, "Few Showing the Way," *Church Times*, no. 7392, 11.05.2004, and the on-line organization *eGodparent*. See e.g., www.egodparent.com. Accessed 02.09.2006.

[11] For the fine detail, see Joseph H. Lynch, *Godparents and Kinship in Early Medieval Europe* (Princeton, NJ: Princeton University Press, 1986).

responsibility for the child's Christian upbringing."[12] But there is more. From the eighth century onwards the godparents (a minimum of two women and one man for a daughter, and two men and a woman for a son) became *co-parents*, along with the child's natural parents. The tie of spiritual affinity between the co-parents and their godchild became sufficiently important and (one assumes) strong, for the co-parents to be included in what became known as the Table of Kindred and Affinity within which marriage was forbidden.

The corollary of this prohibition for our present argument is straight-forward. In the pre-Tridentine Church, godparents were family. They were de facto kin, and they thereby impeded themselves from marriage to one another, unless by special dispensation, to the child's natural parents, to other godparents, and to any relatives among the whole circle of the parties involved. Sexual relations between them amounted to "spiritual incest."[13] The involvement of co-parents helped to ensure the welfare of the child in hard times or through the death of one or both natural parents. Their responsibility did not stop with the confirmation of their godchild, and sub-sequent growth in faith. No argument is offered here for the reinstatement of the office of co-parent. However the historical precedent of co-parenthood allows us to envisage a family form where the boundary between kin and non-kin became deliberately porous, where in fact an institution existed precisely to extend the bonds of kin, and to do so in such a way that the needs of children were placed first. Put this way, the present practice of choosing godparents (or sponsors in the cases of services of thanksgiving) provides access to a rich resource of family extension, of merging the spiri-tual and material interests of children, and strengthening the provision for their care.

Blended and adoptive families

Stepfamilies or blended families provide another example of families being extended beyond immediate kin. Churches worldwide have much catching up to do in recognizing stepfamilies as a growing family form. Their reluc-tance to recognize stepfamilies is rooted in the likelihood that a new stepfamily may have been formed after the divorce of one or more parents.

---

[12] James A. Brundage, "Review: Godparents and Kinship in Early Modern Europe," *American Historical Review*, 92.2, April 1987, pp. 393–4.
[13] Loius Hass, "Il mio buono compare: Choosing godparents and the uses of baptismal kinship in renaissance Florence," *Journal of Social History*, 29.2, Winter 1995 [341–77], p. 341.

The remarriage or "further marriage" of a divorced parent may be held by some Christians to "weaken" marriage and "the family" further. But these reservations, sometimes more damaging when tacit and unspoken, can create further problems for stepfamilies just at the point when they need all the help they can get. This book has strongly advocated marriage as the best family form, for couples, for their children, and for society, but there should be no contradiction in advocating marriage and honoring the hopes and best intentions of postmarried people who choose to form new families.

I have cited stepfamilies as an example of the extension of a family of kin (to a joint family of kin). But in Christian theology, especially pastoral theology, the recognition of stepfamilies is integrally related to what might be called a simple "ministry of understanding." If stepfamilies are not respected and welcomed in "the family of God," or if they are excluded from recognition by narrow (and arbitrary) definitions of what a family is, then they are effortlessly marginalized and "de-validated." Stepfamilies are likely to experience many difficulties in addition to those encountered in biological families. For example, the new family is born out of loss, through divorce or death, of a parent. Relationships with ex-spouses and with the biological parent who lives apart may be problematic (to say the least). The bonding required of a new stepfamily is not that of a couple as in a first marriage: parts of one or two families recombine bringing different, and set, traditions with them. The bond between a child and his or her biological parents predates the new couple's bond. Roles, and rules, within the new family will be unclear at first, and discipline is often the new family's biggest problem.

Violence and incest are more likely in stepfamilies.[14] It is better to be honest about this, not least to understand why and to help to prevent it happening. More than half of all stepfamilies end in divorce. That is a sad statistic, but prior attention to the problems and tensions that arise within stepfamilies, and to appropriate community support for them, remains the way forward. The sharing of understanding and information may lead in some cases to a change of mind about the decision to remarry and to end a marriage that is "good enough." There must be at least a de facto recognition of stepfamilies by the churches, and a conscious decision to accept them in the name of the God who accepts everyone in spite of themselves and their histories. There is surely evidence of much of the theological

---

[14] I have been helped in writing these paragraphs by the Smart Marriages archive, archives.his.com/smartmarriages/. Accessed 02.09.2006. See also the Stepfamily Association of America, www.saafamilies.org/, the publications listed there, and StepFamilies UK, www. stepfamilies.co.uk. Accessed 02.09.2006.

virtues of faith, hope, and love among couples taking the step to form a new family. Churches can help, not by equivocation over their status, but by pointing to sources of grace, healing, and renewal.

The discussion so far has proceeded by showing how a nuclear family may be an open family whose members are drawn more widely than the two-generational kin paradigm suggests. The practice of adopting children widens this family further. Stephen Post has provided an excellent discussion of the theology and practice of adoption among Christians.[15] For every child adopted there is a child relinquished. Many mothers later regret relinquishing their child for adoption. One such Christian mother sent me an anguished letter querying how I, as a Christian theologian, could ever have advocated (in a review article) a practice that, in her case, had led to much subsequent regret, guilt, and remorse. However, as Post points out, a mother may also come to regret taking other available options (abortion, raising the child in very difficult circumstances), and the object of her regret may not be the relinquishment of the child but "that her situation was not otherwise" at the time.[16]

Familiaris consortio commends the adoption and/or fostering of children. The immediate theological grounds supporting the commendation are the universal Fatherhood of God and the one family of humankind; the extending and embracing character of parental love (in which the Spirit is present); and the experience of the divine Fatherhood that the children receive through their new parents.

Christian families, recognizing with faith all human beings as children of the same heavenly Father, will respond generously to the children of other families, giving them support and love not as outsiders but as members of the one family of God's children. Christian parents will thus be able to spread their love beyond the bonds of flesh and blood, nourishing the links that are rooted in the Spirit and that develop through concrete service to the children of other families, who are often without even the barest necessities.[17]

Christian families are marked by their "greater readiness to adopt and foster children who have lost their parents or have been abandoned by them." Such children "will be able to experience God's loving and provident fatherhood witnessed to by Christian parents." God's fatherhood is expressed through *mothers and* fathers, and the "fecundity" of the family is extended beyond immediate kin. There is a "vast field of activity" open to

---

[15] Post, *More Lasting Unions*, chapter 5, pp. 119–50.
[16] Post, *More Lasting Unions*, pp. 137–9.
[17] John Paul II, *Familiaris consortio* (1981), section 41. www.vatican.va/holy_father/john_paul_ii/apost_exhortations/. Accessed 02.09.2006.

Christian families which "broadens enormously" the "horizons of . . . parenthood": for "even more preoccupying than child abandonment is the phenomenon of social and cultural exclusion, which seriously affects the elderly, the sick, the disabled, drug addicts, ex-prisoners, etc."

These emphases accord entirely with the theology for families in the present volume. A further, powerful, theological argument can be added to them. According to Christian faith, all people have become God's adopted children. That belief is the basis of St Paul's mission to the Gentiles, namely that Gentiles are *not* God's chosen people. We are the children of God just because we do *not* belong to God's elect by right, or natural descent. We are the outsiders welcomed without reservation into the family of God through our Brother, Jesus Christ. "The Spirit you have received is not a spirit of slavery, leading you back into a life of fear, but a Spirit of adoption, enabling us to cry 'Abba! Father!' The Spirit of God affirms to our spirit that we are God's children; and if children, then heirs, heirs of God and fellow-heirs with Christ . . ." (Rom. 8:15–17a; and see Gal. 4:5; Eph. 1:5). This affective testimony of the Spirit depends for its effect on all Paul's readers upon them entering imaginatively into the plight of a wretched child, perhaps abandoned or orphaned, who finds her situation transformed by being made a full, dependent member of a new family, with the same entitlements and endowments as if she were born into it. This is the root experience, of freedom from destitution, of relief from poverty, on which the experience of salvation itself is based.

We have already seen how some Christian language use about children, about the *mikroi* or "little ones," about fatherhood and motherhood, and so on, is borrowed from its original settings in order to describe the new family of Kingdom or Church, and the relationship of its members to each other and to the heavenly Father. Once again it is necessary to resist the displacement of meaning that is an unintended consequence of such language use, and to return to the root experiences and real family relations which must first exist to make the articulation of experience in the family of God a linguistic possibility. Adoption is a further case where original root meanings may become obscured in the attempt to record and commend the redeeming action of God in Christ. It is essential that the analogy work both ways. The adoption of a child can be a supremely loving act, an intense example of neighbor-love, a life-changing expression of faith, hope, and love, for parents and child alike. God the Spirit empowers and sanctifies such practice. Our adoption as God's children is also a supremely loving act. It is important for a theology of families to locate the affective testimony of the Spirit *both* in what God does in adopting us *and* in what parents do in adopting a child.

8.2 Families and Neighborhoods

A family then, is broader and more open than its reproductive nucleus. The term "nuclear family" conflates incompatible meanings. It might mean "couple + biological children" or "couple as the nucleus of a network of relations," some of whom are kin while some are not. The families described in the previous section are, at least potentially, open families. Beginning with the couple nucleus they are able to extend their scope outwards, embracing the neighbor and the stranger. Each family member may have friends and acquaintances through contacts at school, college, university, through work, or through clubs, voluntary societies, churches, and so on. The contacts that family members have cannot be confined to kin (or marriages would be impossible!). But however open these families are, they are not open enough for David McCarthy, and the theological fabric I have used to weave this portrait of families (theological personalism) is, he thinks, badly rent. That is why it will be necessary to attend to his strictures in some detail.

McCarthy's first target is "market capitalism and nation-state individualism." These "encroach upon neighborhood reciprocity and the organic (non-voluntary) character of the household."[18] The second target is theological personalism which, despite the weighty backing of Pope John Paul II, "tends to narrow the foundation of family to an interpersonal space (i.e., the couple)." This personal space becomes a dangerous misconception. It "becomes a romantic abstraction when conjugal union is conceived not only as a thing *in itself* but also as a basic social relation *in itself*, outside the practical complexities of the household and other social relations."[19] The "modern narrative of love" is the well-trodden "passage from arousal to cohabitation to dissolution."[20] This narrative lacks "a fitting habitat" for "the germination of conjugal love." Marriage is not founded on love! This "key modern principle" is challenged throughout the book. "Conjugal love is formed within social practices like those of marriage, family, and household management. The 'face-to-face' or 'Me and You' love between two people is secondary to these prior social conditions."

McCarthy inveighs against what he calls "the standard account" of personalism. It has three features. First it "considers the inter-personal, 'Self to Self' relationship the basic (and original) context of true love."[21] Second, it

---

[18] McCarthy, *Sex and Love in the Home*, p. 4.
[19] McCarthy, *Sex and Love in the Home*, p. 5. And see p. 213.
[20] McCarthy, *Sex and Love in the Home*, p. 21. And see p. 216.
[21] McCarthy, *Sex and Love in the Home*, p. 24.

"follows modern trends by highlighting sex and sexual desire as ideal expressions of love." While this account "gives sex and interpersonal love profound theological and human meaning," it is nonetheless unjustified and misconstrued, because, third, "the context for this meaning tends to be a theoretical nowhere place," where "the lovers are abstracted from the conditions of their workaday life."[22] Papal and official writing loads too much on to each act of sexual intercourse, making every occurrence a transcendent event where total self-giving is supposed to be achieved. Rather the meaning of sexual intercourse has to be spread over the course of a lifetime with one's partner,[23] not compounded into each "totalizing moment" of love-making which, ironically, is said to make "day-to-day sexual embodiment semantically superfluous."[24] The standard account relies on "the transparent private self," abstracted from its social habitus. Consequently "it actually takes the joy out of the regular course of things."[25]

The contrast between the private romantic self and the social embedded self is mirrored in two fundamentally contrasting families or households, open and closed. "The closed family understands its health and well-being in terms of emotional and financial independence."[26] The closed family is the nuclear family.

> Another useful conception is the ideal of the nuclear family, defined by narrow lines of kinship and a clear boundary between inside and out. For nuclear households, most kinship relations, grandparents to grandchildren for instance, are considered either positive or unacceptable intrusions, but always as external relationships.

"Open families," by contrast, "have loose and porous boundaries."[27] "Kinfolk, friends, and neighborhood are three distinct, but sometimes overlapping, kinds of networks," and "the critical feature of the open household is its practical dependence on a wider network of exchange, particularly in relation to a dominant cultural and economic narrative that gives privilege to the isolated, self-sufficient home."[28]

In McCarthy's view Catholic social teaching has taken an "interpersonal turn" that "makes the outward disposition of marriage ambiguous and its

---

[22] McCarthy, *Sex and Love in the Home*, p. 25.
[23] McCarthy, *Sex and Love in the Home*, p. 46.
[24] McCarthy, *Sex and Love in the Home*, p. 47.
[25] McCarthy, *Sex and Love in the Home*, p. 64. And see p. 214.
[26] McCarthy, *Sex and Love in the Home*, p. 93.
[27] McCarthy, *Sex and Love in the Home*, p. 97. And see p. 187.
[28] McCarthy, *Sex and Love in the Home*, p. 101.

social character less distinct."[29] "When marriage is defined by inward relations rather than outward roles and duties, connections between inter-
personal harmony and the social function of family become loose."[30] This
criticism is then deployed against the Catholic understanding of the home as
the "domestic church" (below, 9.1) which unwittingly sanctifies the separation of home from neighborhood.[31] The teaching of Augustine, and of Leo
XIII, is to be preferred to Vatican II because both of them saw marriage as
organically related to the wider society. "Leo XIII conceives of all social life
as an ordered whole, so that his references to the roles of family are not set
in contrast to independent economic or political relations, but dependent
upon them."[32] The Vatican doctrine of the complementarity of the sexes is
demolished at a single stroke – "It is impractical to hope that one person can
be completed by another, or that one's spouse would be able to receive the
'total' personality and texture of the other."[33] The expectations created by
complementarity are not just impossible to achieve; they are damaging to
attempt, for "[t]he romantic ideal of mutual absorption threatens to make
friendships and other social relations appear as optional or as intrusions," and
"the self-contained picture of nuptial union cuts the household off from so-
called 'external' relationships between neighbors and kin that constitute
family's [sic] complex and variegated internal forms."

McCarthy has a chapter on the *ordo caritatis* which argues "that love in its
basic and highest form is cultivated in ordinary friendships and duties of
neighborhood and home."[34] Its "basic habitat" is "the household economy,
not necessarily the biological family, but primarily the household of God."[35]
"Love as communion shifts the problem," so that it is defined neither by a
narrow personalism, nor by a disinterested altruism, but "by the intensity of
everyday connections and our common endeavors."[36] What happens to
sexual passion in the household economy? Not much. The chapter devoted
to that question scarcely fizzles: in fact it fizzles out with the assertions that
"enjoyment comes through activities that have internal goods and ends,
such as playing tennis, carpentry, or raising children and managing a home
. . . In this regard, romantic love would not be excluded but recognized as
limited. It is indeed narrow in focus (on one person only) and lacks com-

---

[29] McCarthy, *Sex and Love in the Home*, p. 112.
[30] McCarthy, *Sex and Love in the Home*, p. 113.
[31] McCarthy, *Sex and Love in the Home*, p. 114.
[32] McCarthy, *Sex and Love in the Home*, p. 115.
[33] McCarthy, *Sex and Love in the Home*, p. 123.
[34] McCarthy, *Sex and Love in the Home*, p. 128.
[35] McCarthy, *Sex and Love in the Home*, p. 141.
[36] McCarthy, *Sex and Love in the Home*, p. 149.

plexity."[37] Egalitarian marriage is not spared from the onslaught on personalism. That project is driven by secular "contractual individualism,"[38] which produces a "mere equality of sameness."

Sex and love in the home

Sex and Love in the Home is a remarkable achievement. Its sustained onslaught against personalism and its individualizing influences on theology and society alike is original (and, I am about to argue, seriously overstated). It offers original criticisms of official Catholic theology while remaining obstinately and traditionally Catholic. It heroically debunks romantic love. Locatable in the pre-personalist theology of earlier times, it may be seen to be the ally of very conservative influences in theology, yet it achieves this without jargon and by the route of total immersion in the quotidian chores of child care, housework, fixing the plumbing, and all the while participating in the neighborhood economy and local networks. In order to engage positively with the work, one might first ask whether any readers recognize the kind of neighborhood in which McCarthy lives. His "biographical subtext" is about "the life of neighborhoods and networks of households amid a dominant grammar of self-sufficiency and independence."[39] This life is unlike any neighborhood in which I or my parents, or sisters, or son, or grandparents have ever lived: indeed the absence of such habitats remains a principal problem for families in developed, post-industrial societies. Neither should it be assumed that in earlier times when neighborliness was facilitated by common interests and closer proximity, such common life lacked inquisitiveness, rivalry, and viciousness. The great majority of families need to sustain themselves materially and spiritually in different *milieux* from that described by McCarthy. Consequently he misses the remarkable activities and achievements of members of these families in, for example, non-intrusive friendliness, baby-and-toddler groups, baby-sitting circles, tea dances, parent-teacher associations, community councils, voluntary associations, amateur dramatic societies, neighborhood watch groups, and countless other improvised and *ad hoc* local groups which ought not to exist in the bleak landscape of closed families, capitalist economies, and competitive individuals.

There can be little doubt that conjugal love is celebrated in Roman

---

[37] McCarthy, *Sex and Love in the Home*, p. 161.
[38] McCarthy, *Sex and Love in the Home*, p. 179.
[39] McCarthy, *Sex and Love in the Home*, p. 86.

Catholic personalist thought, and given a prominence from Vatican II onwards. The question is whether this is a welcome innovation or an incautious mistake that sanctifies a narrow coupledom and buys into the secular narratives of love. The answer of course may lie somewhere in between. I welcome the innovation unreservedly.[40] McCarthy's account of the "interpersonal turn" rests in part on the historical case that, prior to Vatican II, marriage was defined more by its outward roles than its inward relations. But that case is not obviously true. Augustine's three "goods of marriage" are at least as much about inward relations as they are about outward roles. The good of the *sacramentum* cannot be broken, because scripture says so (so Augustine thought).[41] It cannot therefore be classified as inward or outward in its significance, but the other two goods clearly can. The good of the "natural society" or "faithfulness" between husband and wife is valuable *to the couple* because "albeit there hath withered away the glow of full age between male and female, yet there lives in full vigor the order of charity between husband and wife." The good of children brings good out of the evil of lust, and tempers lust when they arrive. The goods of marriage are generic to marriage and in that sense social, but they are very much about the personal relationship between the spouses, especially as they negotiate the horrors of sexual intercourse and pay each other the marital debt. Personalism is surely to be preferred?

The interpersonal turn is thought to be completed by the text of *Gaudium et spes*[42] and in particular the much-quoted statement that "the intimate partnership of married life and love has been established by the Creator and qualified by His laws, and is rooted in the conjugal covenant of irrevocable personal consent."[43] But the Latin version of this text, beginning *intima communitas vitae et amoris coniugalis*, recalls a much older understanding of marriage that is "personalist" through and through. The "intimate partnership of married life and love" recalls the medieval doctrine that the essence of marriage is a *consortium totius* [or *omnis*] *vitae*, a phrase incorporated into the revised canon law in 1983. *Communitas* and *consortio* both convey a sense of partnership for the whole of life, and "whole" (*totius*) means both for its entire duration and of every part of it, including of course

[40] See Adrian Thatcher, "Marriage and Love: Too Much of a 'Breakthrough'?," *INTAMS Review*, 8.1, 2002, pp. 44–54, where some of the less obvious implications of theological personalism are also discussed.
[41] Augustine, *de bono conjugali*, 3 (tr. C.L. Cornish) in *Nicene and Post-Nicene Fathers*, Series I, vol. III. www.ccel.org/fathers2/NPNF1–03/npnf1–03–32.htm. Accessed 02.09.2006.
[42] McCarthy, *Sex and Love in the Home*, p. 113.
[43] *Gaudium et spes: Pastoral Constitution on the Church in the Modern World,* section 48. www.vatican.va/archive/hist_councils/ii_vatican_council/documents/. Accessed 02.09.2006.

sexual *intimitas* and *amor coniugalis*.[44] The innovation here is a retrieval of personalism, not the invention of it. "Outward roles" are no more prominent here than in Augustine.

Neither is it obvious that Pope Leo XIII saw marriage as "organically related" to the wider society. In his *Arcanum*, there are many complaints (against the loss of the power of the church over marriage; against divorce, and the loss of holiness of the married state) and assumptions (about male headship, gender roles, the reproduction of the marital order in the social order). McCarthy is silent about these elements of the organic vision. The most that can be claimed is "that God intended it [marriage] to be a most fruitful source of individual benefit *and public welfare*,"[45] but it would be difficult to claim that the latter features prominently in the encyclical. Leo is clear that "the family and human society at large spring from marriage,"[46] and not conversely.

I conclude that the great innovation, that marriage is founded on love, is sound. It is partly a retrieval of earlier wisdom (which can be traced as far back as Ephesians 5). Neither does the frailty and instability of romantic love count against it. The transience of romantic love can (and should) be read as the end of a phase in the growth of love, and the beginning of a new one. Jack Dominian has investigated this process in several books. He calls it "the process from falling in love to loving."[47] Loving, being a process, is analyzable through the shared dynamics between lovers. It requires *sustaining*; brings about *healing*, and induces personal and spiritual *growth*.[48] Each of these overlapping processes contains several components, and central to it all is the "divine liturgy of love"[49] that is sexual intercourse. As the couple grow, the meaning of love-making can grow with it as an "essential component of the ongoing interaction of the couple." Their love is likely to be further affirmed precisely as it is shared more widely with children, more immediate neighbors, and beyond.

The social implications of marriage, especially its contribution to the common good, are vitally important, but there is no need to emphasize these at the expense of the bond of the couple, which has been influenced in Judeo-Christian thought by Genesis 2:24, where "a man leaves his father

---

[44] See Thatcher, "Marriage and Love," pp. 44–8.

[45] Pope Leo XIII, *Arcanum* (Encyclical, "On Christian Marriage," 1880), section 28 (emphasis added). www.vatican.va/holy_father/leo_xiii/encyclicals/. Accessed 02.09.2006.

[46] Leo XIII, *Arcanum*, section 17.

[47] Jack Dominian, *Let's Make Love: The Meaning of Sexual Intercourse* (London: Darton, Longman, and Todd, 2001), p. 71, and see the further references on p. 192.

[48] Dominian, *Let's Make Love*, chapter 10 (author's emphases).

[49] Dominian, *Let's Make Love*, p. 79.

and his mother and cleaves to the wife, and they become one flesh" (RSV). McCarthy over-emphasizes the social embeddedness of marriage and its social purpose, and has disappointingly little to say about the religious, theological, and spiritual meanings of intimacy for couples prior to its outworking in family and neighborhood. He uses a discredited target (romantic love) for some of his strictures, and a similar charge might be made about the self concept that underlies them. The account of the social self offered earlier (above 4.3) provides an alternative, whereby the social embeddedness of the person is unavoidable and so normal.

The problem of priorities is not resolved by claiming that love as communion shifts it. True it remains "defined by the intensity of everyday connections," but even within these there are priorities to be determined. We have already had reason to commend (a version of) Aquinas' teaching that in loving their children, parents are commendably loving themselves (above, 3.3). Children, readers will recall, are too special to be classified as neighbors or special strangers (above, 3.4). But preferences sometimes have to be exercised between children who are kin, and children who are not. Aquinas gives us reasons for choosing kin (should we need them): McCarthy does not. Aquinas says "we ought out of charity to love those who are more closely united to us more, both because our love for them is more intense, and because there are more reasons for loving them."[50] He thinks that "degrees of love" can be measured from the standpoint of the beloved, or from that of the lover. We have a "union" with what or whom we love, and "in comparing love to love we should compare one union with another."[51] This is the theological basis for the notion of kin altruism which is conspicuously absent from McCarthy's work. When we compare love of kin, principally children and parents, with any other love, Aquinas reaches the verdict that

> the union arising from natural origin is prior to, and more stable than, all others, because it is something affecting the very substance, whereas other unions supervene and may cease altogether. Therefore the friendship of kindred is more stable, while other friendships may be stronger in respect of that which is proper to each of them.[52]

---

[50] Thomas Aquinas, *Summa Theologiae*, 2–2, q.26, a.8. Text, translated by the Fathers of the English Dominican Province (Benziger Bros edition, 1947). www.ccel.org/a/aquinas/summa/SS/SS026.html#SSQ26A9THEP1. Accessed 02.09.2006.
[51] Aquinas, *Summa Theologiae*, 2–2, q.26, a.8.
[52] Aquinas, *Summa Theologiae*, 2–2, q.26, a.8.

I think, therefore, that the theological personalism which McCarthy attempts to ravage escapes unscathed. Sex and love in the home flourish better in theological personalism than in this critique of it. The nuclear family/closed household is an easy target, but there are doubtless thousands of suburbias where nuclear families approximate too closely to standardized, routinized, self-contained, and self-destroying norms. Families in this book remain open, but not as open as McCarthy would like. They do not need to be.

8.3 Open Families and the Teaching of Jesus

More importantly are these families open enough to remain faithful to the radical teaching of Jesus that was summarized earlier (above, 3.1)? Is my defense of kin altruism finally sustainable in the light of the relativization of kin ties that is an unmistakeable feature of Gospel teaching? In accordance with our first family-friendly principle for handling biblical material, priority over all biblical teaching must be given to the teaching of Jesus in the Gospels. Given the incipient tendency of interpreters of the Bible (of all theological persuasions) to domesticate all biblical passages that make them uncomfortable, can we be reasonably sure that the exegesis in this volume has escaped a similar tendency?

Stephen Post remains convinced that "Jesus' criticisms of familial ties . . . in no way indicate ambivalence about the meaning of marriage and family . . . Such sayings emphatically do not suggest a diminishment of the centrality of marriage and family in Jesus' teachings . . ."[53] These are brave propositions. They are supported by three strands of argument. First, it is abundantly clear that Jesus opposes divorce. His well-known teaching about marriage (based on Genesis 1:27 and 2:24) forms a "creation principle."[54] In this pro-marriage, pro-monogamy stance, he remains close to the Qumran community. Second, Post acknowledges growing tension in the early Christian communities between those Jews who became followers of Jesus and those who did not. Summarizing Peter Brown he says "After the crucifixion, with the growing estrangement between Jesus' supporters and their fellow Jews, 'the sense that there would be a natural, undisrupted continuity between the present social structures of Israel and those of the new

---

[53] Post, *More Lasting Unions*, p. 57 (author's emphasis).
[54] Post, *More Lasting Unions*, pp. 45–9.

kingdom' was lost, as was the centrality of marriage to the kingdom."[55] Behind the Gospels, then, lies a tension between those disciples who held that marriage would be central to the messianic reign (and in which there would be no divorce), and those who held that the ties of kin were in danger of preventing or circumscribing the reckless generosity and openness of the new Reign of God. Third, these were "crisis conditions," under which many disciples were required to undergo the acid test of choice between families of kin and the family of God. The Gospels acknowledge these tensions, and the purpose of the hard sayings about abandoning one's family (above, 3.1) is to acknowledge and incorporate the itinerant evangelists and former householders who had left their households and kin in obedience to their particular "call." But in these early times and ever since, the great majority of the followers of Jesus remained married.

Given the fluid state of the current discussion about Christian origins, this is surely a plausible account of the tensions within the Gospels themselves between the simultaneous affirmation and renunciation of kin. So far, so good. But difficulties remain. We are told that the criticisms of family ties "in no way indicate ambivalence about the meaning of marriage and family." But it is hard to see how this assertion resolves the tension. A man who leaves behind his wife for the sake of the Kingdom (Lk. 18:29) dumps her. Such practice surely indicates ambivalence about the meaning of marriage in God's Reign? Is there not a further tension between a) the affirmation and renunciation of kin in the Gospels, and b) the replication of this tension in later commentary when it re-appears in a different guise? The tension re-presents itself as the awkward choice facing individual Christians between celibacy (holy) or marriage (worldly), or between the call to the priesthood (holy) or some other vocation (worldly), or between obedience to the heavenly Father (holy) or to one's natural father (worldly). In the primitive community there was disagreement about the place of marriage which, in later generations, became intensified. Why not admit the tension and avoid the pretence that the Gospels speak unambiguously about marriage and families? It may be a positive feature of contemporary Christian life that this tension remains. It may be preferable to the emollient elision of the public tension within history and tradition into the private dilemma for individual Christians between holy and worldly goals. That is an attempt at the resolution of Gospel tension that merely transfers the tension within the historical community onto the individual.

---

[55] Post, *More Lasting Unions*, p. 47, citing Peter Brown, *The Body and Society: Men, Women and Sexual Renunciation in Early Christianity* (London and Boston, MA: Faber and Faber, 1989), p. 41.

The gender basis of the renunciation pole must also be rendered explicit. It is easier to go off and serve the Kingdom if you don't have to look after the children. There is an awkward theological risk to the placing of the Kingdom above kin. On the one hand, several sayings of Jesus undeniably do this, and they may be taken to "convey Jesus' strong reaction to the absolute patriarchal grip on the family in antiquity."[56] But the Reign of God is also evident precisely in the care of parents for children, and in the devotion to their needs. Add to this the care of one who has a disability, or a learning difficulty, or of an elderly relative who joins the household: the outpouring of love upon one's immediate kin itself may become an exhausting, open-ended project. Since this is itself a profound making present of the divine love, great care must be taken not to conceptualize it as secondary to any other work the disciples of Jesus may feel called to do.

Post's confidence in the Gospels' unambiguous support for the family of kin is demonstrated in his account of the "imitation of divine parental solicitude" as the core of Christian ethics. One feature of the Kingdom is "the 'imitation of divine parental solicitude,' since Jesus compared the 'essential benevolence of God to the attitude of human parents.'"[57] Post says "all divine love described in the New Testament exemplifies affective *parental* solicitude."[58] In support of this claim he cites the parables of Jesus, especially the Prodigal Son; the designation of Jesus as "Son" in Gospel narratives; Jesus' use of "Abba" and "Father" in the context of prayer; and the designation of peacemakers as "children of God." The (largely rhetorical) question is raised "How, then, does the literal family fare under this Christian ethic of familial love writ large to the inclusive Christian community and to humanity as a whole?" That question is quickly dispatched: "The particular family is not at all degraded; instead, its meaning is enhanced and transformed." With sweeping self-assurance it is claimed "the genius of Christian biblical ethics is twofold. First, the power of both vertical (parent–child) and horizontal (husband–wife, brother–sister) familial is placed at the very center of the entire spiritual universe, and thereby sets the example for universal solicitude."[59]

So there isn't really a problem after all! These conclusions can apparently be reached by sound biblical exegesis alone. The main difficulty with Post's account, as with other critical familist writings, is not with his conclusions, but with his short way of arriving at them. I remain less confident that

[56] Post, *More Lasting Unions*, p. 58.
[57] Post, *More Lasting Unions*, p. 60. Both quotations are borrowed from Geza Vermes.
[58] Post, *More Lasting Unions*, p. 61 (author's emphasis).
[59] Post, *More Lasting Unions*, p. 62.

family renunciation and family affirmation turn out to be so readily recon-
cilable. Post is right to borrow heavily from critical and historical studies of
the Gospels. I have already borrowed from a range of interpreters (above,
3.1) in coming to a similar conclusion. In the end, however, I think biblical
exegesis requires considerable further doctrinal exegesis and control, and it
is these that guarantee Post the conclusion he seeks.

There is also a problem about the imitation of divine parental solicitude.
There is a much richer, more promising way of bringing divine solicitude to
the center of Christian ethics. Christian ethics is much more than *imitation*.
Imitation or exemplification assumes distance from what is imitated or
exemplified. On this account, God breaks into the world through the gift of
the Son, and reveals the true character and extent of the divine love in the
crucifixion and resurrection of Jesus Christ. Ethics or the Christian life then
consists in imitating this costly, unmerited, and all-forgiving love. The very
different alternative to imitation is *participation*. God's intervention through
the gift of the Son remains the unsurpassable revelation of divine love, but
this love touches, inspires, generates, and embodies all human love by participating in it. There is divine grace in human love, however frail. The
Cross is the historical point of their identity.

The case has already been made for utilizing the *analogia participationis* in
indicating how human parenting and divine parenting belong together
(above, 7.3). That earthly parents locate their parenting within the divine
parenting of the heavenly Father is essential to the Christian understanding
of what they do. Participative analogies operate in both directions. The
Parable of the Prodigal Son is earthed in *human* parenting. It tells us of the
reckless and unimaginable generosity of the heavenly Father, but it does so
by affirming the forgiving actions of the extraordinary human parent,
through which the divine love is also disclosed. The two may be qualita-
tively different but they are not separate.

So, is the teaching of Jesus about families safe in this volume? I seek, as
Post does, to ensure that "familial love is placed at the very center of the
entire spiritual universe." I have sought to add further premises in support of
this conclusion, and these will be familiar enough to readers who have
remained with me thus far. The fabric of the argument has been woven
from the treatment given to love, to children, to the self, to ontological
union between spouses and between spouses and children, to the image of
God, and above all to the Blessed Trinity in Whom we live and move and
love. These fabrics have all been woven from scripture by the church, but it
must be admitted they lack the immediacy of simple engagement with the
Gospel narrative, and may not have been woven together in quite the same
way before. Readers must judge for themselves whether the argument is

faithful to God's revelation in Jesus Christ or is in the end yet another bourgeois accommodation of his radical teaching.

8.4 Choosing Childlessness

A couple voluntarily choosing childlessness might be thought to be a "closed household"; closed, that is, at least to the desirability of producing children. The propriety of choosing childlessness within the Christian community is fraught with controversy and evasion, and has been postponed several times in this volume. Since children have been welcomed unreservedly in these pages as priceless, life-changing, life-enhancing gifts of God, the problematic of chosen childlessness must assume the form, "Why do so many fertile couples refuse the gift?"

A small but significant study of couples in Britain who had chosen childlessness,[60] found different degrees of determination to remain childless among them, and variations in the degree of determination at different stages throughout the period of the woman's fertility. Those couples who were "certain" that they wished to remain childless often said they thought parenting was "disruptive and linked to financial and emotional risk." Some couples "made coolly logical decisions against parenting." They "felt children would create an opposite style of marriage to the one that they had chosen." They had "invested heavily in their houses." Women in particular worried that, with the advent of children, their relationship with their partners might become unequal; there would be restrictions on pursuing a career, and consequent loss of economic independence.[61] Others reported a lack of any "maternal instinct." These findings converge with the conclusion of North American research that "women are less likely to want to marry, stay married to, and bear children with men who are not committed to taking on a large share of responsibilities."[62] The problem of the second shift within marriage has grown to the extent that some women now prefer to avoid marriage altogether.

According to the European Commission a gap exists between the number

---

[60] Fiona McAllister with Lynda Clarke, *Choosing Childlessness* (London: Family Policy Studies Centre and Joseph Rowntree Foundation, 1998). For a summary see "Sociology since 1995: Families and Households." www.connectpublications.co.uk/sociology1995.htm. Accessed 02.09.2006.

[61] "Sociology since 1995," p. 2.

[62] W. Bradford Wilcox, *Soft Patriarchs, New Men: How Christianity Shapes Fathers and Husbands* (Chicago, IL, and London: University of Chicago Press, 2005), p. 208.

of children Europeans would like (2.3) and the number that they actually have (1.5).[63] The Commission depicts the low fertility rate as the result of obstacles to private choices: these include "late access to employment, job instability, expensive housing and lack of incentives (family benefits, parental leave, child care, equal pay)." Member states, it thinks, can remove the obstacles and provide the incentives. It is not questioned whether mothers may wish to cherish their children by refraining for a period from fulltime work. The fertility rate in the European Union is below the threshold needed to renew the population (around 2.1 children per woman), and has even fallen below 1.5 children per woman in some member states including Britain. The chief anxieties of the Commission are the effect of population decline upon economic growth, and the extent to which the shortfall in the labor force will need to be topped up by immigration. From Brussels and Strasbourg comes the new, post-Christian, work ethic. We are all to work more hours, harder, and for more years, in order to sustain the levels of consumption which are damaging ourselves, our children, our population levels, our environment, and our pensions. In France financial incentives are provided to mothers to have children. In Italy, a bonus is paid to mothers who have a second child. In Britain, the most fertile mothers are unmarried teenagers. The government wishes to encourage fertility which thousands of young unmarried mothers appear keen to provide. Yet it wishes to discourage welfare dependency while making no attempt to encourage marriage. There is a growing element within the workforce that resents child-friendly policies. These intentionally childless employees wail against practices like maternity leave, holiday preferences for mothers and fathers, and part-time employment that coincides with school hours and holidays. And, they point out, they pay for schools and universities even though they have no children to send there.

Children: a joy or a burden?

The choice to have fewer or no children rightly worries governments. But the demographic and economic analyses do not tell the whole story. There are theological analyses too, and these diverge. Karl Barth assumed that childlessness is "a lack, a gap in the circle of what nature obviously intended for man . . . Parenthood is one of the most palpable illuminations and joys of

[63] European Commission Green Paper, *Confronting Demographic Change: A New Solidarity between the Generations* (Brussels: March 2005), p. 10. www.europa.eu.int/comm/employment _social/news/2. Accessed 11.26.2005.

life, and those to whom it is denied for different reasons have undoubtedly to bear the pain of loss."[64] Without doubt, Barth enjoyed parenthood and loved his own children. By way of consolation, he continues, childless couples may be reminded that a marriage may nonetheless be "fruitful" without children; that in the light of the New Testament "there is no necessity, no general command, to continue the human race as such and therefore to procreate children;" that "the joy of parenthood should still have a place," even though "this world is passing away." Parenthood is an "optional gift of the goodness of God." "One of the consolations of the coming kingdom" is

> that this anxiety about posterity, that the burden of the postulate that we should and must bear children, heirs of our blood and name and honour and wealth, that the pressure and bitterness and tension of this question, if not the question itself, is removed from us all by the fact that the Son on whose birth alone everything seriously and ultimately depended has now been born and has now become our Brother.

The lack of a child, concludes Barth, "cannot be a true or final lack" for a couple, "for the Child who alone matters has been born for them too."[65]

Barth says he has in mind "all those who broadly speaking" might become parents, "and perhaps would like to do so, but either as bachelors or in childless marriage do not actually fulfil this possibility."[66] It is not entirely clear whether he acknowledges that some individuals and some couples definitely decide to avoid having children. Is the compensation for childlessness the Gospel allegedly offers available to all childless people (all of whom are supposed to want them), or only to that class of people who do want them but cannot have them because of a lack of a partner or because of a fertility problem? Whatever the answer Barth does not envisage the complexity of contemporary attitudes to fertility, for there are a) fertile couples who want children; b) fertile couples who do not want children (for medical or social reasons); c) infertile couples who want children; and d) infertile couples who do not want children. (There are also plenty of single women who want children without the encumbrance of live-in fathers.) Barth addresses condition c) and offers these couples "consolation."[67] If Barth had known about IVF, he surely would have commented on the extraordinary lengths some couples (in condition c)) are prepared to travel down this route to parenthood. But he does not address condition b), and that is where the growth

---

[64] Karl Barth, *Church Dogmatics* III/4, pp. 265–6.
[65] Barth, *Church Dogmatics* III/4, p. 267.
[66] Barth, *Church Dogmatics* III/4, p. 265.
[67] Barth, *Church Dogmatics* III/4, p. 268.

lies. There are couples marrying in Christian churches who intend to avoid having children, and the Protestant churches are silent about them.

Pope John Paul II, however, was far from silent about such matters, but before we turn to his analysis of childlessness, there are further problems with Barth's (largely conventional) treatment of the problem. He erects a false dichotomy between the joy and the anxiety of parenthood, and cannot hold them together in the tension he has created between them. If parenthood really is one of the most palpable joys of life, there is scant compensation for the childless in telling them that by not having children they are not having to deal with anxiety, burdens, pressure, tension, and the like. Either parenthood is a joy, or it is a burden, and if the childless want children because it is a joy having them, it is useless to tell them that they are escaping a burden by not being joyful. Neither does Barth's theology of parenthood leave him with an explanation for this joy. It belongs to the world that passes away: there is only one Child that matters; parenthood is an optional gift of God, and so on. Despite his theology of relation, he cannot bring himself to welcome children without reserve. In these pages the Christ Child is allowed to marginalize real children. Parental love lavished on a vulnerable child cannot be a sign of the Kingdom. It is the sign only of the world that is passing away.

Suppose we hear Barth's compensatory declaration that children are, after all, a burden, not a joy. The account of burdensomeness is no more convincing than the account of joy. The anxiety about raising sons has doubtless afflicted countless patriarchal men who want to hand on either their reigns (Henry VIII is an obvious example), or their estates, households, dukedoms, fiefdoms, earldoms, stocks and shares, businesses, powers and privileges, and so on. Contemporary people with or without children are more anxious about avoiding inheritance *tax* than about raising legitimate heirs or extending their blood lines. Men and women who through faith in Christ refute the patriarchal order should not have ascribed to them the anxieties that that order generates. Children are somewhere between being an unaccountable joy and an archaic burden. The analysis neither honors children nor comforts couples who want and cannot have them. And how is "the Child who alone matters" related to real or longed-for children? The argument of chapter 6 was not that the Christ Child alone matters, but that through the Christ Child alone all children matter. Barth has allowed the spiritual family of the church to usurp real relations within real families. Theology can do better. By making the gift of children unambiguously joyful, the sorrow of those who cannot have them is properly honored in their lack.

Contraceptive and consumer mentalities?

Barth's agenda lay in part in contrasting a Protestant theology with the natalism of Rome. Pope Pius XI had asserted that "Christian parents must . . . understand that they are destined not only to propagate and preserve the human race on earth, . . . but children who are to become members of the Church of Christ, to raise up fellow-citizens of the Saints, and members of God's household."[68] This had been Roman Catholic teaching for centuries.[69] For Barth, "from a Christian point of view the true meaning and primary aim of marriage is *not* to be an institution for the upbringing of children."[70] From Vatican II on, the procreation and education of children is given equal weight with the couple's sharing of life and love, within the purposes of marriage.[71] We cannot discuss here the refusal of contraception in *Casti connubii* (1930) and *Humanae vitae* (1967) and the ensuing controversies. But the widespread availability of cheap and effective contraception, not sexual abstinence, is clearly the major factor in the determination of fertile couples to remain childless. For Pope John Paul II, not only must every act of sexual intercourse between married couples happen within a contraceptive-free zone, the availability and use of contraceptives had produced a "contraceptive mentality" which of itself is a major contribution to the "culture of death."

There is a series of "moral deficit" arguments leading to the conclusion that children are the victims of a culture that is at turns hedonistic, narcissistic, indulgent, selfish, and competitive. These arguments enable the ill-treatment of children, the having of fewer or no children, and the neglectful bringing-up of children, to be identified as the consequences of social evils and trends. The best known of these is based on the contraceptive mentality. In *Evangelium vitae* Pope John Paul II spoke of a "veritable structure of sin" which produces the culture of death, and "is actively fostered by powerful cultural, economic, and political currents which encourage an idea of

---

[68] Pope Pius XI, *Casti connubii [Of Chaste Marriage]* (1930), section 13. www.vatican.va/holy_father/pius_xi/encyclicals/documents/hf_p-xi_enc_31121930_casti-connubii_en.html. Accessed 02.09.2006.
[69] See Thomas Knieps-Port le Roi, "Marriage and the Church: Theological Reflections on an Underrated Relationship," in Adrian Thatcher (ed.), *Celebrating Christian Marriage* (Edinburgh and New York: T&T Clark, 2002), pp. 105–18.
[70] Barth, *Church Dogmatics* III/4, p. 267 (emphasis added).
[71] See for example, *Gaudium et spes: Pastoral Constitution on the Church in the Modern World* (1965), sections 47–52. www.vatican.va/archive/hist_councils/ii_vatican_council/documents/vat-ii_cons_19651207_gaudium-et-spes_en.html. Accessed 02.09.2006.

society excessively concerned with efficiency."[72] Contraception and abortion are closely connected, "as fruits of the same tree." Such practices "are rooted in a hedonistic mentality unwilling to accept responsibility in matters of sexuality, and they imply a self-centered concept of freedom, which regards procreation as an obstacle to personal fulfilment."[73]

This same tree also produces *consumer* and *anti-life* mentalities. Couples may find themselves "imprisoned in a consumer mentality" whereby their "sole concern is to bring about a continual growth of material goods." They "finish by ceasing to understand, and thus by refusing, the spiritual riches of a new human life. The ultimate reason for these mentalities is the absence in people's hearts of God."[74] An all-pervasive "anti-life mentality is born." Later the Vatican complained about "the spread of a 'culture' or a mentality that has lost heart with regard to the family as a necessary value for spouses, children and society." This is due in part to "a secularized atmosphere" and in some countries "the process of de-Christianization."[75]

The consumer mentality has been powerfully criticized by Bonnie Miller-McLemore. She finds that the "powerful controlling logic of market utility" has "invaded domestic and social life."[76] She thinks "people rather unwittingly transfer understandings from the world of production – to compete, win, and be first – to the world of child rearing." Importantly for our analysis of children as gifts, she claims that the market economy

> disturbs the understanding of children as gift. In fact, principles of market exchange rule out the very premise of gift. In such a world, children are not gifts. They become instead artefacts to be produced, owned, managed, cultivated, and invested. The view of children as product is especially disturbing because it transforms them without remainder into a means to another end.[77]

The United States, she thinks, is "a narcissistically hungry society" where parents "increasingly look to children to prove their own worth." They become "hypervigilant about their child's success not merely for the sake of

---

[72] Pope John Paul II, *Evangelium vitae* (1995), section 12. www.vatican.va/holy_father/ john_paul_ii/encyclicals/documents/hf_jp-ii_enc_25031995_evangelium-vitae_en.html. Accessed 02.09.2006.

[73] Pope John Paul II, *Evangelium vitae*, section 13.

[74] Pope John Paul II, *Familiaris consortio*, section 30.

[75] Pontifical Council for the Family, *Preparation for the Sacrament of Marriage* (1996), sections 11–12. www.vatican.va/roman_curia/pontifical_councils/family/documents/rc_pc_family_ doc_13051996_preparation-for-marriage_en.html. Accessed 02.09.2006.

[76] Bonnie J. Miller-McLemore, *Let the Children Come: Reimagining Childhood from a Christian Perspective* (San Francisco, CA: Jossey-Bass, 2003), p. 88.

[77] Miller-McLemore, *Let the Children Come*, pp. 88–9.

the child but for their own self-affirmation, as a sort of proof of their own value." Other people's children in this environment "actually become competitors for limited goods."

Our present concern is with voluntary childlessness, and whether the adult practice of avoiding having them is part of a wider web of negative social attitudes to them. Miller-McLemore blames the "instrumental, consumerist thinking of market capitalism" for three distorted images of children: as products, consumers, and burdens. Reproductive technology, in particular, encourages "the view of child bearing as analogous to making any other purchase in which one selects the most desirable features."[78] It is often lamented, especially by parents, that television advertising treats children as consumers, and bombards them with allurements many of which may be detrimental to their well-being and their parents' household budget. That children are burdens is linked to the impatience of the market with "the unproductive, unsettled nature of childhood." It is explained that "in a two-tiered world that separates those who can produce and consume from those who cannot, children, especially poor children, have a stark disadvantage."[79] These attitudes use children as means to other ends instead of treating them as ends-in-themselves. When these attitudes are emphasized or intensified, children are overtly used for "war, sex, and work," epitomizing "the horrendous and extreme outcome of viewing children as products, consumers, and in the end nonentities."[80] Anyone doubting the corrosive effect of market values upon the human spirit should consider the fate of Christmas which has become "associated with laborious purchases and accumulation of excessive goods." In these circumstances "comparing children with gifts becomes a potentially unhelpful, even harmful, concept."[81]

While Miller-McLemore identifies market values as injurious to children Herbert Anderson and Susan Johnson understand modern societies to produce a culture of indifference to children. There are three types of indifference manifesting themselves in three linked attitudes to children.[82] Children are regarded as "private property." This attitude confuses children with things; it lies behind the justification and practice of the corporal punishment of children, and regards the family as a private domain, free from public scrutiny or reproof. The second attitude regards children as

---

[78] Miller-McLemore, *Let the Children Come*, p. 90.
[79] Miller-McLemore, *Let the Children Come*, p. 91.
[80] Miller-McLemore, *Let the Children Come*, pp. 91–2.
[81] Miller-McLemore, *Let the Children Come*, p. 93.
[82] Herbert Anderson and Susan B.W. Johnson, *Regarding Children: A New Respect for Childhood and Families* (Louisville, KY: Westminster John Knox Press, 1995), pp. 13–16.

"depraved," that is, as inheritors of original sin, requiring correction and conversion. The third attitude regards them as "incomplete." This attitude "gives the appearance of valuing children by creating environments to protect and train them. In fact, however, it overlooks the present needs of children by focusing on preparing them for their future in society." Anderson and Johnson isolate a specific cultural trait that lies at the root of these attitudes. "In a society that glorifies size, strength, and self-sufficiency, anyone who is small, weak, or needful is treated with contempt."[83] They say this atmosphere breeds an "attitude of contempt for the weakness and vulnerability of childhood." It also "underlies the various forms of physical, sexual, and psychological abuse of children. The abuse of anyone less powerful is a way of continuing to repress what we fear in ourselves."

These analyses assume a causal relation between, on the one hand, a web of overlapping social forces, variously called individualism, consumerism, hedonism, narcissism, instrumentalism, indifferentism; and on the other hand, the fertility choices couples make (or fail to make). These are the strands of the single web of market values, and its time-consuming work ethic, and we remain trapped within it. It is difficult to resist the conclusion that their all-pervasive influence *does* impact negatively upon the decision to have children. At the very least the desire for children competes with endlessly stimulated desires for endless commodities.

The "sexual market" and the "children-problematic"

Perhaps the most passionate theological voice in defense of children in Britain belongs to Jon Davies. Davies also identifies a cultural indifference to children for which he gives explanations that are historical, philosophical, sociological, and theological. He claims that Western culture is "now so indifferent to its children" that it "carries serious risks for a steady erosion of the rights and well-being of all."[84] He thinks that "increasing and accelerating instability in intra-familial relationships . . . is a systemic part of our way of life ('late twentieth-century capitalism' if you like), and a quite logical development from earlier arrangements."[85] The Church of England Alter-

---

[83] Anderson and Johnson, *Regarding Children*, p. 15.

[84] Jon Davies, "A Preferential Option for the Family," in Stephen C. Barton (ed.), *The Family in Theological Perspective* (Edinburgh: T&T Clark, 1996) [219–36], p. 226.

[85] Jon Davies, "From Household to Family to Individualism," in Jon Davies (ed.), *The Family: Is it Just Another Lifestyle Choice?* (London: IEA Health and Welfare Unit, 1993) [63–103], p. 63.

native Service Book (1980) is castigated for reversing "two millennia of religious teaching when it demoted children from their first place in the priorities of marriage – it replaces them with the adults." He explains, "*If the point and purpose of marriage is located in a contract between adults, then by definition, children, qua children, can not be parties to the marriage.*"[86] There is an "overwhelming ethos of *Privacy and Appetitive Individualism*" in British society, which causes many of its fertile members to "accept an endless variety of sexual and procreative relationships which lack both internal stability and a clear articulation within society in general."[87]

Davies holds, if I understand him correctly, that there is a narrowing and escalating historical focus on who or what constitutes family. Already the Protestant family is a narrowing of the older and more encompassing "household": the social unit becomes the patriarchal family. But now a further narrowing has occurred: the social unit is the individual, untrammeled by social constraints and expectations regarding fatherhood and marriage. "Late twentieth-century capitalism appears not to need the nuclear family. The 'individual' which was the icon of liberal economics *was generally the nuclear family* . . . The 'individual' is now a 'person' on his or her own."[88] Such emancipated persons are able to enter "the sexual market" where sex has come apart from its "familial and procreational purposes" and from its "involvement in the institutionalization of inter-generational and inter-gender relations."[89] There is a connection between capitalism and the sexual market, here through the endless stimulation and attempted satisfaction of desire: "there is no limit to the empire of the appetite, especially when the appetite, as body, my body, is made the moral arbiter of everything."[90]

Within the sexual market children are the casualties. "Whereas under the traditional Christian regime the interests of adults were sacrificed to those of the child, seen as the future society, under present practices the interests of the child are being sacrificed to those of the adults, the adults in the here and now."[91] Children have become a "problematic": "what is most threatening

---

[86] Davies, "From Household to Family to Individualism," p. 88 (author's emphasis).

[87] Davies, "From Household to Family to Individualism," p. 99 (author's emphasis).

[88] Jon Davies, "Sex These Days, Sex Those Days: Will it Ever End?," in Jon Davies and Gerard Loughlin (eds.), *Sex These Days* (Sheffield, UK: Sheffield Academic Press, 1997) [18–34], p. 26 (author's emphasis).

[89] Davies, "Sex These Days," p. 18.

[90] Davies, "Sex These Days," p. 31.

[91] Jon Davies, "Neither Seen or Heard nor Wanted: The Child as Problematic. Towards an Actuarial Theology of Generation," in Michael A. Hayes, Wendy Porter, and David Tombs (eds.), *Religion and Sexuality* (Sheffield, UK: Sheffield Academic Press, 1998) [326–47], p. 330.

to both the moral systems and life–style practices of this adult world are children: they are a form of existence which *must* be dealt with in order that the
sexual purposes of the adult world may be the more assiduously pursued."[92]
The threefold strategy attributed to reluctant parents for solving the "chil-
dren-problematic" is a) to stop having them ("a womb-strike"[93]); b) to
"nationalize them," that is to treat them "as a 'public good,' just like foot-
paths or street lighting;"[94] and c) to "treat them as adults" so that "they can,
at ever younger ages, be regarded as the proper beneficiaries of that tradition
of possessive or appetitive individualism which has been so radical a liberator
of adult men and women."[95] Theological discussion of sex culpably ignores
children and the deleterious consequences for them of adult sexual indul-
gence.[96] A deliberately offensive and savage acronym is coined to
characterize the threefold strategy and the unforgivable complicity of theology with it: ADORASS. "All of these tactics are both in use and easily
justified by contemporary theology and the vested interest which that theology represents – the Adult Orgasm Association (ADORASS)."[97]

Our review of chosen childlessness ends with a calm *apologia* for it, within
a developing Christian tradition. Helen Stanton reports conversations with
a dozen or so married Christians who chose to remain childless. While
admitting it is an option only for the privileged, she says all of them rejected
consumerism as a reason for remaining childless.[98] These Christians valued
parenthood as a vocation to which they were not called. "Commitment to
Christian, political, and pastoral causes was given as the primary reason why
members of the group had chosen not have children. These other callings
were felt very strongly, and seen as incompatible with the perceived calling
of commitment to be parents."[99] In some cases "lack of empathy with children" was given as a reason for the experienced lack of vocation to have
them. A similarity was drawn with the advantages of celibacy, freeing up
time for the Kingdom. Why marry at all, then? Because their partners,
rather than children, were the divine gifts. "Universally the twelve said that

---

[92] Davies, "Neither Seen or Heard nor Wanted," p. 334 (author's emphasis).
[93] Davies, "Neither Seen or Heard nor Wanted," p. 337.
[94] Davies, "Neither Seen or Heard nor Wanted," p. 339.
[95] Davies, "Neither Seen or Heard nor Wanted," p. 342.
[96] Davies, "A Preferential Option for the Family," p. 220.
[97] Jon Davies, "Welcome the Pied Piper," in Adrian Thatcher (ed.), *Celebrating Christian Mar-riage* (Edinburgh and New York: T&T Clark, 2002) [219–50], p. 242.
[98] Helen Stanton, "Obligation or Option? Marriage, Voluntary Childlessness, and the Church," in Thatcher (ed.), *Celebrating Christian Marriage* [223–39], p. 235.
[99] Stanton, "Obligation or Option?," p. 228.

this was to do with making a life-long commitment to a partner whom they felt in some sense had been given to them by God."[100]

8.5 Chosen Childlessness: an Appraisal

Chosen childlessness, then, is an awkward subject. In secular thought it generates anxiety about the future of work, economic growth, and much else. Among Christians a wide spectrum of opinion has emerged. On the one hand it frustrates God's creative purposes. On the other hand, married Christians can experience the call of God to demanding service for the Reign of God, hitherto reserved for the celibate. Beneath this spectrum lies the uncomfortable series of analyses that accuse us, whether Christian or not, of having succumbed to dominant ideologies whose effectiveness is heightened by their ability to conceal their impact upon us, from us. Let us now try to find a way through this maze.

That married Christians now choose childlessness is a remarkable development of the Christian tradition; indeed it is a severance of the long-held conviction that the having of children was a principal purpose of marriage. One might take issue with some of the reasons given here. Is parenthood a "vocation"? If so how does one test that one does not have it? Is not perceived lack of empathy with children notoriously subject to change, especially when they arrive? Here are Christians assuming responsibility under God for their lives and their childless choices. No criticisms are offered of them. It is possible, however, that they may not have considered the extent to which their reasons are influenced by deeper factors, and to that question we shall need to return.

There is much in the "moral deficit" analyses that is consistent with the themes of this volume. These are the analyses that should perhaps trouble intentionally childless couples more than they apparently do. Marriage is advocated in this volume not least *because* children are more likely to thrive within it. The teaching of Jesus requires adults to put children first. Much sexual theology, or sexual ethics, as Davies accuses, shows no interest in children. It is guilty of child-neglect, and a similar verdict might be passed on most "theological anthropology." These analyses describe the operation of structural sin, whether or not they use the term. Whereas original sin was once thought to be at the root of child rebellion and refusal of authority, now it is structural sin that is thought to strike at the root of their well-being.

---

[100] Stanton, "Obligation or Option?," p. 229.

The stories of "mentalities" (contraceptive, consumerist, hedonist, death-dealing, and so on), "cultures" (of individualism, narcissism, competition, and so on), and social forces impacting upon individuals, uprooting them from the values of community and family, encouraging dissolute behavior and sexual irresponsibility, remain powerful but partial explanations of complex behaviors. With regard to the contraceptive mentality, Anglicans teach that "where there is a clearly felt moral obligation to limit or avoid parenthood, the method must be decided on Christian principles."[101] In the same year (1930), Pope Pius XI called contraception "a criminal abuse."[102] But this continuing disagreement should not be allowed to conceal the conviction of almost all Christians and churches that contraception of various kinds is used to make possible widespread promiscuity which itself leads to deleterious consequences for bodies, persons, children, and society. So a widespread attitude that regards conception as an accident to be avoided rather than a gift to be embraced deserves to be called a "mentality" especially if it routinizes sex apart from either the expectation of conception or marriage. But "Natural Family Planning," which *is* permitted, clearly expresses the intention to limit or avoid parenthood, and so cannot be judged free from contraceptive intent either. Any general condemnation of a contraceptive mentality is bound to marginalize all people, whether Christian or not, who use contraception responsibly and within marriage. There remain good reasons both for postponing the gift of children, and for a couple limiting the number of children they have. While the notion of "planning" a family may seem to be at variance with receiving children as divine gifts, the gift of too many children is also at variance with the "gift-edness" of children. The *Catechism* still regards large families as "a sign of God's blessing and the parents' generosity."[103] Parents suffering poverty or in poor health regard them differently.

The story of the contraceptive mentality is therefore a partial one. Have market values really invaded our domestic and social life, making us hedonistic and incapable of appreciation of the gift? The answer is, almost certainly. But is there not something rather too easy, too *a priori*, again too partial, about this accusation? How would we verify it? How might we compare individuals in market economies with individuals in traditional societies, or in totalitarian or communist ones? Comparable evils were, and

---

[101] Lambeth Conference, 1930, Resolution 15. www.anglicancommunion.org/acns/archive/1930/1930–15.htm. Accessed 02.09.2006.
[102] Pope Pius XI, *Casti connubii* (1930), section 4. www.vatican.va/holy_father/pius_xi/encyclicals/documents.
[103] *Catechism*, section 2343, p. 508.

are, doubtless perpetrated by the people with the power, including the economic power, to do so. Is not the sheer affluence which our economic
system has bestowed upon us, as responsible for our misuse of economic
freedom as the system itself? Is it not greed, a pre-modern and deadly sin,
that is our trouble, fanned by affluence and advertising?

Davies' naming of appetitive individualism and the sexual market is
driven by his passionate and justified belief that children are likely to suffer
badly when they are brought unwanted into the world, or are avoided (or
aborted). I think savage criticism of adults who mistreat children or act
contrary to their interests, or who do not consider them, is justified theologically and in any other way. But I am less convinced that traditional
societies, even Christian ones, were less evil: there were fewer *opportunities*
for evil, but the hierarchical organization of those societies, their patriarchal
values, their public and private cruelty, and the sexual misuse of women,
children, servants, and prostitutes, do not make these societies more envi-
able. True, the apparatus was in place for controlling and repressing sexual
desire and for channeling it toward the procreation of children and the stability of society, but as Davies admits, the adults who espouse libertarian
sexual values today "have a pressing appetite agenda to attend to, not least
because those agendas *have been too long ignored.*"[104] Exactly. The dam has
burst. Some of his targets scarcely threaten what remains of the public sexual
order. Lesbian and gay couples seeking marriage actually want to join the
order, not to weaken it further. If Christianity was once successful in controlling and channeling sexual desire in healthy, positive, child-friendly
ways, it will contribute to that task today by proclaiming the Good News
that is its *raison d'être*. Sexual experience between men and women who
are fertile is a bodily self-giving that requires life-long commitment to
complete its meaning, and to care for the children who, contraceptive mentalities notwithstanding, may nonetheless arrive.

Another missing element in the meta-analyses of structural sin, further
rendering them partial, is the lack of any sense of the abundance of the
grace of the Holy Spirit coursing through humanity, not simply ecclesial
humanity, enabling loving relations between parents, between parents and
children, within and beyond families, all of whom have the Triune God as
their Father, whether acknowledged or not. In a world of sinful mentalities
there is too little praise for ordinary goodness. Evangelism is more likely to
be successful if it begins where God the Spirit already is, and joyfully
announces the surprising presence of God in the care of children that

---

[104] Davies, "A Preferential Option for the Family," p. 221 (emphasis added).

already goes on in millions of homes. There are open families, still highly irregular in papal scripts, which are microcosms of Spirit-given love. Where is the Good News in Davies' strictures?

When social theology names sinful mentalities, it must take care to understand individual people more as *victims* than as accomplices in the havoc these mentalities cause. The New Testament is careful to do this with regard to the "principalities and powers" which are stronger than human resistance to them but are overcome anyway by the power of God through Jesus Christ. In the midst of such social sin there is also resistance to it. People need to be shown something better in order to be persuaded to renounce the mentalities that surround them, yet they need encouragement in their own struggles, often in the privacy of conscience and wordless communication, and in their stubborn commitments to friends, neighbors, and kin. When those struggles are not successful, people need to hear about the grace of God more than about the strident exposure of their failings.

The question therefore remains whether married Christians forgoing children do in all cases fully consider or are even fully aware of the much bigger picture, of the child-indifferent culture and theology, of the mentalities that may silently colonize even their most intimate thoughts and announcements? A similar question however applies to all of us when we seek to examine our convictions. Enough has been said in this book about the desirability of the gift of children, and about the gift of God the Child, to suggest that chosen childlessness needs an exceptional case to be made for it, one which has not yet been fully made.

Chapter Nine

Families and the "Domestic Church"

Recent Roman Catholic theology has advocated the idea of the "domestic church." The Protestant theologian Horace Bushnell taught that families should see themselves as "little churches,"[1] yet there is little comprehension of either idea in contemporary Protestantism.[2] The Roman Catholic Catechism teaches that "The Christian family constitutes a specific revelation and realization of ecclesial communion, and for this reason it can and should be called a *domestic church*."[3] In the first section of this final chapter, the "doctrine" that the Christian family is a domestic church is described, critiqued, compared with the theology of families developed earlier in these pages, and welcomed as a supplement to it, derived from similar theological premises. The remaining sections attempt some practical outcomes of the theology of families for churches and their ministry to families. Section 2 examines the extent to which it is helpful for the local church to consider itself a family, and how families might operate if the Christians who comprise them are churches. Section 3 examines some policy implications for national and global churches.

---

[1] Horace Bushnell, *Christian Nurture* (New York: Charles Scribner, 1861; rep. Cleveland: Pilgrim Press, 1994), p. 10. Cited by Margaret Bendroth, "Horace Bushnell's *Christian Nurture*," in Marcia J. Bunge (ed.), *The Child in Christian Thought* (Grand Rapids, MI/Cambridge, UK: Eerdmans, 2001) [350–64], p. 356.

[2] But see Don S. Browning, Bonnie J. Miller-McLemore, Pamela D. Couture, K. Brynolf Lyon, and Robert M. Franklin, *From Culture Wars to Common Ground: Religion and the American Family Debate* (Louisville, KY: Westminster John Knox Press, 1997), pp. 76, 308.

[3] *Catechism of the Catholic Church* (London: Geoffrey Chapman, 1994), para. 2204 (authors' emphasis), citing *Familiaris consortio*, para. 21.

9.1 Families and the "Domestic Church"

A main source in official teaching for the idea that the Christian family is a domestic church is *Familiaris consortio*. (Florence Bourg provides a survey of magisterial references to it.)[4] John Paul II distinguishes between "the family" and "the Christian family." As we will soon discover, the distinction causes trouble. However it is his generosity toward "the family" that principally marks this exceptional teaching. "Conjugal communion" is a universal, human, reality, *and* a specifically Christian reality. It

> is rooted in the natural bonds of flesh and blood, and grows to its specifically human perfection with the establishment and maturing of the still deeper and richer bonds of the spirit: the love that animates the interpersonal relationships of the different members of the family constitutes the interior strength that shapes and animates the family communion and community.[5]

The bonds of flesh and blood are natural, human bonds, albeit weakened and potentially distorted by sin. The "richer bonds of the spirit" do not directly refer to the Holy Spirit (except insofar as the Holy Spirit inspires the blooming of all human love). The same may be said of "the love that animates" family relationships. The Christian family has an extra, specific experience. It is "called to experience a new and original communion which confirms and perfects natural and human communion." This it finds in "the grace of Jesus Christ" and in the Holy Spirit

> who is poured forth in the celebration of the sacraments, is the living source and inexhaustible sustenance of the supernatural communion that gathers believers and links them with Christ and with each other in the unity of the Church of God. The Christian family constitutes a specific revelation and realization of ecclesial communion, and for this reason too it can and should be called "the domestic Church."

The Holy Spirit, then, operates at the *super*natural level. Christians have additional access to supernatural communion, the communion that is also the mystical union between believers, between believers and Christ, between believers and the Church, and between the Church and Christ. The Christian family is a domestic church because the natural communion

---

[4] Florence Caffrey Bourg, *Where Two or Three Are Gathered: Christian Families as Domestic Churches* (Notre Dame, IN: University of Notre Dame Press, 2004), pp. 43–5.
[5] John Paul II, *Familiaris consortio* (1981), para. 21. www.vatican.va/holy_father/john_paul_ii/apost_exhortations/documents/.

within the family is further deepened and inspired by the supernatural communion which is mediated through the sacraments and is, substantially is, the Holy Spirit. There are two particular points in this rich passage that enrich the themes of this book. First, there are obvious analogies of relation between three pairs of terms: the family/the Christian family; natural or family communion/supernatural or ecclesial communion; and the spirit/the Holy Spirit. These analogies are also analogies of participation (above, 7.3). The Triune God really is present within the dynamism of family relationships. Second, John Paul does not say that the Church or the ecclesial communion reveals what the conjugal Christian family should be like: it is the other way round. "The Christian family constitutes a specific revelation and realization of ecclesial communion . . ." Theologians are accustomed to using the category of revelation when handling what they perceive to have come directly from God and so from outside human thought. Here the revelation is "from below," in the day-to-day tensions of Christian families. They are themselves capable of celebrating and living the supernatural and ecclesial communion that the Church receives and knows in the sacraments. The designation "domestic church" is therefore much more than a metaphorical device for sacralizing families. By allowing that the Christian family is itself a "specific revelation" of ecclesial communion, the communion within the *domus* reveals the communion within the *ecclesia*. The notion of domestic church, then, may be an alternative way of expressing the conviction (above, 7.4) that familial relations really share in the divine Relations.

"All members of the family," the Pope continues, "each according to his or her own gift, have the grace and responsibility of building, day by day, the communion of persons, making the family 'a school of deeper humanity.'"[6] The Holy Spirit adds depth to human familial exchange. The contribution of all members of families to the family communion is welcomed and valued. This communion-making "happens where there is care and love for the little ones, the sick, the aged; where there is mutual service every day; when there is a sharing of goods, of joys and of sorrows," and particularly through the "educational exchange between parents and children, in which each gives and receives." By means of love, respect, and obedience toward their parents, children offer their specific and irreplaceable contribution to the construction of an authentically human and Christian family. The late Pope brings the family and the Christian family together in several ways in this extract, not least by combining them more than once in a single grammatical phrase. He

---

[6] *Familiaris consortio*, para. 21, citing *Gaudium et spes*, para. 52.

emphasizes the positive contribution of children to families. He says "By means of love, respect and obedience towards their parents, children offer their specific and irreplaceable contribution to the construction of an authentically *human and Christian family*."[7] Parents have an "unrenounceable authority" over their children, but John Paul speaks gently of its exercise. It is "a true and proper 'ministry,'" defined as "a service to the human and Christian well-being of their children." Here then is a further extension of the Church into the domestic church. Parents have a real ministry which the Church recognizes, supports, and encourages. Echoing further themes of this book (the "Gifting God," and mutuality in parent–child relations) he tells parents they will be aided in their ministry if they "maintain a living awareness of the 'gift' they continually receive from their children." There is scarcely a comparable passage in Christian theology where parents are addressed with such sensitivity, compassion, theological understanding and sheer human depth.

A further advantage of the idea of domestic church is thought to include the provision of "a healthy balance to other texts (such as Matthew 10:35–6 and 1 Corinthians 7:32–5) that have been used to instill the presumption that religious vocations necessarily draw individuals away from family, rather than incorporating family bonds and everyday lifestyle choices."[8] The history of the use of "domestic church" is described by Lisa Cahill,[9] who notes approvingly how its development by John Paul II both "addresses economic inequities and holds Christian families responsible for just distribution of material and social wealth," and provides for "a sphere of relative gender equity."[10] But, as we will shortly explore, beyond the undoubted empathy and sensitivity the term conveys, there are theological difficulties too. Bourg explores some of these and concludes the domestic church "is primarily a symbolic expression. It should function first and foremost to stimulate imaginations to a deeper appreciation of the mystery of the Church and of how family life figures into God's plan of gracious presence in history."[11] I shall address three difficulties, and then suggest that the doctrinal gains made in earlier chapters give added weight to "domestic church."

---

[7] (emphasis added)

[8] Bourg, *Where Two or Three Are Gathered*, p. 10.

[9] Lisa Sowle Cahill, *Family: A Christian Social Perspective* (Minneapolis, MN: Augsburg Fortress Press, 2000), chapter 4 and throughout.

[10] Cahill, *Family*, p. 85.

[11] Bourg, *Where Two or Three Are Gathered*, p. 25. A recent critical study raises problems of its identity, its theological legitimacy, and its authentic appropriation. See Joseph C. Atkinson, "Family as *Domestic Church*: Developmental Trajectory, Legitimacy, and Problems of Appropriation," *Theological Studies*, 66.3, September 2005 [592–604].

Problems of hierarchy, constitution and ministry, and membership

First, Churches generally are hierarchically organized, whereas families are not. These claims are of course generalizations for there are democratic churches and there remain too many hierarchical households. But the term is old enough to have its roots in times when both institutions were hierarchical, and hierarchical order was a major point of comparison. St John Chrysostom called the Christian household a "little church."[12] Although his later teaching about marriage and families is more positive than that of Augustine, he "does not seriously challenge the hierarchical model of relations in the family transmitted by the Household Codes of the New Testament."[13] Augustine is clear that the head of the Christian household functions like a bishop in the church, exercising leadership, power, and watchfulness.[14] While hierarchy is not a necessary feature of the contemporary use of the expression "domestic church," it remains a latent one. The family historian Stephanie Coontz explains that in the Roman empire heads of household were not members but rulers. "Men were not *in* families; they ruled *over* them." The Christian families of Western Europe adopted the Roman pattern which "helps explain why for so many centuries family advice manuals were addressed to wives rather than husbands. Husbands, it was long thought, didn't need to know how to behave in families. They simply needed to know how to make their families behave."[15]

But the presence of hierarchy is not fatal to the idea of the domestic church. Some episcopal churches elect bishops and/or operate a joint form of episcopal and synodical government. Oversight needs to be exercised in families too, and this needs to be shared wherever there are two parents. Crucially, the history of marriage is also a hierarchy, but the hierarchy has been largely replaced, in the countries of Christendom, by a more equal-regard, egalitarian, institution. Second, questions arise about the constitution of the domestic church and the exercise of its particular ministry of the word and sacraments. Ministry is generally exercised in the Church by ordained (generally male) priests. Are parents unofficially yet specifically "ordained" to the "sacramental" task of nurturing their children in preparation for their adult

---

[12] *Homily 20 on Ephesians*. See David G. Hunter (ed.), *Marriage in the Early Church* (Minneapolis, MN: Fortress Press, 1992), p. 87.

[13] Cahill, *Family*, p. 56, and for a full account of Chrysostom's teaching about families, see pp. 52–7.

[14] See Bourg, *Where Two or Three Are Gathered*, p. 10, and the references there.

[15] Stephanie Coontz, *Marriage, a History: From Obedience to Intimacy or How Love Conquered Marriage* (New York: Viking, 2005), p. 79.

lives? The sacrament of marriage, like the vows that constitute it, is actually administered by spouses to each other (in the presence of a priest, only since the Council of Trent). This sacrament assumes a particularly close and intimate relationship between liturgy and life. The married couple go on ministering their sacrament to each other, and in this they exercise a "priestly" function to each other. Is the economy of domestic churches to be seen as the continuing and continuous ministry of the sacrament of marriage? Is the occasion of a family meal, lovingly prepared, and made into an occasion of communion for family members, "eucharistic"? Do the two sacraments of healing, penance, and anointing of the sick, have their analogates in the communion of family as each member cares for one another in sickness and in health and forgives one another when hurt? Can we say that parents receive their child with joy as the church receives the same child with joy in the sacrament of baptism? And that confirmation has its domestic equivalent in the preparation of children for adult life and their eventual participation within it? How does the domestic church proclaim God's Word? By the reverberations of the divine love that flow through the families to the wider community? The Church is one, but families are many. Is the domestic church related to the wider Church as a cell is related to the body? In that case, how is it an independent center of communion, of action and interaction?

But these questions are not fatal either. During the International Year of the Family (1994) the Roman Catholic bishops of the United States issued a "pastoral message" which developed distinctive answers to some of these questions. New Testament passages about love provide the methodological and exegetical basis for what the bishops have to say about both the constitution and ministry of the domestic church. The great identity statement "God is love" (1 Jn. 4:16) is pressed into service as the constitution of Christian families.[16] While the profound meditation on the love of God in 1 John 4 has a primary reference to the experience of Christians as children in God's family, the bishops are comfortable with a broader interpretation. The chapter assumes Christian believers "dwell" in God because the Holy Spirit is imparted to them and because they have acknowledged Jesus as God's Son (1 Jn. 4:13–15). The bishops' reading of the text is commendably and very broadly inclusive, embracing all families wherever they are and whatever

---

[16] United States Conference of Catholic Bishops, Secretariat for Family, Laity, Women and Youth, *Follow the Way of Love* (*A Pastoral Message of the U.S. Catholic Bishops to Families on the Occasion of the United Nations 1994 International Year of the Family*) (1994). www.usccb.org/laity/follow.shtml. Accessed 01.31.2006. The on-line version has no pagination. Further references are to sections.

form they take. They say with disarming simplicity, "The story of family life is a story about love – shared, nurtured, and sometimes rejected or lost. In every family God is revealed uniquely and personally, for God is love and those who live in love, live in God and he dwells in them (cf. 1 Jn. 4:16)."[17] They would have no problem with principle 7 (above, 2.3) that "all families are able to receive and embody the love of God whether or not they believe in or know God." Families, all of them, whatever their constitution, "are a sign of God's presence."[18] The intended readership of the pastoral message is not confined to Roman Catholics. It is for "Christian families" and "all who can use it toward strengthening their families." They are directly told "What you do in your family to create a community of love, to help each other to grow, and to serve those in need is critical, not only for your own sanctification but for the strength of society and our Church . . . It is holy."

The sacrament of baptism is important for the *domestic* church because the family is said to deepen the union with God that baptism establishes. "Baptism brings all Christians into union with God. Your family life is sacred because family relationships confirm and deepen this union and allow the Lord to work through you."[19] The continuity both of holiness and of union with God flow from the Church to the domestic church and back again. Liturgy and life are linked so that the liturgical action of the Church is re-enacted in the domestic church as the liturgy of love. Following the argument, then, baptism is the formal means whereby ordinary family life is thought to be sanctified. Baptismal grace is not simply given through the sacrament: it continues to be given through the mutual ministries of the domestic church. It has a divine origin, yet grace is one. Given formally in baptism and informally in the domestic church, it forms the characters of that church's members, and forms them mutually. On this basis

> The profound and the ordinary moments of daily life – mealtimes, workdays, vacations, expressions of love and intimacy, household chores, caring for a sick child or elderly parent, and even conflicts over things like how to celebrate holidays, discipline children, or spend money – all are the threads from which you can weave a pattern of holiness.

---

[17] Earlier verses of 1 Jn. 4 receive similar treatment. On the basis of the exhortation (v.11) "Beloved, if God so loved us, we also must love one another," the bishops conclude "Thus, the basic vocation of every person, whether married or living a celibate life, is the same: *follow the way of love, even as Christ loved you* (cf. Eph. 5:2). The Lord issues this call to your family and to every family regardless of its condition or circumstances."

[18] *Follow the Way of Love*, "Families Are a Sign of God's Presence."

[19] *Follow the Way of Love*, "You Are the Church in Your Home."

A family is "our first community and the most basic way in which the Lord gathers us, forms us, and acts in the world." The domestic church has a mission which is carried out "in ordinary ways." These are activities such as believing, loving, educating, praying, forgiving, celebrating, and justly acting within and beyond "the church of the home." "Your domestic church" is said to be incomplete without being "united with and supported by parishes and other communities within the larger church."

The third difficulty is about membership of the domestic church. This difficulty has already been partly removed in the pastoral message. The difficulty arises in official literature when non-traditional families get rebuked (above, 1.3) the boundaries of "the family" are too tightly drawn, or mention of the "genealogy of persons" (above, 8.1) unwittingly excludes all but the intact nuclear family from qualification for membership. The bishops are more inclusive and all-embracing than the Vatican documents, when they come to answer the question which families constitute domestic churches. They answer: if they practise the way of love, all of them do. As the bishops seek to inculcate the understanding of families as domestic churches, they admit to two problems: ignorance and unworthiness. Ignorance about the domestic church is understandable because this teaching of the early Church fell into disuse and was only revived at Vatican II. But unworthiness is dismissed by a sound theology of grace: some families "feel overwhelmed by this calling or unable to carry out its responsibilities. Perhaps they consider their family too 'broken' to be used for the Lord's purposes. But remember, a family is holy not because it is perfect but because God's grace is at work in it, helping to set out anew everyday on the way of love."

The Church itself, and every "little church," have a common "firm foundation, namely Christ's promise to be faithful to those he has chosen." At this juncture the developmental character of the pastoral advice is at its most evident, for the document moves beyond the "irregular situations" of *Familiaris consortio*[20] and its ambivalence about their recognition, to a full-on embrace of single-parent families, divorced people, and adoptive and step-families. While "a committed, permanent, faithful relationship of husband and wife is the root of a family," the grace of God is by no means confined to the approved marital form. "Wherever a family exists and love still moves through its members, grace is present. Nothing – not even divorce or death – can place limits upon God's gracious love." Single parents are affirmed without reserve: they are courageous, determined, and even admired, for

[20] *Familiaris consortio*, para. 65, 79.

"Somehow you fulfil your call to create a good home, care for your children, hold down a job, and undertake responsibilities in the neighborhood and church. You reflect the power of faith, the strength of love, and the certainty that God does not abandon us when circumstances leave you alone in parenting." The bishops are aware of the difficulties faced by blended families (above, 8.1) and wish to learn from them: "Those who try to blend two sets of children into one family face a special challenge to accept difficulties and to love unconditionally. They offer us a practical example of peacemaking."

There is much more in this short message that cannot detain us, especially about "true equality," "sharing power" and household duties,[21] and "the incredible busyness of family life that can take its toll on loving relationships."[22] It may be important to recognize that *Follow the Way of Love* is a local document, designed to address Christians in the United States where, as we have noted, culture wars and a "divorce culture" persist. I think the sacrament of marriage should have featured more prominently in the analysis of the way of love, not least because the priests who administer that sacrament are the couple themselves, who also provide and carry with them the obvious continuity between liturgy and life. I also think the bishops' unreserved welcome of non-traditional families could have been aided by the analysis of "marital values" (above, 5.3) which, it was urged, are capable of being extended beyond the marital norm. But that development may be years in coming.

In conclusion I take the domestic church as a fruitful and attractive idea for emphasizing the divine presence and love within families. It currently enjoys little comprehension among Protestants: among Roman Catholics more commendation is also required. I think it provides an alternative way of arriving at many of the conclusions of this book, about the use of the Bible in the service of families, about relations within God and among ourselves, the social image of God, the gift of children, the tension between the marital and other family forms, parenting, and parental love, and much else. That said I prefer to ground a Christian family ethic in theology, not ecclesiology, in the Trinity rather than in domestic ministry, in the being of God rather than in the being of the Church. That way tricky problems about constitution, ministry, and eligibility, and so on, which are bound to exercise legal minds, are confined if not obviated altogether. But both ways remain open, and each of them deserves the title "The Way of Love." The attempt to ground the domestic church in the reality of the divine love in any case brings both ways together.

---

[21] *Follow the Way of Love*, "Growing in Mutuality."

9.2 Families and the Local Church

Does a family resemble a church, and the church a family? Another disadvantage for a family theology that models families on churches may be the actual condition of some local congregations, the lack of suitable activities for children, the continuing local disunity of and rivalry between the churches, and the credibility gap that undoubtedly exists (in countries like Britain) between public perceptions of the churches and the transformation of personal and public life which the Church of Christ exists to proclaim. The idea of the domestic church provides one answer to the question "Can a family also be a church?" In order to attend to the local church's ministry to families it will be useful to reverse that question and ask "Is the local church a family?"

Is the local church a family?

Peter Selby, an Anglican theologian and bishop, raised the question "Is the Church a Family?,"[23] in order to divest local congregations of similarities to actual families that he thought actually hindered the proclamation of the Gospel. In his trenchant but positive analysis, he warns that chosen terminology involving references to "church family" or "family services" can have a different use, such as inculcating family-like loyalty in the church (when it is in short supply), or "merely signifying an occasion at which account will be taken of the presence of young children."[24] Churches can replicate many features of closed, nuclear families, by being more concerned with themselves, their members, and their squabbles, than with the Gospel in the wider neighborhood.

One such feature, Selby observes, is the behavior of many priests, which perhaps inevitably, is often going to resemble that of the harassed head of a (single-parent) family. The asymmetrical parent–child relationship in the nuclear family is claimed to be the key to understanding the unfortunate dynamics of clergy and laity in the local church:

> the power of parents over children extends itself into every aspect of their
> lives as a result, as psychological and emotional power; and it is this experi-

---

[22] *Follow the Way of Love*, "Taking Time."
[23] Peter Selby, "Is the Church a Family?," in Stephen C. Barton (ed.), *The Family in Theological Perspective* (Edinburgh: T&T Clark, 1996) [151–68].
[24] Selby, "Is the Church a Family?," p. 151.

ence of childhood which also allows for the psychological and emotional extension of the power of the clergy over the laity.

More serious is the fact that this analogy between congregation and family also has the effect of preventing such issues of power and authority being confronted in a mature way.[25]

This "overdeveloped sense of responsibility" can lead to an infantilization of the whole congregation – "in many churches a willingness to be like a child in a family becomes almost an essential qualification for membership." Such parenthood in real families leads to disruptive behavior on the part of children: in congregations it can lead to "the incessant carryover of the power of unacknowledged experiences of the nursery."[26] Some clergy work so hard in the service of the institution that believes in, and supports, family life that their own families are disrupted. Church activity can take parents (and children) away from their families when churches should be actively persuading members of families to spend more time with each other.

Selby advocates the adoption of the model of "public company" instead of family for many of the activities of the local church. Public companies have structures and policies in place for the furtherance of their missions, including policies for the employment of disabled people. The local church "does not give much encouragement to the view that seeing it as a 'family' really assists it in its task, and indeed suggests that other ways of seeing it might make it if anything a more effective environment for human flourishing." The Church's self-understanding as a family "has its origin in the determination of the New Testament to speak of the human situation in terms of relationship, and of the transformation of that situation by the grace of Christ in terms of transformed relationship."[27]

The local church then must be an open church, just as a family must be an open family (above, 8.2). Selby's criticisms of the family model are apposite, and indicate the stultifying dangers of a closed system that chokes the flow of love beyond itself and embraces the neighbor and the stranger. Whether we focus on families from a Trinitarian perspective toward the "communion of persons," or from an ecclesial perspective toward the domestic church, or from both perspectives, the home is, at least potentially, a site of divine love and grace. Part of the ministry of the local church is to sustain family members in the exercise of mutual love, and also to be a community of mutual love which, when its members meet, allows God the Spirit to inspire

---

[25] Selby, "Is the Church a Family?," p. 157.
[26] Selby, "Is the Church a Family?," pp. 158–9.
[27] Selby, "Is the Church a Family?," p. 164.

them in the practice of social holiness in the home and in the wider community. Following Couture (above, 1.2) let us take families as microsystems, and the churches where families worship as mesosystems, and ask how the two systems may integrate with one another in the sustaining of families.

Families, time, and work

Let us allow that the microsystem of a family is illuminatingly explained to itself by means of the idea of "domestic church." What difference might that make to it? Two of several areas that require examination are time and work. Families generally need to make more time for one another. Communion needs time. There is an alarming decline in the time families spend having meals together.[28] A national time diary study of 3,563 children in the United States found that "Time spent in family activities is associated with fewer problem behaviors . . . that children who spent more hours eating meals and sleeping had lower levels of behavior problems than did those who spent fewer hours eating or sleeping." An average of only 45 minutes per week was spent sitting and talking,[29] yet this simple activity was found to be more advantageous in terms of children's well-being than any other in their diaries. William Doherty, an influential social scientist, draws attention to increased working hours for parents, "frantic families" and "over-scheduled kids" who are pushed into a surfeit of "extremely competitive activities."[30] Reminiscent of the analyses of the influence of market capitalism on adult attitudes to children offered by Miller-McLemore and Pope John Paul II (above, 8.4), he explains these trends as an intrusion of market values into family life. "Parenting has become a form of product development in the contemporary world, with parents anxious to provide opportunities for their children in a competitive environment."[31] The importance of time together, regular meals together, family rituals (like nightly bedtime stories for young children), and countless other shared activities are all an expression of "the way of love." Christian families need the help of churches and appropriate devotional publications in order to sustain family prayers or home worship. In some

---

[28] See Robert D. Putnam, *Bowling Alone: The Collapse and Revival of American Community* (New York: Simon and Schuster, 2000).

[29] Sandra L. Hofferth and John E. Sandberg, "How American Children Spend Their Time," *Journal of Marriage and Family*, 63.2 (May 2001) [295–308], p. 307.

[30] William J. Doherty, "Family Life and Civic Bonds: Renewing the 'Very Air Our Loved Ones Breathe,'" *American Experiment Quarterly*, Fall 2003 [21–39], pp. 23–5.

[31] Doherty, "Family Life and Civic Bonds," p. 27. This is a major argument of his well-known work *Take Back Your Kids* (Notre Dame, IN: Sorin Books, 2000).

countries this material is in short supply. While the practice of family prayer is much less common in mainline Protestant denominations than it once was,[32] it requires resourcing with appropriate and participative worship activities that prevent over-reliance on the extempore form.

Doherty addresses the problem of the millions of frantic families who have unwittingly ingested the selfish and competitive market values mediated to them through the consumer culture by the creation of a civic movement, "Putting Family First," whose web-site advertises it as " a grass-roots, community wide organization, raising awareness about finding balance in our over-scheduled lives."[33] It believes that "families can only be a seedbed for current and future citizens if they achieve a balance between internal bonds and external activities," and "that this balance has become gravely out of whack [*sic*!] for many families of all social classes . . ." It seeks "to take back family life from the individualistic, hyper-competitive consumer culture of childrearing."[34] One suspects that the United States provides the strongest example both of the consumer culture and of the networks of "civil society," so "Putting Family First" may not be entirely transposable elsewhere. Nevertheless it provides salutary analyses of the demise of family life under any consumer culture, and in this respect at least it remains steadfastly counter-cultural. These analyses receive too much verification in other consumer cultures too. Churches belong to the network of civil organizations that should encourage such a movement. The Christian beliefs about families that have been explored in this book provide overwhelming reasons for doing so.

Time is inevitably going to be spent in families on essential domestic tasks and basic childcare, and here a gender imbalance still needs to be urgently addressed. Childcare and domestic work can be as different as going on a picnic and cleaning the bathroom. A recent official fact sheet on child care in the United Kingdom reveals that on average, fathers working full-time spend one hour a day on childcare activities during the week and one hour 40 minutes a day at weekends.[35] Full-time working mothers spend two hours a day during the week and two hours 20 minutes a day at weekends. (But this statistic is complicated because "full-time" works out at 47 weekly hours for men, and 40 for women.) Fathers are much more involved with their children than they were two generations ago. (Now 37.2 percent of

---

[32] Browning et al., *From Culture Wars*, p. 308.

[33] *Putting Family First*. For the details, see www.puttingfamilyfirst.org/. Accessed 02.09.2006.

[34] Doherty, "Family Life and Civic Bonds," pp. 33–4.

[35] Economic and Social Research Council, *Factsheet: Parenting in Britain Today* (2004). www.esrcsocietytoday.ac.uk/ESRCInfoCentre/facts/. Accessed 02.09.2006.

fathers change diapers more than once a day: only 8.7 percent never do.) (More fathers in Denmark spend their time looking after their children than in any other Western European country: fathers in Portugal and Greece the least.)

An authoritative study comparing two cohorts of parents, born in 1958 and 1970, when in their thirties, showed that "although the number of fathers taking the main responsibility for children doubled from 1 percent in the 1958 cohort to 2 percent in the 1970 cohort, the number of fathers taking equal responsibility for childcare dropped from 46 percent to 39 percent."[36] This and two additional, meticulous studies "do not support the notion of a 'new dad' who spends more time with his children. In fact, they seem to suggest that fathers today are actually taking a slightly smaller role in childcare." The picture is less one of stubborn male indolence: more that "the 'new dad'" is "a father who wants to be more involved in his child's upbringing but, due to other pressures, finds this is not possible." There is also evidence that men slightly overestimate their involvement with their children.

The popular, media idea of the "new man" or the "new family" may both assume real changes to family life in a more egalitarian direction and also be tinged with idealism and rhetoric. The decrease in paternal involvement, if it is sustained, could lead to an increase in chosen childlessness (above, 8.4–5) among the married *and* the unmarried, for the alternative to "new families" is not a return to "traditional families" but to no families at all, as "women decide that the new marriage bargain – in which they hold a job and remain responsible for all child-care and housework – is a bad deal, and as men decide that filling all the requirements of a traditional breadwinner but getting few of the traditional prerogatives or wifely supports is just as unattractive."[37]

A key to healthy families in the coming decade will be *negotiation* between spouses and partners regarding every aspect of child care and household maintenance. Two-income families are here to stay, and sharing in the breadwinning will be matched by sharing in the shopping, cooking, and cleaning. The parceling-out to one another of domestic tasks and responsibilities does not have to be equal! Paid work outside the home and unpaid work inside the home together form a "quantum" or whole. It is this whole that needs to be discussed, reviewed, negotiated, and settled. More

[36] CLS [Centre for Longitudinal Studies] Briefings, *Parenting*, November, 2005. www.cls.ioe.ac.uk. Accessed 02.09.2006.
[37] Linda J. Waite and Maggie Gallagher, *The Case for Marriage: Why Married People Are Happier, Healthier, and Better Off Financially* (New York: Doubleday, 2000), p. 171.

traditional families settled for "specialization" which usually created unfair burdens for mothers. Specialization can remain, as long as all the work, inside and outside the home, is fairly distributed. This is the policy of the charity and campaigning organization Fathers Direct.[38] It is essential also that employers cultivate, wherever possible, and against the growing backlash from child-renouncing careerists, family-friendly working practices and shifts. It is hard to think of a greater contribution that companies could make to the common good of societies than to reorganize work in order for mothers *and fathers* to be fully involved in child care arrangements. Flexitime, and proper remuneration, status, and promotion for part-time employment all have their part to play.

The influence of gender within the domestic church of course remains immense. But the very close relationship that Roman Catholic theology itself sets up between the domestic church and the Church renders inevitable comparisons between the progress made in involving men within the domestic church and the lack of progress made in involving women in the ministry of the Church at all levels. A rudimentary attempt was made (above, 7.1–2) to place the being of God beyond maleness (and femaleness), and to include the co-equality of the Persons of God among the ingredients of the human *imago dei* that God has chosen to implant within us. A strong theological argument exists for egalitarian marriage. Christian advocates of egalitarian marriage do not merely reflect back the assumptions of contemporary culture after two (or more) waves of aggressive feminism. They believe that respect for the full but different personhood of women better reflects the coming Reign of God than patriarchal regimes, religious or secular, past, present or future, ever can. Christians who are members of churches that ordain women are able to square the circle here, for, at last, in the area of gender, it seems to them that liturgy and life are beginning to synergize each other. There are many reasons why the liturgy and the sanctuary must be gender-sensitive. Change cannot be confined to the kitchen and the nursery. Only when male power in the sanctuary is fully shared will the liturgy of the Church be more fully re-enacted in its domestic counterpart.

At a recent valedictory service for a College principal, the hymn was chosen, "I cannot tell why He, whom angels worship, Should set His love upon the sons of men." Neither he, nor I, nor (thankfully) a sizeable minority of the congregation felt able to endorse these sentiments publicly by singing them. Women who retort that they are untroubled by the blatant

---

[38] Fathers Direct: The National Information Centre on Fatherhood. www.fathersdirect.com. Accessed 02.09.2006.

sexism of so much Christian hymnody do not provide evidence that sexism is not a problem in the sanctuary. They provide evidence of something more sinister. They are either too worn out by the patriarchy it represents to resist it, or they have been so colonized or undermined by it that they *fail to notice* that it generates exclusion on a massive scale. The full visibility of women is required at all levels of church organization and ministry. Neither do congregations need to intone "and was made man."

The local church, ideally of course, should be free from all those tendencies that Selby describes. Churches have to be child-friendly and family-friendly places with worship and activity for all ages. "Family worship" can be a misnomer. Special services for children can also draw attention to the unsuitability of normal worship for them. Children should be included, not patronized. Sunday school or junior church should be available to the children of the area, adequately resourced by trained teachers and superior teaching materials. Churches that practice the baptism of infants should not refuse children communion. The usual excuse, that children need to understand the sacrament before they receive it, is incoherent. Did they understand their baptism? Is the eucharist not a mystery? What could count as an adequate understanding warranting admission? Is not the imaginativeness of children an aid to reception that adults too often lack? In several countries, the local church is likely to be near or below the threshold of viability. A full ministry to families is well beyond the resources of most churches, but not all. In some cases, local churches should be able to do together what they cannot do alone. Marriage preparation, marriage enrichment, and parenting courses are obvious examples.

Exploring marriage, preparing for children

Ministry to families also operates at the meso-level, where national churches and local churches co-operate with one another, and with other agencies. British churches do not prepare couples well for marriage. A recent survey of the marriage preparation practice of 400 churches (of the major denominations) in southern England revealed startling inattention and neglect. Some preparation "amounts to little more than one or two meetings between a couple and the minister to discuss the religious significance of marriage and the wedding ceremony itself."[39] The Roman Catholic Church

---

[39] Roehampton Social Research Unit, University of Surrey Roehampton, *Church Support of Marriage and Adult Relationships in Southern England* (2003), p. iii.

has the best record of marriage preparation with a centrally administered, comprehensive program. Within Protestant churches a lack of time, of outside expertise, of training, and of resources were all regularly blamed for the general paucity of provision, yet there was little evidence either of much inclination to share systemically what resources were available or for the churches to work co-operatively with each other or collaboratively with other agencies. The researchers concluded that the churches had not kept pace with the changes to family structure identified earlier in this book (above, 1.1–1.2); that these changes "can compromise how churches support, for example, divorced, non-married, gay and lesbian couples;" and that "by accident or design, churches support marriage and adult relationships on an exclusive basis."[40] The theology of the churches had not responded well to the changes around and within them and this sometimes resulted in ministers themselves losing confidence in marriage[41] and in the purpose of preparing couples for it. The researchers helpfully recommend that churches "develop packages of support that allow ministers and laity to offer not just marriage *preparation* but marriage *exploration*. Theologically, it also requires an understanding of marriage as a process not an event – and that cohabitation might be part of such a process of couples exploring marriage . . ."[42] The researchers were unable to report what knowledge, understanding, or skills (for example in negotiation or conflict resolution) had been imparted or gained in the course of preparation,[43] and so were unable to assess its effectiveness.

Churches in post-Christian societies must learn to utilize much more effectively those events in the life-course when people seek Christian ministry. One marvelous example of what a determined parish can do comes from Australia. The story runs from a basic marriage preparation course, and free computer disks for couples to design (with guidance) their own liturgies, through to preparation courses for *divorced* people who wish to remarry, to the adult baptisms of inquirers, to baptisms of the children of married couples, and ten-year follow-ups.[44] There can hardly be a more exhilarating case of practical, parish-based, marriage-focused, pastoral care. People in all seven distinct types of family structure (above, 1.1) could

---

[40] *Church Support of Marriage*, p. iv.
[41] *Church Support of Marriage*, p. x.
[42] *Church Support of Marriage*, p. vi.
[43] The report is silent about this, but the point has been well established in conversation with the researchers.
[44] Philip Newman, "An Holistic, Parish-Based Marriage-Ministry," in Thatcher (ed.), *Celebrating Christian Marriage* [71–84].

benefit from "marriage exploration." An understanding of marriage is needed, including what was earlier called "marital values" (above, 5.3), alongside the growing emphasis on skills. Since marriage in Christian understanding is a "vocation," some people are therefore necessarily not called to it. How do they find out? One way of finding out is to undertake a marriage inventory with a prospective partner such as FOCCUS[45] or PREPARE/ENRICH.[46] Where preparation is undertaken by trained people, couples discuss their answers to searching questions. *Marriage Care*, in origin Roman Catholic, provides preparation courses for any couples seeking them: *Marriage Resource* offers training for clergy and lay people who want to be effective in marriage ministry.[47] Inventories sometimes arrange themselves around "the six 'Cs'" – communication, commitment, conflict-resolution, children, career, church.[48] There can be little doubt that inventories are aids to undertaking the self-examination, mutual discussion, and exploration that may be needed if marriage is not to be "enterprised, nor taken in hand, unadvisedly, lightly, or wantonly," but "reverently, discreetly, advisedly, soberly, and in the fear of God."[49] They can test the vocation to marriage, and inform the decision whether or not to commit oneself to another for the rest of one's life.

Some British Christians are adopting a "Marriage Culture Strategy" in the local church (or group of churches).[50] The strategy involves encouraging couples, whether they are marrying in a church or secular venue, to attend preparation classes and to complete a PREPARE or FOCCUS inventory. A marriage enhancement course or event is offered annually, and qualified help is offered for people in difficulties with their marriage or who are undertaking second marriages. Couples are assigned mentors who are themselves couples who have received training in the mentoring role.[51] Couples need rather different support when children arrive. Nearly all first-time parents underrate the changes to their social, domestic, and sex lives that follow the arrival of the first baby. Research on the transition to parenthood is gathering momentum. Susan Pace summarizes how new parents "have great pleasure from their baby, but many suffer significant losses in companionate activities,

---

[45] Facilitating Open Couple Communication, Understanding and Study. www.foccusinc.com/. Accessed 02.09.2006.

[46] PREPARE/ENRICH. www.prepare-enrich.com/indexm.cfm. Accessed 02.09.2006.

[47] *Marriage Care*. www.marriagecare.org.uk. Accessed 02.09.2006.

[48] See Adrian Thatcher, *The Daily Telegraph Guide to Christian Marriage and to Getting Married in Church* (London and New York: Continuum, 2003), pp. 47–61.

[49] The Book of Common Prayer, "The Form of Solemnization of Matrimony."

[50] "Marriage Culture Strategy," *Marriage Resource Briefing*, September 2004.

[51] See Harry Benson, *Mentoring Marriages* (Oxford: Monarch Publications, 2005).

sex, and mutual nurturing and attentiveness. They feel isolated, abandoned, and continuously under duress. The parents' dyad is then at risk, and, if left untended, it may decline to the point of divorce or dissolution."[52] While professional help may be needed in these circumstances, couples are often unwilling to seek it, perhaps because of its intangible or intimate character. In these circumstances, a network of couples in similar circumstances can provide much reassurance. Research findings are ambivalent about the impact of the arrival of children on relationship quality. A "meta-analysis" of 97 studies and 47,692 participants concluded that parents with children experienced significantly lower marital satisfaction than parents without children (55 percent to 45 percent).[53] On the other hand, the methodology of these studies has been criticized for wrongly assuming "that the factors determining marital satisfaction have the same effect before and after the birth of the first child for first-time parents and for childless couples."[54] After appropriate adjustments are made a counter-claim is offered, that "first-time parents were more satisfied with their marriage than the childless group, in both standard and weighted measures." Clearly if the meta-analysis is correct, further light will be shed on the phenomenon of chosen childlessness (above, 8.4). In the meantime, whatever consensus there may be in the next few years, the need for pastoral care of these couples remains constant.

9.3 The Churches and Pro-Family Policies

There has been no space to discuss the broader range of activities, worship and otherwise, that might be appropriate for local churches in their ministry to families. At the level of exo-systems, Christians will want to be active in seeking to bring about various political changes if they can be shown to benefit family life. At this level, co-operation between churches, nationally and regionally, is more likely. The examples in the next few paragraphs are drawn from Britain and Europe, but Christians are likely to have similar agendas in different countries, all of them based on enriching family life. I indicate very briefly six areas of government policy, because they appear to

---

[52] Susan Pace, "Couples and the First Baby: Responding to New Parents' Sexual and Relationship Problems," *Sexual and Relationship Therapy*, 19.3 (August 2004) [223–46], p. 242.

[53] Jean M. Twenge, W. Keith Campbell, and Craig A. Foster, "Parenthood and Marital Satisfaction: A Meta-Analytic Review," *Journal of Marriage and Family*, 65.3 (August 2003) [574–83], p. 574.

[54] J. Guttmann and A. Lazar, "Criteria for Marital Satisfaction: Does Having a Child Make a Difference?," *Journal of Reproductive and Infant Psychology*, 22.3 (August 2004) [147–55], p. 147.

be in conflict with the theology for families that has been worked out in this book. They are the encouragement and enablement of weekend working, the expectation that mothers, partnered or single, will wish to undertake fulltime, paid work: the welfare system that has unintended consequences, the tax system which favors singleness; and the lack of advocacy of marriage in family policy.

A Eurostat report (2002) shows that 40 percent of women and over 45 percent of men undertook paid work on Saturdays, while almost 23 percent of women and just over 26 percent of men worked on Sundays.[55] There had been a marked increase in weekend working in the decade prior to publication. Research from the campaigning organization Keep Time for Children[56] addressed the problem of the decimation of family time at weekends. It concluded that the "potential impact on family life" was worrying, with "significant numbers of children deprived of time with parents or of time as part of a nuclear family group and many couples having limited time that they can spend together." There were further implications, yet to be fully explored, "around the association between parental involvement with their children and their children's development and educational attainment."[57] A majority of mothers want fathers to work shorter hours. Parents of both sexes, and their children, dislike weekend working, and many mothers would prefer to work less or not at all, at weekends.[58]

Within the church and beyond there is a need to recognize that while the so-called "24/7 society" is convenient for consumption and leisure activities, a price for the convenience is being paid by many thousands of families in the likely reduction of their quality of life. When Jesus took issue with the strict observance of the Sabbath day with the remark "The Sabbath was made for man, not man for the Sabbath" (Mk. 2:27) he reclaimed it for humanity: regular, cyclical rest, in the form of the complete cessation of work, is written into the constitution of human being. The disruption to families and the unwillingness of parents to undertake weekend work must be taken as signs: signs perhaps of the unsustainable levels of consumption which appear to require the sacrifice of time and relationship quality. How the

---

[55] Ana Franco and Karin Winqvist, *Women and Men Working Weekends and Their Family Circumstances* (Eurostat, 2002). Cited in National Family and Parenting Institute, *Making Britain Family Friendly* (London: 2003), p. 9. www.nfpi.org. Accessed 02.09.2006.

[56] *Keep Time for Children.* www.keeptimeforchildren.org.uk/NatCen_exec_summary.doc. Accessed 02.09.2006.

[57] A major research project published by the Joseph Rowntree Foundation analyzed 19 studies on work and family life. See Shirley Dex, *Work and Family Life in the Twenty-First Century* (London: Joseph Rowntree Foundation, 2003).

[58] Summary of Dex's work in *Making Britain Family Friendly*, p. 11.

churches might one day become communities of resistance to all-pervasive consumerism is beyond the scope of this volume.

Weekend working is part of a broader problem, the relation between paid and unpaid work, and its long connection with gender. European governments may just be plain wrong in thinking that, in the drive to treat men and women equally, women who are mothers generally want to be equally involved in the work place. Jill Kirby has criticized the assumption of the British government "that men and women should be homogenous and interchangeable." She thinks a perverse vision of family life is assumed by this policy, in which "all adults of working age, regardless of gender or parental status, should ideally be in full-time paid employment, equal earners and taking equal shares in their domestic responsibilities."[59] The vision is distorted, she thinks, because it "ignores the changes which come about in the lives of women when they become mothers. It assumes that, given the choice between work and home responsibilities, women will exercise that choice in the same way as men. In other words, that their priority will be participation in the job market." Evidence is then set out that

> Women today have no difficulty in regarding themselves as equal with men, but they do not consider themselves the same. In particular, on becoming mothers, only a small percentage of women remain centred on their careers. The majority choose a more home-centred pattern of work, either by reducing their working hours, transferring to part-time work or leaving the job market entirely. Large numbers of mothers who remain in work due to financial pressure continue to express a clear preference for more time at home.[60]

A strong case can be made for the view that governments do not honor the preferences of a clear majority of mothers to be *less* involved in the work place than they presently are.[61] These social policy debates are as contested as any comparable debate in theology and ethics, leaving applied theologians baffled and unqualified as they to seek to understand the impact of postmodern culture on family life. If we begin by putting the needs of children first; if we uphold the sacredness of families (as the domestic church doctrine seeks to do); and if we advocate "specialization" (above, 9.2) we are right to question the assumption that the more people, men, and women, who are in fulltime paid work, the better for everyone.

---

[59] Jill Kirby, *Choosing to be Different: Women, Work and the Family* (London: Centre for Policy Studies, 2003), p. 1. www.cps.org.uk/pdf/pub/398.pdf. Accessed 02.09.2006.
[60] Kirby, *Choosing to be Different*, pp. 1–2.
[61] She cites as her source Catherine Hakim, *Models of the Family in Modern Societies* (Aldershot, UK: Ashgate, 2003.)

Women who interrupt their careers for the sake of their children will receive a reduced pension in retirement. One in five single women pensioners risk being in poverty in retirement.[62] This sends the wrong message about the social value of unpaid parenting. It could be recognized by counting toward pensionable service. More controversially, the soaring cost of welfare in developed countries creates intense pressures for reform, that is, toward reduction of the costs of the welfare system. While Christian theology is right to put first the defense of vulnerable people, especially where amoral market forces are given free rein, it is also necessary to examine unintended consequences of the system. One such unintended consequence is that in Britain fiscal policy discourages marriage. The married person's allowance has been abolished. Officially neutral with regard to the problem of family form (above, 1.1, 5.1), the British government's welfare policy is not simply neutral with regard to marriage: it discourages it.[63] The decline of marriage has been harmful to children, while "the cost to the taxpayer of lone parenthood . . . shows how present policies penalise intact families and subsidise lone parenthood on a scale that is not widely appreciated."[64] It is explained that if a family breaks up or if a single woman has children on her own, the annual cost to the rest of society can easily run into many thousands of pounds. The example given is of a single parent with two children who may be entitled to more than £11,000 a year in welfare benefits. Around one million couples in a committed sexual relationship live most of the time at separate addresses so they can cash in on benefits. While soaring welfare bills will always attract criticism from taxpayers, there is a more sinister problem: "the state is increasingly taking on the roles normally expected of a husband – providing a stable income for the mother and doing more and more childcare."[65]

The single, most positive, step that could be taken is for governments to advocate marriage, and to allow support for marriage to influence family, social, and economic policy. There are overwhelming *economic* reasons for

[62] The Equal Opportunities Commission in Britain co-ordinates the Women's Pensions Network which campaigns for unpaid parenting to be recognized as pensionable. www.eoc.org.uk.

[63] Several publications of the Centre for Policy Studies develop and defend this analysis, and their arguments must be fairly assessed (and not automatically assumed to endorse the ideology of the political right). See Jill Kirby, *The Price of Parenthood* (London: Centre for Policy Studies, 2005); Jill Kirby, *Broken Hearts, Family Decline and the Consequences for Society* (London: Centre for Policy Studies, 2002).

[64] Robert Rowthorn, "Foreword," in Jill Kirby, *The Price of Parenthood*, pp. i–ii. Also at www.cps.uk/pdf/pub/396.pdf.

[65] Rowthorn, "Foreword," pp. ii–iii.

this (the sort of reasons that politicians normally find convincing). The *social evidence* has already been reviewed (above, 5.1–5.2). Long before churches and theologians make their contribution to social policy, the evidence is clear that marriage, on balance, is better for everyone: for husbands and wives; fathers and mothers; particularly for children; for the common good; for the public purse; for the private home. There is poor public awareness of these realities. Cohabiting couples have little idea of the low statistical probability of the durability of their relationship when compared with marriage. In fact they are likely to entertain the myth that there is something called "common law marriage," and that it applies to them in cases of relationship breakdown. Information and truth-telling is vital in social policy. We have seen that the positive benefits of being and remaining married are little understood even among the professionals dealing with marital breakdown (above, 5.2). All of us, professional theologians included, need life-long learning, continuous re-training, and help to overcome our reluctance to accept realities that do not accord with unexamined and ageing assumptions.

At the level of macrosystems, what can the churches do? There is no shortage of policies or recommendations. Browning and his team have a ten-point plan for "the critical retrieval of a marriage and family culture,"[66] followed by a seven-point strategy regarding the influencing of public policy.[67] The arguments of this volume lead to a further endorsement of all these policies and recommendations. But the United States has more resources, a much higher record of church attendance (than in Britain and many other countries), a heightened awareness of issues surrounding marriage and families ("culture wars" means nothing in Britain), a lively civic tradition, and a much more vocal evangelical Christian constituency. It has also had the enormous benefit of the Family, Religion, and Culture project, most of whose books are not well known in Britain and Europe. The United States has a huge head-start theologically. Lisa Cahill suggests a five-point "Program for Christian Families,"[68] but this is addressed to families themselves. In both cases, inevitably, there is a high level of abstraction that operates against application. Browning recommends *"More than anything else, churches must retrieve their marriage and family traditions, even though they must do so critically."*[69] Sadly there is little willingness to do this: indeed it is difficult to include marriage and family traditions within crowded theological and

---

[66] Browning et al., *From Culture Wars*, pp. 307–22.
[67] Browning et al., *From Culture Wars*, pp. 322–34.
[68] Lisa Sowle Cahill, *Family: A Christian Social Perspective* (Minneapolis, MN: Fortress Press, 2000), pp. 135–7.
[69] Browning et al., *From Culture Wars*, p. 307 (authors' emphasis).

ethical curricula outside the pastoral components of professional ministerial training. Browning's understanding of "critical" in "critical familism" is sophisticated. That sophistication is not widely shared. Cahill recommends that "Christian families should be grounded in the kinds of human relations that promote family well-being in general." Well, yes, but as part of a program? It is difficult to see how either recommendation (and the other policy points) is much more than an exhortation. Yet at this level of analysis, perhaps that is all recommendations can be.

In *Marriage and Modernization* Browning advocates "a powerful world-wide religiocultural vision that advocates a new critical familism."[70] For this purpose he advocates a particular kind of "analogical thinking," not between human and divine relations as I have attempted here, but between reformist movements within religions. A telling example of the genre is the strand of Islamic thought which finds gender equality within it. Critical familism and the work of the Islamic scholar Azizah al-Hibri have obvious parallels in their reformism and their engagement with patriarchy that can be mutually beneficial to each. They have "resources that point to important analogies – analogies that are sufficiently close to one another to provide for co-operation and the creation of overlapping, if not identical, cultural frameworks."[71] This is clearly an important agenda. Our partners in this dialog will increasingly be found across the religions, among reformist and revisionary seers, instead of the limited and less promising engagement with reactionary forces within our own religion. This is likely to add practical zest to inter-religious conversations. When Browning bravely tackles "world family strategies," he examines global organizations that might potentially carry out such strategies. These include the World Council of Churches, the Roman Catholic Church, and the United Nations. While he finds weaknesses (and omissions) in their analyses, his intention is "to show that ambitious world family programs actually exist and that to enter into an inquiry about a global strategy for families is to venture into a territory that different intellectual and cultural armies are already competing to occupy."[72]

Browning's vision for a global strategy may occupy scholars, religious and secular, for a generation to come. My limited scholarship is confined to the Christian tradition. This narrower work is a contribution to that earlier task of retrieving marriage and family tradition, but coupled with retrieval is the need for innovation. It was written because, with all Christians, the author

[70] Don S. Browning, *Marriage and Modernization: How Globalization Threatens Marriage and What to Do about It* (Grand Rapids, MI/Cambridge, UK: Eerdmans, 2003), p. 144.
[71] Browning, *Marriage and Modernization*, p. 146.
[72] Browning, *Marriage and Modernization*, p. 223.

believes the Christian faith is true. That is, it tells us how it is with God, how it is with God in relation to us, and how it is with us in relation to one another and to God. The truth of God impinges restoratively on families, and in this work I hope to have offered to the Church what I hope are new insights about the presence of God among the families of the world.

Families are fragmenting, and too often children are the victims. But the fragmentation of families provides a problematic, a vital element of culture with which to engage for the sake of the Gospel. When that engagement happens the situation of families themselves appears in a different light, and new light shines out of the tradition as the Church asks new questions of the inheritance of faith. This, of course, is how tradition develops, whether doctrinal, ecclesial, liturgical, or moral. Because much of the book is about theological ideas, it operates at the "macro-level," but I have tried to show, particularly in this last chapter, that the practical implications of such a theology for families and children are considerable.

Any innovation in these pages, I claim, is a potential development of, and not a departure from, tradition. The more theological reading of the New Testament, in which the revelation of divine love attested in the scriptures influences our way of reading them, and finding them family-friendly, is hardly even an innovation. The question of parent–child relations occurred in several places, not least because the tradition says little about these. In this case innovation is inevitable. Our children are not our neighbors, and they have prior entitlement to our love. The teaching of Jesus about children was taken with such unconditional seriousness that it became the basis for a new pro-marriage argument: Jesus wills the flourishing of all children, and *ipso facto* wills the family form which is most likely to make this possible. The remarkable recovery of the doctrine of the Trinity is evident in contemporary theology, even though its connection with family relations has only just begun to be explored. Yet the very names of the Persons of God derive from relations within families, and the linguistic home-field of these names provides the clue to the provision of a Trinitarian theology of the family which in turn is capable of addressing a hiatus in the tradition: how we are to be good parents and how the grace of God assists parents in that task.

There is no need to summarize the themes of the book. It is necessary, though, to observe that the themes are deeply embedded in the doctrines of the Church, even as they sometimes prompt novel uses of it. Radical theology worth the name has to take tradition at least as seriously as so-called "traditionalists" because it goes back to the *radices* or roots of doctrine, and the way back is through tradition. There were uncomfortable moments in the book, not least when, from our very limited vantage point, the tradition seemed to marginalize children, be gripped by patriarchy, and so deploy familial terms and relations in the articulation of relations within the family of God that a real displacement of ordinary families, and ordinary relations within them, occurred.

At other points in the book, connections between the faith of the church and the secular culture simply suggested themselves, awaiting appropriation. A good example is the connection between the belief in the orthodox Christological doctrine that God the Word became a child, and the secular doctrine that all children have rights. Since God the Word Who is light and life for all women, men, and children (Jn. 1:4,9) is the very Word that becomes flesh in Jesus Christ, the presence of Christ in our reception and care of children acquired additional theological weight. The unabashed universalism of rights language was seen to extend in a most practical way the teaching of Jesus about children, especially vulnerable children. The joyful experience of having a child led to a renewed understanding of God the Giver, and a renewed attentiveness to all that God gives. The understanding of children, above all as gifts, was able to throw new light on the vexed question of chosen childlessness and the possible reasons for that choice. The Relations within God allowed deep theological grounding for mutuality within families, and especially within parent–child relations. They were able to counter-balance the more familiar story of willing sacrifice and filial obedience. Crucial to this re-balancing of intra-family dynamics was the convincing testimony of women: women who are Christians, mothers, and theologians.

In the present chapter the theology of, and for, families converged with the Way of Love. The commendable inclusivity of this document finds the redeeming action of God beyond the Catholic Church, beyond all the churches, wherever there are families. *Ubi caritas, deus est.* That is real catholic teaching in several senses. And it is the language of a global ethic in a globalizing world.[73] If there is to be a global strategy for families, the Christian contributions to it will need to be distinctively Christian, and capable of global application. I hope the theology of families developed here will be a contribution to that contribution. While there is much to be learned about families from outside Christendom, there is a Christian understanding of families which is sharable universally, and which in the sharing sets forth "the unfathomable riches of Christ" (Eph. 3:8).

---

[73] William Schweiker, *Theological Ethics and Global Dynamics in the Time of Many Worlds* (Malden, MA, and Oxford, UK: Blackwell, 2004), pp. 16–19.

Bibliography

Achtemeier, Elizabeth, "Exchanging God for 'No Gods,'" in Kimel (ed.), *Speaking the Christian God*, pp. 1–16.

Adams, Marilyn McCord, "Trinitarian Friendship: Same-Gender Models of Godly Love in Richard of St Victor and Aelred of Rievaulx," in Rogers (ed.), *Theology and Sexuality*, pp. 322–42.

Ahearne-Kroll, Stephen P., "'Who Are My Mother and My Brothers?' Family Relations and Family Language in the Gospel of Mark," *Journal of Religion*, 81.1, January 2001, pp. 1–25.

Ainsworth, M.D.S., Mary C. Blehar, Everett Waters, and Sally Wall (eds.), *Patterns of Attachment* (Hillsdale, NJ: Lawrence Erlbaum, 1978).

Albrecht, Gloria, "A Comment in Defense of 'Living Faithfully with Families in Transition'" (2003). www.witherspoonsociety.org/03-may/albrecht.htm. Accessed 02.09.2006.

Anderson, Herbert and Susan B.W. Johnson, *Regarding Children: A New Respect for Childhood and Families* (Louisville, KY: Westminster John Knox Press, 1995).

Andolsen, Barbara Hilkert, Christine E. Gudorf, and Mary D. Pellauer (eds.), *Women's Consciousness and Women's Conscience: A Reader in Feminist Ethics* (New York: Harper and Row, 1985).

Aquinas, Thomas, *Summa Theologiae* (tr. Fathers of the English Dominican Province), 3 vols (New York: Benziger Brothers, 1947). www.ccel.org/a/aquinas/summa/SS/SS026.html. Accessed 02.09.2006.

Atkinson, Joseph C., "Family as *Domestic Church*: Developmental Trajectory, Legitimacy, and Problems of Appropriation," *Theological Studies*, 66.3, September 2005, pp. 592–604.

Augustine, *de bono conjugali* (tr. C.L. Cornish) in *Nicene and Post-Nicene Fathers*, Series I, vol. III. www.ccel.org/fathers2/NPNF1–03/npnf1–03–32.htm. Accessed 02.09.2006.

Australian Government, Australian Institute of Family Studies. www.aifs.gov.au/institute/info/charts/glossary.html#couple. Accessed 02.09.2006.

Barr, James, "'Abba' and the Familiarity of Jesus' Speech," *Theology*, 91, 1988, pp. 173–9.

Barr, James, "'Abba' isn't 'Daddy,'" *Journal of Theological Studies*, 39, 1988, pp. 28–47.

Barth, Karl, *Church Dogmatics*, III/4 (Edinburgh: T&T Clark, 1961).

Bartkowski, John P., "Debating Patriarchy: Discursive Disputes over Spousal Authority among Evangelical Family Commentators," *Journal for the Scientific Study of Religion*, 36.3, September 1997, pp. 393–410.

Barton, John (ed.), *The Cambridge Companion to Biblical Interpretation* (Cambridge, UK: Cambridge University Press, 1998).

Barton, Stephen C., *Discipleship and Family Ties in Mark and Matthew* (Cambridge, UK: Cambridge University Press, 1994).

Barton, Stephen C. (ed.), *The Family in Theological Perspective* (Edinburgh: T&T Clark, 1996).

Bauman-Martin, Betsy J., "Women on the Edge: New Perspectives on Women in the Petrine *Haustafel*," *Journal of Biblical Literature*, 123.2, Summer 2004, pp. 253–79.

Beattie, Tina, *God's Mother, Eve's Advocate* (London and New York: Continuum, 2002).

Bendroth, Margaret, "Horace Bushnell's *Christian Nurture*," in Bunge (ed.), *The Child in Christian Thought*, pp. 350–64.

Benson, Harry, *Mentoring Marriages* (Crowborough: Monarch Publications, 2005).

Bentham, Jeremy, *An Introduction to the Principles of Morals and Legislation* (1780).

Blankenhorn, David, Don Browning, and Mary Stewart Van Leeuwen (eds.), *Does Christianity Teach Male Headship? – The Equal-Regard Marriage and Its Critics* (Grand Rapids, MI/Cambridge, UK: Eerdmans, 2004).

Board for Social Responsibility of the Church of England, *Something to Celebrate: Valuing Families in Church and Society* (London: Church House Publishing, 1995).

Boff, Leonardo, *Trinity and Society* (Tunbridge Wells: Burns and Oates, 1988).

Book of Common Prayer (1662).

Bourg, Florence Caffrey, *Where Two or Three Are Gathered: Christian Families as Domestic Churches* (Notre Dame, IN: University of Notre Dame Press, 2004).

Bowlby, John, *Attachment and Loss 1: Attachment* (New York: Basic Books, 1969).

Brown, David, *The Divine Trinity* (London: Duckworth, 1985).

Brown, Peter, *The Body and Society: Men, Women and Sexual Renunciation in Early Christianity* (London: Faber and Faber, 1989).

Browning, Don S., Bonnie J. Miller-McLemore, Pamela D. Couture, K. Brynolf Lyon, and Robert M. Franklin, *From Culture Wars to Common Ground: Religion and the American Family Debate* (Louisville, KY: Westminster John Knox Press, 1997).

Browning, Don S., *Marriage and Modernization: How Globalization Threatens Marriage and What to Do about It* (Grand Rapids, MI/Cambridge, UK: Eerdmans, 2003).

Browning, Don S., "Empty Inclusivism," *Christian Century*, 120, 13 (June 28, 2003), pp. 8–9.

Browning, Don S., "The Problem of Men," in Blankenhorn et al. (eds.), *Does Christianity Teach Male Headship?*, pp. 3–12.

Brundage, James A., "Review: Godparents and Kinship in Early Modern Europe," *American Historical Review*, 92.2, April 1987.

Bunge, Marcia J. (ed.), *The Child in Christian Thought* (Grand Rapids, MI/Cambridge, UK: Eerdmans, 2001).

Bunge, Marcia J., "Introduction," in Bunge (ed.), *The Child in Christian Thought* (Grand Rapids, MI/Cambridge, UK: Eerdmans, 2001), pp. 1–28.

Bunge, Marcia J., "Education and the Child in Eighteenth-Century German Pietism: Perspectives from the Work of A.H. Francke," in Bunge (ed.), *The Child in Christian Thought*, pp. 247–78.

Bushnell, Horace, *Christian Nurture* (New York: Charles Scribner, 1861; repr. Cleveland, OH: Pilgrim Press, 1994).

Butler, Joseph, *Analogy of Religion* (1736).

Cahill, Lisa Sowle, *Sex, Gender and Christian Ethics* (Cambridge, UK: Cambridge University Press, 1996).

Cahill, Lisa Sowle, *Family: A Christian Social Perspective* (Minneapolis, MN: Fortress Press, 2000).

Campbell, B. (ed.), *Sexual Selection and the Descent of Man* (Chicago, IL: Aldine Publishing Co., 1972).

Carr, Anne and Mary Stewart Van Leeuwen (eds.), *Religion, Feminism, and the Family* (Louisville, KY: Westminster John Knox Press, 1996).

Carter, Warren, *Households and Discipleship: A Study of Matthew 19–20 (Journal for the Study of the New Testament* Supplement 103) (Sheffield, UK: JSOT Press, 1994).

Cashman, Hilary, *Christianity and Child Sexual Abuse* (London: SPCK, 1993).

Catechism of the Catholic Church (London: Geoffrey Chapman, 1994).

Center for Marriage and Family, *Time, Sex and Money: The First Five Years of Marriage* (Omaha, NE: Creighton University, 2000).

Cere, Daniel Mark, "Marriage, Subordination, and the Development of Christian Doctrine," in Blankenhorn et al. (eds), *Does Christianity Teach Male Headship?*, pp. 92–100.

Chrysostom, John, *On Marriage and Family Life* (tr. Catherine P. Roth and David Anderson) (Crestwood, NY: St Vladimir's Seminary Press, 1986).

Chrysostom, John, *Homily 20 on Ephesians*, in Hunter (ed.), *Marriage in the Early Church*.

Chrysostom, John, *Homily 1 on Marriage*, in Rogers (ed.), *Theology and Sexuality*, pp. 87–92.

Church of England, *Common Worship*, "Marriage Service." www.cofe.anglican.org/worship/liturgy/commonworship/texts/marriage.html. Accessed 02.09.2006.

Church of England, *Common Worship*, "Prayers of Intercession at Holy Communion." www.cofe.anglican.org/worship/liturgy/commonworship/texts/hc/intercessions.html. Accessed 02.09.2006.

Church of England, *Common Worship*, "Thanksgiving for the Gift of a Child." www.cofe.anglican.org/worship/liturgy/commonworship/texts/initiation/thanksgiftchild.html. Accessed 02.09.2006.

CIVITAS, *Does Marriage Matter?* (London: undated).

Clapp, Rodney, *Families at the Crossroads: Beyond Traditional and Modern Options* (Leicester: Inter-Varsity Press, 1993).

Clarke, L. and C. Roberts, "The meaning of grandparenthood and its contribution to the quality of life of older people," in Walker and Hennessy (eds.), *Growing Older*, pp. 188–208.

Clement of Alexandria, *Paidagogos [The Instructor]* (tr. Roberts-Donaldson). www.earlychristianwritings.com/clement.html. Accessed 02.09.2006.

CLS [Centre for Longitudinal Studies] Briefings, *Parenting*, November 2005. www.cls.ioe.ac.uk. Accessed 02.09.2006.

Coakley, Sarah (ed.), *Re-Thinking Gregory of Nyssa* (Malden, MA, and Oxford, UK: Blackwell, 2003).

Coakley, Sarah "Introduction – Gender, Trinitarian Analogies, and the Pedagogy of *The Song*," in Coakley (ed.), *Re-Thinking Gregory of Nyssa*, pp. 1–14.

Compact Oxford English Dictionary. www.askoxford.com. Accessed 02.09.2006.

Coontz, Stephanie, *Marriage, a History: From Obedience to Intimacy or How Love Conquered Marriage* (New York: Viking, 2005).

Cooper-White, Pamela, *The Cry of Tamar: Violence against Women and the Church's Response* (Minneapolis, MN: Fortress Press, 1995).

Cosgrove, Charles H., *Appealing to Scripture in Moral Debate* (Grand Rapids, MI/Cambridge, UK: Eerdmans, 2002).

Couture, Pamela D., *Seeing Children, Seeing God: A Practical Theology of Children and Poverty* (Nashville, TN: Abingdon Press, 2000).

Crispin, Ken, *Divorce: The Forgivable Sin?* (London: Hodder and Stoughton, 1988).

Cunningham, David S., *These Three Are One – The Practice of Trinitarian Theology* (Malden, MA, and Oxford, UK: Blackwell, 1998).

D'Angelo, Mary Rose, "Abba and 'Father': Imperial Theology and the Jesus Traditions," *Journal of Biblical Literature*, 111/4, Winter 1992, pp. 611–31.

D'Angelo, Mary Rose, "Intimating Deity in the Gospel of John: Theological Language and 'Father' in Prayers of Jesus," *Semeia*, 85, 1999, pp. 59–83.

David, Miriam E. (ed.), *The Fragmenting Family: Does It Matter?* (London: Health and Welfare Unit of the Institute of Economic Affairs, 1998).

Davies, Jon (ed.), *The Family: Is It Just Another Lifestyle Choice?* (London: Health and Welfare Unit of the Institute of Economic Affairs, 1993).

Davies, Jon, "From Household to Family to Individualism," in Davies (ed.), *The Family* pp. 63–103.

Davies, Jon, "A Preferential Option for the Family," in Barton (ed.), *The Family in Theological Perspective*, pp. 219–36.

Davies, Jon, "Neither Seen or Heard nor Wanted: The Child as Problematic. Towards an Actuarial Theology of Generation," in Hayes et al. (eds.), *Religion and Sexuality*, pp. 326–47.

Davies, Jon, "Sex These Days, Sex Those Days: Will it Ever End?," in Davies and Loughlin (eds.), *Sex These Days*, pp. 18–34.

Davies, Jon, "Welcome the Pied Piper," in Thatcher (ed.), *Celebrating Christian Marriage*, pp. 219–50.

Davies, Jon and Gerard Loughlin (eds.), *Sex These Days* (Sheffield, UK: Sheffield Academic Press, 1997).

Davis, Ellen F. and Richard B. Hays (eds.), *The Art of Reading Scripture* (Grand Rapids, MI/Cambridge, UK: Eerdmans, 2003).

Davis, Muller, "Is the Genie out of the Bottle?," in Wall et al. (eds.), *Marriage, Health and the Professions*, pp. 90–107.

Dawkins, Richard, *The Blind Watchmaker* (London: Penguin Books, 1988).

de Vaus, David, *Diversity and Change in Australian Families: Statistical Profiles* (Australian Institute of Family Studies, 2004). www.aifs.gov.au/inst/pubs/diversity/main.html. Accessed 11.23.2004.

Deddo, Gary W., *Karl Barth's Theology of Relations – Trinitarian, Christological, and Human: Towards an Ethic of the Family* (New York: Peter Lang, 1999).

Dennis, Norman, *Rising Crime and the Dismembered Family: How Conformist Intellectuals Have Campaigned Against Common Sense* (London: Health and Welfare Unit of the Institute of Economic Affairs, 1993).

Dennis, Norman and George Erdos, *Families without Fatherhood* (London: Health and Welfare Unit of the Institute of Economic Affairs, 1993).

Dex, Shirley, *Work and Family Life in the Twenty-First Century* (London: Joseph Rowntree Foundation, 2003).

Doherty, William J., *Take Back Your Kids* (Notre Dame, IN: Sorin Books, 2000).

Doherty, William J., "Family Life and Civic Bonds: Renewing the 'Very Air Our Loved Ones Breathe,'" *American Experiment Quarterly*, Fall 2003, pp. 21–39.

Doherty, William J. and Jason S. Carroll, "Health and the Ethics of Marital Therapy and Education," in Wall et al. (eds.), *Marriage, Health and the Professions*, pp. 208–32.

Dominian, Jack, *Let's Make Love: The Meaning of Sexual Intercourse* (London: Darton, Longman, and Todd, 2001).

Dominian, Jack, *Living Love* (London: Darton, Longman, and Todd, 2004).

Drane, John and Olive M. Fleming Drane, *Family Fortunes: Faith-full Caring for Today's Families* (London: Darton, Longman, and Todd, 2004).

Economic and Social Research Council, *Factsheet: Parenting in Britain Today* (2004). www.esrcsocietytoday.ac.uk/ESRCInfoCentre/facts/. Accessed 02.09.2006.

Economic Lifestyle. www.economiclifestyle.co.uk. Accessed 02.09.2006.

eGodparent. www.egodparent.com. Accessed 02.09.2006.

Elliott, John H., "Jesus Was Not an Egalitarian. A Critique of an Anachronistic and Idealist Theory," *Biblical Theology Bulletin*, 32.2, 2002, pp. 75–91.

Elliott, John H., "The Jesus Movement Was Not Egalitarian but Family-Oriented," *Biblical Interpretation*, 11/2, 2003, pp. 173–211.

Equal Opportunities Commission, Women's Pensions Network. www.eoc.org.uk. Accessed 02.09.2006.

European Commission Green Paper, *Confronting Demographic Change: A New Solidarity between the Generations* (Brussels: March 2005). europa.eu.int/comm/employment_social/news/2. Accessed 11.26.2005.

Eurostat yearbook 2004. epp.eurostat.cec.eu.int/. Accessed 11.17.2004.

Ewing, A.C., *Ethics* (London: English Universities Press, 1953).

Facilitating Open Couple Communication, Understanding and Study. www.foccusinc.com/. Accessed 02.09.2006.

Farley, Margaret, "Marriage, Divorce, and Personal Commitments," in Thatcher (ed.), *Celebrating Christian Marriage*, pp. 355–72.

Fathers Direct: The National Information Centre on Fatherhood. www.fathersdirect.com. Accessed 02.09.2006.

Fiorenza, Elisabeth Schüssler, *In Memory of Her: A Feminist Theological Reconstruction of Christian Origins* (New York: Crossroad, 1983).

Fitzgerald, Valpy, "The economics of liberation theology," in Rowland (ed.), *Cambridge Companion to Liberation Theology*, pp. 218–34.

Ford, David, *Self and Salvation* (Cambridge, UK: Cambridge University Press, 1999).

Fotiou, Stavros S., "Water into Wine, and *Eros* into *Agape*: Marriage in the Orthodox Church," in Thatcher (ed.), *Celebrating Christian Marriage*, pp. 89–104.

Fowl, Stephen E., *Engaging Scripture* (Malden, MA, and Oxford, UK: Blackwell, 1998).

Franco, Ana and Karin Winqvist, *Women and Men Working Weekends and Their Family Circumstances* (Eurostat, 2002).

Frye, Roland M., "Language for God and Feminist Language," in Kimel (ed.), *Speaking the Christian God*, pp. 17–43.

Frykberg, Elizabeth A., "The Child as Solution: The Problem of the Superordinate–Subordinate Ordering of the Male–Female Relation in Barth's Theology," *Scottish Journal of Theology*, 47.3, 1994, pp. 327–54.

Garrett, William R., "The Protestant Ethic and the Spirit of the Modern Family," *Journal for the Scientific Study of Religion*, 37.2, June 1998, pp. 222–34.

Gaudium et spes: Pastoral Constitution on the Church in the Modern World (1965). www.vatican.va/archive/hist_councils/ii_vatican_council/documents/vat-ii_cons_19651207_gaudium-et-spes_en.html. Accessed 02.09.2006.

Gittins, Diana, *The Family in Question* (2nd edition) (London: Macmillan, 1993).

Glancy, Jennifer A., "Family Plots: Burying Slaves Deep In Historical Ground," *Biblical Interpretation*, 10.1, 2002, pp. 57–76.

Grandparents' Association. www.grandparents-association.org.uk/. Accessed 02.09.2006.

Green, Garrett, "The Gender of God and the Theology of Metaphor," in Kimel (ed.), *Speaking the Christian God*, pp. 44–64.

Grenz, Stanley J., *The Social God and the Relational Self: A Trinitarian Theology of the Imago Dei* (Louisville, KY, and London: Westminster John Knox Press, 2001).

Greven, Philip, *The Protestant Temperament, Patterns of Child-Rearing, Religious Experience, and the Self in Early America* (New York: Alfred A. Knopf, 1977).

Greven, Philip, *Spare the Child: The Religious Roots of Punishment and the Psychological Impact of Physical Abuse* (New York: Alfred A. Knopf, 1991).

Gudorf, Christine E., "Parenting, Mutual Love, and Sacrifice," in Andolsen et al. (eds.), *Women's Consciousness and Women's Conscience*.

Gudorf, Christine E., "Dissecting Parenthood: Infertility, in Vitro, and Other Lessons in Why and How We Parent," *Conscience* 15.3, Autumn 1994.

Gudorf, Christine E., "Sacrificial and Parental Spiritualities," in Carr and Van Leewen (eds.), *Religion, Feminism, and the Family*, pp. 294–309.

Gundry-Volf, Judith M., "The Least and the Greatest: Children in the New Testament," in Bunge (ed.), *The Child in Christian Thought*, pp. 29–60.

Gunton, Colin, "Proteus and Procrustes," in Kimel (ed.), *Speaking the Christian God*, pp. 65–80.

Guroian, Vigen, "The Ecclesial Family: John Chrysostom on Parenthood," in Bunge (ed.), *The Child in Christian Thought*, pp. 61–77.

Gutierrez, Gustavo, "The Task and Content of Liberation Theology," in Rowland (ed.), *The Cambridge Companion to Liberation Theology*, pp. 19–38.

Guttmann, J. and A. Lazar, "Criteria for Marital Satisfaction: Does Having a Child Make a Difference?," *Journal of Reproductive and Infant Psychology*, 22.3, August 2004, pp. 147–55.

Guyette, Fred, "Families, Pastoral Counseling, Scripture: Searching for the Connections," *Journal of Pastoral Counseling*, 38, 2003, pp. 5–33.

Hackstaff, Karla B., "How Gender Informs Marital Fragility," *INTAMS Review*, 10.1, 2004, pp. 33–47.

Hahn, Scott, *First Comes Love: Finding Your Family in the Church and the Trinity* (London: Darton, Longman, and Todd, 2002).

Hakim, Catherine, *Models of the Family in Modern Societies* (Aldershot, UK: Ashgate, 2003.)

Hallett, Garth, *Priorities in Christian Ethics* (Cambridge, UK: Cambridge University Press, 1998).

Halsey, A.H., "Foreword," in Dennis and Erdos, *Families without Fatherhood*, pp. ix–xiii.

Harden, Rachel, "Few Showing the Way," *Church Times*, no. 7392, 11.05.04.

Harrison, Verna E.F., "Male and Female in Cappadocian Theology," *Journal of Theological Studies*, 41.2, October 1990, pp. 441–71.

Harvey, J.H. and M.A. Fine, *Children of Divorce: Stories of Loss and Growth* (Mahwah, NJ: Erlbaum, 2004).

Hass, Loius, "Il mio buono compare: Choosing Godparents and the Uses of Baptismal Kinship in Renaissance Florence," *Journal of Social History*, 29.2, Winter 1995, pp. 341–77.

Hastings, Adrian, Alistair Mason, and Hugh Pyper (eds.), *The Oxford Companion to Christian Thought* (Oxford, UK: Oxford University Press, 2000).

Hauerwas, Stanley, *Suffering Presence: Theological Reflections on Medicine, the Mentally Handicapped, and the Church* (Notre Dame, IN: University of Notre Dame Press, 1986).

Hayes, Michael A., Wendy Porter, and David Tombs (eds.), *Religion and Sexuality* (Sheffield, UK: Sheffield Academic Press, 1998).

Heiman, Carrie J., *The Nine-Month Miracle* (Liguori, MO: Liguori Publications, 1986).

Hinze, Christine Firer and Mary Stewart Van Leeuwen, "Whose Marriage Whose Health? A Christian Feminist Ethical Response," in Wall et al. (eds.), *Marriage, Health and the Professions*, pp. 145–66.

Hofferth, Sandra L. and John E. Sandberg, "How American Children Spend Their Time," *Journal of Marriage and Family*, 63.2, May 2001, pp. 295–308.

House of Bishops, *Issues in Human Sexuality* (London: Church House Publishing, 1991).

House of Bishops' Group on "Issues on Human Sexuality," *Some Issues in Human Sexuality: A Guide to the Debate* (London: Church House Publishing, 2003).

Hunter, David G. (ed.), *Marriage in the Early Church* (Minneapolis, MN: Fortress Press, 1992).

Institute for American Values, *Why Marriage Matters: Twenty-One Conclusions from the Social Sciences* (New York: 2002).

International Obesity Task Force, Report, *Obesity in Children and Young People: A Crisis in Public Health* (London: 2004).

Jerome, *The Perpetual Virginity of Blessed Mary: Against Helvidius* in Nicene and Post-Nicene Fathers, series II, vol. VI (undated). www.ccel.org/fathers2/NPNF2–06/. Accessed 02.09.2006.

John Paul II, *Familiaris consortio* (1981). www.vatican.va/holy_father/john_paul_ii/apost_exhortations/. Accessed 02.09.2006.

John Paul II, *Mulieris dignitatem* (1988). www.vatican.va/holy_father/john_paul_ii/apost_letters/index.htm. Accessed 02.09.2006.

John Paul II, *Letter to Families* (1994). www.vatican.va/holy_father/john_paul_ii/letters/. Accessed 02.09.2006.

John Paul II, *Evangelium vitae* (1995). www.vatican.va/holy_father/john_paul_ii/encyclicals/documents/hf_jp-ii_enc_25031995_evangelium-vitae_en.html. Accessed 02.09.2006.

John Paul II, *The Theology of the Body according to John Paul II: Human Law in the Divine Plan* (Boston, MA: Pauline Books, 1997).

Johnson, Elizabeth, "Ephesians," in Newsom and Ringe (eds.), *The Women's Bible Commentary*.

Keep Time for Children. www.keeptimeforchildren.org.uk/NatCen_exec_summary.doc. Accessed 02.09.2006.

Kimel, Alvin F. Jr (ed.), *Speaking the Christian God: The Holy Trinity and the Challenge of Feminism* (Grand Rapids, MI: Eerdmans/Leominster, UK: Gracewing: 1992).

Kirby, Jill, *Broken Hearts, Family Decline and the Consequences for Society* (London: Centre for Policy Studies, 2002).

Kirby, Jill, *Choosing to be Different: Women, Work and the Family* (London: Centre for Policy Studies, 2003). www.cps.org.uk/pdf/pub/398.pdf. Accessed 02.09.2006.

Kirby, Jill, *The Price of Parenthood* (London: Centre for Policy Studies, 2005).

Knieps-Port le Roi, Thomas, "Marriage and the Church: Theological Reflections on an Underrated Relationship," in Thatcher (ed.), *Celebrating Christian Marriage*, pp. 105–18.

Küng, Hans, *Does God Exist?* (New York: Vintage Books, 1981).

Lambeth Conference Resolutions, 1930. www.anglicancommunion.org/acns/archive/1930/1930–15.htm. Accessed 02.09.2006.

Lawler, Michael G., "Perichoresis: New Theological Wine in an Old Theological Foreskin," *Horizons* 22.1, 1995, pp. 49–66.

Lawler, Michael G., *Family: American and Christian* (Chicago, IL: Loyola Press, 1998).

Lawler, Michael G., "Towards a Theology of Christian Family," *INTAMS Review*, vol. 8.1, Spring 2002, pp. 55–73.

Leo XIII, *Arcanum* (Encyclical: "On Christian Marriage"), 1880. www.vatican.va/holy_father/leo_xiii/encyclicals/. Accessed 02.09.2006.

Lynch, Joseph H., *Godparents and Kinship in Early Medieval Europe* (Princeton, NJ: Princeton University Press, 1986).

Maas, Robin, "Christ as the Logos of Childhood: Reflections on the Meaning and Mission of the Child," *Theology Today*, 56.4, January 2000, pp. 456–68.

Macmurray, John, *The Self as Agent* (London: Faber and Faber, 1957).

Macmurray, John, *Persons in Relation* (London: Faber and Faber, 1961).

Macquarrie, John, *Principles of Christian Theology* (London: SCM Press, 1966).

Malina, Bruce J., *The New Testament World: Insights from Cultural Anthropology* (Louisville, KY: Westminster John Knox Press, 1997).

Marion, Jean-Luc, *God Without Being* (tr. Thomas A. Carlson) (Chicago, IL, and London: University of Chicago Press, 1991).

Marriage Care. www.marriagecare.org.uk. Accessed 02.09.2006.

Marriage Culture Strategy, *Marriage Resource Briefing*, September 2004.

Marriage: A Teaching Document from the House of Bishops of the Church of England (London: Church House Publishing, 1999).

Marshall, Kathleen and Paul Parvis, *Honouring Children: The Human Rights of the Child in Christian Perspective* (Edinburgh: Saint Andrew Press, 2004).

McAllister, Fiona with Lynda Clarke, *Choosing Childlessness* (London: Family Policy Studies Centre and Joseph Rowntree Foundation, 1998).

McCarthy, David Matzko, *Sex and Love in the Home* (London: SCM Press, 2001).

McFadyen, Alistair I., *The Call to Personhood: A Christian Theory of the Individual in Social Relationships* (Cambridge, UK: Cambridge University Press, 1990).

Milbank, John, "Can a Gift be Given? Prolegomena to a Future Trinitarian Metaphysic," *Modern Theology*, 11.1, January 1995, pp. 119–62.

Milbank, John, *Being Reconciled: Ontology and Pardon* (New York and London: Routledge, 2003).

Miller, Alice, *For Your Own Good: Hidden Cruelty in Child-Rearing and the Roots of Violence* (tr. H. and H. Hannum) (New York: Farrar, Straus, and Giroux, 1983).

Miller, John W., *Calling God "Father": Essays on the Bible, Fatherhood and Culture* (New York/Mahwah, NJ: Paulist Press, 1999).

Miller, John W., "The Problem of Men, Reconsidered," in Blankenhorn et al. (eds.), *Does Christianity Teach Male Headship?*, pp. 65–73.

Miller-McLemore, Bonnie, *Also a Mother: Work and Family as Theological Dilemma* (Nashville, TN: Abingdon Press, 1994).

Miller-McLemore, Bonnie J., "'Let the Children Come' Revisited: Contemporary Feminist Theologians on Children," in Bunge (ed.), *The Child in Christian Thought*, pp. 446–73.

Miller-McLemore, Bonnie J., *Let the Children Come: Reimagining Childhood from a Christian Perspective* (San Francisco, CA: Jossey-Bass, 2003).

Molnar, Paul D., "Love of God and Love of Neighbor in the Theology of Karl Rahner and Karl Barth," *Modern Theology*, 20.4, October 2004, pp. 567–99.

Moltmann, Jürgen, *History and the Triune God* (London: SCM Press, 1991).

Monti, Joseph, *Arguing About Sex: The Rhetoric of Christian Sexual Morality* (New York: State University of New York Press, 1995).

Morgan, Patricia, *Farewell to the Family? Public Policy and Family Breakdown in Britain and the USA* (London: Health and Welfare Unit of the Institute of Economic Affairs, 1995).

Morgan, Robert, "The Bible and Christian Theology," in Barton (ed.), *The Cambridge Companion to Biblical Interpretation*, pp. 114–28.

Moxnes, Halvor (ed.), *Constructing Early Christian Families: Family as Social Reality and Metaphor* (New York: Routledge, 1997).

Moxnes, Halvor, "What is Family? Problems in Constructing Early Christian Families," in Moxnes (ed.), *Constructing Early Christian Families*, pp. 13–41.

Muncie, John, Margaret Wetherell, Rudi Dallos, and Allan Cochrane (eds.), *Understanding the Family* (London: Sage, 1995).

National Family and Parenting Institute, *Making Britain Family Friendly* (London: 2003). www.nfpi.org. Accessed 02.09.2006.

National Statistics. "Living in Britain." www.statistics.gov.uk/lib2002/default.asp. Accessed 02.09.2006.

National Statistics. Census 2001. www.statistics.gov.uk/census/default.asp. Accessed 02.09.2006.

Newman, Philip, "An Holistic, Parish-Based Marriage-Ministry," in Thatcher (ed.), *Celebrating Christian Marriage*, pp. 71–84.

Newsom, Carol A. and Sharon H. Ringe (eds.), *The Women's Bible Commentary* (Louisville, KY: Westminster John Knox Press, and London: SPCK, 1992).

Ngien, Dennis, "Richard of St Victor's Condilectus: The Spirit as Co-Beloved," *European Journal of Theology*, 12.2, 2003, pp. 77–92.

Ontario Consultants on Religious Tolerance, "Corporal Punishment of Children – Spanking." www.religioustolerance.org/spanking_menu.htm. Accessed 02.09.2006.

Osiek, Carolyn, "*Pietas* in and out of the frying pan," *Biblical Interpretation*, 11.2, 2003, pp. 166–73.

Osiek, Carolyn, "Did Early Christians Teach, or Merely Assume, Male Headship?," in Blankenhorn et al. (eds.), *Does Christianity Teach Male Headship?*, pp. 23–7.

Osiek, Carolyn and David L. Balch, *Families in the New Testament World: Households and House Churches* (Louisville, KY: Westminster John Knox Press, 1997).

Pace, Susan, "Couples and the first baby: responding to new parents' sexual and relationship problems," *Sexual and Relationship Therapy*, 19.3, August 2004, pp. 223–46.

Pais, Janet, *Suffer the Children: A Theology of Liberation by a Victim of Abuse* (New York/ Mahwah, NJ: Paulist Press, 1991).

Palkovitz, Rob, "The 'Recovery' of Fatherhood?," in Carr and Van Leeuwen (eds.) *Religion, Feminism, and the Family*, pp. 310–29.

Peachey, Paul, *Leaving and Clinging: The Human Significance of the Conjugal Union* (Washington, DC: University Press of America, 2001).

Pellegrino, Edmund D., "The Family as a Clinical Entity," in Wall et al. (eds.), *Marriage, Health and the Professions*, pp. 130–45.

Perdue, Leo G., "The Israelite and Early Jewish Family: Summary and Conclusions," in Perdue et al. (eds.), *Families in Ancient Israel*, pp. 163–222.

Perdue, Leo G., Joseph Blenkensopp, John J. Collins and Carol Meyers (eds.), *Families in Ancient Israel* (Louisville, KY: Westminster John Knox Press, 1997).

Pius XI, *Casti connubii [Of Chaste Marriage]* (1930). www.vatican.va/holy_father/ pius_xi/encyclicals/documents/hf_p-xi_enc_31121930_casti-connubii_en.html. Accessed 02.09.2006.

Pontifical Council for the Family, *Preparation for the Sacrament of Marriage* (1996). www.vatican.va/roman_curia/pontifical_councils/family/documents/rc_pc_family_ doc_13051996_preparation-for-marriage_en.html. Accessed 02.09.2006.

Pontifical Council for the Family, *The Family and Human Rights*, December 9, 1999.

Pope, Stephen J., "The Order of Love and Recent Catholic Ethics: A Constructive Proposal," *Theological Studies*, 52.2, June 1991, pp. 255–89.

Popenoe, David and Barbara Dafoe Whitehead, "The Personal Costs of Divorce," in Wall et al. (eds.), *Marriage, Health and the Professions*, pp. 33–46.

Post, Stephen, *A Theory of Agape: On the Meaning of Christian Love* (Lewisburg, PA: Bucknell University Press, 1990).

Post, Stephen, *Spheres of Love: Toward a New Ethics of the Family* (Dallas, TX: Southern Methodist University Press, 1994).

Post, Stephen G., *More Lasting Unions: Christianity, the Family and Society* (Grand Rapids, MI/Cambridge, UK: Eerdmans, 2000).

Post, Stephen G., "Health, Marriage, and the Ethics of Medicine," in Wall et al. (eds.), *Marriage, Health and the Professions*, pp. 108–29.

PREPARE/ENRICH. www.prepare-enrich.com/indexm.cfm. Accessed 02.09.2006.

Presbyterian Church (USA), General Assembly Special Committee on Human Sexuality, *Keeping Body and Soul Together: Sexuality, Spirituality and Social Justice* (1991).

Purvis, Sally B., "Mothers, Neighbors and Strangers – Another Look at Agape," in Thatcher and Stuart (eds.), *Christian Perspectives on Sexuality and Gender*, pp. 232–46.

Putnam, Robert D., *Bowling Alone: The Collapse and Revival of American Community* (New York: Simon and Schuster, 2000).

Putting Family First. www.puttingfamilyfirst.org/. Accessed 02.09.2006.

Pyper, Hugh, "Children," in Hastings et al. (eds.), *The Oxford Companion to Christian Thought*, p. 110.

Rahner, Karl, "Reflections on the Unity of the Love of Neighbour and the Love of God," *Theological Investigations*, vol. 6 (Baltimore: Helican Press; London: Darton, Longman, and Todd, 1969), pp. 231–49.

Rahner, Karl, "Experience of Self and Experience of God," *Theological Investigations*, 13 (New York: Crossroad, 1974).

Roehampton Social Research Unit, University of Surrey Roehampton, *Church Support of Marriage and Adult Relationships in Southern England* (2003).

Roels, Shirley J., "Reconstructing Home: Business Responsibility for the Family," in Wall et al. (eds), *Marriage, Health and the Professions*, pp. 254–82.

Rogers, Eugene F., Jr, *Sexuality and the Christian Body* (Malden, MA, and Oxford, UK: Blackwell, 1999).

Rogers, Eugene F., Jr (ed.), *Theology and Sexuality* (Malden, MA, and Oxford, UK: Blackwell, 2002).

Rowland, Christopher (ed.), *The Cambridge Companion to Liberation Theology* (Cambridge, UK: Cambridge University Press, 1999).

Rowland, Christopher, "Preface," in Rowland (ed.), *The Cambridge Companion to Liberation Theology*, pp. xiii–xv.

Rowland, Tracey, "Divine Gifts to the Secular Desert," *Reviews in Religion and Theology*, 11.2, April 2004, pp. 182–8.

Rowthorn, Robert, "Foreword," in Kirby, *The Price of Parenthood*.

Rubio, Julie Hanlon, *A Christian Theology of Marriage and Family* (Mahwah, NJ: Paulist Press, 2004).

Ruether, Rosemary Radford, *Sexism and God-Talk: Toward a Feminist Theology* (Boston, MA: Beacon Press, 1983).

Ruether, Rosemary Radford, *Christianity and the Making of the Modern Family* (Boston, MA: Beacon Press, 2000).

Ryan, Maura A. and Todd David Whitmore (eds.), *The Challenge of Global Stewardship: Roman Catholic Responses* (Notre Dame, IN: University of Notre Dame Press, 1997).

Salzman, Todd A., Thomas M. Kelly, and John J. O'Keefe (eds.), *Marriage in the Catholic Tradition – Scripture, Tradition and Experience* (New York: Crossroad, 2004).

Schweiker, William, *Theological Ethics and Global Dynamics in the Time of Many Worlds* (Malden, MA, and Oxford, UK: Blackwell, 2004).

Seim, Turid Karlsen, *The Double Message: Patterns of Gender in Luke and Acts* (Nashville, TN: Abingdon Press, 1994).

Selby, Peter, "Is the Church a Family?," in Barton (ed.), *The Family in Theological Perspective*, pp. 151–68.

Shivanandan, Mary, *Crossing the Threshold of Love – A New Vision of Marriage* (Edinburgh: T&T Clark, 1999).

Smart Marriages Archive. archives.his.com/smartmarriages/. Accessed 02.09.2006.

Soskice, Janet Martin, "Can a Feminist Call God 'Father'?," in Kimel (ed.), *Speaking the Christian God*, pp. 81–94.

Soskice, Janet Martin, "Trinity and 'the Feminine Other,'" *New Blackfriars*, 75, January 1994, pp. 2–17.

Southern Baptist Convention, "The Baptist Faith and Message." www.sbc.net/bfm/bfm2000.asp#xviii. Accessed 02.09.2006.

Stackhouse, Max L., "Familial, Social, and Professional Integrity in Relationship to Business," in Wall et al. (eds), *Marriage, Health and the Professions*, pp. 233–53.

Stanton, Helen, "Obligation or Option? Marriage, Voluntary Childlessness, and the Church," in Thatcher (ed.), *Celebrating Christian Marriage*, pp. 223–39.

StepFamilies UK. www.stepfamilies.co.uk. Accessed 02.09.2006.

Stepfamily Association of America. www.saafamilies.org/. Accessed 02.09.2006.

Stortz, Martha Ellen, "'Where or When Was Your Servant Innocent?': Augustine on Childhood," in Bunge (ed.), *The Child in Christian Thought*, pp. 78–102.

Thatcher, Adrian, *The Ontology of Paul Tillich* (Oxford, UK: Oxford University Press, 1978).

Thatcher, Adrian, *Marriage after Modernity: Christian Marriage in Postmodern Times* (Sheffield, UK: Sheffield Academic Press, and New York: New York University Press, 1999).

Thatcher, Adrian, "Forming a Family," *Christian Century*, November 1, 2000, pp. 1122–6.

Thatcher, Adrian (ed.), *Celebrating Christian Marriage* (Edinburgh and New York: T&T Clark, 2002).

Thatcher, Adrian, *Living Together and Christian Ethics* (Cambridge, UK: Cambridge University Press, 2002).

Thatcher, Adrian, "Marriage and Love: Too Much of a 'Breakthrough'?," *INTAMS Review*, 8.1, 2002, pp. 44–54.

Thatcher, Adrian, *The Daily Telegraph Guide to Christian Marriage and to Getting Married in Church* (London and New York: Continuum, 2003).

Thatcher, Adrian and Elizabeth Stuart (eds.), *Christian Perspectives on Sexuality and Gender* (Leominster, UK, and Grand Rapids, NJ: Gracewing and Eerdmans, 1996).

Thatcher, Adrian and Elizabeth Stuart, *People of Passion – What the Churches Teach about Sex* (London: Mowbray, 1997).

Therborn, Göran, *Between Sex and Power: Family in the World, 1900–2000* (London and New York: Routledge, 2004).

Torrance, Thomas F., "The Christian Apprehension of God the Father," in Kimel (ed.), *Speaking the Christian God*, pp. 120–43.

Traina, Christina L.H., "A Person in the Making," in Bunge (ed.), *The Child in Christian Thought*, pp. 103–33.

Trivers, Robert, "Parental Investment and Sexual Selection," in Campbell (ed.), *Sexual Selection and the Descent of Man*.

Turner, Denys, "Tradition and Faith," *International Journal of Systematic Theology*, 6.1, January 2004, pp. 21–37.

Tutu, Desmond, "Restoring Justice," *The Tablet*, February 21, 2004.

Twenge, Jean M., W. Keith Campbell, and Craig A. Foster, "Parenthood and Marital Satisfaction: A Meta-Analytic Review," *Journal of Marriage and Family*, 65.3, August 2003, pp. 574–83.

UNICEF, *Building a World Fit for Children* (New York: United Nations Children's Fund, 2003). www.unicef.org/publications/. Accessed 02.09.2006.

United States Conference of Catholic Bishops, Secretariat for Family, Laity, Women and Youth, *Follow the Way of Love* (*A Pastoral Message of the U.S. Catholic Bishops to Families on the Occasion of the United Nations 1994 International Year of the Family*) (1994). www.usccb.org/laity/follow.shtml. Accessed 02.09.2006.

Van Leeuwen, Mary Stewart, "Is Equal Regard in the Bible?," in Blankenhorn et al. (eds.), *Does Christianity Teach Male Headship?*, pp. 13–22.

Vanhoozer, Kevin J. (ed.), *The Cambridge Companion to Postmodern Theology* (Cambridge, UK: Cambridge University Press, 2003).

Vanhoozer, Kevin J., "Theology and the Condition of Postmodernity," in Vanhoozer (ed.), *The Cambridge Companion to Postmodern Theology*, pp. 3–25.

Vergote, Antoine, *The Religious Man: A Psychological Study of Religious Attitudes* (Dublin: Gill and Macmillan, 1969).

Vergote, Antoine, "The Parental Figures: Symbolic Functions and Medium for the Representation of God," in Vergote and Tamayo (eds.), *The Parental Figures and the Representation of God*.

Vergote, Antoine and Alvero Tamayo (eds.), *The Parental Figures and the Representation of God: A Psychological and Cross-Cultural Study* (The Hague: Mouton, 1981).

von Balthasar, Hans Urs, "Jesus as Child and His Praise of the Child," *Communio*, 22, 1995, pp. 164–70.

Waite, Linda J., "The Health Benefits of Marriage," in Wall et al. (eds.), *Marriage, Health and the Professions*, pp. 13–32.

Waite, Linda J. and Maggie Gallagher, *The Case for Marriage: Why Married People Are Happier, Healthier, and Better Off Financially* (New York: Doubleday, 2000).

Walker, A. and C. Hagan Hennessy (eds.), *Growing Older: Quality of Life in Old Age* (Milton Keynes: Open University Press, 2004).

Wall, John and Bonnie Miller-McLemore, "Health, Christian Marriage Traditions, and the Ethics of Marital Therapy," in Wall et al. (eds.), *Marriage, Health and the Professions*, pp. 186–207.

Wall, John, Don Browning, William J. Doherty, and Stephen Post (eds.), *Marriage, Health and the Professions: If Marriage Is Good for You, What Does This Mean for Law, Medicine, Ministry, Therapy, Business?* (Cambridge, MA: Eerdmans, 2002).

Weaver, Darlene Fozard, *Self Love and Christian Ethics* (Cambridge, UK: Cambridge University Press, 2002).

Webb, Stephen H., *The Gifting God: A Trinitarian Ethics of Excess* (New York: Oxford University Press, 1996).

Whelan, Robert (ed.), *Just a Piece of Paper? Divorce Reform and the Undermining of Marriage* (London: Health and Welfare Unit of the Institute of Economic Affairs, 1995).

Whitmore, Todd (with Tobias Winwright), "Children: An Undeveloped Theme in Catholic Teaching," in Ryan and Whitmore (eds.), *The Challenge of Global Stewardship*.

Wilcox, W. Bradford, *Soft Patriarchs, New Men: How Christianity Shapes Fathers and Husbands* (Chicago, IL, and London: University of Chicago Press, 2005).

Williams, Fiona, ESRC CAVA Research Group, *Rethinking Families* (London: Calouste Gulbenkian Foundation, 2004).

Williams, Rowan D., "The Body's Grace," in Rogers (ed.), *Theology and Sexuality*, pp. 309–21.

Witte, John, Jr, "The Goods and Goals of Marriage: The Health Paradigm in Historical Perspective," in Wall et al. (eds.), *Marriage, Health and the Professions*, pp. 49–89.

Wojtyła, Karol, *Sources of Renewal: The Implementation of the Second Vatican Council* (tr. P.S. Falla) (San Francisco, CA: Harper and Row, 1980).

Zinn, Grover A. (tr. and introduction), *Richard of St Victor* (New York: Paulist Press, 1979).

Index of Scriptural Citations

Index of Names

Index of Subjects